JOE CRONIN

To George –

Thanks for reading and
For your own contributions.

Take care,

Mark L. Ar

JOE

CRONIN

A LIFE IN BASEBALL

MARK ARMOUR

University of Nebraska Press \ Lincoln and London

Library of Congress Cataloging-
in-Publication Data
Armour, Mark L.
Joe Cronin : a life in baseball
/ Mark Armour.
p. cm.
Includes bibliographical
references and index.
ISBN 978-0-8032-2530-5
(cloth : alkaline paper)
1. Cronin, Joe, 1906–
2. Baseball players—United
States—Biography. 3. Baseball
player-managers—United
States—Biography. 4. American
League of Professional
Baseball Clubs—Presidents—
Biography. I. Title.
GV865.C7A76 2010
796.357092—dc22
[B]   2009037270

Set in Janson by Kim Essman
Designed by Nathan Putens

To my father, Laurence, who was never too tired to play catch, and my mother, Elizabeth, who encouraged my writing as early as the fourth grade. You made this book possible, and I only hope I have learned half of what you taught me.

CONTENTS

Illustrations

Following page 182

ACKNOWLEDGMENTS

The number of people who contributed to the research and writing of this book is staggering, but I will try to make a go of it here. Three friends read drafts of the entire book: Dan Levitt, my frequent collaborator, who also spent many hours talking through many of the stories I wanted to tell; Rob Neyer, who helped me smooth over some writing habits; and Bill Nowlin, who knows the Red Sox and style. The finished work is much better for their efforts.

Carl Haas, a man I did not know when this project began, gave me a tour of Joe Cronin's childhood San Francisco neighborhood one day in 2007, made several trips to the library, told me about the history of baseball in the city, and read the relevant material in this book. The news of his passing in May 2009 came as a jolt—I so wanted Carl to see what I had done with all of his help. He was a true gentleman.

David Smith, the czar of Retrosheet, the most beneficial endeavor since the Brooklyn Bridge, provided me with Joe Cronin's dailies—the day-by-day statistical record of his career. Dixie Tourangeau made several trips to the Boston Public Library digging for a particular story I needed.

Two other men with whom I discussed parts of my research unfortunately passed away before they could see the results of our conversations. Dick Thompson, an expert on the Red Sox of the 1930s, suggested that I write this book more than ten years ago, a notion that startled me at the time. Jules Tygiel, one of our most revered historians, specialized in the subject of baseball integration—a subject I dreaded tackling. An exchange of emails with Jules helped convince me that I was on the right track. I sincerely hope I have written a book that Dick and Jules would have appreciated.

I acknowledge the continual efforts of Gabriel Schechter at the Baseball Hall of Fame Library, who sent me files a number of times and gave me some unexpected items when I visited Cooperstown in 2008. For photographs I thank Michael Ivins and Megan Labella of the Boston Red Sox; Mary Brace; Steve Steinberg; John Horne of the Baseball Hall of Fame; and Aaron Schmidt of the Boston Public Library.

The following friends or fellow researchers helped me answer one or more questions over the course of the few years I was working on this project: David Vincent, Bob Dorin, Rich Morris, Jan Finkel, Mark Brown, Dave Eskenazi, Warren Corbett, Dick Beverage, Glenn Stout, Louis Kokernak, Walter Kephart, Cappy Gagnon, Charlie Bevis, Jeff Bower, Larry Tye, Ron Anderson, Rod Nelson, Geri Strecker, Wayne McElreavy, Andy McCue, Craig Calcaterra, Larry Gerlach, Steve Gietschier, Rick Huhn, Don Zminda, Lew Lowenfish, Larry Lester, Bobby Plapinger, and Jim Walsh.

I was fortunate to hear the recollections and insights of Joe Cronin's four children, Thomas Cronin, Corky Cronin, Maureen Cronin, and Kevin Cronin, as well as three of his grandchildren, Trevor Hayward, Chris Hayward, and Joe Hayward. I especially want to thank Maureen, who welcomed my father and me into her home in early 2007 and who enthusiastically fielded several follow-up phone calls.

I corresponded with a number of people who played for, dealt with, or otherwise knew Joe Cronin, none of whom was as helpful and gracious with their time as John Harrington, who endured two lengthy and fruitful phone interviews. Also generous to me were Bobby Doerr, Mel Parnell, Dom DiMaggio, Johnny Pesky, Don Gutteridge, Boo Ferriss, Matt Batts, Ellis "Cot" Deal, Sam Mele, John Underwood, Gus Zernial, Dick Bresciani, Buzzy Bavasi, Bowie Kuhn, Lou Gorman, Al Salerno, Bill Valentine, Roland Hemond, Jerome Holtzman, John Rice, and Marvin Miller.

Rob Taylor and the folks at the University of Nebraska Press have been helpful and encouraging throughout the process.

Finally, I thank my family—Jane, Maya and Drew—who allowed me to indulge myself in this book for a few years. They complete me.

JOE CRONIN

Prologue

TUESDAY, MAY 29, 1984, WAS A DAMP AND miserable night at Fenway Park. The Boston Red Sox were playing host to the Minnesota Twins, and it was Jimmy Fund night, an annual affair from which the Red Sox donated all net proceeds to the team's long-time charity. Making the event historical, the Red Sox planned a pregame celebration to retire the uniform numbers of Ted Williams (9) and Joe Cronin (4), the first players they had ever so honored. Only 15,472 tickets were sold, however, and fewer than ten thousand fans braved the conditions to head to the park for a game that might not be played. In the *Boston Globe* the next day, Peter Gammons referred to the dismal crowd as "the bittersweet part of the occasion" and reflective of "the state of the franchise's current interest."[1] Though the season was just eight weeks old, the club was already seventeen games out of first place.

The Red Sox decision to retire the two numbers, announced the previous November, had been met with some confusion. No one had worn Williams's number since his dramatic home run twenty-four years earlier in the final at bat of his storied career, and most fans believed that his number had already been retired. In fact, the club had never held a ceremony, made a public pronouncement, or recognized the number anywhere in the park. They had just never let anyone else wear it. As for Cronin's 4, it had been worn regularly in the thirty-seven years since Cronin took it off in 1947, most recently by Carney Lansford in 1982. Few fans would have known what number Cronin had worn.

John Harrington, a team consultant and future CEO, had pushed for this night. He had lobbied Haywood Sullivan and Jean Yawkey, the team's two principal owners, both of whom were initially reluctant. Once you start retiring numbers, they felt, when does it stop? To combat this argument, Harrington set out to develop a strict set of criteria, for which he enlisted Dick Bresciani, the club's public-relations director and historian. The two men came up with three: membership in baseball's Hall of Fame, ten or more years playing for the Red Sox, including the last five of their playing career. When Harrington presented his proposal to Yawkey and Sullivan, he told them that only two men qualified for the honor: Cronin and Williams.[2]

The decision to retire the numbers was made in the fall of 1983, and a formal event was planned for the following spring. Had the event been for Williams alone, it might never have come off—he was generally uninterested in ceremonies or honors, especially when they involved him. Convincing Williams to give up a few days of fishing would not have been easy. But the main impetus for the evening was not to honor Ted Williams, who had been honored plenty; it was to honor Joe Cronin. Cronin was very ill, confined to a wheelchair, and suffering from cancer that would take his life less than four months later. For Cronin, a beloved former teammate, manager, and general manager, Williams enthusiastically signed on. He would be there. The night would go on.

Williams and Cronin made for an interesting pairing. They had very little in common within baseball or outside it. Williams joined the Major Leagues as an extraordinary once-in-a-generation talent but spent his entire career battling bouts of rage and immaturity. No one ever accused Joe Cronin of being immature—he behaved like a ten-year veteran when he broke in and was managing a Major League team at age twenty-six. Cronin was a family man, a devoted churchgoer, a gentleman who wore suits and watched his language in front of women. Williams was none of those things and never would be. Williams was a rebel. Joe Cronin did not have a rebellious bone in his body.

Cronin loved nothing more than being around baseball people, attending baseball games and functions, and talking with the press. Williams was a student of the game and could talk for hours if you wanted to talk about hitting, but he spent very little time with baseball people unless he had to and feuded with the press his entire career. When the season was over, Williams would practically disappear until spring training, off fishing somewhere. Cronin's off-season was a whirlwind of meetings, baseball dinners, and socializing. When he became general manager of the Red Sox he instituted a weekly press briefing—there was rarely news, but it gave him an excuse to talk baseball.

Though very different men, Cronin and Williams grew to respect and love each other. Williams later admitted wishing he'd had some of what Cronin had—the family life, the friends, the peace and happiness. It is not hard to imagine Cronin wistfully admiring Williams's rebelliousness, wondering what it would be like to discard the tie before dinner, to fling the bat, to yell at the crowd that booed him. What the two had in common—a love of baseball and their teammates and fellow players and extreme personal generosity—would sustain them through Williams's many rough patches.

The big night still almost did not come to pass. Cronin lived an hour and a half from Boston, in Osterville on Cape Cod, and resisted making the trip almost to the minute he had to leave. Cronin dearly wanted to see all of his old friends but not in his deteriorating condition. Finally, the day before the event, he and his wife Mildred were driven by a neighbor, Laura O'Neill, to the Park Plaza Hotel in Copley Place. When he arrived, he was greeted by several members of the Twins' front office. Cronin had requested the night involve the Twins, for the club's two principal owners—Calvin Griffith and Thelma Haynes—were Mildred's brother and sister, and many other family members worked for the team. The Cronins' oldest son, Tommy, worked in sales for the Twins and was in Boston for the big event. "The next morning," Mildred later related, "that darling Ted Williams came up to the hotel room, and Ted and Joe spent two hours talking about old times."[3]

That evening, the Cronin entourage all made it to the park in time for the 7:30 ceremony. Though he badly wanted to, Cronin decided at the last minute that he could not go out on the field, instead sitting with Mildred in a luxury box above the third base stands. On the field below them sat a ring of dignitaries, including commissioner Bowie Kuhn, American League president Bobby Brown and his predecessor Lee MacPhail, Sullivan, Yawkey, and former teammates Johnny Pesky and Bobby Doerr. Representing Cronin were his four children and several grandchildren, some of whom were running around second base. Williams had three children during his three marriages, but on this night was joined only by John Henry, a fifteen-year-old son he hardly knew.

Mrs. Yawkey, whose late husband had purchased Cronin for a record-setting price fifty years earlier, spoke briefly, saying: "Joe, Ted, we of the Red Sox organization always loved you as do the fans of New England. We will always love you because you are the Red Sox." Both men received the Thomas A. Yawkey Award for their many years of support to the Jimmy Fund. In presenting the award to Williams, Pesky also spoke to his old manager: "Joe, thank you for letting me play. Those were great years." Doerr presented Cronin's award to his daughter Maureen, while thanking Joe for "giving me a look in 1937 for the Red Sox." When Cronin's name was announced the organist played the Disney song "When You Wish upon a Star," a favorite of his.[4]

But the person everyone wanted to hear, as always, was Williams, and the great slugger devoted most of his remarks to his fellow honoree. "One of the best things about playing in Boston," Williams told the crowd, "was I got to play for manager Joe Cronin. You don't realize what an impact he had on me. I have great respect for a very, very wonderful man. Joe Cronin was a great player, manager, and wonderful father and nobody respects you more than me." Visibly emotional as he gestured to Cronin in his box above, he added, "In my eyes you're a great man." Cronin returned the wave, equally moved. Finally, the Red Sox unveiled the two huge numbers, in their classic Red Sox font, on the right-field façade below the ever-present Jimmy Fund billboard.

The ceremony delayed the start of the baseball game until 8:30. At the end of four innings the Twins had built a 5–0 lead, the Red Sox managing just one hit and eight strikeouts against Frank Viola. When the Red Sox took the field in the top of the fifth, the rains that had pelted the city all day and washed out batting practice came back with a vengeance. After a delay of an hour and forty-one minutes, the umpires called the game, wiping out the Twins likely victory. Cronin and Williams, whose ceremony had delayed the game, had helped the club one final time.

"Joe to me was the main concern," related Williams during the rain delay. "Talking with Joe and seeing him smile made the night. I've talked to him on the phone and the greatest thing that could happen to him now is to hear from old ballplayers or get out to see a game like he did tonight."[5] Williams and Cronin would speak on the phone regularly the rest of the summer but would never see each other again.

After the ceremony, Cronin was helped to the pressroom, where he had spent so much time in the previous fifty years. He had a message to deliver to the fans: he had so wanted to be down on that field one more time, to tell the fans how he much he loved them, and to return the complements Williams had paid. But his body simply could not do it. "It was too tough," he said. Cronin also denied any difficulties dealing with Williams: "He was perfect. He never missed a bus, never missed batting practice, never missed anything. He never griped either."[6]

The old shortstop glowed that night. His friends and family still recall how happy he was seeing old friends, being at Fenway Park. He told his children how appreciative he was that the Red Sox had gone through so much trouble for him, long past the time of his contributions to the club. They had honored him with on-field ceremonies twice before: in 1938, to recognize his excellence as a player and manager (he received a silver service, and an Irish terrier that he named Red Sox), and in 1956, to celebrate his induction into baseball's Hall of Fame. This time was better. Williams was right: Cronin needed this night, needed to be around baseball, the game that had meant everything to him for nearly all of his seventy-seven years.

1 San Francisco

AT 5:12 A.M. ON APRIL 18, 1906, A MASSIVE earthquake rocked the vibrant city of San Francisco, California. The devastation wrought by the tremors, along with the resulting fires that burned for four long days, created one of the largest natural disasters in American history, comparable in scope and cost to Hurricane Katrina in 2005. The city of San Francisco reported only 498 deaths, but this figure was almost certainly a deceit by officials concerned about real-estate prices and potential investments in the recovery efforts. Later estimates raised the figure to at least 3,000 dead, but many immigrants in the city—especially the Chinese—would never be properly accounted for. The true death toll may have been 5,000 to 10,000.[1]

At the time of the earthquake, nearly 400,000 people lived in San Francisco,[2] the ninth-largest city in the United States and the cultural and financial center of the American West. Four days later, 490 city blocks, containing an estimated two-thirds of the property value of the city, had been destroyed, leaving 250,000 people homeless. Nearly all of the banks, hotels, and retail stores lay in ruins, along with most of the city's oldest and most fashionable neighborhoods.[3]

As difficult as it might be to imagine today in light of the Katrina disaster, various state and federal agencies acted quickly to rebuild San Francisco and helped organize massive volunteer efforts. The first relief train arrived from Los Angeles on the first night, and the next day the U.S. Congress approved funds that allowed the army to begin sending trains filled with supplies, rations, and tents. Relief soon flowed from Great Britain and Europe. Within three years twenty thousand new buildings had sprung up. In 1915 the city hosted the Panama-Pacific International Exposition, a world's fair, ostensibly to celebrate the opening the previous year of the Panama Canal but more to show the world the city's remarkable recovery. Eighteen million visitors attended the fair, making it a memorable success.[4]

Part of the public-relations strategy of the civic leaders was to place the blame for the city's terrible destruction completely on the fires, most of which resulted from natural-gas mains broken by the tremors. A week after the disaster the real-estate board met and agreed to a resolution that the term "the great earthquake" could no longer be used. It was the "great fire."[5] Any city can have a fire, the reasoning went, so building a home or a business in San Francisco was no more risky than anywhere else. This deception was only partly successful. Though the city rebuilt quickly, most of the West's industry and population growth was diverted south to Los Angeles, which soon replaced San Francisco as the West Coast's economic center. However, San Francisco did restore its reputation as a destination for travelers from all over the world.

Among San Francisco's many homeless after the earthquake was the family of Jeremiah Cronin, a teamster whose horses surely came in handy in the city over the next few years. Born in 1870 in County Cork, Ireland, Jeremiah made his way to San Francisco in 1886. As with many immigrants of this period, things did not work out exactly as he had hoped. Work days were long and difficult even before the quake and fires, and for men like Jeremiah, the city's working poor, the rebuilding of their city meant even more work and ever longer days. Jeremiah's wife, the former Mary Caroline, was a native San Franciscan, born in 1870. Mary's parents had emigrated from the old country, County Athlone.[6] At the time of the city's devastation, Jeremiah and Mary had two sons, twelve-year-old Raymond and nine-year-old James, and Mary was expecting a third child in the fall.

Like most people who lived through the fires, the Cronins had their story to tell. Their home in the heart of the city was destroyed, forcing the family of four to move in with Jeremiah's sister, Hannah Coughlin. Hannah and her family had a small house on Twenty-ninth and Sanchez streets in the Mission District, and it had been thankfully spared. The only object Jeremiah saved from his house was an old rocking chair, which stayed in the family for years and played a prominent role in most family reminiscences about the city's famous earthquake.[7]

A story was later told of Jeremiah watching the city burn from a bar he frequented on Russian Hill, not far from where the family lived.[8] Jeremiah was not happy in San Francisco and often regretted his decision to leave Ireland for a better life that had not come. Seeing the city being destroyed in front of his eyes, he knew that he would have steady work for the foreseeable future but that his days would be hard ones. For many years, teams of horses, run by men like Jeremiah Cronin, carried tons of debris from the heart of the city to the bay, creating or defining the city's famous bay fronts and wharves and making room for many of the buildings that mark the city today.[9]

The Cronins' third son, Joseph Edward Cronin, was born on October 12, at the family's temporary home with his aunt in the Mission District. After the christening Jeremiah playfully shook a fist at little Joe and warned, "If I ever catch ya near a horse, I'll shoot ya."[10]

When Joe was a few months old, the family of five moved into their own home, a small two-story house that still stands at 412 Persia Avenue in the city's Excelsior District. The Excelsior is in the far-southern end of the city, about two miles west of Candlestick Point, and a century ago was a neighborhood of farms and inexpensive homes. The neighborhood was relatively untouched by the earthquake, and became a destination for many displaced families.[11] The Cronins were one such family, and they stayed in the house on Persia Avenue for nearly thirty years. It was located in a quiet neighborhood away from the active urban renewal going on to the north. Young Joe raised rabbits and chickens in his backyard.

The central elements in young Joe's life were church and school. He attended the Roman Catholic Church of the Epiphany a few blocks away at least once a week throughout his childhood and remained a regular churchgoer for the rest of his life. The Cleveland School, which Joe attended through eighth grade, was also a short walk from his house. With his father working long hours, Joe's mother Mary was the central figure in his childhood, a strong woman who preached traditional values about God and education. Joe loved his mother dearly and spoke of her often to his own children decades later.[12]

But from a very early age Joe Cronin wanted nothing more than to play sports. There is no indication that either of his brothers, each several years older, were athletes. By the time Joe was a few years old his brothers were teenagers and holding down jobs. While his father worked, his mother kept the house running. When it came to making his way in the new neighborhood, Joe was more or less an only child.

The Excelsior Playground, equipped with a baseball diamond and tennis courts, was just one block away from Joe's house and part of a well-managed recreational system in the city. Each neighborhood had its own playground, and each playground employed a caretaker in charge of maintaining the grounds and a director who organized teams at various levels in several sports. Each playground fielded teams in baseball, basketball, soccer, and several other sports with the staff doubling as coaches and umpires. The rivalries with other playgrounds were intense.[13]

Joe Cronin, possessing an excess of nervous energy and with no siblings near his age, spent hours at the playground every day and played on every team he could. He participated in soccer, ran track, and played basketball. In 1920 at age fourteen, he won the city's tennis championship for his age group, a story he retold often in later years. "I never had the price of a pair of tennis shoes, but one year when I was 14," Joe recounted, "Stella Harris, our playground director, bought me my first pair out of her own pocket. I won the city-wide championship in those shoes." Harris remained a lifelong friend.[14]

But like most San Francisco boys of his time, baseball was the most important sport. "I cannot remember a day," he later recalled, "when I didn't want to be a ballplayer."[15] In San Francisco, with its mild winters and cool summers, there were leagues all year-round. He began his career as a pitcher and was, by all accounts, a good one. He became a shortstop, writer Joe Williams later reported Joe told him, "because he could not see eye-to-eye with the umpire."[16]

The Pacific Coast League (PCL) was born three years before Joe, and to the boys of the city there was no greater aspiration than to someday play for the Seals, the Coast League's San Francisco franchise. The local heroes played in Recreation Park, located at Fifteenth and Valencia, and Joe was not alone in trying to see them any chance he got. Joe never took much interest in his schoolwork, but when the Seals began giving tickets to local schools for students who exhibited good attendance and behavior, the promotion had the intended effect on young Cronin, who earned the tickets several times.[17] Joe later referred to the park as "the hallowed ground of Willie Kamm," referring to the third baseman who played four years for the Seals starting when Joe was twelve and who was sold by the Seals to the White Sox for a record price of $100,000 while Joe was in high school. "Yeah, I idolized Willie—so did half my friends—and then years later I found myself playing in the major leagues against him."[18]

Though San Francisco was nearly two thousand miles from the nearest Major League team, the city had a rich baseball tradition exemplified both by the Seals and by the number of excellent players who grew up there and were in the Major Leagues during Cronin's childhood. Ping Bodie, another of Joe's childhood heroes, had grown up in the Cow Hollow neighborhood, played for the Seals, and starred for the White Sox and Yankees in the 1910s. Harry Heilmann led the Seals to the 1915 PCL championship, then embarked on a great career with the Detroit Tigers. George Kelly began his long career with the Giants in 1915. Babe Pinelli played eight years in the Majors, followed by twenty-two years as a National League umpire. Lefty O'Doul, the pride of Butchertown, made it to the Seals in 1917 and played and managed in the city for thirty years before and after his own fine Major League career. All of these men, and several others, returned to San Francisco every winter and were role models for aspiring schoolboy baseball players.

For Joe Cronin, nothing could compare with watching the Seals play at Rec Park. In fact, Joe would often jump on the back of passing trucks to get to the games. "Funny thing about that," Joe recalled sixty years later, "I learned that you could get into Recreation Park if you went down there early and helped the man who was in charge of the turnstiles. So I went down bright and early one day and helped this fellow set up, and sure enough he let me in. I was the first person in the ball park, and I went out to the bleachers to watch the players warm up." Unfortunately, Joe got so excited when a loose ball came near him in center field that he jumped onto the field, retrieved the ball, and tossed it back to the players. "After dreaming all night long about how I was going to get in free, I got myself kicked out before the game even started."[19]

Besides Bodie and Kamm, Cronin later recalled having one other baseball idol as a boy: Tony Lazzeri. Lazzeri, just three years older than Joe, grew up in Cow Hollow like Bodie had and starred in several sports for Jackson Playground. Joe could not keep his eyes off him. "It was Tony who booted the ball to win the soccer match, or got the hit that won the ball game, or carried the pigskin for the touchdown," Joe later recalled. "I was always imitating Tony."[20] Lazzeri did not go to high school, instead working alongside his father at a local iron-works factory. When his local playground needed him, he got off work and, more often than not, provided what his team needed to win.

As soon as Joe was old enough, he had to help out the family by delivering newspapers, running errands for the local merchants, or just helping his mother keep the house running. But no doubt his athletic notoriety helped him earn a job working for Stella Harris, the Excelsior Playground's director. By the age of nine he had begun showing up to games early to help Harris roll the baseball diamond for two cents, but within a few years he held an official position on the staff and eventually became a roving substitute with other playgrounds in the city. When playground directors in the city were sick or vacationing, Joe was called upon to take their place for a day or a week. He often tutored future Major Leaguers like Frank Crosetti, Eddie Joost, and Dario Lodigiani.[21] The idea that he would someday play for the Seals was a dream that kept Joe working at baseball every day.

After graduating from Cleveland Grammar School in 1920, Joe attended Mission High School for two years, about a four-mile trolley ride to the north but fortuitously just a few minute's walk from Recreation Park and the Seals. As a sophomore at Mission he teamed with future National League star Wally Berger to help win the city public-school baseball championship—Berger played third base and Cronin second base.[22] (Another teammate, Jack Shelley, later served eight terms in the U.S. Congress before becoming San Francisco's mayor.) Not long after winning the 1922 baseball title, Mission High School burned to the ground, an event Joe later jokingly blamed on various school chums.

While Mission High was being rebuilt the next fall, classes were temporarily held in a local Protestant church. This turn of events was too much for a devoted Catholic like Mary Cronin to bear, so the family transferred Joe to the parochial Sacred Heart High School, about six miles north in the heart of the city. Heilmann and Pinelli had attended Sacred Heart a few years earlier. Dolph Camilli was a student there two years after Joe. Former heavyweight boxing champion Gentleman Jim Corbett might have been the school's most famous graduate.

Joe played baseball, soccer, and basketball for his new school, and earned extra money working as a basketball referee. "I played anything that didn't cost anything," Joe later recalled.[23] By this time Joe had played these sports all over the city, so he knew many of the athletes at his new school and elsewhere. "I used to carry my spikes to school, and when we had the time we would organize what we called 'hitting leagues,' with a boy taking 20 minutes at bat and then shagging flies."[24] His 1924 baseball team won the city-wide prep-school championship, with Joe acting as captain.

In addition to the organized playground leagues, the city also had several other sandlot baseball circuits organized by local companies. In 1923 Joe joined the Columbia Park Boys Club, which had a great team in a high-quality league that was run by the *San Francisco Examiner*. Joe's team was organized by a local philanthropist, who took the team on an annual trip down the Pacific Coast, stopping several times along the way to play local semipro teams. This trip marked Joe's first excursion away from the Bay Area. The club was followed by several scouts from the Pacific Coast League and the Major Leagues. The winners of the *Examiner* league each received a Bill Doak–model glove, providing additional motivation for the boys while making

Doak, a dependable but unspectacular National League pitcher of the time, one of the better-known players in the city. Cronin's club won the gloves in 1923.

During the spring of 1924, Joe's senior year, he was offered a baseball and basketball scholarship by Slip Madigan, the athletic director at St. Mary's College. St. Mary's was a private Roman Catholic school in Oakland (it moved to Moraga in 1929), which had sent many players to the Major Leagues, including Harry Hooper and Dutch Leonard. Joe had little interest in college, but his family urged him not to turn the offer down right away and give it some thought. In the meantime, Joe was playing baseball for his high school and several sandlot teams.[25]

At this early age Joe had already begun to exhibit the work ethic that would sustain him into his Major League career. Possessed of great athletic ability and a genuine love of baseball and other sports, he nonetheless outworked everyone at every level up the baseball ladder. This nature would inform his philosophy as a manager and general manager in later years, to the point that he believed that mediocre players could become very good players by working harder. After all he had done that very thing. Of course this discounts his obvious baseball talent, and Joe would eventually learn that sometimes hard work was not enough to make a player as good as he had been.

In the summer of 1924 Joe earned money playing baseball for the first time, with a semipro club in Napa, north of the city. Before he graduated from Sacred Heart, he played under the name of Joe Smith, reverting to his real name when high school finished. The club played on Sundays, and Joe eventually made $12.50 per game. In addition to this stipend, he also earned money by continuing to help out at various playgrounds and held a part-time job as a bank teller. All of this money went to his parents to be used just like any other money that came into the household.

In order to get to the Sunday games in Napa, Cronin first went to 6:00 mass at his neighborhood parish, got on a trolley at 6:30, which took him to the waterfront on the northern end of the city, then took a two-hour ferry ride to Vallejo, and finally a one-hour trolley to

Napa.[26] (San Francisco was still largely landlocked—the Bay Bridge and the Golden Gate Bridge opened in the late 1930s.)

The seventeen-year-old Joe Cronin was nearly six feet tall but weighed no more than 140 pounds, with dirty blond hair, striking Irish blue eyes, and his trademark cut jaw. Skinny as a rail, he was nonetheless the Napa team's star, and the battle for the league championship with San Mateo drew quite a bit of local attention. The title contest, played in San Mateo to the south, was of such interest that Joe's parents paid the twenty-five-cent streetcar fare to come watch him play. Unfortunately, Joe had badly injured his ankle in a game a few days earlier and was not able to take the field. Late in the game he was put in to pinch hit and slugged what would have been a home run, but Joe had to settle for a game-winning single after he hobbled to first base. This story and Joe's picture were in the city papers the next day.

In the fall of 1924 Cronin played for the San Leandro club in the Eastbay League and continued to gather attention for his play. "In the game at the Coast League park last Sunday afternoon," reported the *Oakland Tribune*, "[Joe] hammered out a pair of triples to the right field fence and got a single. He is a tall boy, who has a wonderful pair of hands, and knows what it is all about when he gets into action."[27]

Joe's family could hardly believe that their seventeen-year-old son was making more money than his father for playing baseball and helping out in the playground. One Sunday Joe came home with $12.50 for playing a game that day. "If I had only known that a few years ago," exclaimed the impressed Mrs. Cronin, "I would have made both Jim and Ray become ballplayers." By 1920 Joe's brother James had joined their father as a teamster, while Raymond was a clerk. The reasonable expectation was that Joe, no great scholar, would eventually, perhaps after some time at St. Mary's, have to learn a trade. This all changed in the summer of 1924, when the pro scouts first showed up at the door on Persia Avenue.

Joe still dreamed of playing for his hometown Seals. By the summer after his graduation he had become enough of a local star that he would not have been surprised when Seals' president Charlie Graham came to call on the Cronin family. Graham, from nearby Santa Clara, played briefly with the Boston Americans (later named the Red Sox) in 1906 but made his mark in baseball with his thirty-year association with the Seals. He managed the team for four years beginning in 1918, but after he became the team's czar, the club won four PCL titles in the 1920s, with some of the better teams in Minor League history. Graham would have been a very impressive figure in the Cronin house, even more so when he offered Joe $300 per month to sign with the Seals for 1925. But the family did not sign right away, waiting to see if any other offers were forthcoming.

The other interested team was the Major League Pittsburgh Pirates, represented by scout Joe Devine. A native of San Francisco, Devine had had small stints as a player, including with the Oakland Oaks in 1915, and had managed Calgary in the Western Canada League in 1920 and 1921. By 1923 he was back in his native region, working as Pittsburgh's Bay Area scout. When he approached the Cronins the next year, he had not yet achieved his great fame as a scout—his biggest coup thus far had been his inking of longtime Oakland Oak Ray Kremer to a contract a year earlier. His big signings for the Pirates—including Harold Rhyne, Paul Waner, Lloyd Waner, Dick Bartell, and Arky Vaughan—were in the near future. After a stint managing the PCL Mission Reds, Devine later scouted for the New York Yankees and helped land a succession of West Coast standouts, including Joe DiMaggio, Bobby Brown, Jackie Jensen, and Gil McDougald.[28]

But all of that was in the future. Cronin had nearly made up his mind to sign with Graham when he agreed to meet Devine one final time at Klawan and McMullen's, a sporting-goods store at Mission and Fourth that operated as the social center for the city's sports enthusiasts. Devine offered Cronin a $200 bonus and $400 per month for 1925, easing Joe's decision by besting the Seals' terms. Cronin barely kept his emotions in check, telling Devine he would speak with his family at home that evening.

Mary Cronin had reservations about her son hanging around with "sporting characters" but had finally reconciled herself to his playing with the Seals, at least staying in the city. Pennsylvania was another matter, and Mrs. Cronin did what all good Irish mothers of the time would do: she sought the advice of the family priest. "Don't you worry," consoled the Father. "He's going to be a fine ballplayer. It won't be long before you're the proudest mother in San Francisco."[29]

So the Cronins accepted Devine's offer, putting the $200 bonus towards the family's mortgage.[30] Joe Cronin, still a boy, would now begin a new life in professional baseball, far away from the only world and people he had ever known.

2 Pittsburgh and Other Places

THE PROFESSIONAL BASEBALL WORLD THAT
Joe Cronin entered in 1925 included the two Major Leagues, and
twenty-five independent Minor Leagues collectively made up of 172
teams. These teams owned and controlled most or all of their rosters.
The Minor Leagues, organized as the National Association, were
further arranged by classification, from the lowest Class-D leagues to
the three strong Double-A circuits. As "farm systems" had yet to be
established, the Minors and Majors had formal agreements that regu-
lated how players could be controlled or advanced through the Minor
Leagues and to the Majors. These agreements were not static—the
arrangements were often altered from the 1910s through the 1930s.

For a promising young amateur ballplayer, there were still two main
paths to the Major Leagues, though neither path offered the player any
control of his career once he signed his initial contract. The first and
most common path consisted of signing a deal with a Minor League
team, often near the player's hometown, having a good season or two,
getting sold to a higher league, and then repeating this process up the
ladder until the player reached the Major Leagues. For example, Joe
Cronin's old rival Tony Lazzeri signed with Salt Lake City (Pacific
Coast League) in 1922 and was sold to the Yankees after four seasons.
This path was not always a straight one—Lazzeri was twice optioned
to lower leagues during these years, with Salt Lake City still having
control of his contract and future. After a breakout season in 1925,
New York paid $50,000 to Salt Lake for Lazzeri's contract.

Had Joe Cronin chosen to take the offer from the Seals' Charlie
Graham, he would have been the property of San Francisco, but the
eighteen-year-old would have been unlikely to stick with the PCL
club. The Seals of this era fielded some of the greatest teams in Minor

League history. The 1925 team, ranked by baseball historians Bill Weiss and Marshall Wright as the tenth best ever, was led by Paul Waner, whose .401 batting average that season was the first .400 season ever in the Pacific Coast League.[1] The team had several other star players as well. Cronin's competition at shortstop on the Seals would have been Harold "Hal" Rhyne, who hit .315 in 188 games in his fourth season of regular duty. Cronin would not have unseated Rhyne, who was seven years older and a key player on several great Seals teams. More likely, Cronin would have been farmed out to the Utah-Idaho league like many young PCL prospects of the time.[2]

Joe Cronin followed the alternative path available to only a select few prospects; he signed directly with a Major League team. A club in the 1920s could have twenty-five players on its active roster and could "option" up to eight additional players to the Minor Leagues for later recall. No player could be optioned more than twice. As an illustration, the New York Yankees signed local college star Lou Gehrig in 1923, optioned his contract to Hartford in both 1923 and 1924, and finally kept him on the Major League roster in 1925. New York could not have optioned Gehrig a third time; had they chosen not to keep him, an unlikely scenario given his great season with Hartford in 1924, Gehrig could have been signed by any other team.

On rare occasions an amateur player would sign with a Major League team and stick with the club immediately. The Giants inked a seventeen-year-old Mel Ott from a semipro team in 1926 and kept him on the Major League roster for a couple of years before playing him regularly. The Giants at this time signed a lot of amateur players, and the option limits restricted their development options. Ott was not really a Major League player—he stuck with the team because the Giants could not option him and didn't want to lose him.[3]

The Major League draft, begun in 1892 as a way for the Major Leagues to select players from the Minors for a set fee, rather than engaging in a bidding war, was abrogated by the Minors in 1919. From 1919 until 1931 the status of the draft changed many times; in the mid-1920s each Minor League could opt out of the draft, which all three Double-A leagues did. Regardless of a league's stance on this matter, any player obtained by the Minors from the Majors could be drafted in the following off-season. In 1931 the draft was reinstituted for all leagues, and it remains in effect today as the Rule 5 draft.[4]

These ever-changing rules evolved because of the conflicting goals of Major and Minor League teams. The Minors wanted to field competitive teams and make money, sometimes by selling their players to higher-classification teams or to the Majors. Major League clubs wanted to control as many good players as they could, storing some for later, sifting through all of them to field the best team every year. Kenesaw Mountain Landis, baseball's commissioner, was purportedly looking out for the players and wanted the best players to be able to work their way up the chain with little impediment. The notion of a Major League ballclub using the Minor Leagues as a "farm system" was on the near horizon and would butt up against Landis's wishes repeatedly in the next twenty years.

Meanwhile Joe Cronin, wholly owned by the Pittsburgh Pirates, headed south in March 1925 to Paso Robles, California, where the Pirates held their annual spring training camp. Cronin was accompanied by his good friend Eddie Montague, a fellow San Franciscan against whom Cronin had played many times and whom Joe Devine had also signed for the Pirates. Montague was a year older than Cronin and had attended the city's Polytechnic High. He had also played for the Sunset Federals in the *Examiner* league, a rival to Cronin's Columbia Park Boys Club, and briefly for the Seals in 1923. Montague had been released by the Seals in 1924 because of an unexpected glut of talent on their roster.[5] Now the two San Franciscans were teammates, two infielders competing against each other for a spot with the Pirates. The Pirates could option either or both men and could do so for two years.

The Pirates of this era were a quality team, especially in the infield. The 1924 team had finished a strong third, just three games behind the champion New York Giants. The incumbent shortstop was twenty-four-year-old Glenn Wright, who after a single season had established himself as one of the stronger shortstops in the National League, not missing a single inning and hitting a solid .287. The rest of the infield did not offer any opportunities either. Pie Traynor, the twenty-five-year-old third baseman, was just getting started on his seventeen-year Hall of Fame career with the Pirates. The club had acquired second baseman George Grantham from the Cubs in the recent off-season but planned to move him to first base. Eddie Moore had hit .359 in seventy-two games in 1924 and looked to be the second baseman.

As Cronin and Montague took the train two hundred miles south, they probably understood the odds. According to his later accounts, Cronin was well treated by his veteran teammates in camp and at least some evidence bears this out. Cronin began his habit of making lifelong friends in the game at every stop he made, and he would later hire Bill McKechnie, Glenn Wright, and Kiki Cuyler, three men he met at his first camp. Cronin later had kind words for the way he was treated by Wright, and also by Fred Clarke, a long-time Pirate player and manager who had returned that season as a coach.[6] Cronin played well enough in camp to draw the attention of the *Los Angeles Times* ("the 18-year-old Frisco phenom")[7] and the *Washington Post* ("a marvel").[8]

But he was not going to make the team. McKechnie told reporters on March 19, "Cronin has been the sensation of the camp. He needs seasoning, and will be farmed out for future use."[9] The team broke camp in early April, and Cronin remained with the team on the long trip back east, playing briefly in various exhibition matches and even riding the bench for a couple of weeks after the season started. Finally he was ordered to report to Johnstown, Pennsylvania, which had a team in the Middle Atlantic League. Cronin had stuck with the Pirates into the late spring because the Middle Atlantic did not start its season until mid-May, and the Pirates did not have to cut down to a twenty-five-man roster until June 15.[10]

Johnstown, a city of about seventy-five thousand people, was just seventy-five miles away from Pittsburgh and was most famous for the Great Flood of 1889, when the collapse of a dam unleashed twenty thousand tons of water into the town.[11] After several years of recovery efforts, Johnstown had rebuilt itself into a comfortable hard-working city, which primarily produced and fabricated steel at its Cambria Iron Company. No reminiscences survive of what Cronin might have done off the field, but surely there would have been movie houses and dance halls to get a young man through the hot summer.

Traveling in the Middle Atlantic League was not difficult—six clubs made up the circuit, and the towns were all within one hundred miles of each other.[12] The team likely would have used a couple of large automobiles to get around (the roster consisted of about fifteen men) or perhaps an old bus. Cronin was joining a Class-C league, a long way from the Major Leagues but having much higher caliber competition than he had faced in the strong semipro organizations in the Bay Area.

Eddie Montague accompanied Cronin to Johnstown, where they remained all summer, living in the same boardinghouse a few miles from the ballpark.[13] The team's star was twenty-one-year-old center fielder James "Ripper" Collins, who hit .327 with 15 home runs near the start of his twenty-four-year professional career. Although the Pittsburgh and Johnstown clubs had a loose affiliation, most of the players—including Collins—had contracts with Johnstown. Cronin's contract was, of course, with the Pirates. The left fielder on the club was Nat Hickey, a versatile athlete who played professional basketball for many years and still holds the record for being the oldest player in NBA history. Hickey also became Stan Musial's first Minor League manager in 1938 in the Mountain State League. Later asked if he had taught Cronin and Collins how to hit while at Johnstown, Hickey responded, "Yeah, I helped them—it was like teaching a duck to swim."[14]

Johnstown's Johnnies, led by manager Norm McNeill, went 64-31 and ran away with the pennant. The league played a split season schedule, but as Johnstown won both halves of the season there was no playoff.[15] Cronin was the everyday shortstop and hit .313, with just 3 home runs but 11 triples and 18 doubles in ninety-nine games. Montague played third base and hit .248.

After the conclusion of the Middle Atlantic League schedule, Cronin and Montague worked out with the Pirates for the rest of the season, watching the Major Leaguers wrap up the league pennant easily over the Giants. The two youngsters even had a seat on the bench when the Pirates beat the Senators in a tight seven-game World Series.

Cronin had a right to be satisfied with his first professional season as he traveled back home to his family. That winter, Cronin and Montague played for the Oakland Roofers, a club owned by local contractor Del Webb (who would later become a real-estate and construction tycoon and co-own the New York Yankees). Cronin also continued to work for San Francisco's playground system, organizing teams and umpiring games.

Despite his fine maiden season, Cronin's chances of making the Major Leagues in the short-term had not improved much. Glenn Wright once again had played every game at shortstop, hitting .308 with 18 home runs and 121 runs batted in. Eddie Moore had played second base for the champions, batting .298 with 36 errors. After the season Joe Devine purchased the contracts of outfielder Paul Waner and shortstop Hal Rhyne for the Pirates, placing another more experienced infielder in Cronin's path.

Nonetheless, Cronin returned to Paso Robles in March 1926 with the goal of making the big league club. After another impressive showing, he broke camp with the Pirates and even got into some game action. On April 29 in Pittsburgh's Forbes Field against the Reds, Cronin pinch-ran for catcher Earl Smith in the sixth inning, his first Major League appearance. He pinch-ran again the next day and twice more in early May. On May 10 the Pirates traveled to Johnstown for an exhibition game, and McKechnie let Cronin play against some of his old mates, including Eddie Montague. Cronin responded with a pair of two-run home runs to lead the Major League squad to a 5–0 victory.[16] Nonetheless, a few days later he was optioned to New Haven, Connecticut, to play in the Eastern League. At the time of his demotion, Cronin's Major League career consisted of four pinch-running appearances and two runs scored.

New Haven was a city of about 160,000 people,[17] a place with more diversions than Johnstown but of course fewer than Cronin's hometown. The Eastern was a Class-A circuit, the second highest Minor League classification at the time and a big promotion from the Middle Atlantic. The league was geographically concentrated, bounded by Albany to the north and west, and Providence to the east, again limiting travel to two-hour car rides. One of the better teams, New Haven was managed by Jack Flynn, who had briefly played with the Pirates and Senators in the early 1910s. The strong organization was ably led by thirty-year-old team president George Weiss, near the start of a fifty-year association with the game that would eventually earn him a plaque in the Hall of Fame.

Weiss and Cronin would later become friends and rivals running Major League clubs, and the two would often be asked to reflect on their time together in New Haven. "Cronin was 19 and a tremendous prospect," recalled Weiss. "Joe was well behaved, was always in bed early, and came to the park ready to play. He was the ideal type player." For his part, Cronin remembered that Weiss drove a Cadillac, one of two cars used by the team when it traveled to road games, the other being Flynn's Hudson. "On the days we won, everybody tried to climb into the Caddy because we knew George was going to pick up the dinner checks," recalled Cronin. "When we lost, everybody ran for the Hudson."[18]

More than twenty years later, on the occasion of Cronin being honored at a dinner in New Haven, Sam Hyman, a roommate of Cronin's in 1926, spoke to a reporter about his old teammate. "There never was a rookie like Cronin. That's all he wanted to talk—baseball. That's all he wanted to do. He got so he went to the park every morning to practice hitting and he dragged me along to do the pitching. On the way out we would pick up kids to do the shagging. I never saw a young ball player with more ambition."[19]

In his first Eastern League game, on May 14 in Springfield, Massachusetts, Cronin played shortstop and hit a double and triple in two official at bats.[20] He kept hitting, climbing to .320 by midsummer. On June 12, his bases-loaded home run helped win a game at Providence, 10–2. Looking back on his days in New Haven years later, Cronin credited his double-play partner Bill Gleason, a Major League infielder a few years earlier, for working with him and encouraging him at shortstop and at the plate.[21]

Around the Eastern League, a hard deluge of rain was referred to as "Joe Cronin weather" because Cronin insisted on practicing every day, even in the worst conditions. As his teammates backed away one by one, Cronin worked out with kids that were hanging around the park. The term "Joe Cronin weather" was used in the league for years afterwards.[22] The hard work paid off when Cronin learned of his recall to the Pirates on July 15. By agreement he played a few more games in New Haven; in his final one, on the eighteenth, his three hits helped beat Springfield, 5–3.[23]

The Pirates were in first place on July 24 but were overtaken by the Cardinals at the end of August and finished third. Shortstop Glenn Wright and rookie second baseman Hal Rhyne were fighting injuries, and Eddie Moore, backup at both positions, was not hitting or fielding well. A few days after Cronin's arrival, Moore was sold to the Braves, making Cronin a top middle-infield reserve. Though Cronin later claimed to have never manned second base, he played twenty-seven games there (along with seven at shortstop) after his promotion. Cronin hit .265 in his trial and fielded both positions well. He got his first Major League hit, a single, on August 4 off Bob Smith of the Boston Braves.

The Pirates' failure to repeat as National League champions in 1926, coupled with a bizarre internal controversy involving several players and Pirate icon Fred Clarke, caused owner Barney Dreyfus to fire manager McKechnie after the season. To take over the reins, Dreyfus tapped Donie Bush, a sixteen-year veteran shortstop who had skippered the 1923 Washington Senators. Cronin had played no part in the internal bickering and likely took no joy in the sacking of the well-respected McKechnie, who had given him twenty-five starts in September.

Cronin returned to San Francisco after the season, playing baseball when he could and helping out on the playgrounds. According to his later accounts, he spent much of that off-season trying to get bigger and stronger—drinking eggnog and creams and eating his mother's oatmeal. He hiked in the nearby woods and chopped down trees, and played semipro baseball through the winter. The next spring he was ten pounds heavier, and much stronger.[24]

Cronin returned to Paso Robles in 1927, ready to battle for the second base job. Rhyne was the incumbent, but the position had been the Pirates' weakest in 1926. Cronin might "spur Rhyne on," felt a *Sporting News* correspondent. "Cronin looks mighty good, and, no doubt some day is going to be a real ball player, but there are still some crudities about his work. . . . Perhaps another season in the minors will polish him off."[25] In fact, the Pirates could not send Cronin to the Minors for a third time without risking losing him to another Major League club.

In spring camp, Bush liked what he saw in his young infielder. "I am sure that second base is going to be well taken care of," said Bush, "no matter whether I finally assign Joe Cronin or Hal Rhyne to the keystone sack."[26] Cronin had played as well as Rhyne in 1926, though in many fewer games. In any event Rhyne won the everyday job, with Cronin remaining as his backup. At least that was what observers believed.

When Rhyne developed a bad cold that forced him to the bench in early May, Cronin might have assumed it was his chance to get some playing time. Instead, Bush shifted veteran first baseman George Grantham to second base and installed Joe Harris, Cronin's roommate, at first. This was not as bold as it sounds—Grantham had been a regular at second base as recently as 1923, and Harris at the time of trade was a .318 lifetime hitter with power and patience. Though no one had anticipated this move during the spring, Bush did not hesitate to make the switch, and both Harris and Grantham hit well at their new positions. When Rhyne got healthy, Bush kept his new infield in place. On the year, Harris hit .326, while Grantham hit .305. The Pirates reclaimed the pennant in 1927, and Bush's decision to realign his infield was considered the key move of the year.

Cronin watched this fine team from a spot on the bench, playing in just twelve games, most of them partial games, while remaining with the club all season. He stroked three hits in a rare start at shortstop on July 2, earning a shot again the next day when he went hitless with three errors, all on high throws. Overall he managed just 5 hits in 22 at bats for a .227 batting average. Cronin played the final (meaningless) game of the year at first base after having not played at all in more than two months. For exercise that season, Cronin often resorted to playing tennis with Doc Marks, an assistant football coach at Carnegie Tech.

Still he continued to work hard at baseball. Cronin later credited clubhouse attendant Socko McCarey, a one-time aspiring pitcher, "who used to go out and pitch to me morning, noon and night. Socko was a little guy, but I could never wear him out. He wouldn't quit and so I refused to quit." Cronin's experiences that summer and his eventual success strengthened his belief that ballplayers could be made by hard work. (Years later, Cronin hired McCarey as a Red Sox scout, and they would remain friends until the end of Cronin's life.[27])

The Pirates won a tight four-team race but fell quickly to the powerful New York Yankees in the World Series. For Cronin, who never left the bench in the Series, the silver lining to the season was his full World Series share of nearly $4,000—far more money than his yearly salary.

After the season Pittsburgh traded right fielder Kiki Cuyler to the Cubs for two players, including second baseman Sparky Adams. Cuyler, a great hitter, had been involved in a bitter dispute with Bush that led to his benching for the last two months of the season and the World Series. More importantly for Cronin, whatever remaining flicker of hope he had of playing in Pittsburgh was extinguished by the acquisition of Adams, one of the league's better second basemen.

Cronin spent another winter in the Bay Area playing ball and preparing for the season, come what may. He ran into his friend Eddie Montague and learned that Eddie had joined the Indians organization. Though Cronin had a much more impressive Minor League record, he knew his friend had a better path to more playing time in the big leagues, and Cronin longed to move anywhere rather than go through another year like 1927. While still only twenty-one, he was losing patience with his situation.[28] Practically speaking, 1927 had been a wasted year in Cronin's journey to whatever he was to become.

For the fourth straight year, he traveled to Paso Robles in March, hoping for more playing time even if it meant returning to the Minor Leagues. Cronin competed for a backup infield job with Dick Bartell, one year younger than Cronin and from Alameda, California, just across the Bay from San Francisco. Bartell had signed with Joe Devine in 1926 and had spent 1927 at Bridgeport, hitting .280.[29]

On April 1 while the Pirates were staying at the Rosslyn Hotel in Los Angeles and preparing for their long trip east, Cronin got the news he had been waiting for: a note from Bush telling him he had been sold to Kansas City. The Pirates had used up their two options on Cronin and could not send him to the Minor Leagues without losing all rights to him, so they worked out a deal with the Kansas City club. The note came with a train ticket. He later recalled being both relieved and disappointed at his failure to make good with the Pirates. In any event, Cronin packed his bags and headed east.[30]

A Pirate correspondent cast a hopeful tone to the news. "Joe is one of the most popular young players ever with the Buccaneers," said the writer. "Relations between the Pirates and Blues are friendly, and it is possible Pittsburgh would be given first opportunity to repurchase Cronin in case he should find himself."[31]

The Kansas City Blues played in the American Association, one of three Double-A circuits in the Minor Leagues. The league in 1928 consisted of eight teams, playing in second-tier cities throughout the Midwest. The Blues were the property of local millionaire George E. Muehlebach, owner of a large brewery, a famous downtown hotel, and Muehlebach Stadium, which he had built for his baseball team.

Dutch Zwilling, a former big-league outfielder, returned for the second year of what would be a six-year run as skipper of the Blues. The team Cronin joined already had a shortstop—Topper Rigney, who had played the past six years with three teams in the American League—and a second baseman—Bill Wambsganss, a thirteen-year

AL veteran. So Cronin would switch positions once again, this time playing third base.

Strictly speaking, one might consider Cronin's sale to the Blues as a demotion, but in reality he had never played regularly in a league as advanced as the American Association. Furthermore, he had not seen much game action over the previous year and one-half. Despite the impression that his career had stalled, Cronin was only twenty-one. There was still time.

Cronin played nearly every day for Kansas City, mostly at third base and occasionally at shortstop. He worked on his hitting and fielding before every game with Chick Fraser, a long time Major League infielder twenty years earlier. Nevertheless, he struggled in the advanced league after his long layoff, hitting just .245 in seventy-four games. Cronin was frustrated, broke (he was sending nearly all his money back to his parents), and worried about his future.[32] Apparently the Blues were considering optioning Cronin to Wichita of the Western League.[33]

It was later said of Joe Cronin that he was a fortunate man, that he had the Luck of the Irish. Of course this ignores the fact that he spent more than three years working his tail off without experiencing any luck at all. Nevertheless, the next passage in Joe Cronin's story is one of the life-changing events that led to his later reputation for being "lucky." One day in early July, after another hot ballgame, Fraser approached Cronin and told him to go upstairs to see Joe Engel. "Who's Joe Engel?" Cronin wanted to know. "You'll find out when you get there." Cronin did as he was told, fearing the news that he was being demoted and that his career had taken yet another detour. Instead Engel, chief scout for the Washington Senators, told Cronin he had just purchased his contract, and they needed to get back to DC immediately. The happily stunned Cronin quickly cleared out his apartment and was ready to go.[34] He was returning to the Major Leagues.

As both Cronin and Engel became famous baseball personalities in the years ahead, many versions of this deal were recounted; in fact, it became a signature story in each man's baseball life. A few facts can be stated with confidence. Engel was on a routine scouting trip in the Midwest, always on the lookout for players. He stopped in Kansas City, and heard from Muehlebach and business manager John Savage that Cronin had been a disappointment. Engel remembered watching Cronin practice with the Pirates the previous season and decided to make an offer. After some haggling, the parties settled on $7,500.[35]

Engel later claimed that Senators owner Clark Griffith blew up when he telegrammed the news of the purchase price—$7,500 for a .245 hitter!—and told Engel that he would have to pay the $7,500 himself. Engel decided to take his time getting back to Washington, hoping that Griffith would calm down. This part of the story is almost certainly exaggerated; Engel and Griffith were friends, and the great scout knew his baseball talent—he had signed many fine players for the Senators, including Joe Judge, Bucky Harris, Ossie Bluege, Fred Marberry, and Buddy Myer. Griffith had every reason to trust Engel's judgment as it had helped him win two pennants in the past four years.

Griffith may well have been surprised but would not have tried to back out of the deal. On the other hand he was not overly enthusiastic. "I have just bought Joe Cronin, a shortstop from Kansas City," he told the press. "I don't know whether he'll be much good, but we may be able to use him in a deal next spring. He looks like pretty fair trading material."[36]

Engel also often recounted that the Blues were dying to get rid of Cronin, which is also at least somewhat exaggerated given the price Engel paid. It is true that he was available, and the Kansas City club had offered him to Pittsburgh and Detroit just before the deal with the Senators.[37] Although Cronin was not hitting particularly well, the Blues had paid $7,500 for him just three months earlier, and as a former Major Leaguer, he would have been eligible for the Major League draft the next winter. The Blues knew that Cronin might be lost at the end of the season anyway.

Minor League sales at the time often resulted in the player being delivered at the end of the season; in this case, the Blues did not object to Engel taking Cronin immediately, so the two men boarded a train and headed for Washington.[38] Engel, a natty dresser, did not approve of Cronin's paltry wardrobe. Wanting his new shortstop to make a favorable impression on his new employer, Engel gave Cronin one of his own suits and had it tailored on their way home. They did not go directly to the capital, for Engel had more scouting to do. They stopped in Akron, and while at the ballpark Engel asked Cronin to sit elsewhere, so they could compare notes after the game.

One reason for Cronin's surprising break was that the Senators were in sudden need of a shortstop, due oddly enough to an injury to their left fielder. Leon "Goose" Goslin was the team's best player—a star hitter with a great throwing arm. That spring Goose had been fooling around with a shot-put on a neighboring field and hurt his arm badly enough that he could barely lift it. Management hoped that the arm would improve as the weather heated up. It did not. As the club could not afford to take Goslin's bat out of the lineup—he would lead the league that season with a .379 batting average—manager Bucky Harris had his young shortstop, Bobby Reeves, run out to left field on any ball hit to Goslin and relay Goose's soft underhand toss to the infield.[39] Writers began to call Reeves "Goslin's caddy."

Reeves, a star prospect who had joined the club directly from the campus of Georgia Tech in 1926, soon wore down. Though hitting well over .300 in June, he began to lose weight rapidly, and at the very least the team needed a capable reserve.[40] As Engel wandered around the Midwest, he surely was aware of all this and looking for a shortstop. Cronin's batting slump made him available, but what Engel needed most was a defensive shortstop, and his recommendation was based largely on what he had seen of Cronin in Pittsburgh. Engel purchased Cronin to help Reeves get through the season.

One final story needs to be told here, as it turned out to be the most important story of all. Mildred Robertson, Clark Griffith's niece, had been working the past three years as her uncle's secretary. Mildred knew Engel well, and the two often joked about his finding her a husband on his travels. Once Engel had made arrangements with Griffith about his new infielder, he sent a letter to Miss Robertson:

Dear Mildred,

Am bringing home to you a real sweetie in Joe Cronin, so be dolled up Wednesday or Thursday to meet him. Tall and handsome. Hold all my mail. Don't show this to anyone.

Yours,

Joe

On July 16, 1928, a Monday it turned out, Joe Engel and Joe Cronin (wearing his new suit) arrived in Washington. Engel brought his new shortstop into the office to meet Clark Griffith and Griffith's dolled-up niece.[41] Joe Cronin's ship had come in.

3 Washington

JOE CRONIN MADE HUNDREDS OF FRIENDS during his years in the game, people to whom he would remain close and loyal for decades. None would approach Clark Calvin Griffith in their influence on Cronin's life and his career. Griffith was a much older man, fifty-eight years old when Cronin first met him. Griffith had struggled before establishing a fine career as a player, then he climbed his way to the very pinnacle of power in the sport. As the boss of the team in Washington, he befriended presidents and other leaders, becoming the face of baseball in the nation's capital for forty years.

Having grown up very poor in Missouri and Illinois, Griffith began his professional career as a pitcher in 1888 in Bloomington, Indiana. After pitching well for several years in an era of unstable teams and leagues, he joined Cap Anson's National League Chicago Colts in late 1893. Over the remainder of the decade, Griffith became one of the game's best pitchers, finishing his career with a record of 237-146, and earning the enduring nickname "The Old Fox." "The nickname," wrote Shirley Povich, "was a tribute to his canny pitching, his awareness of the batters' weaknesses, his calmness under pressure, his sly tampering with the ball, and all the other tricks which in those days were permissible."[1]

Although by 1928 he had become a symbol of the baseball establishment, Griffith had a subversive past. An outspoken critic of the National League's treatment of players and its maximum $2,400 salary, Griffith in 1901 became a key figure in the establishment of the American League as a "major" circuit, traveling the country to convince nearly forty National Leaguers to jump to the fledgling league. He was rewarded with a job as player-manager of the new Chicago White Sox, who won the league's first pennant in 1901, thanks in part

to Griffith's twenty-four pitching victories. When the AL put a team
in New York in 1903, league president Ban Johnson tapped Griffith
to lead the Highlanders. After six up-and-down seasons in New York,
Griffith managed the Cincinnati Reds for three years.[2]

After the 1911 season Griffith turned forty-two years old and dearly
wanted to move into ownership, as former players Connie Mack and
Charles Comiskey had done before him. When an opportunity came
up in Washington, Griffith mortgaged his ranch in Montana, bought
10 percent of the Senators, and took over as manager. In his first
season, the club improved by twenty-seven wins. Seven years later
he acquired a controlling interest in the franchise and made himself
team president. After the 1920 season he relinquished the manager's
job but ran the Senators until his death in 1955.[3]

The 1920s saw the emergence of the general manager, as a few
owners with no background in the game hired experienced baseball
men to run their organizations. Branch Rickey with the Cardinals,
Bill Veeck Sr. with the Cubs, and Ed Barrow with the Yankees worked
for owners who had no experience in baseball prior to taking over
their teams. On the other hand, Clark Griffith did not need a general
manager. He remained in complete control of the Senators organization, working closely with his managers on decisions about roster
composition and playing time.

Though the Washington Senators established a reputation as a
perennial doormat (the phrase "First in war, first in peace, and last
in the American League" had gained currency by the first decade of
the twentieth century), this characterization should not be applied to
the Griffith years. The Senators did not finish in last place in his first
thirty-two years in charge, and they were often quite competitive.
For Griffith, it became a matter of pride that his team would *never*
finish last, and it didn't until 1944, when World War II had decimated
Major League rosters.[4]

Griffith was also fiercely loyal. When someone emerged as a dependable player, he stayed around for years. Walter Johnson, Clyde Milan,
Sam Rice, Joe Judge, Ossie Bluege, Joe Kuhel—all played ten or more

years in Washington, and several of them ended up managing the club. His managers, coaches, and staff were mainly former players.

Griffith married Anne Robertson in 1900, but the couple did not have any children of their own. Anne had a brother in Montreal, James Robertson, who had seven children but struggled to feed his family, at least partly because he had a severe alcohol problem. In 1921 two of the Robertson children—eleven-year-old Calvin and nine-year-old Thelma—were moved to Washington to live with their aunt and uncle. Though never officially adopted, both children legally changed their last names to Griffith and were treated as Clark and Anne's family.[5]

The next year James Robertson died, leaving his wife Jane and five other children. In November 1925 Griffith moved the remaining Robertsons from Canada into a new house in the Takoma Park section of Washington DC,[6] about ten minutes from the Griffith family home. Calvin and Thelma continued to live with Clark and Anne, not with their mother and siblings. The change in fortune for these seven children would read like a Charles Dickens novel—a poor family suddenly living in luxury, sleeping in huge bedrooms, riding ponies.[7]

The children had never met their aunt or uncle before moving to Washington but were taken in as full family members. Clark and Anne did more than give the children a house. "I was backward," Calvin later admitted. "I didn't have a good foundation so Griffith's family had me tutored so I learned my ABC's and things like that. It was quite a thing for me to go through."[8]

Besides schooling and church, the children were taught the family business. "He was a man to be admired in many ways," remembered Shirley Povich, who knew the family well. "While they were privileged there was always the sense that there was work to do. Nobody had a free ride."[9] For the Griffiths and Robertsons, "work" meant baseball, and all the children ended up working for Griffith's team, some for decades.

Mildred Robertson, the oldest child, was fourteen when her father died, and three years later became her uncle's personal secretary. On July 16, 1928, when Joe Engel and Joe Cronin entered the Senators' offices, Mildred was on the job. In fact, it was her twentieth birthday.

After brief introductions, Cronin headed to the park and worked out with the team before their game against the Browns that day.[10]

Though Clark Griffith did not believe he had purchased anything other than a no-hit backup infielder, Cronin made a positive first impression on his new manager, Bucky Harris. Four years earlier the twenty-seven-year-old second baseman had been Griffith's surprise choice as the team's manager, and Harris had led his club to pennants in his first two years, including a victory in the 1924 World Series. Now thirty-one and in his fifth year on the job, Harris had skippered the team to a 36-50 record through July 17, twenty-seven games behind the Yankees.

Cronin played in a doubleheader against the Tigers on July 19, getting 2 hits in 8 at bats. Harris had not given up on Reeves, who played third base that day, the *Post* reported; the incumbent had simply worn down from acting as "assistant left fielder."[11] Cronin kept hitting, using an eight-game hitting streak to get to .353 (12 for 34) on July 26. Even after his hitting tailed off, Harris kept Cronin in the lineup.

While the club was on a long road trip in the Midwest, Griffith wired Harris that Reeves would never develop as a player if he did not play. Harris wired back, "Neither will Cronin." By mid-August Harris occasionally benched himself and played Reeves at second base. Veteran first baseman Joe Judge was sold on Cronin. "He's smart," said Judge. "He handles himself well, has a great arm and he'll start hitting one of these days."

"That kid is a natural fielder," said Harris, "and a much better hitter than he is given credit for being. He has saved any number of games since he has been with us by brilliant fielding and, unless I miss my guess, will furnish plenty of competition against all comers who try to get him out of next year's lineup."[12]

In the sixty-nine games after his recall, Cronin played shortstop in sixty-three. For the season Cronin hit .242, while Reeves, playing sixty-six games at shortstop and another thirty-six elsewhere, batted .303 with more power than Cronin. But manager Harris wanted Cronin in the lineup to shore up the team's defense, and the statistics there tell a different story: Reeves made 36 errors in his sixty-six games, while Cronin made just 16 in sixty-three games. The team was 36-50 when Cronin showed up, but 39-29 thereafter.

Nonetheless, Cronin's job was by no means secure. Harris was fired immediately after the season (though Griffith helped him get the manager's job in Detroit), perhaps partly due to his defiance of Griffith in playing Cronin over Reeves.[13] Many observers believed that Reeves had a brighter future, that his defensive issues were completely related to the arm problems of Goslin, and that with Harris out of the picture he would win his job back.[14] In his search for a new manager, Griffith seriously considered veterans Sam Rice and Joe Judge. In the end, the Old Fox gave the job to Walter Johnson.

Johnson, the legendary "Big Train," had pitched twenty-one years for the Senators, retiring after the 1927 season, and may well have been the greatest pitcher who ever lived. He won 417 games, including 110 shutouts, despite pitching for mainly mediocre teams—his clubs won 90 games just four times in his twenty-one seasons. More importantly, he was a beloved figure in Washington and in baseball. "With all the glory that was his," wrote Frank Young in the *Post*, "he never lost his modest and unassuming manner and was the idol of fans and players alike."[15]

Johnson spent the 1928 season managing the Newark Bears in the International League, overcoming a nearly fatal kidney infection that caused him to miss the first month of the season. Griffith offered Johnson the Senators job as early as July—an offer Johnson declined—before turning to him again after the season. The dismissal of the well-liked Harris was not a popular one in the capital city, but the hiring of Johnson stemmed any grumbling. The Big Train, the team's greatest hero, was back.[16]

Meanwhile, Joe Cronin returned to San Francisco in 1928 as a bona fide Major Leaguer. Much like the previous few years, his off-season was devoted to improving his physical condition. At the end of the season Bucky Harris had told him, "You'll be a regular next year, Joe.

You can't miss. Just put on a little more weight and you'll be as good a hitter as you are a fielder."[17] Over the holidays Cronin sent a letter to team trainer Mike Martin saying that he was hiking in the local mountains, adding weight and muscle. "I'm rarin' to go," reported Cronin.

In early December the Senators reacquired Buddy Myer, further muddying their infield for 1929. Two years earlier Griffith had swapped shortstops with the Red Sox, dealing the twenty-three-year-old Myer for thirty-year-old Topper Rigney. Rigney was now in the Minor Leagues, while Myer had hit .288 and .313 for Boston, the latter season as a third baseman. Griffith now determined to get Myer back, and in early December acquired him for five players: pitchers Milt Gaston and Hod Lisenbee, outfielder Elliot Bigelow, and shortstops Reeves and Grant Gillis. Reportedly, the final holdup in the deal was the Red Sox insisting on Reeves *and* Cronin, before finally settling on Gillis as a substitute for Cronin.[18]

Despite his slim hold on his position, Cronin was involved in his first contract dispute at the end of the 1928 season. During the previous off-season Cronin had signed a contract with Pittsburgh for $3,000 plus the cost of transportation home to San Francisco. When Cronin was sold to Kansas City he agreed to the same terms, and when he arrived in Washington, he reminded Griffith of the provision. Griffith balked, claiming that the player's agreement for transportation was with Kansas City, and appealed to Judge Landis, baseball's commissioner. There followed a stream of letters involving Cronin, Griffith, officers of the Kansas City club, Joe Engel, and the commissioner that did not end for more than a year. Landis eventually denied Cronin's claim to any additional money, on the grounds that Griffith had raised his salary by $500 after acquiring him, which more than covered the cost of his trip home.[19] For 1929 Cronin received a raise to $4,000 per year.[20]

In the spring of 1929 there was considerable speculation about the makeup of the Senator infield. Myer and Ossie Bluege were third basemen, but both had experience at shortstop and it was assumed that one, probably Bluege, would shift there. With Harris gone, the team also needed a second baseman, with Jackie Hayes and Stuffy Stewart the leading contenders. When new manager Walter Johnson was asked at the start of the spring camp about Joe Cronin, he allowed as he had never seen Cronin play.[21]

A few weeks into the Senators spring camp, held in Biloxi, Mississippi, the *Washington Post* reported that Cronin was "looking like a million dollars," perhaps forcing Bluege to second base. Johnson was more cautious, saying, "He is a real ball player and it is just his hard luck that he has a fellow like Bluege to beat out. Joe would be a regular on several clubs in our league. . . . I wish I had nine Cronins on my team."[22] By the end of the spring, Johnson had settled on Judge, Hayes, Bluege, and Myer in his infield, with Cronin as the top reserve. Cronin had shown surprising bat strength, and according to the *Washington Post*, "If [Cronin] continues to field and hit as he has been doing, it is hard to see how Manager Johnson can keep him out of the lineup."[23]

The Senators entered the 1929 season full of optimism, largely because of the return of Johnson. Realistically, the club had finished twenty-six games behind in 1928 and had added only Buddy Myer to the cause. The team had several veteran stars who could still play—notably thirty-nine-year-old right fielder Sam Rice, thirty-five-year-old Judge, twenty-eight-year-old Goslin, and thirty-six-year-old pitcher Sam Jones—but needed contributions from its younger players.

On April 27 Ossie Bluege turned his ankle in a game in Boston, a seemingly minor injury that kept him out of action until May 9. Cronin performed well in his absence, especially on defense. When Bluege's injury had healed, he moved to second base in place of the slumping Jackie Hayes. Cronin did not hit right away, getting just 9 hits in his first 54 at bats (.167 average), but soon embarked on a fifteen-game hitting streak that sealed his place in the lineup.

"One of the most important players on the Washington club this season," the *Washington Post* reported in mid-May, "is Joe Cronin, who suddenly has blossomed into a slugger."[24] Cronin hit his first Major League home run on May 24 off George Earnshaw at Philadelphia's Shibe Park. By the end of May he was hitting fifth or sixth in the lineup.

In the middle of June, it was reported that Cronin "has the whole league talking."[25] Although Cronin's place on the club was now secure, Bluege's season-ending knee injury in early July left no doubt that Cronin would not be sitting down again. Ironically, given that he was purchased the previous year as a good-field–no-hit solution, Cronin began to suffer from "erroritis," occasional lapses in the field.[26] At this point in his career many of his spectacular plays drew comment, but he was prone to bobbling the routine grounder.

Cronin had his best game of the season on Sunday, September 2 at Boston's Braves Field. (The city of Boston first allowed professional baseball to be played on Sundays in 1929, but Sunday games at the Red Sox's Fenway Park were still prohibited because it stood within one hundred yards of a church. The prohibition was not lifted until 1932 after someone thought to ask the minister of the church if he objected, and the minister allowed that baseball would have no effect on his services, which were completed before the game would start. In the meantime Red Sox Sunday games were played at Braves Field, a little over one mile away.[27]) In the first game of the day's double-header, Cronin smashed five hits in five at bats, including a single, two doubles, a triple, and a home run, one of just two times in his career he would hit for the cycle.

For the 1929 season Cronin batted .281 with surprising power: 8 home runs, 8 triples, and 29 doubles. Cronin hit all of his home runs on the road—Griffith Stadium, the Senators' home park, deflated home runs tremendously for most of its existence, and the Senators hit only 10 there in 1929.[28] Cronin also showed wonderful plate discipline, walking 85 times, fifth most in the league. Defensively, he led the league's shortstops with 62 errors, and also with 459 assists.

Although there were undoubtedly a few people who believed Joe Cronin would develop into a Major League hitter, including Joe Devine and Joe Engel, his breakthrough in 1929 caught most observers by surprise. Looking back years later, Cronin credited hard work: "Al Schacht used to pitch to me before and after games. Any time I wanted to do any hitting, Al was available. Fred Marberry and Milt Gaston used to do a lot of pitching to me too, and Muddy Ruel was very valuable, catching batting practice."[29] Schacht focused on the curve ball, pitched to all corners of the plate, taught Cronin how to read every pitcher in the American League, and preached waiting for a pitch he could hit.[30] As Ed Linn later wrote, "no man ever worked at any profession harder than Joe Cronin worked to make himself a success in baseball."[31]

Despite the breakthrough of their young shortstop, the season brought mostly disappointment for the Senators and their faithful. By August 1 the team was twenty games below .500 and in sixth place. While Johnson was willing to take the blame, Griffith came out forcefully in his skipper's defense. "How foolish are these stories about Walter's softness. Why, Johnson has the heart of a lion." Late in the season Johnson instituted morning drills before games, and the club closed the last two months at 35-24, to finish 71-81 overall.[32]

After Cronin's fine season, Clark Griffith rewarded him with a new contract calling for a $6,000 annual salary, a $2,000 raise. Interestingly, a provision of the contract stipulated that "Player agrees he will not play golf at any time during the championship season."[33] Cronin paid the down payment on a new home for his parents in the more upscale Balboa Terrace section of San Francisco, about two miles west of their home of the past twenty-three years.

Had Joe Cronin merely held on to the gains he made as a twenty-two-year-old in 1929, perhaps cut down on the errors and developed a little more power, he would have had a fine, though perhaps unappreciated, career. An above-average hitter who can play shortstop is a valuable player in any era. Cronin, however, took another leap forward in 1930, becoming one of the very best players in the game. He began once again by working all winter on his body, showing up in the spring with 180 pounds on his six-foot frame, most of it muscle. In the preceding few off-seasons he had put on thirty hard pounds.

The Washington club essentially returned the same players who had finished thirty-four games behind the Philadelphia Athletics in 1929, and there was little reason to hope for much better this time around. Bluege had recovered from his knee surgery and would join Judge, Myer, and Cronin in the infield. Goose Goslin, Max West, and Sam Rice were back patrolling the outfield. The pitching staff, led by Fred Marberry, was principally the same group as the previous season. "If [Johnson] can get [Washington] out of the second division," wrote one scribe, "it will be proof of managerial genius."[34]

The Senators had a great spring training in Biloxi, winning seventeen of nineteen games. After losing their regular-season opener against the Red Sox on April 14, the two clubs played the next two days in Boston, with the Senators winning each game. They finished April at 10-3, including winning four of five against the Athletics.

The Athletics of this era were one of baseball's greatest teams, managed by Connie Mack and featuring stars such as Jimmie Foxx, Lefty Grove, Mickey Cochrane, and Al Simmons. The Senators stuck with this great club for a while, holding first place as late as July 12. Cronin's all-around game was a primary reason they could stay close. On May 2 he clubbed two doubles and a triple to help beat the Browns in St. Louis. On the twenty-sixth at Yankee Stadium he singled off Hank Johnson with one out in the seventh, stole second base, went to third on a ground ball, and then stole home.[35] Manager Walter Johnson thought Cronin "the ideal type of player to have around."[36]

The club had fallen to third place on June 13 when Griffith made a blockbuster deal, sending Goose Goslin to the Browns for pitcher Alvin "General" Crowder and outfielder Heinie Manush. The trade was a great one for the Nats—Goslin might have been a better hitter than Manush, but Crowder became the Senators' best pitcher for the next four seasons. Washington briefly regained the American League lead in mid-July, but after a brief stumble—losing thirteen of twenty to end the month—they were suddenly eight games back and the race was essentially over. The Senators finished 94-60, eight games behind the Athletics, who went on to beat the Cardinals in the World Series.

Meanwhile, Cronin kept up his heroics. He had two home runs and two singles in a victory over the Athletics on July 23, four hits in beating the White Sox on August 8, a two-run home run to beat Lefty Grove 3–2 on August 25, and ended a win over the Yankees with a diving defensive play with the tying run on third on September 2. "The biggest surprise of the year," said Johnson, "was the work of Joe Cronin, who seemed to find himself almost overnight. Fans probably are wondering whether or not this was a merely a flash, but I don't think that it is. When a player unexpectedly has a good year it is usually the result of flashes between slumps, but Cronin has been hitting and fielding well all year, with practically no slump."[37] Cronin credited his additional batting strength to extra muscle across the shoulders and chest and a more powerful batting stance and stroke.[38] He later said that he learned his new stance playing pepper, when he realized that hitting flat-footed produced harder contact.[39]

Tragically, Walter Johnson was not able to fully enjoy his team's big turnaround, as his beloved wife Hazel died on August 1. She had taken ill a week before with what the doctors diagnosed as complete exhaustion, and finally her body just gave out. Johnson was left with five children. Inconsolable, he did not leave her body for four days. He returned to his job on August 8, but his friends believed he never truly recovered.[40]

For the season Cronin played all 154 games at shortstop, leading the league in assists and put-outs, while dropping his error total from 62 to 35. At the plate he hit .346, with 13 home runs and 41 doubles among his 203 hits, scoring 127 runs and driving in 126. For good measure he finished third in the league in stolen bases and fourth in sacrifice hits. With the Senators improving by twenty-three victories, the baseball writers voted Cronin the league's MVP, ahead of Al Simmons and Lou Gehrig. It was not until 1931 that the writers' award became the "official" MVP award, but Cronin was recognized in the press as the recipient in 1930.[41] *The Sporting News* also awarded Cronin with its Player of the Year honor.

"Nature gave me a good start," Cronin said, "but it has taken a lot of hard work and a willingness to listen to advice to enable me to make the grade in the American League."[42] Rescued from the Minor Leagues just two years before, Cronin was acclaimed as the game's greatest shortstop and one of its greatest players. After the season, he signed a new one-year contract for $10,000.

Other than baseball, the principal excitement in Cronin's life was Mildred Robertson. As Joe Engel prophesied, Joe and Mildred had taken to each other right away, though it was anything but a whirlwind romance. Cronin began by dropping in to the office more often than necessary, but their courtship became more traditional in the spring of 1930 in Biloxi. Cronin had bet pitcher Bobby Burke that he could get a date with Mildred. "Bobby lost the bet," Mildred later recalled.[43]

By the time they returned to Washington in 1930, the couple was dating twice a week when the team was in town, but Cronin was adamant that the relationship remain a secret lest anyone write that he was trying to get in good with the boss. Mildred complained later that when couples on the team got together for group outings, Joe would not invite her. Though Mildred went to every home game, the two would not even speak at the ballpark. Joe used a hand signal to communicate that he would call her after the game. On a few occasions they would go out dancing at some out-of-the-way place, but Joe was particular about not tiring himself out before games and would want to be in bed by ten o'clock.[44]

By the end of the 1930 season, Mildred and Joe had an informal understanding of their future together, but Joe was focused on making enough money to buy his parents' home in San Francisco, and Mildred was providing some support to her own family. When Joe returned to California, they wrote each other three times a week and talked on the phone when they could. Both were anxious to get to Biloxi in 1931.[45]

During the off-season, Joe Cronin's story began to gather more attention in the press and public. Although Glenn Wright had looked as if he would hold down the job in Pittsburgh for another decade or more, he developed a sore arm in 1928—soon after Cronin had been discarded—and missed fifty games.[46] In December 1928 the Pirates dealt Wright to the Dodgers, handing their shortstop job to Dick Bartell. Two years later, in November 1930, Bartell was sent to

Philadelphia for another shortstop, Tommy Thevenow. Naturally, the loss of Cronin, universally hailed as the game's best shortstop less than three years after the Pirates had given up on him, became a popular topic.

John Kieran, writing in the *New York Times*, asked the opinion of Jewel Ens, a Pirate coach during Cronin's time there and at that time the team's manager. "They talk about young Joe Cronin suddenly becoming a great ball player," said Ens. "Why, it was years of hard work that made Joe Cronin a good player. When we had him years ago as a kid he used to be out for hours in the morning learning to hit and field."

Walter Johnson, at a speaking engagement in Pittsburgh in December 1930, tried to find humor in the situation, which was easier for him to do than it was for Ens. "I wonder if the Pirates are developing more young ballplayers like Joe Cronin who they don't intend to keep," said the Big Train. "If so, I'd like to be tipped off to them. I'll grab them in a minute."[47] The stories of Cronin's recruitment by Joe Devine and (especially) Joe Engel also began to be circulated with various details emphasized to make Cronin's rise seem as unlikely as possible.

Cronin's off-season was filled with the usual baseball and exercise, but as a full-fledged baseball star, his time was in more demand. On January 14 the San Francisco Elks Club had a luncheon in his honor with many baseball dignitaries in attendance.[48] There were undoubtedly many more events like this throughout the winter. He finally arrived in Biloxi on March 9 after a three-day train trip from San Francisco.[49]

The Senators and their star shortstop entered 1931 with higher expectations than they had faced the previous year. The Nats began the season with the same lineup they had had at the end of 1930: Judge, Myer, Cronin, and Bluege in the infield; Manush, Sam West, and Rice in the outfield; and Roy Spencer at catcher. Though Judge batted .326 in 1930, in August Griffith had purchased Joe Kuhel from Kansas City. Kuhel was in his seventh Minor League season and third full year with the Blues (he and Cronin had been teammates in 1928). In his three seasons in Kansas City, Kuhel had hit .327, .325, and .372.

Judge kept his job in the spring of 1931, but a couple of weeks into the season Judge had an appendicitis attack in Boston's Fenway Park, resulting in Kuhel's promotion to everyday duty.

Cronin started the 1931 season on the same roll he had been on the previous year. He finished April at .331 (19-58) then took off on perhaps the hottest stretch of his career. Cronin hit in each of the first fourteen games in May, going 28 for 65 (.431) with 12 extra-base hits. On the sixteenth, he hit a double and home run in regulation, before belting a two-run triple in the eleventh to beat the Browns 11–9 in St. Louis.[50]

The Senators were playing well, but again were up against the historic excellence of the Athletics. After starting the season with 10 wins and 11 losses, Washington won twenty-nine of thirty-five games, reaching 39-17 on June 17. Unfortunately, over this same stretch they actually lost ground to the Athletics, who at one point won seventeen straight games. The Senators inched to within a game of Philadelphia in late June but ultimately could not keep up the torrid pace. They lost their last four games of the season and were nipped at the wire by the New York Yankees for second place. The Senators finished 92-62, sixteen games behind the Athletics.

Their shortstop made good use of his new fame. Cronin was a featured guest at a dinner in the city in mid-May and displayed the gee-whiz sense of humor expected of heroes at the time. "Somebody once called upon Jack Dempsey for a speech," began Cronin, "and he replied that he could not make a speech, but he would fight anyone in the house. Ladies and gentlemen, I can't make a speech or fight, but if anyone here will produce a bat I will show you how Lefty Grove struck me out with three men on base."[51]

By June 10 Cronin was leading the league with 74 hits, 53 runs batted in, and 8 triples. His eighteen-game hitting streak was stopped on June 11 when he was hit in the left shoulder by a pitch from Cleveland's Mel Harder and had to leave the game without an official at bat.[52] It was assumed he would miss a few days, but he was back in the lineup the following afternoon, getting three more hits. In a 14–1 victory over the Red Sox on July 9, Cronin had 3 hits and 6 runs batted in, including a long three-run inside-the-park home run off Ed Durham at Griffith Stadium.[53]

For the second straight year Cronin played in every Senators game, although one of his 156 games in 1931 was as a pinch hitter. His batting average dropped from .346 to .306 which, in keeping with the understanding of the time, led to the impression that he had suffered a big drop-off. However, there was a league-wide reduction in offense from the historic levels of 1930, and Cronin's value was not tied up solely in his batting average. He still hit 12 home runs, drove in 126 (equaling his 1930 total), and increased his doubles, triples, and walks. He finished seventh in the official balloting for the Most Valuable Player Award, won by Lefty Grove.

After being named for the second consecutive year the shortstop on *The Sporting News* Major League All-Star team, Cronin headed back home to San Francisco. He had become not only one of the game's great players but also one of the most well liked.[54] Nonetheless, he had to spend to the next five months without the company of Mildred Robertson, having to be satisfied with letters and the occasional phone call. Cronin spent the winter working out and hanging around with all his baseball friends. After signing a new contract, the twenty-five-year-old would earn $12,000 for his services in 1932.

The only significant change to the Senators heading into 1932 was the acquisition of outfielder Carl Reynolds, acquired in December in a five-player deal with the White Sox that cost Washington veteran pitchers Sam Jones and Bump Hadley. Reynolds's arrival was recognition that Sam Rice, a forty-two-year-old veteran, had finally begun to slow. Griffith felt that the team had gotten overly left-handed, as Kuhel, Myer, and the entire outfield of Manush, West, and Rice swung from the left side. Joe Judge, also left-handed, had recovered from his appendicitis to fight for his first base job with Kuhel.

It was the pitching that caused the most anxiety in camp, a concern expressed by both Griffith and Cronin. The shortstop did allow that he was excited about the promise of rookie hurlers Monte Weaver and Bob Friedrichs.[55] As for Cronin himself his hitting and fielding were the talk of spring camp from the moment he arrived, with Griffith saying he was "in top form."[56] The club mainly played Minor League teams, not facing a big league club until a game with Brooklyn on April 2. The next day the Senators headed north, playing a series of exhibition contests en route.

On April 4 in Chattanooga, Cronin was stricken with a sinus attack and rushed ahead to Washington. A few days later he was sent to Georgetown University Hospital with a high fever. "Some toxic poison is in his system," reported the *Post*, "and last night it was not known just how much longer he would have to be classed as an invalid."[57] He missed the first four regular-season games before taking his place in the lineup on April 17, getting two hits in his first action.

During a brief slump in late May, Cronin experienced the darker side of baseball fame. On May 26 in Griffith Stadium, the Senators' Alvin Crowder was locked in a duel with the Yankees' Red Ruffing in the sixth inning. With two outs and a runner on, Cronin booted a routine ground ball by Joe Sewell to keep the inning alive. Crowder walked Ruth, but Lou Gehrig followed with a grand slam to effectively ice the game for the visitors. On Cronin's next appearance at bat, wrote Shirley Povich, he "was the object of the greatest salvo of boos since the declining days of Bucky Harris with the Washington club."[58] According to Povich, Cronin (hitting over .300 at the time of the booing) had been struggling both at bat and in the field. By June 3, however, his "return to batting form was encouraging."[59]

After having missed those few games at the start of the season, Cronin suffered from a more severe physical problem two months later. On June 4 in Boston, Red Sox pitcher Ed Durham hit Cronin on the left thumb with a pitch, chipping a bone. Excepting a single pinch-running appearance and another as a pinch hitter, Cronin was out until June 16, when he returned only because his replacement Johnny Kerr got spiked and could not play. Cronin volunteered to return early, playing with a rubber bandage on his left (glove hand) thumb. In his first game back, his two-run triple helped Lloyd Brown beat Earl Whitehill and the Tigers in Detroit, 4–0.

After a period of adjustment during which his average fell below

.300 for a few weeks, Cronin picked it up at the end of July and closed out the season hitting as well as usual. He hit no home runs after July 4 but made up for it with 12 triples over the second half of the season. He finished the season with just 6 homers, but he still hit 43 doubles and a league-leading 18 triples despite the illness and injury. His 116 RBI were sixth in the circuit and his .318 batting average was tenth.

One of the more newsworthy events of the Senators' season took place on July 4, when they swept a doubleheader against the first-place Yankees at Griffith Stadium. In the first game Lefty Gomez was riding an eleven-game winning streak and up 3–0 when Cronin hit a two-run home run in the fourth. In the seventh, Carl Reynolds singled, reached third on another single, then tried to score on a botched squeeze play. When catcher Bill Dickey's throw attempting to nab Reynolds hustling back to third got away, Reynolds scored after a collision at home plate. Dickey got up, ran over to Reynolds, and slugged the Senators' right fielder in the face, breaking his jaw. Reynolds had walked away and was greeting the batboy at the time of the punch. He missed seven weeks of action, while Dickey was suspended for thirty days.

The Senators had started the 1932 season on a hot streak (19-5), before settling into a three-month funk that brought them to 61-51 on August 14, fifteen and a half back of the Yankees and in fourth place. They finished strong (32-10) and ended up with another fine record, 93-61, the third-best season in franchise history to that point. At the end of the season, Griffith called on Johnson and asked him how he was doing financially. Assured that his friend was secure, Griff told Johnson he'd like to make a change in managers.[60]

The Big Train had managed the team to three straight ninety-win seasons—of the eight such seasons the franchise would have in sixty years in Washington. Despite Johnson's calm demeanor, the club had performed well for him while competing against historically great teams. Cronin admired Johnson highly as a manager and as a man, and it was Johnson who created the atmosphere in which Cronin had become a superstar. He and other observers could only wonder who Johnson's replacement would be.

4 Player-Manager

Upon the announcement of Walter Johnson's dismissal as Senators manager on October 4, 1932, speculation about his successor began immediately. The focus in the newspapers turned to the veteran players on the team, with the two longest tenured—Sam Rice and Joe Judge—considered the leading contenders. Rice and Judge had played together on the Nats for eighteen years, the second-longest run for two teammates in baseball history and were well-liked and respected.[1] Two other possibilities were Bucky Harris, who had lost the job in 1928 because Griffith thought he had softened since his earlier success in the role, and Griffith himself. Griffith did not categorically rule out a return, saying he would consider it "only if I am unable to find the man that I want."[2]

Joe Cronin, the young shortstop, rated a mention early on as well. "Cronin, who will be 26 years of age a week from today," wrote the *Post* on October 5, "has all of the qualities which Harris showed about the time he was given the job. Besides being a prime favorite with the Washington club owner, he is a fighter, is brim full of pep, has gradually absorbed most of the fine points of baseball, is popular with his mates and, above all, gives every indication of being a leader." Furthermore, "On the field during the past season, it was Cronin who was out there spurring on the Nats; it was Cronin who yelled who was to make the catch when two players were after the ball, and it was this same young shortstop who frequently came in to steady faltering pitchers and who appeared to have much to say about the playing of the game."[3]

The *Post* went so far as to include a poll in their October 7 edition, listing Judge, Rice, and Cronin, plus a spot for a write-in candidate. The newspaper allowed a full week, until the fourteenth, for their readers to mail the ballots to the newspaper.[4] The next day, the paper reported that Judge was leading with 337 votes, followed by Cronin (155), Rice (46), Rogers Hornsby (46), Harris (30), and Donie Bush (15).[5] There would be no further balloting, as Griffith dramatically named the young Cronin his new manager on October 8.

"I like these scrappy youngsters as leaders," Griffith related upon the announcement. "Cronin is a fellow who is interested in nothing but baseball. He may not know as much as an older and more experienced man, but he is the type that studies and thinks baseball at all times. . . . From the minute he joined us near the end of the 1928 season, he was taking responsibilities, pepping up the team, and putting fight into it. And, while he was doing this, he was asking questions, figuring out plays and otherwise showing that he was the type that was going to get somewhere here in baseball aside from the playing angle."[6] Griffith did not mention his own lack of enthusiasm upon first acquiring Cronin in 1928.

One of the suspected reasons for Griffith's firing of Harris four years earlier was the belief that the scrappy leader had grown soft after his high-society marriage. In October 1926 Harris had married Elizabeth Sutherland, the daughter of U.S. senator Howard Sutherland of West Virginia.[7] To some observers Harris's relationship with his team—and his comrades—began to change. In the later recollection of Heywood Broun, "There were infielders and substitute catchers whom he would not quite care to ask to his house for dinner." Of Cronin, Broun wrote, "I hope he won't marry a Senator's daughter."[8]

Cronin seemed to be taken off guard, and he had to reschedule his already delayed trip back to San Francisco. After the season he had remained in Washington to have his tonsils removed. This allowed him more time with Mildred Robertson, but he was surprised at the offer from his girlfriend's uncle. "I've had ambitions to be a manager," Cronin admitted, "but never had any idea that I would get the chance this soon. I realize that I am quite young for the job and that there are a lot of things to learn, and I am mighty lucky to have such veterans around as Joe Judge, Sam Rice, Heinie Manush and Ossie Bluege to call on." Cronin was besieged with congratulations, including a phone call from the deposed Johnson.[9]

Cronin had a long series of meetings with Griffith on the ninth (a Sunday) and tenth to discuss what changes needed to be made to the club. "We agreed that we need strength in the box [pitching] and behind the bat [catching] if we are to be serious contenders in the coming race." Cronin took a 4:00 p.m. train on the tenth to San Francisco. Unlike past years, he would be returning east in December for the winter meetings.

Observers did not fail to notice that Clark Griffith stood to save a lot of money with his managerial shift. Cronin received a salary boost for his new duties, from twelve to eighteen thousand, which was not nearly enough to offset the savings of Walter Johnson's reported $25,000 salary. The Senators' attendance had decreased from 614,000 in 1930, to 492,000 in 1931, to 371,000 in 1932, trends consistent with what was happening in other big league cities. Now Cronin was being asked to perform two jobs for the price of one salary.

The worsening economic times in the 1930s at least partially led to a sharp increase in player-managers. While once common—57 percent of managers in the 1900–1909 period also played—by 1929 the player-manager was nearly extinct. Outfielder-manager Billy Southworth had thirty-two at bats as a reserve for the Cardinals in 1929 before being relieved of both duties in midsummer. At the time of the stock market crash in October 1929, there were no player-managers in Major League Baseball.[10]

By 1932 there was increased momentum for the dual role. Star first baseman Bill Terry had replaced John McGraw as manager with the New York Giants. The White Sox's Lou Fonseca and the Red Sox's Marty McManus were doing both jobs. Charlie Grimm took over from Hornsby with the Cubs and led his club to the 1932 league championship. In the next couple of years several star players—Mickey Cochrane, Frankie Frisch, Pie Traynor, and Jimmie Dykes—would follow Cronin to the player-manager job, and men in these roles would win the next three World Series. Oddly, by 1940 the player-manager was nearly extinct again, and has been almost unknown in the decades since.

After an abbreviated two-month stay in San Francisco, Cronin left his home city on December 6 for Washington and then to New York City for baseball's winter meetings. The meetings were much anticipated by Senators followers because Griffith had told the press upon Cronin's hiring that the two men were determined to make big changes to the team's roster. The two had huddled in October but obviously had not seen each other for two months prior to Cronin's arrival in DC on December 10.[11]

Cronin and Griffith were happy with most of the team that had won ninety or more games the past three seasons. They had Joe Kuhel, Buddy Myer, Cronin, and Ossie Bluege returning in the infield, with Heinie Manush, Sam West, and Carl Reynolds set in the outfield. All were solid players, though Cronin and Manush were the only real run producers. Catcher Roy Spencer was no hitter (.246) and had spent the previous summer fighting off injuries and illness, including a case of malaria.[12] Cronin wanted to upgrade the catching position and find another slugger if possible.

General Crowder had broken through with twenty-six wins in 1932, and Monte Weaver added twenty-two. Other than those two, the only dependable pitcher was Fred Marberry, who had thrown 197 innings in his dual role as starter and reliever. In Cronin's mind in order to combat the Yankees' left-handed power, the club needed to find some dependable left-handed pitching—the only two lefties on the roster at the end of the season were Lloyd Brown and Bobby Burke, neither of whom were the caliber of pitcher that Cronin required.

In any event the Senators negotiated three significant trades at the winter meetings. The club sent pitchers Marberry and Carl Fischer to the Tigers for left-hander Earl Whitehill, a sixteen-game winner in 1932. The Senators next traded outfielders Sam West and Carl Reynolds, with pitcher Brown, to the Browns for outfielders Goose Goslin and Fred Schulte and left-hander Lefty Stewart. Finally, they sent young first baseman Harley Boss, who had hit .338 with 35 doubles for Chattanooga in 1932, to the Indians for pitcher Jack Russell and first baseman Bruce Connatser.

Cronin and Griffith were both elated. They had acquired the two southpaw starters they wanted while also upgrading the offense with the reacquisition of Goslin. "Joe got the men he wanted and I am satisfied," said Griffith. "Those new faces ought to please the fans, too." Cronin acknowledged that the Senators had to pay a price for all the new talent, but "I don't think we did badly." In particular Cronin did not like having to part with West, a great defensive centerfielder and one of the more popular Washington players.[13]

His work thus completed, after a stopover in Washington for further meetings with Griffith (and, undoubtedly, a dinner or two with Mildred), Cronin returned to San Francisco for another two months. His schedule that winter included boxing, indoor tennis, and daily mass. The *Post* reported in January: "Joe Cronin writes that he has been keeping his arm in shape writing replies to letters from unemployed baseball players." He also wrote Mildred often and continually pored over possible lineups for his ballclub.[14]

In early January, Griffith after consulting with Cronin made one final deal—sending catcher Spencer to the Indians for catcher Luke Sewell. Sewell, the brother of Yankee third baseman Joe Sewell, could not hit much but was considered a great handler of pitchers and much more durable than the banged up Spencer. If any proof were needed, this deal was further indication that the Senators intended to take on the Yankees and Athletics in 1933.

Upon Joe Cronin's arrival in Biloxi on February 21, he was greeted by an unusual ceremony prepared by Mike Martin and Frankie Baxter, the club's trainers. The two "hired the most ebonized boys in the stronghold of the great American shrimp, armed them with retired tomato cans, gazoos, battered mandolins and a couple of hybrid musical instruments and set them on the sun-washed station platform with instructions to play, 'Hail the Conquering Hero Comes.'" It is not known how Cronin felt about this absurdity as he got off at the front of the train and witnessed the scene without being noticed.[15]

Washington's new manager and players led to added excitement in camp and around the league. Yankees manager Joe McCarthy, training in St. Petersburg, Florida, thought that Washington had replaced Philadelphia as the top competition for his team, allowing only that the Senators would miss Fred Marberry.[16] (The Athletics had begun their self-demolition, selling Al Simmons and Jimmie Dykes to the White Sox the previous fall.) Connie Mack, forty-four years older than Cronin, had praised his fellow manager's intelligence and work ethic, recalling how often the player had stopped Mack to ask him questions about the game. "He's a smart young fellow, I want to tell you," Mack said. "A nice-mannered chap, too. Joe Cronin's a gentleman—a great ball player. I wish him luck."[17]

Cronin never was much for luck, but he did believe in hard work. As early as October Cronin pledged that his team would work on stealing more bases, taking extra bases on hits, the hit and run, sacrifice bunting, and other forms of aggressive baseball. He wanted to drill more on cutoff plays and smart defensive positioning and tactics. "If we play smart, peppy baseball," said Cronin, "added to our already tight defense, we're going to win a lot of games."[18] At the start of camp Cronin reported that he was happy with the players' conditioning.[19]

One of the challenges for a new player-manager, especially one so young as Cronin, was to lead and inspire men who recently had been his peers and who just a few years earlier had helped him break into the Major Leagues. Judge had been sold to the Dodgers, but Rice was nearly seventeen years his manager's senior. Besides believing in hard work, the young manager believed in chatter—he talked constantly on the field to his teammates. One imagines a Little Leaguer yelling encouraging words to his pitcher. "No batter, no batter, he can't hit, he can't hit . . ." In fact, this might not be far off. "Cronin was an aggressive manager and he could pick up a man's spirit," remembered Ossie Bluege decades later. "I was never much for chatter but he got me to talk some—although I was never a holler guy. It was not my nature."[20]

Although the lineup and rotation pitchers appeared to be set, Cronin had a few interesting battles to resolve in camp. In February the team had purchased Kansas City shortstop Bob Boken, a .280 hitter who could back up Cronin and Myer. Catcher Cliff Bolton hit .339 for Chattanooga and was slated to fight for time with Sewell. The most intriguing prospect in camp was nineteen-year-old infielder Cecil Travis from Georgia, who had batted .360 in just more than one season with Chattanooga. For a time it looked as though Travis could challenge Bluege at third base, but Cronin felt the youngster needed more work on his defense.[21]

As the team closed its spring camp and prepared to head north, Cronin was particularly excited about his catching corps of Sewell, Bolton, and Moe Berg. Sewell, who Cronin felt was "the best receiver in the business,"[22] would get the bulk of the time. Bolton was the best hitter but considered behind the others as a catcher. Berg, who would spend most of the next decade working for Cronin, was a solid defensive player and spoke several languages.[23] "I can't see where any of our rivals possess a trio of receivers of such high class," enthused the manager.[24]

On the eve of the season, both Griffith and Cronin were optimistic. "What I believe will put us over," allowed the team president, "is that I look for four comparable youngsters—Cronin, Myer, Kuhel and Schulte—to find themselves this season and play their top games."[25] *The Sporting News* was less sanguine, picking the Nats to finish third. "There are some who say [Cronin] hasn't the temperament to be a manager," noted the paper, "and that should things break badly for his club he would collapse and his team with him."[26] The New York Yankees, who had won 107 games and the World Series in 1932, were overwhelming favorites to repeat.

The Senators hosted the Athletics in the traditional baseball season opener April 12, with new president Franklin D. Roosevelt on hand to throw out the first ball. Cronin handed the president a ball to throw, but, unable to decide amongst the many waving arms, including those of Vice President John Nance Garner, Roosevelt casually tossed the ball to the ground untouched. Reserve infielder Johnny Kerr won the ensuing scramble.[27] Once the game began, the Senators prevailed 4–1, with their new manager collecting three hits.

When the Yankees came to town on April 23, the champions were 7-0, with the Senators in fourth place at 4-5. Cronin, hitting .265, had yet to record an extra-base hit. Washington won two hard-fought games, 5–4 and 11–10, before being crushed 16–0 in the finale. This last game, on April 25, may have turned the season around.

The Yankees and Senators had some bad blood from the previous year, when Bill Dickey had broken Carl Reynolds's jaw. In the first game of this series, Cronin had challenged Babe Ruth after Ruth slid hard into third base, and the Yankees also thought Buddy Myer had spiked Lou Gehrig at first base.[28] But things boiled over completely on the twenty-fifth when the Yankees Ben Chapman slid hard into Myer, cutting the second baseman's ankle. The enraged Myer proceeded to kick Chapman several times before the Yankee retaliated with several punches of his own. Cronin pulled Chapman away, and the umpires restored order temporarily, ejecting both Myer and Chapman.

In order to leave the field, Chapman had to enter a passage next to the Senators' bench. Before he got there pitcher Earl Whitehill yelled something at him, and soon Chapman and Whitehill were belting each other, leading to a general free-for-all among both teams, several policemen, and bat-wielding spectators. It took twenty minutes to sort everything out, after which the Yankees completed their rout. Chapman, Myer, and Whitehill all received five-game suspensions.[29] Coincidentally or not, the Senators beat the Yankees twice more the next weekend and played well enough to keep close to New York over the next six weeks.

Lending cover to those who thought managing would hurt his play, Cronin hit just .246 in April, but he made his season in a five-week stretch beginning on May 25. Over the next thirty-two games manager Cronin hit .463 with 28 extra-base hits and 45 runs batted in, while his team moved from two and a half behind the Yankees to one and a half ahead. At the end of June Cronin was hitting .354, and his team had a one-game lead, all but the Yankees having fallen well off the pace.

On July 4 the Senators visited Yankee Stadium to play a holiday doubleheader, holding a slim half-game lead over their rivals. In the first game Lefty Gomez had the visitors down 5–2 into the eighth, but the Senators won in the tenth. Walter Stewart tossed a five-hitter in the second game to complete the sweep before 77,365 fans, the second largest in Major League history to that point. Cronin finished the double-header four for eight with a home run. That evening the Senators returned to Washington, where five thousand fans met them at Union Station. Cronin did not accompany the team south—instead he and Alvin Crowder traveled west to Chicago.[30]

In that summer of 1933, Chicago hosted a six-month World's Fair, called the Century of Progress International Exposition. Arch Ward, the sports editor of the *Chicago Tribune*, had been asked to think of an event that would bring sports fans to the city. Ward had conceived of a Game of the Century, matching the best players in each league with all proceeds going to charity. The two leagues agreed to Ward's brainchild and rearranged league schedules so that the game could be played July 6 at Chicago's Comiskey Park. Newspapers around the country conducted fan balloting to select the lineups. Cronin was the easy winner as the American League's shortstop.[31]

Although there were more famous stars present at Comiskey Park on July 6, men like Babe Ruth and Lou Gehrig, there was no bigger story in baseball at the time than Joe Cronin. The twenty-six-year-old entered the game hitting .362 while managing the team with the best record in baseball. He played the entire game at shortstop and singled and walked in four plate appearances. Witnessed by more than forty-seven thousand people, the American League won the game 4–2 backed by a two-run home run by Ruth in the third inning. At the time, no one knew if there would ever be another All-Star game. After the game Cronin and Crowder, who had pitched three innings for the winners, returned to Washington to continue their season.

The concerns that Cronin's managing would detract from his playing had abated, but there were occasional voices questioning just who was running the show in Washington. "It is not my idea to take so much as a tiny morsel of credit away from young Joe Cronin," said Stoney McLinn in the *Philadelphia Record*, before taking away more than a morsel, "but it is my opinion that Griff is the man primarily responsible for the success of the team." The writer went on to allow that Cronin deserved credit for talking to his boss regularly, implementing Griffith's advice, and earning the respect of his players.[32]

Shirley Povich thought Cronin's strengths greater than that. "Joe Cronin is a master strategist," said the writer in late July. "Did you ever see him pat a faltering pitcher on the back with one hand while using his other hand to wave to another pitcher to warm up in the bullpen?"[33] A theme of Cronin's life in baseball was his obsession with knowing everything he could about the game. To that end, it was observed, he read piles of out-of-town newspapers every day.[34]

One writer considered stretching the point even further. "Cronin has few interests outside of baseball. There are those who say he scarcely is conversant on any subject other than baseball, though this is perhaps a harsh observation."[35] His soft-handed approach off the field also drew comment. He allowed beer and card playing on the trains, and even gambling. Cronin did not partake in these activities, instead talking ("mostly baseball") with other nongamblers like Moe Berg, Fred Schulte, and Monte Weaver.[36]

On the field, the rookie manager kept his club on its toes. "The man never stands still," wrote John Drebinger in the *New York Times*. "He is always moving around, fussing with his belt, his glove or the peak of his cap. His rah-rah tactics finally became infectious. The staid veterans of the team forgot that a young upstart had been placed above them and began to pull on the oars at once."[37] He also had the team's back—according to Povich, he was a "fiery, fighting and inspiring leader," and a "consummate crab" to the umpires.[38]

The Senators were remarkably healthy all season. When hit with a few minor injuries to the infielders in May, the Senators briefly recalled Cecil Travis from Chattanooga. In his first Major League game, May 16 at home against the Indians, Travis hit 5 singles in his first five trips to the plate, finishing 5 for 7 in the twelve-inning game.[39] Monte Weaver, a twenty-two-game winner in 1932, missed several starts in midsummer with a sore arm but pitched well both before and after his ailment. For the most part, Cronin was able to put his best players on the field every day.

After sweeping the Athletics in Philadelphia to move a game ahead of the Yankees, Cronin and the Senators returned home for a crucial four-game series with New York beginning July 27. The Nats took the first game 3–2 on a pinch-single by Cliff Bolton, and the second 11–5 to build their lead to three games. But the Yankees cut their deficit back to one with victories over the weekend, 7–2 and 13–9.

A week later the teams met for four games in New York, and after the Yankees took the opening doubleheader, winning both games in the bottom of the ninth inning, some writers sensed an impending shift in the race. "[The Yankees'] answer," wrote Joe Vila in *The Sporting News*, "was so convincing as to cause many to feel that August 7 witnessed the definite turning point in the American League race and that McCarthy's team will again be on top when the schedule ends."[40] Instead, August 7 would be the Bronx Bombers' last gasp. Washington took the next two contests, 5–1 and 4–1, behind the brilliant pitching of Earl Whitehill and Monte Weaver and then won its next eleven games as well.

J. G. Taylor Spink, the editor of *The Sporting News*, spoke for many in his "letter" to Cronin in the August 17 issue. "Kid, you can take it," began Spink. "After the razzing the New York scribes gave you, following the loss of that double-header, you kept your chin up and came right back. I had some misgivings about turning the greatest shortstop in the game, only 26, into a leader. But Griff had the correct dope, and if you win, he'll have the laugh on a lot of folks."

The *New York Journal*'s Bill Corwin thought the kid was holding up well under the pressure: "If piloting a pennant contender through the crucial days of a red-hot race is proving a strain on the Cronin boy, he does not show it in his looks or actions."[41] In fact, Cronin went into a terrible hitting slump during this period, hitting just .168 in 119 at bats in August, dropping his .347 batting average to .306.

At the conclusion of their thirteen-game winning streak on August 20, the Senators were eight and a half games in front and the race was essentially over. The Yankees did not get within six games again until after being eliminated from the race. The pennant-clinching game was a 2–1 victory over the Browns on September 21. After an extended celebration in the clubhouse, Cronin escaped via the field but found himself chased by a large number of female fans. The bachelor had to scurry out a door deep in the outfield before finally reaching his car and speeding away, most likely to a date with Mildred.[42]

The Senators, winners of ninety-nine games, were a remarkably well-balanced team. The pitchers that Cronin had asked for the previous fall came through: Earl Whitehill finished 22-8, Lefty Stewart 15-6, and Jack Russell 12-6 with a league-leading 13 saves.[43] The Nats won nine of the fourteen games that left-handers Whitehill and Stewart started against the Yankees, a principal reason for their acquisitions. General Crowder won twenty-four games, while Monte Weaver battled injuries to finish 10-5.

On offense, the club led the league with a .287 batting average and finished third in runs scored. Cronin's .309 was backed with 118 runs batted in, 87 walks, and a league-leading 45 doubles. Heinie Manush led the league with 221 hits and fashioned a thirty-three-game hitting streak. Joe Kuhel added a .322 average and 107 runs driven in. Buddy Myer, Goose Goslin, and Fred Schulte also had fine seasons.

The 1933 World Series matched the Senators against the New York Giants, led by their own player-manager, first baseman Bill Terry. This was the first Series that pitted two player-managers since 1906, when Frank Chance's Cubs battled Fielder Jones's White Sox. The Giants fielded some strong hitters, including Terry and Mel Ott but were led primarily by a spectacular pitching staff, anchored by the incomparable Carl Hubbell.

Hubbell, the thirty-year-old King Carl, had enjoyed a fine five-year start to his career, twice winning eighteen games, before putting together his finest season in 1933. He won twenty-three games, a league-leading ten of them by shutout, while posting a 1.66 ERA, the lowest in the National League between 1917 and 1968. Hubbell threw a famous screwball, a pitch considered so remarkable that the Senators hired Garland Braxton, a ten-year veteran who had last pitched briefly with the Browns earlier that season, to throw them screwballs in batting practice. How well Braxton may have done is unknown, but one thing is certain: he was no Carl Hubbell.

The 1933 World Series began at New York's Polo Grounds on October 3, a Tuesday, and was scheduled to take place over (if necessary) seven consecutive days—there were no "travel" days. On the strength of their much better record (ninety-nine wins versus ninety-one), and the overall reputation of the American League, the Senators were installed as 7–5 favorites by at least one oddsmaker.[44]

To oppose Hubbell in the first game, Cronin pitched Lefty Stewart, trying to counter the left-handed bats of Terry and Ott. Stewart allowed a two-run homer to Ott in the first inning and departed in the third, while Hubbell struck out ten en route to his 5–2 victory, both Senators runs unearned. Cronin had two of the Senators' five singles in the one-sided contest. The next day the Giants used Hal Schumacher, the somewhat overshadowed number-two starter who had won nineteen games, and he threw his own five-hitter in an easy 6–1 victory.

With the teams moving 250 miles south for Game 3, twenty-five thousand fans turned out, including President Roosevelt and a large delegation of congressmen. Cronin delivered a fiery pep talk before the game, challenging his team to play better than they had in New York, to not let down the fans who had supported them all season long. Re-enacting the scene from the regular-season opener, Roosevelt tossed the ball onto the field and various Senators scrambled after it, Heinie Manush emerging with the baseball.[45] Earl Whitehill got the Senators back on track with a five-hit shutout, backed by the Senators nine hits (including four doubles).

The next day the Giants brought Hubbell back on just two days rest, while Cronin countered with Monte Weaver. The two battled toe-to-toe for ten innings, the Senators matching Terry's fourth-inning home run into the deep centerfield bleachers with an unearned tally in the seventh. After the Giants took a 2–1 lead in the top of the eleventh, the Senators loaded the bases with one out in the bottom half, with pitcher Jack Russell due up. Cronin sent reserve catcher Cliff Bolton up to hit, and he grounded into a double play to end the game.

Down three games to one, Cronin chose Alvin Crowder to face Hal Schumacher in Game 5. The Giants took a 3–0 lead into the bottom of the sixth, but Fred Schulte hit a three-run home run to tie the score. From then on it was a relief pitching battle between Russell and forty-two-year-old Dolf Luque. Russell pitched four scoreless innings before allowing a solo home run to Ott with two out in the tenth. Luque finished it off, ending with four and a third shutout innings and the Series-clinching victory. Cronin hit three singles in the game, including the Senators' only two hits off Luque.

The Senators were vanquished primarily because they could manage only 11 runs in five games. The pitching held its own, posting a 2.74 ERA, but the offense could not overcome the great pitching of Hubbell (twice), Schumacher, and Luque. That said, the final two games went to extra innings and were certainly winnable. Joe Cronin hit .318, with 7 singles in 22 at bats.

The most controversial move Cronin made in the Series was pinch-hitting Bolton in the bottom of the eleventh of the fourth game. Sam Rice, the forty-three-year-old veteran who had hit .285 in a reserve role that season, was on the bench and available. Rice batted just once in the Series, getting a pinch single off Schumacher in Game 2. Bolton hit .410 in 39 at bats during the regular season, including 9 for 22 (.409) as a pinch hitter, but was hitless in both his Series appearances. Bolton was a left-handed hitter and was sent in to face Hubbell, a left-hander himself, albeit one whose screwball was at least as difficult for right-handed batters.

No less an authority than Connie Mack came to Cronin's defense over the strategy, saying, "You always use the 'hot' man in a pinch." Mack instead pointed to two occasions when the Senators failed to execute sacrifice bunts, once by Goslin in the fourth game, and again by Bluege in the fifth, that cost the team two victories.[46] Writer Dan Daniel, a critic of several of Cronin's moves in the Series, thought Mack was being overly generous: "Had Connie found himself in that situation he would have called on the crafty and fast Sam Rice. It was an inexcusable error."[47]

Cronin's disappointment at losing the World Series was abated somewhat when he signed a new three-year contract to continue as shortstop and manager at $22,000 per year.[48] At the World Series, Cronin had been offered thirty-five thousand to spend ten weeks speaking on a vaudeville tour. When Cronin turned it down, saying, "I'm a ballplayer," writer Tom Meany commented, "Thirty-five thousand dollars is a lot of dough in these times. Or in any other for that matter. In return for his refusal, Joe has only his own self-respect. And it's not difficult to discover just how highly he values it."[49]

Cronin soon learned he had finished a strong second in the voting for the league's Most Valuable Player Award, trailing only Jimmie Foxx, who had won the Triple Crown, and finishing just ahead of his friend and teammate Heinie Manush. In addition to his fourth consecutive great season with the bat, Cronin also led the league's shortstops in fielding percentage for the second straight year. Of Cronin's many years in the game, very few, if any, topped 1933.

A few days after the end of the World Series, Cronin traveled alone as far as Chicago, changed trains there, and rode the rest of the way back to San Francisco with Lefty O'Doul, who had played for the Giants in the just-completed Series. Lefty had just one at bat in the Series, but it was a huge one—a two-run pinch single in Game 2 off Crowder that gave the Giants a 2–1 lead in the sixth inning. O'Doul was no bit player to the people of San Francisco—he was already one of the more popular baseball men in the city's history, even though he had yet to begin his long stint as Seals manager.

Upon their arrival in San Francisco, O'Doul and Cronin were given keys to the city, starred in a parade, and were feted at a large banquet.[50] On October 15, fifteen thousand fans crowded into Seals Stadium to watch an all-star game pitting a group of Major League players, managed by Ty Cobb, against a team of Minor League stars. The Majors team included Cronin, O'Doul, Chick Hafey, Tony Lazzeri, Gus Suhr, Willie Kamm, Ernie Lombardi, Lefty Gomez, and Dick Bartell among many others. The Minors group included the Seals' Joe DiMaggio and the Missions' Babe Dahlgren. The Minor League stars won the game, 5–3, all proceeds from the game going to local charities.[51]

Cronin spent a bit too much time as the guest of honor at banquets that winter and later admitted to having put on fifteen unwanted pounds. He spent his usual time golfing and hiking,[52] but the weight problem was something he was destined to fight for the rest of his life. He had spent several off-seasons in his early twenties eating heavy proteins and fats in order to get bigger and stronger. At twenty-seven, his days as a skinny kid were long-gone. His remaining spring trainings, and some of his summer months too, would be spent trying to work off an ever-growing waistline.

During the off-season Cronin put another large sum of money into his parents' home in San Francisco's Balboa Terrace. With his mother and father now financially secure, he finally decided to ask Mildred Robertson to marry him. They had been dating for four years, albeit only during home stands in the spring and summer. When he proposed that March in Biloxi, she was not surprised, as they had spoken frankly about their future many times. Mildred, a Protestant, began taking classes to convert to Joe's Catholicism.[53] They planned to be married at the end of the upcoming season. No formal announcement was made, but their friends and family were all made aware of the news.

A national radio interview Cronin gave in April 1934 testified to the lack of publicity surrounding his engagement. Margaret Santry of the *Washington Post*'s women's department, a baseball novice, asked Cronin ("a charming and handsome young man") a number of questions about his childhood, how he learned the game, and whether he recommended baseball as a career. According to Santry, "he refused flatly to be quoted on whether he likes blondes or brunettes." She also queried him about how many "mash notes" he received from adoring female fans. He allowed that he had only received one or two, but that Moe Berg was the most popular bachelor on the club.[54]

Coming off the American League pennant, Cronin and Griffith targeted fewer changes to their club than they had the previous winter. Goose Goslin, reacquired a year earlier to provide another big bat, had hit just .297 with 64 RBI and argued with Cronin a few times when he had not been in the lineup. In a game near the end of the season Goose left the bench to go nap on the trainer's table, and on his way he asked Cronin to let him know if he needed a pinch hitter. He might be available. Then again, he might not.[55] Goslin had also been forced to play right field for the first time in 1933, a move that stretched his defensive abilities. In December Griffith dealt Goslin to the Tigers for John Stone, who was as good a hitter at that point as Goose, and a natural right fielder. This would turn out to be one of Griffith's better deals. Sam Rice, with nineteen years of service in the capital but disappointed over not being used in Game 4 of the recent World Series, was released in January.[56]

Cronin was optimistic about his club's chances, especially after the strong performances of his pitching staff in the spring.[57] The rotation of Crowder, Whitehill, Stewart, and Weaver returned intact, backed by the strong work of Jack Russell of whom Cronin said, "He's the greatest relief pitcher since Marberry was mowing 'em down nine or ten years ago."[58] As for the rest of the league, Cronin looked to New York first of all, but also to Boston. The Red Sox, long-time league doormats, had recently added Lefty Grove. "[They] may have their weak points," said Cronin, "but overlooking their pitching staff is as easy as overlooking Kate Smith."[59]

Cecil Travis, now twenty years old and fresh off another big year at Chattanooga, returned to camp to challenge Bluege at third base. Bluege and Cronin both worked with Travis on his defense and positioning, while Cronin also recommended he switch to a lighter bat. Most of Travis's hits were singles to the opposite field, and Cronin hoped to see Travis begin to slug drives into the spacious Griffith Stadium power alleys—as Cronin himself had learned to do. Based on his great defense and incumbency, Bluege won the job in the spring, but after a brief slump by Bluege, Cronin gave Travis a shot on April 26. The youngster made the most of it, getting two hits, and Cronin kept him in the lineup. For his rookie season, Travis hit .319 in 109 games.[60] Bluege became a capable backup at both shortstop and third base since, according to Shirley Povich, "he can field rings around Cronin even at the shortstop position."[61]

Travis proved to be one of the few bright spots for the 1934 Senators. The club suffered a series of injuries, beginning with catcher Luke Sewell's broken finger in the spring that cost him two months of action. Both Jack Russell and Buddy Myer suffered spike wounds in separate on-field incidents early in the season; both returned after missing a couple of weeks, but Russell never rebounded to form. Joe Kuhel, who had driven in 107 runs in 1933, broke his ankle sliding in mid-June and missed three months.[62]

Alvin Crowder had won fifty games for the Senators over the previous two years, but a sore arm in 1934 limited him to a 4-10 record with a grisly 6.79 ERA in one hundred innings. In early August the Senators finally cut their losses and waived Crowder to the Detroit Tigers. (As luck would have it, the General went 5-1 down the stretch, won sixteen games the next season, and pitched in two more World Series for the Tigers.) The rest of Washington's pitching slumped as well, and the team's earned-run average jumped from 3.82 in their pennant season to 4.68.

Joe Cronin struggled with his own game. Like 1933 he started slowly, but this time the slump persisted a bit longer. At the end of May he was hitting just .215, causing Cronin to drop himself to the seventh spot in the batting order for a while. He made three errors in consecutive games on May 11 and 12. The Senators, meanwhile, stayed in contention because no team had caught fire. At the end of May they were 21-19, but just two and a half games behind the surprising first-place Indians. Answering a query concerning the Senators slow start, Cronin responded, "The team isn't leading because Cronin isn't hitting."[63]

In June Cronin finally began to hit. He started a twenty-two-game hitting streak on June 8, to highlight a .362 month. In a doubleheader sweep of the White Sox on June 13, Cronin drove in 10 runs on 3 singles, 2 doubles, and a home run, part of a 6-for-9 day. At the All-Star break he had 73 RBI in his team's seventy-seven games.

On June 20 Cronin and Bill Terry were named by their respective leagues to manage the upcoming All-Star Game, to be held at New York's Polo Grounds on July 10.[64] Cronin turned sentimental in the selection of his two coaches: Walter Johnson, who had made Cronin a regular shortstop in 1929 and whose Cleveland Indians had surprised early in 1934, and Al Schacht, one of Cronin's own coaches and his roommate in his early days with the club.[65]

Both Cronin and Terry did not adhere to the voting of the fans in a few cases. Cronin replaced Chicago's Jimmie Dykes, the fans' selection at third base, with Jimmie Foxx, a first baseman but likely the best player in the American League at the time, and substituted Al Simmons for Earl Averill in center field. Similarly, Terry bypassed catcher Al Lopez and outfielder Chuck Klein in favor of Gabby Hartnett and Kiki Cuyler. (The fan voting was considered advisory in 1934.) The Senators on the club included Cronin and Heinie Manush, both starters, and relief pitcher Jack Russell. Earl Whitehill was upset at his manager's decision not to select him, beginning another tradition that would cause headaches for All-Star managers for decades to come.[66]

The 1934 All-Star Game remains one of the most famous such contests, a highlight of Cronin's baseball life. Cronin is most famous in this game for striking out in the second inning. Carl Hubbell started for the National League. After allowing a single to Charlie Gehringer and walking Heinie Manush, Hubbell proceeded to strike out the next five players to face him. Not just any players, either—he fanned Babe Ruth, Lou Gehrig, Jimmie Foxx, Al Simmons, and Joe Cronin. For the rest of Cronin's life, whenever the All-Star Game rolled around, the story of Hubbell's achievement was retold, and Cronin would graciously "brag" about hitting a foul ball off the great screwballer, whom he referred to after the game as "unquestionably the greatest pitcher I have ever seen."[67]

Cronin would occasionally have to remind the questioner that the American League came back and won the game. Hubbell left after three innings with a 4–0 lead, but the AL battered Lon Warneke and Van Lingle Mungo for eight runs over the next two innings and held on for a 9–7 victory. The real pitching star of the day was not Hubbell, but Mel Harder, who pitched five scoreless innings to finish off the Nationals. Cronin drove in the first AL run with a single in the fourth, and the last with a double in the sixth. Cronin's American League squad remains the only one to start nine future Hall of Famers.

There was little remaining excitement for the Senators in the 1934 season. The team was 36-31 and in third place on June 26, but they faded quickly. An 8-21 July left them sixteen games behind the Tigers and Yankees, who were staging a great pennant race. Cronin lifted his average up to .285 at the end of July, but he could never quite get to the coveted .300 circle he had reached the previous four seasons. His frustration came out in a 13–7 loss at Detroit on July 11, when his repeated yelling from the bench led to his ejection by umpire Bill McGowan. It was the first ejection of Cronin's career.[68]

In August it was announced that following the season Babe Ruth would lead a team of All-Stars on a trip to British Columbia, Hawaii, Japan, China, and the Philippines. Connie Mack was organizing the trip, but Ruth, who was angling for a big league managerial job, would be the bench manager. Cronin, who planned to marry right after the season, signed up, figuring this would be a suitable honeymoon for a baseball couple.[69]

Despite a number of bumps and bruises, including taking a Mike Higgins ground ball to the face in a loss at Philadelphia on July 31, Cronin missed just one game through the end of August that season. His luck ran out on September 3 in the first game of a doubleheader against the Red Sox. Batting in the eighth inning, Cronin beat out an infield single. While crossing the first base bag, he collided with Red Sox pitcher Wes Ferrell and took a hard somersaulting tumble. He came up holding his left forearm. He finished the game, but X-rays revealed a break that ended his playing season.[70]

For the 1934 campaign, Cronin hit .284, his lowest average since hitting .281 in 1929, his first as a regular. Despite playing just 127 games, he managed 30 doubles and 101 RBI, his fifth consecutive year over 100. Also for the fifth straight year he was named by *The Sporting News* as the shortstop on their Major League All-Star team.

While recovering from his broken arm, Cronin spent a week away from the club in the hospital, turning over the managerial reigns to Schacht. Cronin returned on September 10 in Chicago, but his season was interrupted again on the advice of Clark Griffith. Knowing of Joe and his niece's longing to get married, in mid-September Griffith suggested that they go ahead and do it earlier than planned, and take the rest of the season off. "I'm not a quitter, Griff," said Cronin.[71] With the support of Mildred, Griffith eventually talked Joe into taking an early break. In any event, Cronin missed only the last three games, a home series against New York that included Babe Ruth's last home run and last game with the Yankees.

Joe Cronin and Mildred June Robertson married on Thursday, September 27, at 10:00 a.m. at St. Mathews Catholic Church, about four blocks from the White House. (St. Mathews became a cathedral in 1939, and hosted the funeral mass for President John F. Kennedy in 1963.[72]) The Reverend T. J. Murray from Branford, Connecticut, performed the wedding service. Murray had befriended Cronin when he played for New Haven in 1926 and had attended every Senators game in New York in subsequent seasons.[73] The best man was Arthur Crowley, the son of a former Boston police chief and Cronin's friend since 1928. Mildred's sister Thelma Mae Griffith, who would take over Mildred's job as their uncle's secretary and marry a ballplayer herself, served as the maid of honor. Because Mildred's father was deceased, her uncle Clark walked her down the aisle to his waiting manager.[74] September 27 was an off day for the Senators, which allowed many players and officials to attend the nuptials.

Because Cronin's broken arm forced him to pull out of Ruth's Japan tour, the young couple planned a different honeymoon. After a drive to New York City, they embarked on a long cruise through the Panama Canal to San Francisco, not arriving in Cronin's hometown for a month. Cronin's family and western friends had not attended the hastily arranged ceremony, and none of them had ever met Mildred. The Cronins planned to reside in San Francisco in the winter, and obviously Washington in the summer. Soon after Joe and Mildred arrived, they were presented with some startling news.

Clark Griffith, back in Washington, had been anxiously waiting for the married couple to reach San Francisco. Griffith had been offered $250,000, plus shortstop Lyn Lary, by the Boston Red Sox for Cronin. Griffith wanted to speak with Joe about it before making the deal official. Griffith also related that the Red Sox would give Cronin a five-year contract as player-manager for $27,000 per year, compared with the $22,000 he was to make in Washington.[75] Though Joe and Mildred were both shocked, in the end Cronin urged Griffith to make the deal.

Red Sox owner Tom Yawkey first approached Griffith with an offer during the World Series in Detroit, which would place the meeting between October 3 and October 9. Griffith initially turned Yawkey down, but a week after the Series they met again in Yawkey's office in midtown Manhattan, a meeting also attended by Boston general manager Eddie Collins. Yawkey again asked for Cronin, raising his offer to $250,000, and this time Griffith demanded Lary, the Red Sox shortstop. Yawkey initially refused but gave way when it was clear that Griffith was prepared to leave the office.[76]

"Cronin has put in seven years of valiant, conscientious service to the Washington Baseball club," Griffith told the press. "Cronin has been a great ball player for us and a great manager. He is one of the finest boys I ever knew, and I am wishing him all the success in the world."[77] In an interview near the end of his life, Griffith admitted that the Senators owed $124,000 to a bank after a disastrous financial year for the club. Most baseball teams were losing money throughout the 1930s, leading to many top stars being sold. Unlike Connie Mack, who sold several top stars in the mid-1930s in order to right his financial ship, Griffith felt he could solve his problems immediately with this one trade.[78]

Griffith also believed the deal was best for Cronin and his new bride. Yawkey could pay him more money and provide more security. Cronin had kept his relationship with Mildred quiet for so long because he was concerned about how he would be treated if it were known he was dating his boss's "daughter." Now that they were married Griffith read many accounts that referred to Cronin as his son-in-law, a foreboding depiction of their relationship. The nepotism charges would grow louder, Griffith felt.[79]

So Griffith made the deal. It got his team out of debt, it made

Joe and Mildred more secure, and the $250,000 would allow him to keep his team strong. Writer Dan Daniel felt certain that this move foretold other player sales, or perhaps that the $250,000 price included "additions to this deal that Washington is not quite ready to announce." Perhaps Joe Kuhel, or Buddy Myer.[80] In any event, in more than four decades of running the Senators, Clark Griffith sold only one star player: Joe Cronin. Although he often operated at a financial disadvantage to many of the more affluent teams, especially the Yankees and later the Red Sox, he remained committed to winning pennants until the day he died.

Cronin was upbeat. "Naturally, I hate to leave Washington," he told the press on the twenty-sixth. "Mr. Griffith was like a father to me. But as long as I am moving, I'm mighty happy it is Boston. Boston is one of the greatest sports towns in the world. A fellow with an Irish name like mine ought to get along there." His new bride added, "I'd be happy to go with Joe to Oshkosh." Mildred did wonder about her new baseball role. "Now I am a girl with divided loyalties," she told her uncle Clark. "Whom will I root for, Washington or Boston?" Clark advised that she cheer on both teams, which Mildred did for many years.[81]

In the meantime, Joe and Mildred Cronin rented a house on Monterrey Boulevard, not far from his parent's home. While Joe Cronin was the center of most baseball conversations on the East Coast that off-season, he and his bride were nearly three thousand miles away, starting their new life together.

5 Rich Kid

JOE CRONIN'S NEW BOSS, TOM YAWKEY, could hardly have been more different than his old one. While Clark Griffith had spent forty years in the game before Cronin met him; Yawkey was just a few years older than Cronin and had been involved in baseball less than two years. While both men genuinely loved the game, baseball was Griffith's life, while to Yawkey it was something like a hobby.

Thomas Yawkey Austin was born in 1903 into a wealthy family that held substantial timber and mining lands in the Midwest. His father died soon after Tom was born, and the boy lived most of his childhood with his uncle William Yawkey, his mother's brother. William lived in Manhattan and mostly neglected the family business. He co-owned the Detroit Tigers for several years, and loved to hunt, attend ball games, drink, and gamble on horses, often in the company of his players. When Tom's mother died in 1918, Tom was formally adopted by Uncle William and his wife Margaret, and his name was changed to Thomas Austin Yawkey. A year later William too died. Suddenly the sixteen-year-old boy was filthy rich, with a fortune estimated at somewhere between $7 million and $20 million.[1]

There was a catch. All of the money would be maintained by conservators until Tom's thirtieth birthday—February 21, 1933. For the intervening fourteen years, Tom lived the life of leisure expected of rich young men in the Roaring Twenties. In 1920 he graduated from the Irving School, a prestigious prep school in Tarrytown, New York. He earned a degree from Yale in 1925, after five years, according to a classmate, "of fast cars, pretty girls, drinks and laughs."[2] In a social environment of mainly wealthy people, Yawkey was wealthier than most and could often be found leading whatever merriment might be going on. After leaving Yale he married a former beauty queen and began spending some of his time working in the family business. He did little—Yawkey Enterprises was well run by other people, mainly buying and selling lands and stock. While he was bear hunting with his friends, his wealth continued to accumulate.[3]

Tom Yawkey loved baseball. He had lived with William when his uncle owned the Tigers and had known and idolized famous ball-players his entire life. It was Ty Cobb who first suggested to Yawkey that he consider buying a baseball team. That was in 1926, several years before Tom would get his inheritance. Yawkey's biggest idol in baseball was Eddie Collins, a great second baseman in the 1910s and 1920s, who had preceded Yawkey at the Irving School by more than a decade. Yawkey played ball himself at Irving and was a pretty good athlete. Years later Yawkey met Collins at a school function and asked Eddie, then a coach with Connie Mack's Athletics, to let him know if a baseball team came up for sale.

By late 1932 the Boston Red Sox were in dire straits. In the early 1920s owner Harry Frazee had decimated a great team by selling or trading all its best players to the New York Yankees. When he sold the wreck of a club to Robert Quinn in 1923, the cupboard was bare. Quinn owned the Red Sox for ten seasons, finishing last eight times and losing money every year. After the club finished sixty-four games out of first place in 1932, Quinn decided he had had enough. During the World Series he ran into Collins, who arranged a meeting with Yawkey.[4]

The price for the team and Fenway Park was $1.25 million, a lot of money for a struggling franchise in 1933. The sale was announced on February 25, four days after Yawkey's thirtieth birthday. Yawkey would love the game for the rest of his life, but he knew nothing about running a team and never really would. Before making the deal Yawkey convinced Collins to be the team's vice president and general manager, running the club's day-to-day operations.[5] The stories in the local papers played up the role of Collins over the unknown Yawkey. "Eddie Collins and 30-Year-Old New York Millionaire Buy Red Sox Club," announced one headline.[6]

In March 1933 as Joe Cronin was conducting his first spring training as Senators manager in Biloxi, Yawkey and Collins were checking out their new team in Sarasota, Florida. There wasn't much to see—the team was fresh off a 111-loss season. As the Red Sox had literally no farm system and until recently, no money to buy players from the Minor Leagues, the club was nothing more than a collection of players other teams did not want.

Yawkey quickly let it be known that he wanted to buy ballplayers, and as most of his fellow owners were either losing money or holding on to it, there was no shortage of sellers. In May 1933 the Red Sox purchased catcher Rick Ferrell and pitcher Lloyd Brown from the Browns, and pitcher George Pipgras and Bill Werber from the Yankees. These four players cost about $125,000, an astronomical sum of money in 1933. Thus fortified, Yawkey's first club improved by twenty wins and advanced to seventh place.

In December the team made even larger headlines when they dealt two unneeded players and another $125,000 to the Athletics for pitchers Lefty Grove and Rube Walberg and second baseman Max Bishop. Walberg and Bishop were no longer the fine players they had been, but Grove had won twenty-four games in 1933 and remained one of baseball's best pitchers. In May 1934 Collins acquired another star pitcher by trading two players and $25,000 to the Indians for Wes Ferrell, Rick's brother. Wes had won twenty or more games his first four seasons but had an injury-plagued 1933 and was holding out rather than accept the huge salary cut the Indians offered.

In 1934 many writers picked the Red Sox to finish third behind Washington and New York, largely because of the big trade with the Athletics. Unfortunately, Grove reported to camp with a sore arm, the first of his long career, and the injury stayed with him all season. Grove finished with eight wins and a 6.52 ERA, and at thirty-four years old appeared washed up. The other two players Collins received from the Athletics were also disappointments—Walberg won six games and Bishop hit .261. Wes Ferrell pitched the way the Red Sox had expected Grove to pitch. All things considered, the team did well to finish fourth at 76-76, twenty-four games behind the Tigers. It was their first nonlosing season since 1918.

Largely by replacing bad players with average players, the Red Sox had improved by a remarkable thirty-three wins in two years. The 1932 Red Sox had started a shortstop who hit .211 and an outfielder who hit .264 with zero home runs. Two years later, the Red Sox had acceptable Major League players dotting the roster. Within the game and in the media, they had become relevant.

Yawkey had also spent $1.5 million on a total reconstruction of Fenway Park. It should be noted that all this money meant very little to Yawkey—in 1933, his aunt (and adoptive mother) Margaret died, leaving Tom another $4 million, dwarfing all his recent investments in his team.[7] The country's economic depression continued, but Thomas Yawkey kept getting richer.

Yawkey and Collins's next big coup was the deal for Cronin in October 1934. Eddie Collins liked Cronin as a player, but just as important Collins did not get along with Bucky Harris, the team's current manager whom Yawkey had hired—without consulting Collins—just a year earlier.[8] The man Yawkey wanted to manage the club was Babe Ruth, who had slowed down considerably as a player. The Yankees would not stand in the way of Ruth moving on for a manager's job, but Collins had no interest in dealing with Ruth and pushed instead for Cronin.[9] "That he should have been preferred to Ruth," wrote the *Brooklyn Eagle*, "an idol and always a tremendous attraction in the Hub, is something not easily explained."[10]

Not to be denied was the fact that Cronin was very popular among his fellow Irishmen in the city—his visits to Boston over the years had included many dinners and speeches that led to lasting friendships.[11] "If Cronin could not draw the Irish of Boston through the gates," *The Sporting News* later wrote, "then never a man from Antrim to Kerry, nor from Clare to Kildare, could."[12] Joe Cronin knew his way around Boston long before he joined the Red Sox.

In early December, Cronin headed east for baseball's winter meetings, first stopping in Boston to see his new bosses. Arriving on December

7, Cronin attended a lunch reception for the press at Fenway Park. He expressed delight at coming to the Red Sox, said he felt the team was in pretty good shape (except perhaps the right side of the infield), and suggested that the team's hopes lay mainly with the comebacks of Grove and Pipgras.[13]

In reality the Red Sox had a long way to go. On offense they now had four good players: Cronin at shortstop, Werber at third base, Rick Ferrell at catcher, and Roy Johnson in left field. Werber had been the team's best player in 1934, hitting .321 with 129 runs scored, 200 hits, and a league-leading 40 stolen bases. Ferrell was one of the league's best-hitting catchers, while Johnson was a consistent .300 hitter with extra-base power, and one of the few good players remaining from the team Yawkey purchased two years earlier. The incumbents at first and second bases, Ed Morgan and Bill Cissell, had moved on and not been replaced. The rest of the outfielders—Carl Reynolds, Moose Solters, Dusty Cooke, Mel Almada—did not hit enough to rank among the better outfielders in the league.

The pitching staff had holes as well. The twenty-six-year-old Ferrell was an ace, and had won fourteen games for the club after his May acquisition. Fritz Ostermueller, Gordon Rhodes, and Johnny Welch were promising youngsters who had won ten, twelve, and thirteen games while hurling 624 innings between them. The club needed to have some contribution from either Grove, who had won only eight games, or Pipgras, who pitched just three innings.

In any event the Red Sox made no additional Major League deals that off-season. "I am through buying," said Yawkey. "Eddie Collins and I are all set now. We've got a club we are confident will go places."[14] One holdup for the Red Sox was that Yawkey and Collins, now that they had a decent collection of players, were willing to make trades, but their fellow owners were holding out for cash. The club hoped to land second baseman Oscar Melillo from the Browns, and offered Solters and Cooke, but the Browns wanted money too. Yawkey's early spending had created an expectation of riches for his fellow owners.[15] After a few months of trying the club later acquired Melillo in May, for Solters and cash.

Back in San Francisco in time for the holidays, Cronin kept in shape with the usual golfing and hiking. He also played tennis with his first baseman Babe Dahlgren, whom the team had acquired from the San Francisco Missions of the PCL.[16] On February 3 Cronin was the player-manager in a charity game matching the San Francisco All-Stars and the East Bay All Stars. His club included Lefty O'Doul, Willie Kamm, Tony Lazzeri, Gus Suhr, and several other Major Leaguers. His opponents, coached by Dick Bartell, included Ernie Lombardi, Chick Hafey, Dolph Camilli, and Augie Galan.[17]

In mid-February Joe and Mildred headed for Sarasota, driving to Los Angeles and then taking a train east. En route they stopped in Biloxi to spend some time with Clark Griffith and see old friends. One familiar face joining Cronin with the Red Sox was Al Schacht, a long-time Washington coach who had helped Cronin when he was breaking in with the Senators. Schacht and fellow coach Nick Altrock had spent many years entertaining Washington fans on the field and in night clubs, but the two had had a serious falling out and had not spoken in years. Now their on-field act had come to an end. The new Red Sox coach was calling himself "O'Schacht" in honor of Boston's Irish.[18] Just before the season began the club signed another ex-Senator, Moe Berg, the mysterious catcher/intellectual who would serve the remainder of the decade as Cronin's third-string catcher.

The Red Sox opened the 1935 season with a 1–0 victory at Yankee Stadium, behind Wes Ferrell's two-hitter. After taking two of three from New York and three straight in Washington, the club hosted the Yankees at Fenway Park on April 23. Cronin was presented with a large floral piece as part of an elaborate ceremony. Gov. James Michael Curley threw out the first ball. After the Red Sox won its fourth straight to improve to 6-1, the *New York Times* reported: "While arrangements for a Boston world series have not exactly been started yet, there does not seem to a doubt hereabouts that they will be in due time."[19]

After a loss on the twenty-fifth, Lefty Grove took on Earl Whitehill and the Senators the next day. The Senators won easily 10–5, though Grove gave up just two earned runs. The Red Sox made five errors behind him, including three by Cronin—two on balls hit right at him, the third on an easy toss from Grove. The fourteen thousand fans booed Cronin throughout the latter part of the game. When he removed Grove in the seventh inning, the fans cheered Lefty's retreat, then resumed their booing. In the eighth inning a meaningless Cronin triple calmed the crowd only briefly. According to Shirley Povich, "Quarter-million-dollar shortstops were being quoted at a nickel along about the seventh inning here today."[20] According to at least one writer, Mildred Cronin left her box seat in tears.[21]

Cronin's image and reputation had crossed into a new realm. No longer was he the scrappy overachieving kid who drove himself to baseball stardom. His extraordinary sale price and fat contract led the fans and media to expect him to play like the best player in baseball, or perhaps the best player ever. Like Alex Rodriguez several decades later, his effort and talent would no longer be enough. The flaws in his game were magnified, and—as the highest-paid veteran on a team of veterans—the flaws of the team were laid at his feet.

His defensive shortcomings began to draw more attention. Cronin had a reputation as someone who would occasionally muff a ball hit right at him, but he also made a lot of hustle plays and had a great throwing arm. Statistically, he was a fine shortstop—his fielding percentage had always been better than the league average, and he also made more plays than the average shortstop. But in 1935 he was below the league average in both categories for the first time.

Two days after Cronin's three-error game behind Grove, Wes Ferrell took a 3–1 lead into the ninth against the Senators. Two Cronin errors and four singles led to four Washington runs and the ballgame. Ferrell was storming around the mound for most of the inning and Cronin, feeling somewhat responsible, had to go to the mound to calm his pitcher down. "Cronin himself has had a terrible time of it," reported the *Boston Globe*. "Under the pressure he has lost, for the time being, his easy-going manner in the short field, and his nonchalance."[22]

After the Ferrell loss on the twenty-eighth, which gave Cronin seven errors in four games, Cronin did not make another error for a month. On the season, he committed 37 errors, a typical total for him—he had made between 32 and 43 errors in the previous five seasons. His errors had not received quite so much attention before the $250,000 sale and before he was playing behind temperamental stars like Grove and Ferrell.

His veteran pitchers not only did not care for his mistakes, they also didn't care for his managing, and they were not shy about airing their views. "Word from Boston," wrote *The Sporting News* in July, "is that Bob Grove and Wes Ferrell have not been taking any too kindly to Joe Cronin's instructions on how to pitch to certain hitters. Having been around the American League for quite a spell, they feel they should know a little more about the weaknesses of opposing hitters."[23]

Robert Moses Grove did not suddenly become difficult to deal with when Joe Cronin became his manager and shortstop. Lefty spent the first ten years of his career pitching for Connie Mack, a man thirty years his senior and as well respected as any skipper in the game's history. No matter. As Eddie Collins later remembered of Grove, "he thought it was an outrage when Connie Mack ordered him to walk a batter."[24]

Jimmie Dykes, Grove's long-time shortstop in Philadelphia, recalled a time in 1929 when a couple of infield errors caused Grove to begin lobbing the ball in to the batter, a not-too-subtle message that if no one else was trying he wasn't going to either. Back in the dugout, Mack got into it with his star pitcher, an argument that led the taciturn manager to say, "And to hell with you, too, Robert." According to Dykes, this was the only time he ever heard his manager cuss. Lefty laughed, returned to the mound, and won the game.[25]

Grove lost a 1–0 game in 1931 when reserve left fielder Jimmy Moore misjudged a line drive in St. Louis. Had Grove won, he would have set a league record with his seventeenth straight victory. When the game ended, Mack advised the young Moore to remain on the bench for a while to allow Grove time to calm down. While Moore waited, Grove destroyed lockers, chairs, light bulbs, shower heads, his uniform, and anything else he could get his hands on. He cussed out Al Simmons, whose injury kept him from taking his usual place in left field, as well as Mack, who had had the temerity to play Moore in the outfield that day.[26] Forty-four years later, Grove recalled the incident to writer Donald Honig: "Still gets me mad when I think about it."[27]

Ferrell, the club's other veteran pitching ace, was no better. Ferrell also stormed around and stared at teammates who erred while he was pitching. He had had many run-ins with manager Roger Peckinpaugh in Cleveland, once drawing a ten-game suspension for refusing to leave the mound when Peckinpaugh came out to relieve him. After the game the manager suggested Ferrell had not been bearing down.[28] When Walter Johnson took over the Indians in 1933, Ferrell's temper and disposition had not improved. In the words of one scribe, "When you can't get along with Walter, something is really out of kilter with your endocrines and your pituitary gland."[29]

Unlike Mack and Peckinpaugh, Cronin had to deal with Grove and Ferrell as a player as well as a manager. Both pitchers tolerated no fielding errors behind them, and no player on the field makes more errors than the shortstop, no matter how accomplished he might be. They also hated being advised how to pitch or even being spoken to on the mound. Cronin talked constantly and was used to going to the mound often to discuss the hitter and situation with the pitcher. Cronin had been a rival youngster just a few months ago, one who had called these men "Mr. Grove" and "Mr. Ferrell."[30]

The situation reached its nadir on July 21 in Boston, with the Red Sox facing the Tigers, Lefty Grove battling Tommy Bridges. After a few lead changes, Grove led 4–3 entering the top of the ninth. With two outs and a man on second, Cronin decided to walk Hank Greenberg, despite the strong objections of his pitcher. Grove next allowed three straight hits before getting the final out, now trailing in the game 6–4. As he walked off the field, Grove heaved his glove into the crowd, ripped off his uniform top and smashed one of Cronin's bats on the edge of the dugout before storming into the clubhouse. Remarkably the Red Sox pulled out the victory when Wes Ferrell, pinch-hitting for Grove in the bottom of the ninth, hit a three-run home run over the left-field wall.[31] Ferrell later recalled what happened next:

So we all rush into the clubhouse, laughing and hollering, the way you do after a game like that. And here's Lefty, sitting there, thinking he's lost the game. When he saw all the carrying-on, I tell you, the smoke started coming out of his ears.

Then someone says, "Hell, Lefty, we won it. Wes hit a home run for you."

Well, I was sitting across the clubhouse from him, pulling my uniform off, and I notice he's staring at me, with just a trace of a smile at the corners of his mouth. He doesn't say anything. I give him a big grin and pull my sweat shirt over my head. Then I hear him say, "Hey, Wes." I look over and he's rolling a bottle of wine across to me. I picked it up and thanked him and put it in my locker.[32]

Cronin had three singles in support of his pitcher, but there is no evidence that he received any wine on this or any other occasion. On August 7 Cronin's three-run homer in the bottom of the ninth off the Yankees' Johnny Broaca won a game for Grove that he did not deserve to win.[33] On September 2 Wes Ferrell, down seven runs in the third inning against the Senators, had to be yanked only to watch as the Red Sox stormed back to win the game in extra innings. Cronin contributed three hits and drove in six runs, including a grand slam in the eighth off Bump Hadley.[34]

The Red Sox did not contend in 1935, as several good seasons by their stars were balanced by lackluster contributions from the supporting cast. The club finished 78-75, just marginally better than their 76-76 under Bucky Harris in 1934. "Boston fans were well satisfied," wrote *The Sporting News* late in the season, "that even if Joe Cronin did not produce a winner he has molded the Red Sox into a real fighting outfit."[35]

Lefty Grove had a marvelous comeback season, following up his injury-filled disaster in 1934 with a 20-12 record and a league-leading 2.70 ERA. His fellow mound terror Ferrell finished 25-14 with a league-leading thirty-one complete games. Only two other Red Sox pitchers won more than five games—Johnny Welch at 10-9 and Fritz Ostermueller at 7-8—but the stars were enough to make the pitching staff among the best in the league. But the offense did not score enough runs for the team to compete.

After a slow start Cronin hit .295 with 60 extra base hits and 95 runs batted in. The arm injury he had suffered the previous September bothered him early in the season and may have lingered longer than he would admit.[36] He started his third consecutive All-Star Game, going hitless but playing all nine innings in the American League's 4–1 win in Cleveland.

Cronin's knack for driving in big runs failed him on September 7 against Cleveland, but his failure was a memorable one. Down 5–1 in the bottom of the ninth, the Red Sox rallied for two runs and had the bases loaded for Cronin with still no one out. A single would likely tie the game, and extra-base hit would likely win it. Facing Oral Hildebrand, Cronin hit a rocket off the forehead of third baseman Odell Hale. Unfortunately, the ball deflected into the hands of shortstop Bill Knickerbocker without touching the ground, and the Indians quickly turned it into a game-ending triple play.[37]

Cronin's first year in Boston had been an uneasy one. While he had drawn praise for his handling of the veteran players in Washington, things were much more difficult in Boston. It is worth noting that while Griffith had been quick to get rid of players who might have clashed with Cronin's managerial decisions, specifically Rice and Goslin, Yawkey and Collins were much less sensitive to the situation. While he and Collins always backed Cronin publicly, Yawkey would not discipline the likes of Lefty Grove, whom Yawkey idolized, went hunting with, and drank with. After the season Bill Werber told the press that he wanted out of Boston—he did not like Cronin as a manager and did not like playing next to such a lousy shortstop.[38] Clark Griffith would have dealt Werber immediately. In Boston Werber was allowed to stay and complain for another year.

Heading into the off-season, there were differing views as to Tom Yawkey's state of mind. *The Sporting News* reported confidently that Yawkey was at the World Series looking to buy more players,[39] while the *Chicago Daily Tribune* reported that the Red Sox owner was no longer willing to spend "big money" on "big names."[40] Rumors flew that fall that Collins was talking to Connie Mack again, this time about center fielder Doc Cramer and shortstop Eric McNair.

Cronin had played the closing doubleheader of the season in New York at first base. This was considered a signal of Cronin's future plans, and the acquisition of McNair would be consistent with the idea that Cronin would shift to another position in 1936. Though just turning twenty-nine years old in October, Cronin's weight had slowed him down considerably in 1935, after also drawing comment his last season with Washington. Cronin thought it worthwhile to wire the Boston press from San Francisco to say that there were no deals imminent despite the rumors.[41]

Nonetheless, at the winter meetings Collins dropped a bombshell by acquiring first baseman Jimmie Foxx and pitcher Johnny Marcum from Philadelphia in exchange for pitcher Gordon Rhodes and $150,000. A few weeks later the two clubs made another big deal, the Red Sox sending two little-used players and $75,000 to the Athletics for McNair and Cramer. In between these two transactions the Red Sox sent outfielders Carl Reynolds and Roy Johnson to the Senators for Heinie Manush. Cronin had lobbied for several months for Manush, a close friend and roommate during their years together in Washington.

This series of deals, Yawkey's biggest haul yet, caused many people to anoint the Red Sox as pennant contenders. Jimmie Foxx was the big prize—a midcareer slugger, the best hitter the team had had since Babe Ruth had been traded sixteen years before. Cramer was an excellent defensive outfielder who hit .300 every year, while Manush was a year removed from a .349 season. And better yet, Marcum had won seventeen games for a poor team in 1935, hopefully giving the Red Sox a third excellent starting pitcher.

There was considerable speculation as to where everyone would play. If Cronin remained at shortstop, McNair would have to move to second or third base. If Cronin or McNair played third, Werber, the team's best defensive infielder, would move to right field. One odd man out was Babe Dahlgren, the incumbent first baseman and Cronin's tennis partner in San Francisco the previous winter. Dahlgren complained about the Foxx deal and blamed his poor hitting in 1935 on being forced to change his batting style, further mentioning that he had spent too much time at first base fielding bad throws by Cronin and others.[42]

Cronin again spent the winter playing tennis in San Francisco (presumably not with Dahlgren), intending to show up to camp in-shape and earn the shortstop job.[43] "When Joe sloughs off some of the extra pounds of easy living," wrote one scribe, "perhaps he may regain the speed and power that made him the greatest shortstop in the league."[44] He was delighted with the new trades, predicting that Foxx (the "greatest player in the game") would hit sixty home runs.[45] He played an occasional game of baseball, including a charity game matching the best players in San Francisco against the best from the East Bay.[46]

In early 1936 Mildred Cronin authored a magazine story telling of her life as a baseball wife. A spouse was a crucial component to a player's success, related Mildred, especially by insisting that he stay home, eat the right food, and stop smoking cigars. A wife could become a handicap by getting too attached to her home, a home the family might have to abandon when the husband was traded to another team. More importantly, a wife should never gossip with other wives, a problem for which "ball teams have been rent asunder." Mildred also provided a detailed recipe for getting a ballplayer out of a slump, with proper cajoling and flattering—but never irritation. Finally, a baseball wife should usually become the business manager of the family, as "players in the main are not good business men because their training has been along other lines."

Mildred conceded that her own husband had been fifteen pounds overweight in 1935. "This interfered with speedy movement around his position, that of a shortstop." Although she had heard all of the voices saying her husband needed to move to first base, she knew better. When they got to San Francisco that fall, she put Joe on a strict diet. "We eliminated potatoes, bread, and all starches from his diet," reported Mrs. Cronin, "and concentrated on lamb chops, lean meats, vegetables—and baked apples! I have baked enough apples to last me for the rest of my life." Cronin would report to camp at 174 pounds, his old playing weight.[47]

Cronin traveled from San Francisco to Sarasota in mid-February to work his retooled team into shape. The biggest distraction was the holdout of Werber, who signed on March 12 but still demanded to be traded—Collins again decided that the team needed the dissident, though the club was bursting with infielders. St. Louis Browns manager Rogers Hornsby saw trouble ahead. "Joe Cronin is going to have a helluva time keeping all his big shot stars in line," predicted the former star. "If he starts booting the ball around and they begin thinking he's losing the pennant for them, he's going to have it hard."[48]

In a poll of American League managers before the season, the Tigers were the consensus pick to win their third consecutive pennant, followed by New York, Cleveland, and Boston—the same order the clubs had finished the past two seasons.[49] Shirley Povich, for one, picked the Red Sox to win the pennant.[50] As thing turned out, Cronin would have no more discouraging year in baseball than 1936.

The Red Sox started the season with Cronin at shortstop, McNair at third, and Werber in right field. They began by beating the Athletics 9–4 in Philadelphia, despite two errors each by Cronin and McNair. In their second game two days later, Cronin made another error, then broke his thumb later in the same inning tagging Mike Higgins on a play at second base. McNair and Werber returned to their old positions, while Cronin missed six weeks of action.

Literally adding insult to injury, the *Los Angeles Times* considered the mishap good news for the team's pennant hopes: "He is the most unsteady fielder in the junior circuit."[51] Shirley Povich, who had thought the Red Sox on their way to the flag, piled on the injured star. Cronin was unpopular in Boston, thought the writer, and the fans were anxious to see the team without him. Cronin had injured himself after yet another bobbled ball required a late tag of Higgins. The mystery, thought Povich, was how the twenty-nine-year-old could be washed up so young.[52]

As it happened, the Red Sox played well in Cronin's absence. Led by the pitching of Lefty Grove (who started the year 7-1 with a 0.83 ERA and four shutouts), the club was 31-18 on June 6, just one and a half games behind the Yankees. After trying to return on May 27, Cronin returned full-time to the lineup on June 2 and soon settled in at shortstop. He played well, hitting .327 through the end of June with only an occasional error. In late June the Red Sox began a seven-game losing streak, and fell to eleven and a half games behind on July 2. The Yankees' lead was never threatened again.

Cronin continued to have trouble with his veteran pitchers, who did not like his fielding or his managing. Elden Auker, who pitched for the team in 1939, later wrote that Cronin's nervous chatter and movement behind him was a constant distraction. "After the pitch, he would run onto the mound, grab the resin bag, throw it down, and say something like, 'Keep the ball down. Make him hit a curveball. Make him hit the fastball.' He was always on the mound and it drove us pitchers crazy." Auker claimed Cronin would do this to all pitchers except Grove.[53]

The Sporting News wrote that "Joe Cronin saves Bob Grove the embarrassment of waving him off the mound when he loses his stuff by allowing Mose to walk out of the box of his own volition."[54] In effect, it seemed that Cronin was afraid of Grove, and he was not alone—it affected the entire team. "That Lefty was a terror," said Oscar Melillo. "So there we'd be in the ninth, and so scared of that wild man you could hear our knees knocking. I'd say to myself, 'I hope this guy hits it to Joe Cronin,' and I knew Cronin was hoping he'd hit it to Jimmie Foxx, and Foxx was hoping he'd hit it to Bill Werber."[55]

At the All-Star break the Red Sox were 42-34, tied with the Tigers for second place, ten games out. As in 1935 the club's performance was fueled by Grove and Ferrell, who were a combined 22-11 in midsummer. For the first time Cronin was not chosen to play in the All-Star Game, his shortstop spot taken by Chicago's Luke Appling. In a nice gesture, AL manager Joe McCarthy picked Cronin as a coach, allowing him to be in uniform in Boston's Braves Field on July 7.

On July 17 Cronin left the club to visit his ill mother in San Francisco. He arrived on the nineteenth and was at her bedside with his brothers and father when Mary Cronin died of pneumonia on July 20 at the age of sixty-five. Cronin and his mother had been very close, close enough to keep Joe in San Francisco in the off-season every year. Cronin was away for ten days, rejoining the club in St. Louis on July 28 after the game had begun. He was back at shortstop the next day. In early August the thumb he had broken in April began to bother him again, and he missed a few more weeks. Cronin played mainly third base for a month, then played infrequently in September.

Cronin's problems with his veterans continued in the second half. At one point Ferrell called his manager to the mound to tell him he would not throw another pitch until the reliever warming up in the bullpen sat down.[56] "What the ritzy Red Sox need," wrote the *Los Angeles Times*, "is a rough, tough, skipper who'll poke a few of these prima donnas right on their snooty snouts, and then hit 'em where it hurts most—right in the pocket book." Grove continued to bawl out his fielders, Ferrell at one point thumbed his nose at the booing fans, and another unnamed star (likely Foxx) was spending too much time in night clubs.[57]

On August 16, Ferrell was pitching the eighth inning of a 3–3 game at Fenway against the Senators. After the visitors loaded the bases, Cecil Travis hit a slow ground ball up the middle that barely eluded McNair playing shortstop and became a double because center fielder Cramer was playing deep. Ferrell thereupon walked to the dugout, his efforts apparently over, though the Red Sox had no one warming up in the bullpen.[58] There was no follow-up to this action—in fact, Ferrell pinch-hit in the second game of the doubleheader that day.

Five days later Ferrell got the ball in Yankee Stadium. The game was tied in the eighth when the Yankees put runners on first and third with two outs. Jake Powell hit a ground ball to shortstop that McNair could not handle. After a walk and a ground single, Ferrell "fired his hat and glove into the air and marched off the field." Again, there was no reliever warming, and this time Ferrell left the clubhouse and went back to his hotel.[59] "I'm through with him," announced Cronin to the press. "He's going to be fined $1,000, suspended and sent home.

I don't care if he goes to Boston, to his North Carolina home, or to the Fiji Islands. I'm washed up with that guy."[60]

Ferrell's initial reaction was to threaten his skipper. "I'm going to punch Cronin in the jaw as soon as I can find him. I didn't walk out on him at all. Cronin ordered me out."[61] He claimed that he thought that Cronin had signaled him to leave the game. He also denied his similar walk-off five days earlier. He said he was upset and didn't bother to look around once he saw the supposed calls to the bullpen. "They can suspend me or trade me," said Wes. "but they're not going to get any dough from me."[62] Upon hearing of Wes's threat, Cronin told reporters that he would be passing through the lobby of the hotel at six o'clock on his way to dinner. In any event, Cronin appeared in the lobby and his pitcher did not.[63]

After a meeting with Cronin and Yawkey, Ferrell said it would all soon blow over. "It was a huge mistake, in which probably I am mostly to blame."[64] Collins said that the fine would stick at least until the end of the season, when it would be up to Cronin whether to levy it.[65] Cronin apparently offered Ferrell to the Yankees, but Joe McCarthy had no interest. "I'm getting rid of those guys as fast as I can," said McCarthy.[66] Ferrell won five of his last six decisions, which got the fans back on his side.

The press was very sympathetic to Cronin, believing the club's prima donnas needed to be put in their place. "The fine and suspension have served to bring the situation to a head, and from now on we may see recessions of ego, and plans for vital changes," said one writer.[67] Cronin himself seemed shaken by all that had gone on. "I've learned a lot about ball players these past two seasons," said Cronin. "When I was named manager [in Washington] the players seemed to be tickled to death that I was given my chance and I had all the co-operation in the world. They were out there hustling all the time and so we did pretty well. When I was bought by the Red Sox I naturally thought that the same practice would work here. I'd be one of the players and would not act the manager. But these weren't the fellows who grew up with me and I finally found out that kindliness isn't always the cure."[68]

Once again, the primary problem with the Red Sox was their lack of hitting punch. While Foxx had come through with his typical season (.338, 41 home runs, 143 RBIs), and Rick Ferrell had an excellent year (.312), the rest of the team was terrible at the plate. In the high-scoring 1930s, players who hit .300 with no power or walks (especially in Fenway Park) were below-average hitters, and the Red Sox were loaded with players like this. Manush hit .291 and Cramer .292, but without a home run between them. Manush, a big disappointment in his only year with the club, was released after the season. Werber finished second on the team with just 10 home runs. Playing in the best hitter's park in the league, the Red Sox finished next-to-last in runs scored.

The terribly frustrating season ground to an even more disappointing conclusion for the Red Sox. After going 43-34 in the first half of the season and looking like they had a shot at second place, the Red Sox could finish only 31-46 in the second half and wound up in sixth place, twenty-eight and a half games behind the Yankees. Cronin played just eighty-one games, sixty at shortstop and twenty-one at third base. He hit just .281 with little power and committed 23 errors at shortstop in less than half a season.

Billy Werber, speaking at YMCA meeting after the season, told a (likely apocryphal) story that gives a glimpse of Cronin's personality and image. Cronin had already struck out a couple of times when he was waiting his turn in the dugout to bat a third time. While doing so, he was swearing elaborately to himself in earshot of the spectators, including Father O'Donnell, a Catholic priest and personal friend. "Come here, Joe," the priest called to Cronin from the front row. "You've been swearing all day without results. Let's try a prayer." Cronin agreed with his friend and joined him for a brief prayer. Stepping to the plate, Cronin soon smashed a long home run to left field. No one was more taken by the event than the priest, who cheered the hit and fell back to his seat shouting, "Good Lord!"[69]

In December the Associated Press polled their writers to determine the biggest disappointment in sports for the year 1936. The Red Sox "won" the poll easily, far outdistancing Joe Louis's loss to

Max Schmeling in June at Yankee Stadium.[70] Two seasons after Tom Yawkey purchased Cronin for $250,000, one would have had to conclude that the deal was a bust. The team had not improved since his arrival, Cronin seemed to be over his head with his players, and he looked to be washed-up as a player himself.

6 Comeback

For the first several years after his purchase of the Boston Red Sox, Tom Yawkey spent millions of dollars on veteran ballplayers for the stated purpose of winning a championship. As his the team could never catch the Tigers or (later) the Yankees, disappointing both himself and the team's fans, one could conclude that his free spending had been an abysmal failure.

Applying a broader look at the early Yawkey years might lead to a more sympathetic judgment. Yawkey and Collins took over a nearly bankrupt franchise coming off a 43-111 season and got the club to .500 two years later. Though the rise stalled over the next two years, most of the star players Yawkey had purchased, including Grove, Foxx, and the Ferrell brothers, had performed well in Boston. Cronin could have been considered a bust thus far, though his play had been seriously affected by the broken arm he suffered just prior to the deal and by his broken thumb in 1936.

The real problem with Yawkey's strategy was that, decades before free agency came to Major League Baseball, there weren't enough great players on the market to make it work. Acquiring Jimmie Foxx was a big help, but to compete with the Yankees—who had Lou Gehrig, Joe DiMaggio, Tony Lazzeri, and Bill Dickey—the Red Sox needed a few more players nearly as good as Foxx, and such players were not typically available. Yawkey's purchases dramatically improved the team and could not realistically have been expected to improve it much more than they did.

Yawkey bought a team that had no Minor League players to help fortify the team. (Only the St. Louis Cardinals had a true "farm system," though many clubs had players on option to independent Minor League teams.) To make the Red Sox respectable in the short-term

Yawkey had to acquire good Major League players, and he could do that only by spending money. He might have spent less money than he did, and he could have been more discerning about some of the players he purchased. But without Yawkey opening his wallet, the Red Sox would have remained terrible for many years. The expectations of the media and fans, that purchasing a bunch of veteran players would put them on par with the New York Yankees, were not realistic. Yawkey was not misguided to spend money as he did, but he and everyone else should have recognized that his approach was nothing more than a reasonable first step.

Yawkey remained perfectly content with his chosen hobby. "Some men like to spend their dough on fast horses and other things that go fast," he told writer Dan Daniel in early 1937. "Some men like to go in for polo, for example, and spend thousands of dollars on ponies. Some go nuts for paintings, and give half a million for a hunk of canvas in a fancy frame, which maybe never is painted by the guy which is supposed to do the job 500 years ago. But my passion is baseball. My idea of heaven is a pennant winner. Boston would go nuts over a winner, and maybe someday we'll get all the dough back. But in the meantime, don't let anybody tell you Tom Yawkey is a sucker."[1]

At the time the press and public were supportive. Yawkey had purchased a dying franchise and made it relevant again without causing more than a ripple in his own substantial bank account. "The fact is," wrote Joe Williams in 1938, "it would be better for baseball—much better—if there were more Tom Yawkeys in it. What do you think a Yawkey would do for the dismal situation in St. Louis, as regards the Browns? When a young fellow comes along and decides to take the rubber band off the bank roll, for some reason the first people to scoff at him are the wise guys."[2]

The Red Sox in the late 1930s were sometimes called the Gold Sox, or the Millionaires, and many stories written about them in this era referred to their opulent salaries. This characterization is misleading. In 1933 Yawkey's first year in charge, the team's payroll was $145,896, sixth of eight teams in the league, and far behind the Yankees' $294,982. Six years later in 1939, when most of Yawkey's high-priced purchases were still on the team, their payroll had risen to $227,237, only the fifth highest in the league, while New York was paying out $361,471. The team's reputation was fueled completely by the prices Yawkey paid to purchase some of his players, but was not reflected in the club's payroll. The Yankees were the team loaded with high-priced stars, many purchased from Minor League teams, and their great success was a tribute to the expensive talent they had acquired.

In the mean time by 1937 Red Sox were beginning to work young players onto their team. The club hired Billy Evans, long-time American League umpire and recently the general manager of the Indians, to build and oversee a farm system. The club had only one Minor League affiliate in 1933: the Reading Red Sox in the New York–Penn League. By 1936 there were nine affiliates, and the next season eleven. Evans spent $50,000 in 1936, but warned that the system would yield nothing for the next couple of seasons. Possibly, he allowed, there would be "two or three prospects" in 1939.[3]

A few youngsters had begun to show up even before Evans. Fritz Ostermueller joined the rotation in 1934 and had several good seasons. The 1935 team had started two rookies—Babe Dahlgren at first base and Mel Almada in center field, neither of whom hit much. Jack Wilson joined the pitching staff that year and gradually assumed a large role. Bobby Doerr, a nineteen-year-old second baseman, was just about ready. One does not develop a farm system overnight, but after a few years of lavish spending on Major Leaguers, Yawkey and Collins were ready to give the system more attention.

After only three thousand people watched the season-ending doubleheader with the Athletics in 1936, *The Sporting News* reported, "[Yawkey] has grown sick and tired of temperamental athletes who seem to be a law unto themselves."[4] The first to go was Werber, who had argued with Cronin on the field in September after being called out for not hustling.[5] Werber was dealt for another third baseman, Mike Higgins, a similar player but easier on his managers.

Yawkey announced in November that he, Collins, and Cronin had agreed that Joe would play third base in 1937, "very definitely."[6] The Werber-Higgins trade a few weeks later led to speculation that Higgins would be traded elsewhere, perhaps to Cleveland for hard-hitting outfielder Joe Vosmik. The Red Sox needed outfielders more than infielders.

After spending much of the fall with Mildred's family in Washington, attending the winter meetings, and joining his father for the holidays, Cronin was back in Boston in January 1937 for meetings with Collins and Yawkey. Cronin spoke to a press gathering at Fenway Park on the fourteenth. According to Cronin, the club had four set positions: Foxx at first base, Ferrell at catcher, Cramer in center field, and McNair at shortstop. "I will never go back there unless he meets with some unexpected setback," assured Cronin. He planned to try Doerr at second base, and Higgins at third. If Doerr was not ready, he'd shift Higgins to second base and play third himself.[7] Cronin was now thirty years old, a lifetime .301 hitter, and one year removed from his third straight All-Star assignment but apparently could find no place for himself in the lineup.

In Sarasota for spring training, Cronin was much happier and more relaxed than he had been in 1936 when expectations for the team were much higher. "This spring," said Cronin, "we are just another ball club. And I prefer it that way." Writer Fred Lieb compared the Red Sox's 1936 spring atmosphere to Babe Ruth's first camp with the Yankees in 1920.[8] That same month Eddie Collins, speaking to a group in Roxbury, Massachusetts, had to respond to criticism for rift between himself and his manager. "Cronin is one of the best managers in baseball," said Collins. "He carries on as a player himself. He is one of the finest characters I know, and I admire and love him."[9]

Although Cronin and Collins had essentially ruled out the possibility over the winter, Cronin ended up moving back to shortstop to start the season. Eric McNair had lost his wife in January, soon after she had given birth to their son. With his young shortstop an emotional wreck all spring, Cronin played a few games at short to give McNair time to recover, and a combination of his own fine play and McNair's depression kept him there. "He sure has played as well as he did in Washington," said Collins. "The club seems to have more life with him in action. There isn't anything wrong with Cronin's wrist, and his mental condition is vastly better than last spring when he thought the club was going to win the pennant and then collapsed."[10]

Cronin had his own tragedy to deal with in early April. Mildred gave birth to twins (a boy and a girl) in Sarasota on April 7, but both children died and she herself spent a day in serious danger. The Red Sox broke camp on the eighth, with several exhibition matches planned on the route north, but Cronin stayed behind with Mildred. He tried addressing the team before they left but broke down in tears.[11] A few days later the Cronins went to Washington so Mildred could recuperate with her mother and family. Cronin rejoined the team in time for their season opener in Philadelphia on April 20, though Mildred remained in bed for several more weeks.[12]

Besides Cronin, the surprise of the camp had been the great play of second baseman Bobby Doerr, who turned nineteen early in the season. Doerr grew up in Los Angeles and had already played three years in the Pacific Coast League. In the winter of 1935 the Red Sox bought options on the contracts of Doerr and shortstop George Myatt. In August 1936 Eddie Collins went out west to do some scouting and checked in on Doerr's San Diego club while they were in Portland. He decided to exercise the club's option on Doerr (who hit .342 that season) but not on Myatt. While Collins was in Portland, he also made a deal with team president Bill Lane to have first crack at a seldom-used outfielder named Ted Williams.

Doerr later recalled meeting Cronin soon after the club purchased his option. Cronin was in Los Angeles visiting a friend, the famed songwriter Harry Ruby, and invited both Doerr and Myatt to Ruby's house for dinner. "Do you bleed baseball?" Doerr recalls Cronin asking. "Do you really bleed it?" Doerr idolized Cronin and had pictures of him on his boyhood bedroom wall.[13]

The promotion of Doerr marked the start of a changing of the guard. As the old veterans began to be replaced with young players, players actually younger than their manager, Cronin's life on and off the field became much more pleasant. Cronin mentored Doerr, and it must have been satisfying to discover someone who actually wanted to be helped, someone as enthusiastic about talking baseball as he was. He worked with Doerr on how to play second base, how to turn the double play. He also convinced Doerr to hit flat-footed with a more open stance, the way Cronin himself hit. Cronin advised him how to hit Bob Feller (concede the outside of the plate and forget about looking for a particular pitch), advice Doerr used to good success. When Doerr was struggling during a game, Cronin would walk over to him at his position, and say, "Bobby, relax. Sing a song." Doerr recalled that he used this expression all the time with the younger players.[14] For his part Cronin loved Doerr as a player and a man, and it is easy to see the parallels between the two men and the lives they chose to lead.

The bad news out of training camp was the condition of Jimmie Foxx, who had became ill at the end of March with severe sinus problems and pneumonia and was eventually hospitalized for ten days. Foxx joined the club on April 30 but did not fully recover that season from his illness, during which he lost twelve pounds.[15] His training methods likely did not help his cause, and after a setback in early May it was reported, "The night dampness of the local track caused Jimmie Foxx' relapse, about which the Boy Manager is more than a little disturbed."[16] Foxx's notorious nightlife would become more of a problem as his career wound down.

Reversing the trend of the past several years, Cronin started the season on fire. He had two doubles and a single in the season opener, five hits in a 15–5 thrashing of the Athletics on April 30, and had an average of over .400 in late May. On May 17 before a game in Washington, Cronin was struck in the face by a Mike Higgins throw. His face was badly cut, and he left in an ambulance for Georgetown Hospital, accompanied by Clark Griffith.[17] Fortunately, there was no fracture, and he missed just a few days of action. In his first game back he had three hits.

He was also fielding much better—he made fewer plays than he had in his Washington years, but he was no longer making errors on easy chances. The complaining from his pitchers had stopped, and the critical press from the previous year had softened. "Manager Joe Cronin handled seven chances in masterly fashion," reported the *Washington Post* in late May.[18] Shirley Povich, a harsh critic of Cronin's play in 1936, now gushed: "Somehow, somewhere the fellow has untracked himself," wrote Povich, "and, two years after he was supposed to add a devastating batting punch and brilliant defensive play to the wobbly Red Sox, he is actually doing it."[19]

Though Cronin was back to starring at shortstop, the situation on the other side of the infield was problematic. Perhaps slowed by his beaning by Washington's Ed Linke in late April, Doerr had to be benched a month into the season for poor hitting. The nineteen-year-old appeared to be over his head in his initial trial and finished the season at .224 in 147 at bats. Eric McNair took over at second for most of 1937 and had a fine season.

In the early part of the year, a few hot starts (Cronin, Rick Ferrell, Grove) were negated by a few slow ones (Doerr, Wes Ferrell, Foxx), and the club was just 19-19 on June 10. The next day Collins pulled off a big deal with the Senators, trading the Ferrell brothers and Mel Almada for outfielder Ben Chapman and pitcher Bobo Newsom. Talentwise, this proved to be a fine deal. Wes Ferrell had a sore arm and would never again be the pitcher he had been, though the loss of his brother Rick—one of the game's best catchers—was a big blow. Though the same age as Wes Ferrell (twenty-nine), Newsom had many more productive seasons in his right arm. Chapman was the best hitting outfielder the team had enjoyed since Cronin arrived.

Unfortunately, both Newsom and Chapman had their own personality issues, especially Newsom. "By swapping those pitchers," one writer mused, "Joe Cronin and Bucky Harris traded a case of poison ivy for the barber's itch."[20] Newsom won thirteen games the remainder of the year, while Chapman hit .307 with extra-base power.

The Red Sox began to win right after the trade, and when Grove and Newsom led a sweep of the Athletics in a July 4 doubleheader they were 35-26 and just five and a half games out. After dropping two in New York the next day, the Red Sox hung within range of the Yankees through early August. On August 11 they were 57-38, nine games behind the Yankees when New York headed to Boston for two doubleheaders. In the first the Red Sox were swept in front of nearly forty thousand pennant-starved fans, dropping eleven games out and effectively finishing the season. The team struggled down the stretch, ending at 80-72 and in fifth place. Nonetheless, this was the best Red Sox record since 1918.

One of the highlights of Cronin's comeback season was his selection to the 1937 All-Star Game after a year off. Playing in front of his old fans at Washington's Griffith Stadium, he played all nine innings (there were no other shortstops on the roster) and managed a double in four at bats in the AL's 8–3 victory. For the season, Cronin hit .307 in 148 games, with 40 doubles, a career-high 18 home runs, and 110 runs batted in.

The Red Sox offense improved by 46 runs in 1937, largely due to Cronin's recovery. Mike Higgins hit .302 and drove in 106 runs in his first year with the club, and Ben Chapman hit .307 after his June acquisition. Foxx had his worst year of the 1930s but still hit .285 with 36 home runs. On the mound, thirty-seven-year-old Grove finished 17-9 with a 3.02 ERA. Johnny Marcum and Newsom won thirteen games apiece, while jack-of-all-trades Jack Wilson finished 16-10 with seven saves.

In August the *New York Journal-American* ran a blockbuster story claiming that Cronin was in line to take over for Clark Griffith as Washington team president and that "it would surprise no one in the baseball world if the Senators bought off Cronin's contract (which has two more years to run) and he showed up at Washington next year." According to the story, Cronin was becoming frustrated by the "dominance of the front office," meaning Eddie Collins. Clark Griffith, according to the newspaper, stated, "Joe has nothing to worry about. No matter what happens in Boston, he will wind up with me. Joe is a fine boy, a great executive and one of the family. He will someday succeed me as president of the Senators."[21]

All the parties involved denied their part of the story. Griffith called it "pure, unadulterated bunk," pointing out that Cronin was happy and doing a fine job where he was. Yawkey also protested, saying "it's all somebody's pipe-dream" and that he was more than satisfied with

Cronin as his manager. Collins was the most upset. "It's my business to round up the talent and run the business end of the club," said Eddie, "and that's a bigger job than managing the team. I've been maligned plenty and I want to tell you it's no fun." Eddie continued, "Joe is having a great year as a player and as a manager."[22]

Shirley Povich, who knew both Griffith and Cronin well, believed that most of the story was fabricated but that Cronin would one day succeed Griffith—it was just a matter of when.[23] Griffith was sixty-seven and in good health, and Cronin had two years to go on his contract. The two men had been close before Cronin married Griffith's niece, and they remained close. Though such rumors persisted off and on for many years, Griffith remained in charge of the Senators until his death in 1955.

The Cronins spent the fall of 1937 in Washington, and Joe golfed with Griffith nearly every day, surely talking baseball. He scored a 79 and 99 on consecutive days at the Congressional, vowing after the latter score never to play again. As a change of pace, he and Bucky Harris participated in a game of duckpin bowling for charity that winter—Harris won the match 115–98. Mildred had recovered from her tragic childbirth of the previous spring but was pregnant again and taking it much easier this time around.

Clark Griffith had organized an informal men's group called the Seventh and Florida Avenue Pleasure Club, or SFAPC. The members included Cronin, Calvin Griffith (Mildred's brother), Bucky Harris, radio announcer Arch McDonald, trainer Mike Martin, and several others. They held meetings every Wednesday afternoon at the offices at Griffith Stadium to just talk, plan golf outings, and challenge other clubs to bowling matches.[24] It is telling that Cronin, now just thirty-one years old, had already developed the hobbies and habits of a much older man. The stereotype of the 1930s ballplayer—hunting, fishing, drinking, and chasing women—never fit Cronin. His closest friends were his wife and her sixty-eight-year-old uncle.

When the Red Sox triumvirate arrived at baseball's winter meetings in Milwaukee in December, their principal need was an outfielder who could hit. In Cronin's three years in Boston, no Red Sox outfielder had hit more than 7 home runs or driven in more than 66 runs in any season. Accordingly, on December 2 the club dealt Bobo Newsom, incumbent left fielder Buster Mills, and infielder Red Kress to the Browns for outfielder Joe Vosmik. One of the benefits of the deal was getting rid of Newsom. "Big Buck has an incurable habit of putting the manager on the spot with his blatant outbursts," wrote Shirley Povich.[25] Newsom did not leave quietly, saying, "There's two managers on the Red Sox, Cronin and Collins, and I am glad to be away from both of them."[26]

The Red Sox had spent two off-seasons trying to land Vosmik. He was not a home-run hitter, but his 47 doubles and 9 triples had helped drive in 93 runs in 1937. With Doc Cramer and Ben Chapman, observers believed the club had its best outfield since their legendary group from the 1910s—Duffy Lewis, Tris Speaker, and Harry Hooper.[27]

The big story in Sarasota in 1938, briefly, was the arrival and presence of Ted Williams, the outfielder Collins had purchased from San Diego. Williams was now nineteen and had hit .291 with 23 home runs in 1937 for the Padres. He had taken a train from San Diego, meeting up with Bobby Doerr in El Paso en route. Doerr was just four months older, but the difference seemed more like ten years. Possessing neither tact nor grace, Williams managed to alienate most of his veteran teammates. Rookies were supposed to shut up, wait their turn, and smile when the older players abused them. Williams talked incessantly, cut in front of the batting practice line, and gave the veterans as much abuse as they gave him. He called everyone "Sport," even Cronin.[28]

He also knew he could out-hit all of them, except perhaps Foxx. Despite this within a few weeks Williams was sent to train with the Minneapolis Millers, the Red Sox's top farm club. He drove every one batty there too, including manager Donie Bush, his teammates, and the local writers. He also won the league's Triple Crown, hitting .366 with 43 home runs, and 142 runs batted in. Had he stayed with the Red Sox he likely would have been one of the top handful of hitters in the Major Leagues. Cronin sent him out hoping he would grow up. Williams would be back.

Another youngster that created a more positive stir was twenty-one-year-old pitcher Jim Bagby Jr., whose father had pitched nine seasons in the big leagues and won thirty-one games for the 1920 Indians. The son had spent three years in the Red Sox's fledgling farm system, winning twenty-one games for Hazleton in 1937. He was the Red Sox's best pitcher in Sarasota in 1938 and was one of the youngsters who helped create the impression of more hustle and spirit in the camp.[29] Bagby started opening day and beat the Yankees in his debut.

With Bobby Doerr slated to take over second base duties in 1938, Eric McNair did not sign his contract right away, hoping to force a trade. One can understand McNair's frustration: he had lost his short-stop job a year earlier largely because of a personal tragedy, moved to a new position and played it well, hit a career-high .292, and was still just twenty-nine years old. Nonetheless, Doerr was a great two-way prospect, and the club felt he had to play. The Red Sox tried to deal McNair in a package to land Cleveland pitcher Mel Harder but failed. McNair went to the bench.[30]

Cronin had his best training camp in years. The team appeared to be on the right track, and Cronin was coming off a fine year and not concerned about deserving his job. Most of the veteran trouble-makers were gone, and the insubordination had lessened. Of course, it hadn't disappeared entirely. When Cronin turned to position left fielder Chapman in a spring game, the outfielder yelled back, "You do the shortstopping, Cronin, and I'll attend to the outfielding."[31] It became a common joke that Cronin had to play Chapman because he was afraid of the damage to team morale if he was left on the bench with the other players.[32]

An eight-year veteran from Alabama, the fiery Chapman was one of the most hard-nosed players of the 1930s. A four-time All-Star, he had played six years with the Yankees but lost his center-field job with the emergence of Joe DiMaggio in 1936. An aggressive and physical base runner, he had led the league in stolen bases four times, and scored 90 or more runs nine times in the 1930s. In 1933 he had been a principal in one of the era's biggest fights, against Cronin's Senators, tangling first with Buddy Myer and then with Earl Whitehill in a brawl that eventually involved both teams, several spectators, and policemen.

On May 5, 1938, Chapman got into it again, this time with Tiger catcher Birdie Tebbetts. When Chapman questioned a couple of strike calls by home-plate umpire Joe Rue, Tebbetts began taunting the outfielder, and soon they were throwing punches at each other and rolling around in the dirt. Each combatant was fined $25 and suspended for three games. Reportedly, it was the first on-field fight at Fenway Park since 1920 (when umpire George Hildebrand struck Bob Shawkey with his mask when the pitcher rushed him).[33]

The day after the fight, Cronin left the team to join Mildred in Washington. The next day she delivered a baby boy, Thomas Griffith Cronin, who carried the names of Cronin's last two baseball bosses. After missing just two games (both victories), Cronin got back into action on May 9 and helped run his team's streak to eight wins in a row. Through May 29 Cronin was batting .355, among the league leaders, with more than half his hits for extra bases.

In 1938 the Red Sox and Yankees were not "rivals" in the way that they would become later. Only once had both clubs finished in the top two spots in the standings: in 1904 the Red Sox edged the Yankees on the last weekend of the season. Many people date the creation of the rivalry—or at least an important stage in its creation—to the events of May 30, 1938.

The Red Sox were visiting Yankee Stadium for three games: a Memorial Day doubleheader followed by a single game on the thirty-first. Cleveland was in first place, with Boston two and a half back and New York three and a half behind. For the Monday twin bill, 83,533 people showed up, including an official 81,841 paid admissions, an all-time regular season record crowd at the time. The first game pitted Lefty Grove, who was already 8-0 on the season, against 6-1 Red Ruffing.

It was no contest. The Yankees battered the great Grove for a run in the second, two more in the third, and chased him with a bases-loaded single by Gehrig in the fourth. With the score 5–0, Archie

McKain entered for Boston, and his first two pitches were stroked for singles by Bill Dickey and Myril Hoag. His third pitch was a fastball toward Jake Powell's head, causing the outfielder to dive into the dirt to avoid a beaning. The next pitch hit Powell in the stomach. Powell picked himself up and, according to Gerry Moore in the *Boston Globe*, "the onetime Senator stormy petrel headed straight for McKain." According to John Drebinger in the *Times*, "McKain seemed more than willing to meet him halfway."[34]

Not long after the players met, Cronin appeared on the scene. "In fact," wrote Drebinger, "he opened fire on Jake, and, with the latter retaliating, there was a spirited struggle until umpires and players pulled the combatants apart." Once order had been restored both Powell and Cronin were banished. Powell left the field first, but Cronin had to first huddle with coach Herb Pennock, who would take over running the team. Strategies settled upon, Cronin headed for the clubhouse.

To get to the Boston dressing room, Cronin had to go through the Yankee dugout and down a walkway under the grandstand. When he got into the tunnel, Powell was waiting for him. So were several of Powell's teammates. Cal Hubbard was umpiring at first base, and as he later told the story, he looked over and noticed that there were no Yankees in the dugout. "I do believe," thought Hubbard, "that young Irish lad may be in need of assistance." By the time the umpire could get to the fracas, Cronin had several scratches on his face and bruises on each arm. "That's where the other boys got me off Powell," said Cronin of his bruises. "They did more damage than Powell and I did together."[35] Cronin played the next day.

If Cronin had not earned the respect of his players before, he earned it that day. "The guy would be there in a minute if anything was wrong," recalled Charlie Wagner years later. "The minute you saw Powell charge our player, you knew he'd be there." Bobby Doerr remembered it the same way. "He was a pretty aggressive type," said Doerr. "He would do anything to protect his players. We should have made sure we had some of our players go down the runway with him."[36]

In the aftermath of the fight, Powell was fined and suspended for three days. Cronin was not punished, which did not draw a protest from the Yankees or anyone else. "The Memorial Day fight between Joe Cronin and Jake Powell," wrote Arch Ward, "was looked upon as a poor match, because few want Powell to even get a draw every time he goes."[37] Reportedly, the Yankee players were getting tired of bailing out Powell every time he picked a fight.[38] (Several weeks later Powell got into worse trouble when he used some racially offensive language on a pregame radio show and drew a ten-game suspension.)

Although the fight might have helped stoke the rivalry between the clubs and have enhanced Joe Cronin's image with his teammates and fans, it had no immediate effect on the fortunes of the team. The club dropped both games of the doubleheader and another the next day. The Red Sox played fairly consistent baseball all season, remaining within five and a half games of the lead through the end of July. New York, however, went 20-5 in July and 28-8 in August to put the race away. The second-place Red Sox ended up at 88-61, by far their best season since 1918, nine and a half games behind the powerhouse Yankees. Other than the brief hiccup in 1936, the Red Sox had improved every year of the Yawkey regime.

"The Red Sox are a crowd of normal happy young men," crowed Ed McAuley in the *Cleveland News*, "as high spirited as any in the league. Jimmie Foxx looks five years younger, Lefty Grove jokes with photographers, and Cronin himself has lost the tension of years past. Cronin is entitled to special commendation, for if ever a boy was sent on a man's errand, Cronin undertook such a mission when he was given charge of the stars that came bouncing out of Yawkey's bank book."[39]

For Cronin the player, the season was even more satisfying. Unlike past years which had been marked by hot and cold streaks, Cronin hit well the entire season. His batting average for the season's six months: .342, .333, .316, .275, .357, and .318. On the season Cronin hit .325 with 17 home runs and 94 runs batted in. He led the league with 51 doubles and established a career high with 91 walks. He played 142 games at shortstop and fielded his position admirably and without incident all season. In July he was selected to start his sixth All-Star

Game, at Cincinnati's Crosley Field. Cronin played all nine innings, collected 2 hits, and drove in the lone AL run with his double in the ninth.

Cronin had plenty of help on the offensive side as the club scored a team-record 902 runs. Jimmie Foxx won his third Most Valuable Player award after clubbing 50 home runs, driving in 175 runs (still the fourth highest total of all time), and winning the batting title with a .349 mark. Joe Vosmik led the league with 201 hits and batted .324. Cramer had 198 hits, Mike Higgins drove in 106 runs, and Ben Chapman hit .340 with 40 doubles. Doerr hit .289 in his first year as a regular. There wasn't an easy out in the lineup.

The pitching was equally good, as the Red Sox allowed just 751 runs, the second lowest total in the league despite playing half their games in hitter-friendly Fenway Park. Jack Wilson (15-15), Jim Bagby (15-11), and Fritz Ostermueller (13-5) all posted decent ERAs. Lefty Grove pitched as well as ever for the first half of the season. On July 14 he beat the Tigers 12–1 to bring his record to 14-3 with the season not yet half over. Unfortunately he had to leave that game early because he suddenly could not feel his fingers. He tried pitching briefly a few times in August but finished just 14-4 while pitching enough innings to win his eighth ERA title. But the old Lefty finally appeared to be all done.[40]

Joe Cronin enjoyed some additional personal honors in 1938. Late in the summer the Kellogg Company conducted a nationwide All-American Baseball Poll, with fans sending in selections for each position. Kellogg gave a new Buick automobile to the leading vote getters at each position: Lou Gehrig (1B), Charlie Gehringer (2B), Mel Ott (3B), Cronin (SS), Joe Medwick (LF), Joe DiMaggio (CF), Pete Fox (RF), Bill Dickey (C), and pitchers Red Ruffing, Carl Hubbell, Johnny Vander Meer, Lefty Grove, and Tommy Bridges.

On September 7 the Red Sox held a Joe Cronin Day at the Fenway Park and presented the manager with a $1,000 set of silverware, and an Irish terrier, symbolic of Cronin's heritage and his temperament. Jimmie Foxx hit two homers and drove in eight runs in the 11–4 win.

After the season Cronin was voted as the shortstop on *The Sporting News* yearly All-Star team, his sixth selection but first since 1934.

Shirley Povich, a keen observer of Cronin's ups and downs over the previous decade, was effusive in 1938. "He has been the power on the Red Sox offense all season," wrote Povich, "and again has taken rank as the best fielding shortstop in the league. And another thing. When all the votes are counted, Joe Cronin may be the fellow convicted of doing the best managerial job in the American League this season."[41]

Before leaving Boston at the end of the year, Cronin hosted a banquet for the writers, as a show of appreciation for their support.[42] "Considering the added pressure," wrote Joe Williams, "we thought Cronin qualified as the most valuable man in the league [in 1938]. Evidently managing the club does not affect Cronin's play, and you have [Joe] McCarthy's testimony that as a field general he is getting better all the time."[43]

The months following the 1938 season were the first for the Cronins as parents. The family stuck pretty close to Washington in the fall, spending even more time with the Robertsons and Griffiths now that they had a baby boy to be doted on. The *Post* referred to young Thomas in a photo caption as "the favorite grandson of Clark Griffith," employing the common assumption that Griffith was Mildred's father.[44]

Cronin and Griffith continued to be constant companions and to play golf daily, usually at India Springs Golf Course. They often played with Marion Brown and Helen Dettweiler, the two most recent winners of the District Women's Golf Championship. In early November the two men prevailed in an arranged match, Cronin scoring a 79 to lead the charge, and staked their claim as the "Women's Champions." The same four players had a rematch a week later using match-play scoring at a different course, and this time the men were routed 13 and 11.[45]

At the winter meetings in December, held at New York's Waldorf-Astoria Hotel, the Red Sox were looking for pitchers. While they had a very good lineup and a few hitting prospects on the way, the team was not counting on Lefty Grove returning to form in 1939. Though Collins remained the general manager, Cronin was playing a larger role in making trades and had developed a reputation as a difficult trading partner. "I taught him too much about making deals when he was manager of the Washington club," complained Clark Griffith.[46]

The Red Sox made two important moves during the meetings. First they dealt Ben Chapman, coming off his .340 season, to the Browns for pitcher Denny Galehouse and shortstop Tommy Irwin. The same day, third baseman Mike Higgins was shipped to the Tigers for pitcher Elden Auker in a five-player swap. Thus the Red Sox acquired two starting pitchers while opening up two holes in their everyday lineup. "We will be gambling at third base and right field next year," said Cronin, "but the extra pitching we have acquired possibly will offset the gamble we are taking."[47] A few years earlier the Red Sox would have looked around for a couple of veteran hitters to buy. Not now. They had solutions in the organization they were ready to show off.

The Red Sox farm system, which had recently produced a starting second baseman (Bobby Doerr) and a fifteen-game winner (Jim Bagby) was ready to pop out a few players from Minneapolis. Twenty-two-year-old Jim Tabor, a third baseman from Alabama, had hit .330 for the Millers, and now had a clear path to an everyday job. Center fielder Stan Spence hit .322 with 19 home runs and was likely capable of taking Chapman's place in right field. Ted Williams had won the American Association Triple Crown and appeared ready for the Majors.

Cronin did not return to San Francisco for the holidays in 1938. In early December Cronin joined Herb Pennock and others for a week of hunting at Yawkey's thirty-two-thousand-acre nature preserve in coastal South Carolina.[48] In late January he headed to Hot Springs, Arkansas, to join a few of his players for additional training before camp opened in Sarasota. For many years Hot Springs was an early spring destination for ballplayers looking to take off their winter fat by climbing nearby hills and soaking their aching muscles in the famous springs. Among the Red Sox contingent were Foxx, Galehouse, Grove, and Jack Wilson. Cronin spent three weeks there, arriving in Sarasota in late February.

Of all the personnel moves made by Joe Cronin and the Red Sox during their long association, few have been more criticized then their handling of Pee Wee Reese in 1939. Men who run baseball teams make hundreds or thousands of decisions to acquire or discard ballplayers, and invariably many of them will not work out as hoped. The story of Reese has stayed alive because the Red Sox manager also played shortstop and played the same position as the team's hot prospect.

Harold "Pee Wee" Reese was born and raised in Louisville, Kentucky, playing sandlot baseball and shooting marbles (which is how he acquired his nickname). In 1938 the nineteen-year-old shortstop signed with the Louisville Colonels, an unaffiliated Double-A club in the American Association, and hit .277 while playing great defense. He was one of the brighter prospects in the Minor Leagues.

The Louisville club had been having money problems for many years and was up for sale. Donie Bush, who managed the Minneapolis club for the Red Sox in 1938, wanted to buy the team but needed financial backing. He called Eddie Collins, who got Tom Yawkey to agree to join a partnership with Bush as part of the ongoing strengthening of their farm system.[49] Yawkey bought a one-third interest in the Louisville team (Bush and Frank E. McKinney, an Indianapolis banker, each also owned a third). Boston transferred their American Association affiliation from Minneapolis to Louisville for the 1939 season. The price was not revealed, but it was reported to be less than $200,000 for the team, the players, and the ballpark.

Most of the Louisville players from 1938 were ultimately not retained, but eight made the 1939 club, including three future Major Leaguers: Yank Terry, Wes Flowers, and Reese. It was often written later that the Red Sox bought the franchise in order to acquire Reese, but it is unlikely that this was completely true. Reese's name was not mentioned in either of the stories in *The Sporting News* about the sale. The Red Sox were looking to invest in a team, and Louisville was available at a very low price. The Associated Press account reported Collins's opinion that Reese was one of the bigger assets on the team.[50] Mel Webb, in a *Boston Globe* story written the next spring, might have been the first to suggest that Reese was the primary reason for the purchase.[51]

In 1939 Major League Baseball fans and the press did not have anything like the knowledge of the players in the Minor Leagues that they would have in the twenty-first century. When the Red Sox traded Sam Chapman in December 1938, Shirley Povich wrote that Chapman's replacement would be either Fabian Gaffke or Les Non-nenkamp, not even mentioning Ted Williams, a once-in-a-generation prospect.[52] The transfer of the Red Sox affiliation to Louisville took place this same winter, and it is unlikely that many fans or writers around the team had ever heard of Pee Wee Reese.

In spring training that year, Reese trained with the Colonels in Arcadia, about fifty miles east of the Red Sox camp in Sarasota. Louisville played the Red Sox three times in Florida that spring. On March 20 in Sarasota, Reese got a double in five at bats and recorded six errorless chances in a 10–7 Boston victory.[53] A week later, the Red Sox thrashed the Colonels 24–2 in Arcadia, with Reese making two errors and failing to get a hit. The Boston papers focused mainly on the Red Sox hitting attack, saying only that the Colonels' pitchers were overmatched. Both Yawkey and Billy Evans attended this ballgame, partly because Bush had been begging the Red Sox for more reinforcements for his Louisville club. This game likely helped make his case.[54]

By the time the clubs met back in Sarasota three days later, the Red Sox had optioned several players to the Colonels, including Stan Spence, Charlie Wagner, and Paul Campbell. This time Louisville won 5–4, Reese getting a single in four trips and turning two double plays.[55] The *Boston Post* referred to Reese as a "brilliant fielding short-stop," and "the logical successor to Joe Cronin." On the other hand, *The Sporting News*'s extensive coverage of the Red Sox that spring, including talk of rookies Ted Williams, Jim Tabor, and Woody Rich, did not once mention Reese's connection to the Red Sox club.

Reese played the entire season with Louisville again in 1939, hitting .279 with 18 triples and by all accounts playing excellent defense. But his future changed dramatically on July 18, when the Louisville club traded his contract to the Brooklyn Dodgers for four players to be named later and cash, believed to be $35,000.[56]

A story grew out of this transaction that laid the blame, at least indirectly, on Joe Cronin. Cronin was the Red Sox shortstop, and Reese represented a threat to his job. According to an unpublished interview Billy Evans later gave to the writer Harold Kaese, Cronin had over-reacted to Reese's poor performance in the 24–2 game, thought the player too small and insisted that the Red Sox get rid of him. Yawkey backed his manager, and a deal was eventually made.[57] At the very least, Cronin's reputation has been hurt to this day by the natural perception on the part of many people that he used his position to protect his own job. Make no mistake, this was a misjudgment on the part of Cronin and the Red Sox. If Cronin thought Reese too small to play shortstop, he would be proved wrong on this count. Reese had a Hall of Fame career ahead of him.

That said, one should consider this situation from the Red Sox's point of view. Joe Cronin was the best shortstop in the Major Leagues, by universal acclamation, at the time of the Reese deal in July 1939. He had been voted as such by the Major League managers in 1938 and would be again in 1939. He was thirty-two years old. Pee Wee Reese was nowhere near the player Cronin was in 1939, and it would not have been unreasonable to think he would not be for some time. Contemporary opinion and the statistical evidence suggests that Cronin had recovered from his problems of 1935 and 1936 and was once again a good shortstop in the late 1930s. In fact, in 1939 Cronin tied a record by playing twenty-five consecutive errorless games at shortstop.[58] There is no credible evidence that Joe Cronin needed to be replaced then, or would be anytime soon.

The Reese episode highlights a fundamental problem with a team employing a player-manager. Joe Cronin was in charge of his own playing career, deciding when he needed to be benched and ultimately when it was time to give up his position. Self-confidence is a strength for a professional ballplayer but can clearly lead to problems for a person who has the dual role. In this case, it should have fallen to Cronin's superiors to step in and help evaluate Cronin the ballplayer.

Evans blamed Cronin and Yawkey, who he claimed acted against the desires of Eddie Collins and Evans himself. Yawkey later was willing to accept all of the blame, saying he believed the team did not need Reese, that Cronin was still a great shortstop, and that the deal was completely his decision.[59] Cronin would later openly own up to his misevaluation, saying simply that he believed he had another five years of fine shortstop ahead of him.

To get even further ahead of our story, when it became clear to everyone that Joe Cronin did need to step aside, when he stopped being the best shortstop in the American League, he would hand the job to rookie Johnny Pesky without incident or any need for urging from his bosses. Pee Wee Reese would turn out to be a fine player, as would Pesky, but one cannot really blame Joe Cronin for thinking himself the better player in 1939. In his first full season as a regular, two years later, Reese hit .229 with a league-leading 47 errors while Cronin had another All-Star season. Though the loss of Reese would prove to be a mistake, the extent of the mistake has been exaggerated—it would be more than a decade before the Red Sox would not have an All-Star caliber shortstop.

Once again in 1939 the Red Sox sent Ted Williams a train ticket to get from San Diego to Sarasota, but this time he chose to drive his new Buick. He got as far as New Orleans before getting knocked down by the flu and a 102-degree temperature. Williams spent three days in the hospital and was the last member of the team to make it to Sarasota. No one had quite recovered from his act at last year's camp, though one of his chief antagonists, Ben Chapman, had been traded so that Williams could have his job. Williams was still a nonstop bundle of energy, a motor mouth, and (it was thought) a newspaperman's dream.

The first controversial incident in what would be a career filled with them came on April 1 in Atlanta. When chasing a lazy pop foul down the right-field line, Williams misjudged the flight of the ball and then had trouble picking it up off the grass. When he finally got hold of it, he threw the ball over the right-field grandstand. Doc Cramer, who had a good view of the events in center field, picks up the story:

> I had to hold my hand over my mouth to keep from laughing. Then I look around and sure enough, he was coming—Cronin. Walking out from shortstop ver-r-r-y slow.
>
> So I said, "Ted, here comes Cronin. Now keep your mouth shut. Don't say anything. 'Yes' him. That's all there is to it."
>
> Cronin didn't say much. Wasn't much he could say. He just took Ted right out there and sat him on the bench. It didn't bother Ted too much, except he wanted to stay in and hit. That boy loved to hit. With good reason.[60]

After the game Cronin gave his rookie a lecture about life in the big leagues. The next day Williams was back in the lineup in the same ballpark, and hit a long home run. A pattern was born.

Ted Williams would dominate the personality and image of the Red Sox for the next two decades. Along with his extraordinary talent, part of the Williams package was an occasional outburst of immaturity or profanity, sometimes during a game on the field. Joe Cronin was often the guy who had to try to pick up the pieces. Williams always apologized, and his contrition was genuine—he knew that he should not have thrown the ball over the grandstand, he knew that this did not reflect well on himself or his team, and he genuinely wished it hadn't happened. But it did happen, and something like it was always going to happen again. Cronin was often criticized for his leniency with Williams, but as Cronin saw it, the person harmed most by Williams's frequent outbursts was Williams himself. Otherwise the youngster did what he was told, generally got along with his teammates and managers, and got to park ready to play and on-time every single day.

After six seasons as a Major League manager, in 1939 Cronin was still the youngest skipper in baseball and the only remaining player-manager in the American League. Cronin felt good about his team, especially as each new season brought more young players and fewer malcontents. "On the bench," wrote John P. Carmichael, "Cronin gives the impression of life conflicting with inertia. The body sprawls at ease, but the eyes never miss a thing and the jaws never miss a punch at the wad of gum without which Joe won't start a game."[61]

The pitching had been fortified in large part because of concerns about Lefty Grove's left arm. "Any game that Lefty can win this year will be all velvet to us," said Cronin at the start of the season. "We're not counting on him." As it happened, the fortifications disappointed, and Grove came back strong. The brilliant left-hander lost 2–0 on opening day in New York, pitched well nine days later, and continued to take the ball about once a week for the rest of the season. For the year, the thirty-nine-year-old pitched only twenty-three times, but threw seventeen complete games, and finished 15-4 with a 2.54 ERA. It was his ninth ERA championship, and the fourth in five years with Joe Cronin as his manager.

Cronin struggled to find other reliable starters. Elden Auker finished just 9-10 with a 5.36 ERA, and after the season told Tom Yawkey he could no longer play for Cronin. Auker liked the man and respected the manager, but he felt Cronin spent too much time coming to the mound giving him advice. After the season Auker was sold to the Browns, for whom he won forty-four games over the next three seasons. Jim Bagby followed up his excellent rookie season with a terrible start in 1939. With a 5-5 record and 7.09 ERA in late June, he was sent to Little Rock to finish the year. Woody Rich, a twenty-three-year-old from North Carolina, was a phenom in Sarasota and started the third game of the season. By late May he had a sore arm, and by August he was pitching for Louisville. Fritz Ostermueller, Jack Wilson, and Denny Galehouse all had their moments, but none could complement Grove as a top-flight starter. Auker led the club with twenty-five starts, while Ostermueller and Wilson each won eleven games, second on the team to the once-per-week Grove.

Williams and Tabor hit well enough to more than make up for the losses of Chapman and Higgins. Williams smacked 31 home runs in his rookie season, with a .327 batting average and a league-leading 145 runs batted in. Tabor drove in 95 runs despite being suspended in June for "breaking training." Though Williams drew all the attention, it was Tabor who caused Cronin the most headaches that season (and in the future) as he battled problems with drinking and late-night carousing. Jimmie Foxx hit .360 with 35 home runs, but missed thirty games with a sinus infection, stomach ailments, and appendicitis.

Overall the Red Sox started 1939 well, but once again the Yankees started even better. Through the end of May, Boston had a fine 21-12 record, but was already six and a half games behind the red-hot New Yorkers (29-7). At the end of June their lead was thirteen and a half games over the second-place Red Sox. Boston would have one final gasp before expiring; and it would be both memorable and historic.

As a prelude, in early July Boston swept the Athletics in Philadelphia, by scores of 17–7, 18–12, and 6–4. The first two games made up a July 4 doubleheader, in which Jim Tabor went 6 for 10 with 4 home runs and 11 runs batted in, including 2 grand slams in the second game. The Red Sox next went to New York, still down by eleven and a half, to play five games, a single contest on the seventh and then consecutive doubleheaders. Cronin had developed a bit of a complex about the Yankees, and it stayed with him for many years. "I'll tell you what is happening," said Cronin in June. "Every other club is conceding the pennant to the Yankees. They aren't pitching their best pitchers against New York. It's a battle for second place, and they're saving their best pitchers to work against the Red Sox."[62]

Taking matters into their own hands, the Red Sox stepped up and won five straight well-pitched games: 4–3, 3–1, 3–2, 4–3, and 5–3. "Joe Cronin certainly takes a lot of convincing," began the *New York Times* story after the final doubleheader. "About the only one in organized ball who wasn't convinced the Yankees were a shoo-in for the American League flag, the lantern-jawed Californian yesterday took steps that were more than adequate to demonstrate his skepticism." Cronin had won the first game of the twin bill with a two-run home run in the eighth.[63] The deficit was now just six and a half games.

Boston got it down to five and a half a few days later and were still within five and a half as late as August 10, before they finally fell back. Cronin might have had a point about the rest of the league—the Red Sox finished the season 11-8 against the Yankees, a team with a 106-45 record, while New York beat every other team at least thirteen times. Boston won eighty-nine games but finished seventeen games behind.

Cronin enjoyed another great individual season, hitting a career-high 19 home runs, driving in 107 runs (his seventh season over 100), and batting .308. He played nearly every day until turning his ankle on September 10—he twisted it on a base while running out a home run. He missed several games but hit well after his return. With the defensive problems of his early Boston years behind him, Cronin again had a higher fielding percentage and made more plays per game than the average shortstop. He was selected to play in his sixth All-Star Game, and after the season he was named by *The Sporting News* as the Major Leagues' best shortstop for the seventh time in ten years.

As a manager Cronin seemed to handle his supposed biggest challenge well: dealing with Ted Williams, his new prodigy. Late in the season Cronin told *The Sporting News*, "Williams, tough to handle? Why that's silly." But Cronin admitted to some difficulties. For one thing he had trouble giving signs to Williams because he was always talking to the catcher. Cronin removed Williams from a game in Philadelphia for not hustling and planned to sit him down for a few games, but Williams came to him and apologized and asked to stay in the lineup. Cronin admired Williams's work habits, his drive to succeed.[64] The rest of his act, to Cronin, was not detrimental to the team.

The 1939 season marked the end of Cronin's five-year contract. Two years into it there was doubt whether he would make it through his term, as both his play and his handling of the team were called into question. But after three great seasons on the field and three improved seasons for the team, it did not come as a surprise when Cronin signed a new five-year contract in October. "I'm more than satisfied with Joe Cronin's managerial record," said Yawkey in his announcement, "and I am sure the Boston baseball public agrees with me."[65]

7 Winding Down

AFTER JOE CRONIN SIGNED HIS SECOND FIVE-
year contract with the Red Sox, he and Mildred began building a new
house in the Boston suburb of Newton Center. The new contract
convinced the couple that they should settle in Boston, reducing their
off-season travel and providing stability for their family of (so far)
three. The completed house at 77 Lake Avenue, located adjacent to
Crystal Lake, would have four thousand square feet of living space on
three and one-half acres and would be the principal family residence
for the next thirty-five years.

It is worth considering here just how well compensated Joe Cronin
was during his baseball career. His years as a star player line up perfectly
with the Great Depression. Between 1931 and 1940 U.S. unemploy-
ment rates fluctuated between 14.3 and 24.9 percent, and the average
production worker, if he was fortunate enough to have a job, had a
salary of about $17 per week. The first federal national minimum wage
was established in 1938 at twenty-five cents per hour.[1]

Joe Cronin, on the other hand, was making more than thirty times
the wages of the average employed worker, drawing a $27,000 annual
salary by the time he reached the age of twenty-eight and staying at
that level for the rest of his career. He grew up in a working-class
family and certainly knew hardship from his childhood, but those
days were long behind him by the 1930s, and he would never again
be anything but a rich man.

If Cronin's salary made him stand out in the terribly difficult 1930s,
Cronin's behavior also stood out among ballplayers in his era. Cronin
could not legally enjoy an alcoholic beverage until 1933, when Prohibition was repealed, but drinking would have been a simple matter.
"They didn't have cocktail parties or beer in the clubhouse," Cronin

later recalled of Prohibition. "A lot of players were not drinking at all. Of course if a guy wanted to find it, he found it."[2] Nonetheless, Cronin was a conspicuous nondrinker until his playing career was over.

After his playing days Cronin was known to have a social beer or Scotch, but there are no funny stories of Cronin going out drinking or carousing during his career like there are about many of the players of the 1930s. He did not gamble, rarely fished or hunted, and had no particularly expensive habits. He smoked cigars most of his adult life, enough to keep his family out of his smoke-filled den.

Cronin's biggest vice was his appetite. Once a skinny young player, Cronin spent several off-seasons in the 1920s eating meat and fatty foods to try to put weight on his frame, and he became one of baseball's best-conditioned and strongest athletes by 1930. This accomplished, he spent the rest of his life fighting an ever-increasing waistline. His salary afforded him the opportunity to eat at great restaurants, and Mildred was both an accomplished cook and a lover of great food herself.[3]

It is also likely no coincidence that Cronin's weight problems began when he was first named to manage the Senators. As a player, Cronin's tireless work ethic often drew comment. He worked on his hitting, his fielding, his base running, and his conditioning during and after the season. When he became manager, he essentially had a second job, and in retrospect it seems naïve to assume that this second job would not affect his ability to perform the first. He now spent much of the off-season in league meetings or with his bosses. During the season he did not have nearly as much time to work at staying in shape.

And, just as likely, the unrelenting stress of the job, especially once he got to Boston, led Cronin to a second helping of potatoes once or twice. Many of the game's better managers turned to alcohol to get them through the dog days of the seasons, but Joe Cronin did not drink. He ate. His weight drew a bit of attention in 1934 (at the time of his sale to the Red Sox, Joe Williams wrote, "His girth has expanded eight inches in the past three years"),[4] and increasing comment during his first couple of years in Boston, especially in 1936 when he and the team failed to live up to expectations. Cronin turned it around in the late 1930s, with three straight excellent offensive and defensive seasons and few managerial difficulties. The press was very kind to Cronin as a manager and player in this period.

Cronin spent several weeks in the fall of 1939 in San Francisco with his father. While out west he played several charity baseball games in the Bay Area, including managing a group of Major Leaguers against Lefty O'Doul's Minor Leaguers in Recreation Park.[5] One of O'Doul's players was Dominic DiMaggio, who had followed his brother Joe as the centerfielder for the Seals. Unlike his slugging brother, Dominic was a slight five feet nine and 160 pounds and wore glasses. Nonetheless, the twenty-two-year-old hit .360 for the 1939 Seals and was named the Most Valuable Player in the Pacific Coast League. Cronin had his eye on DiMaggio throughout this series of games, and in early November he negotiated his purchase, along with that of pitcher Larry Powell, for $40,000 and two players to be named later. The Red Sox were startled when Dom turned down their initial contract offer, but he eventually came to terms.

The signing of DiMaggio caused a bit of a stir, if only because of his famous surname. Brother Joe had played four years with the New York Yankees and established himself as baseball's best player, having led his team to four world championships and winning the league's MVP award in 1939. Brother Vince had three years under his belt in the National League, though at a lesser level. "He can do everything Joe can do except in batting," said Cronin of Dominic. "He's the best young outfielder I have seen in a long time."[6]

The acquisition of DiMaggio put Cronin on the spot in much the same way as the situation with Reese had. In both cases Cronin was criticized for overruling the more expert members of the organization. In Reese's case Cronin apparently disagreed with the consensus of opinion in the farm system. Similarly, the Red Sox signed DiMaggio on Cronin's lone recommendation after the Red Sox scout, and scouts for several other teams including the Yankees, had thought he was not a Major League prospect. Joe Williams, citing the two separate cases, wrote, "We don't know of any other manager in baseball who would ignore the testimony of everybody else in his organization and build up his own case as Cronin did with respect to DiMaggio and Reese." Contrary to his judgment on Reese, Cronin would turn out to be right about DiMaggio.

Despite his recommendation, Cronin coyly pointed out at the time of the deal that the Red Sox outfield was full—with Vosmik, Cramer, and Williams—and that Dom would have a utility role.[7] This remained the party line until early February, when Vosmik was sold to the Dodgers for $25,000. Cronin then intended DiMaggio to play right field, with Williams shifting to left.

During the fifteen years that Babe Ruth played for the New York Yankees the club won four World Series. This was an impressive achievement, but not historically so—the Red Sox of the 1910s had won four championships in just seven years, and even during the height of the dominance of Babe Ruth and Lou Gehrig, the Philadelphia Athletics had put together a great team and bested the Bronx Bombers three years in a row (1929–31). The Yankees of the late 1930s were another matter entirely—four consecutive championships, each more impressive than the last.

Other teams, especially in the American League, were understandably frustrated. The Boston Red Sox, risen from the ashes in the seven years of Tom Yawkey's ownership, were still miles from catching the New Yorkers. With eighty-eight and eighty-nine victories in 1938 and 1939, and a 22-19 record over the Bombers in those years, the Red Sox had nonetheless finished nine and a half and seventeen games out of first. What's more, the Yankees were introducing new All-Star caliber players every year, bringing in Joe DiMaggio (1936), Tommy Henrich (1937), Spud Chandler (1937), Joe Gordon (1938), and Charlie Keller (1939) in only four seasons.

Clark Griffith, who had managed New York for several years in the first decade of the century without winning a pennant, had become determined to thwart the current juggernaut. At the league meetings in Cincinnati in 1939 he pushed for two rules that he thought would help the cause. The first would prohibit the American League pennant winner from trading during its entire reign as champion. The second would limit each team to having only one Minor League affiliate at each classification level.[8] The first proposal passed but the second failed.

The Yankees were not big traders at the time, although Griffith felt that the Yankees always drove up the bidding for other teams. At the time of the meetings, Griffith was trying to pry first baseman George McQuinn from the Browns, offering Cecil Travis and others. The Yankees, who had just lost Lou Gehrig to the illness that would soon take his life, reportedly were willing to part with Babe Dahlgren, Tommy Henrich, and Phil Rizzuto, a deal that would have helped the rest of the league immensely had it transpired.[9] The trading ban passed unanimously and was effective immediately. Any deals the Yankees might have been working on, reportedly including both McQuinn and Bobo Newsom, were kaput.

In addition, the league decided to forego the tradition of having the pennant-winning manager lead the All-Star team the next summer. Joe Cronin was named to skipper the 1940 team, and the league announced all future selections would be made by consensus of the owners. Reactions to this decision were mixed. One writer considered it "another reminder of how popular the Red Sox skipper is throughout the junior circuit."[10] On the other hand, a National League partisan joked, "Cronin knows he's not going to win the pennant anyway, see, so he can concentrate on preparing for the All-Star game."

After the meetings, Cronin joined his family in Washington, waiting for their new house to be built. Cronin's primary form of exercise, in keeping with his recent off-seasons, was daily golf, often with Clark Griffith. In early February he spoke at the Boston baseball-writer's dinner, honored for his feat of leading his team to the five-game sweep of the Yankees. Ted Williams also spoke, after receiving a plaque as Boston's most valuable player. Ted wore a tuxedo, which he joked about, wowed the crowd with his charm, and praised Cronin.[11] This was an annual event for Cronin, as was the New York dinner he attended soon after. A few days later, Joe sent Mildred and Tommy on to Sarasota while he went to Hot Springs to work on his conditioning. He arrived in Sarasota early, weighing 189 pounds, 5 pounds more than his goal.[12]

Heading into the season, the Red Sox offense looked to be as good as ever, with Foxx seemingly recovered from his appendectomy, joined by Doerr, Cronin, Tabor, Williams, and Cramer. Cronin worried about the catching—the incumbents, Gene Desautels and Johnny Peacock, were mediocre solutions—and the pitching. Their best pitcher, Grove, turned forty that spring and could be counted on for twenty starts at most. The rest of the staff—Ostermueller, Wilson, and Galehouse being the leading returnees—were established league-average hurlers.

Cronin was hoping for help from Jim Bagby, the rookie phenom of 1938 who had washed back to the Minors in 1939, and Woodrow Rich, who began the 1939 season so well before hurting his arm in late May. Both had fine springs.[13] In addition, the Red Sox had two new rookies: Herbert Hash and Bill Butland, who had won twenty-two and nineteen games respectively for Minneapolis in 1939.

The team suffered a setback early in spring training when Dom DiMaggio hurt his ankle sliding into home plate. Originally thought to be a day-to-day injury, DiMaggio ended up missing all of the spring-training games, curtailing his hopes for landing a starting spot. Lou Finney, acquired the previous year to spell the injured Jimmie Foxx at first base, took over in right field and had a sensational first half. Hitting over .350 in midseason, Finney's play kept DiMaggio on the sidelines when his ankle healed.

The Red Sox jumped out to a quick start in 1940, which, coupled with the Yankees' poor start, brought new optimism to Boston. The Red Sox led the league from May 6 through June 19, holding off Cleveland and Detroit, but a seven-game losing streak in late June knocked them out of first, and an eight-game losing streak at the end of July put them out of the race. The Red Sox finished at just 82-72, tied for fourth and eight games behind the Tigers. Boston picked a poor time to have an off year, the one year in eight that the Yankees faltered.

The Achilles heel for the 1940 Red Sox was their pitching. Grove and Bagby began the year with consecutive shutouts in Washington, but both were hit hard in their next outings. Those two pitchers led the club with just twenty-one starts each, and sixteen different pitchers started at least once. Early in the season, while the club was winning, Cronin received credit for his handling of all of his mediocre pitchers but later drew fire for not having enough patience as they began to falter.[14] Grove finished just 7-6 with a team-best 3.99 ERA. Bagby, the only pitcher who threw more than 160 innings, finished 10-16.

In early August with Desautels and Peacock struggling, Jimmie Foxx volunteered to catch, allowing the club to shift Finney to first base, move Cramer to right field, and play DiMaggio in center. Foxx played forty-two games behind the plate, which likely contributed to a severe batting slump in September.[15] He still managed to hit 36 home runs, including his five hundredth on September 24 in Philadelphia.

The Red Sox had another good offensive year, led by Foxx, Williams, Doerr, Cronin, and Tabor. Every regular infielder hit 20 or more home runs, the first time a team ever accomplished this. In particular, Bobby Doerr established himself not merely as a fine second baseman who could get an occasional hit but as a middle-of-the-order slugger, driving in 105 runs with his 37 doubles, 10 triples, and 22 homers. Dom DiMaggio hit .301 with 46 extra-base hits in only 108 games. DiMaggio, like Doerr, has fond memories of breaking into the big leagues under Cronin. "I had known Joe before getting to Boston, and there is no one I'd rather have played for," DiMaggio recalled in 2007.[16]

Cronin had another fine year with the bat himself, clubbing a career-high 24 home runs, while also scoring 104 runs and driving in 111. He hit two homers in a 14–5 win in Chicago on June 16, a game in which pitcher Jack Wilson also homered twice. On August 2 Cronin hit for the cycle for the second time in his career, the first having come in 1929 in his first full season. Better yet, he began this day with a double and triple against old nemesis Bobo Newsom, who had remained publicly critical of Cronin since his half-season with the Red Sox in 1937.[17] Cronin's defensive statistics at shortstop were again fine—he was right at the league average for both fielding percentage and plays per game. In the last game of the season, on September 29 against the Athletics, he stole home in the sixth inning. He promptly replaced himself in the lineup, ending his own season in spectacular fashion.[18]

Named over the winter the manager of the AL All-Stars, Cronin enjoyed that opportunity in July at Sportsman's Park in St. Louis. He lost in the fan's shortstop voting to Chicago's Luke Appling and did not choose himself as a reserve. Of his Red Sox, Foxx and Williams were starters, and Cronin added Finney and Cramer to the squad. Though getting to manage the game for the second time was an honor, it was not without its headaches. Bobo Newsom threatened to bolt the AL team when Cronin chose Ruffing to start the game, though Newsom ended up pitching three innings.[19] Cronin did not play Doc Cramer, something Cramer was still stewing about decades later.[20] The AL lost 4–0, getting just three hits.

Doc Cramer, it must be said, was one of the men from Cronin's early years in Boston who did not like his young manager and whose poor opinions of Cronin shaped some of the histories written long after Cronin had died.[21] According to Cramer, Cronin didn't like the former Philadelphia players, including Cramer himself. Cramer was a .300 hitting center fielder who offered very little else on offense, but who Cronin played every day and picked for the All-Star team. That same summer Cronin shifted Cramer to right field, replacing him in center field with DiMaggio, a far superior defensive player.

The club had created some news at the start of the 1940 season when they installed bullpens in right-center field, thereby reducing the distance to the fence from home plate by twenty-three feet.[22] As Ted Williams was the only left-handed power hitter on the team, he would theoretically be the chief beneficiary of the new bullpens, which were dubbed "Williamsburg." Whether he altered his swing or not, Williams's home runs dropped from 31 to 23, while the Red Sox pitchers allowed 47 more home runs than they had in 1939 (77 to 124). Nonetheless, Williams hit .344 and drove in 113 runs, another great season at the start of his career.

Williams's difficulties were mainly off the field. The moody star began the season slowly and some fans, expecting more, began booing him. He publicly sulked and blamed his slow start on batting third, ahead of Jimmie Foxx, rather than the reverse as he had the previous year. In May while all this was going on, Harold Kaese of the *Boston Transcript* wrote a highly critical column and even questioned Ted's decision not to visit his parents during the previous off-season. Williams had a very difficult family life, which he did not talk about, and Kaese's article infuriated him. Williams never forgave Kaese, and he tended to blame every writer for the sins of one. His relationship with the press would never recover.[23]

In August Williams gave a national interview in which he said he'd like to quit baseball and become a fireman, like one of his uncles, leading to a torrent of abuse and ridicule from fans and players around the league. A few weeks later he unleashed a torrent of abuse on Austen Lake of the *Record American* in which he swore his hatred for the fans, the weather, the trees, the press, and everything else about Boston.[24]

Joe Cronin had to deal with all of this, his greatest player and his biggest headache all rolled into one. Cronin would spend twenty years attending to Williams in all his complexities, but at no time was it more difficult than in 1940. He called out Williams for not hustling a few times, the first on an early-June western trip.[25] On June 30 Cronin had to deal with the repercussions of Williams cussing out fans in left field.[26] In late July in St. Louis, he lectured Williams about his fielding and suggested that getting along with the fans and media would make his life, and the team's, much easier.[27] Cronin and Eddie Collins came in for their own share of criticism for their handling of Williams then and later. Cronin lectured or bawled him out many times but never resorted to benching his best hitter. Cronin's other charges, according to at least one writer, wanted Williams to be benched or otherwise disciplined.[28] Cronin believed, in 1940 and later, that Ted was helping the team a lot more than he was hurting it. The press did not agree.

As related in his autobiography nearly thirty years later, Williams wanted more support from management than he received:

Cronin was a big good-looking Irishman who could just swoon you. He could suave those writers to death. If it were me, if I'd been the general manager, I'd have nipped it right now. I'd have called in the writers and said, "Look, this kid is going to be a hell of a player. But he's twenty years old. Give him a break. We're getting on his ass. You don't have to put every little mistake in the paper so that every son of a bitch in Boston knows about it." I couldn't, though, and I sure wasn't getting any help from the front office.

On the other hand, Williams was self-aware enough to realize that there were two sides to the story. "When he chewed me out I am sure I deserved it," he wrote in the same book, "and I'm sure if I told him I felt he should have protected me more—which is true—he would say, 'Protect *you*? For crying out loud, that's all I ever did was protect you.'"[29]

In October 1940 Tom Yawkey fired Billy Evans as farm director and replaced him with Herb Pennock, who had been Evans's assistant. Yawkey's apparent reasoning was a growing dissatisfaction with the lack of pitchers being developed and an expectation that Pennock, a former star pitcher, would be better suited to the task. Evans, in a later interview, claimed that Yawkey called him up drunk one night and fired him without warning. What's more, Yawkey had recently given Evans a raise and moved him to Louisville to run the Double-A club. Evans blamed the firing on a deteriorating relationship with Cronin that began with the handling of Pee Wee Reese in 1939.

Glenn Stout and Dick Johnson, in their history of the team, accept Evans's claims uncritically,[30] but they (or Evans) get the chronology and some of the facts wrong (they place the firing in 1941, for example). For example, Evans claimed that Cronin was angry when Evans told him that Johnny Pesky, leading the American Association in hitting, was going to take Cronin's shortstop job. Pesky was in the Piedmont League in 1940—he did not reach the American Association until the next year, after Evans was gone; furthermore Pesky missed the batting title by 45 points. Similarly, Stout and Johnson blame the

Red Sox for using Ted Williams's pursuit of a .400 batting average as a distraction to keep the firing out of the papers—again, this is a year off. Cronin does not appear to have commented on the firing in October 1940.

Stout and Johnson also point out that the Red Sox farm system was most productive during the Evans years, 1936 through 1940, and suffered thereafter. This claim is misleading. The best players to come along for the Red Sox in these years were Doerr, Williams, and DiMaggio, an impressive threesome of Californians. The first two were scouted and acquired by Eddie Collins and joined the organization almost fully formed. DiMaggio was scouted and purchased at the direction of Cronin and, like Doerr, never played a game in Evans's farm system. It stretches credibility to credit Evans for the development of any of these three players. The best players actually "developed" during Evans's tenure were Tex Hughson and Johnny Pesky, neither of whom had yet played in the Major Leagues at the time Evans was fired. Overall, the players coming through the farm system were not helping the team much.

Surely Evans is not wholly to blame for the problems in the system. The Red Sox front office apparently had some disagreements and ill-defined roles among Yawkey, Collins, Cronin, and Evans. Yawkey lost confidence in Evans perhaps because of Cronin's input, perhaps not. This turmoil seems perfectly normal among four strong men. Yawkey believed that the team was not developing pitchers and ultimately decided Evans was largely to blame for it. There is nothing in the record to suggest that Evans's performance was especially good. Talented baseball people have been fired for less.

More telling are the comments of Shirley Povich, who commented on the firing at the time, rather than decades later. "Yawkey had opened his money bags for Evans. No price for a pitcher was too dear to pay. So Evans traipsed the land and brought back to the Red Sox only the choicest no-account pitchers that ever infested a major league dugout. In fact, he came up with nothing." On the other hand, Povich admitted, "the greatest element of success in pitcher-hunting is luck."[31]

An important story for the Red Sox in this period was the continual deterioration of the pitching staff, even while they were breaking in several outstanding hitters. The club received a lot of teasing in the press when Bobo Newsom won twenty-one games for the pennant-winning Tigers, and Elden Auker won sixteen for the lowly Browns. Both men, though especially Newsom, had been critical of the way they were managed by Cronin, and people started to wonder if perhaps the manager also deserved some of the blame for the lack of development from some of the youngsters. Jim Bagby, Woody Rich, and Herb Hash had all joined the team, showing some promise, but they had not developed.[32] Accurately apportioning blame among the scouts, the Minor League development system, and the Major League staff for the Red Sox's failure to produce Major League caliber pitchers is, of course, impossible.

One of the particular criticisms Cronin received was that he did not allow his young pitchers to work out of trouble, that he had a quick hook. Lending credence to this was the fact that the club was last in the league in 1940 with just fifty-one complete games. Cronin appeared to accept the validity of the criticism when he vowed to reverse course in 1941 and let pitchers finish more games early in the season. He would take the best pitchers in Sarasota, work them in a regular rotation, and keep them in the games.[33] The previous couple of years, a rotation had been difficult to maintain because Grove was used once a week or less, and others had to work around him.

In December the Red Sox sold Fritz Ostermueller and Denny Galehouse to the Browns for $25,000, and Cronin vowed to build a new pitching staff. In a significant three-team trade with the Senators and Indians, the Red Sox dealt Doc Cramer, Gene Desautels, and Jim Bagby for catcher Frankie Pytlak, infielder Odell Hale, and pitcher Joe Dobson. Cramer had grumbled about losing his center-field post to DiMaggio, Desautels had failed to hold the catcher's position, and Bagby had bombed after his impressive debut in 1938.[34]

The key to the deal for the Red Sox was Pytlak, expected to be Boston's best catcher since Rick Ferrell. He would allow Jimmie Foxx to remain at first base and Finney to return to the outfield to replace

Cramer. Dobson would be one of many pitchers given a chance in the spring.

For the first time since he left San Francisco in 1925, Joe Cronin moved into a year-round home in 1940, in Newton Center. Joe's father Jeremiah visited the family in their new house that November, staying for several weeks. It was his first visit to the East Coast. To get ready for the season, Cronin was playing as much as thirty-six holes of golf every day (weather permitting), except now he was doing so around Boston, without Clark Griffith.[35] He also took up ice skating on the lake across from his new house, as well as handball and racquetball. It was reported in January that he still wanted to lose fifteen or twenty pounds.

Meanwhile, Tom Yawkey was instrumental in convincing Cronin to play at least one more season at shortstop. Cronin still was a great hitter, finishing sixth in the league in RBI and had played passable shortstop, though not covering the ground he once had. The club acquired Skeeter Newsome from the Phillies in the off-season—a good-field, no-hit shortstop who could relieve Cronin at the end of games.[36] Yawkey thought Cronin's buying a house in Boston a good sign. "I think he'll profit considerably from having one set place to live," said the Red Sox owner. "He can watch his diet and eat the right food. I expect he'll report next spring in much better shape than for several years."

In fact Yawkey was decidedly optimistic about his manager and shortstop. "Cronin isn't getting any younger, but I think he can do the job until our two youngsters, Pesky and [Eddie] Pellagrini are ripe." Both players were shortstops that looked to be a year away.[37] Pesky, who had hit .325 at Rocky Mount in 1940, was promoted to Louisville. "He can hit .300 in any league," claimed Heinie Manush, his 1940 manager. "And I include the American."[38]

Once again Cronin was a featured speaker at the Boston writers' annual dinner banquet. The headliner was Branch Rickey, long-time general manager of the St. Louis Cardinals and one of the more respected and erudite people in the game. Rickey spoke mostly of the world crisis, with Germany holding dominion over all of Europe and Japan aggressively eyeing East Asia. In summing up, however, he turned to baseball, saying he would "rather his children admire Joe Cronin than the career of Napoleon Bonaparte."

After his annual sojourn to Hot Springs to take in the baths, Cronin headed to Sarasota for the seventh time. The theme of his camp was his search for pitchers, and he vowed to work them hard all spring. "A pitcher is only as good as his legs. You've got to run and keep on running."[39] With much of his 1940 staff scattered to the winds, Cronin brought twenty-one pitchers to camp in 1941, vowing to sift through and find the best ones.

Mickey Harris, winner of ten games in Scranton in 1940, was one of the rookies hoping to stick. Dick Newsome, thirty-one years old, had been purchased from San Diego, having won twenty-three games there. Most interesting was Mike Ryba, a thirty-seven-year-old former coal miner from Pennsylvania, who had spent fifteen years kicking around pro ball as a pitcher and catcher, including some time with the Cardinals in the 1930s. He had been called a "one-man ball club," because he could pitch every day in any role and fill in behind the plate. He had won twenty-four games in Rochester in 1940. After Ryba's brilliant spring, Cronin believed that his club would have captured the 1940 pennant had they acquired the right hander a year earlier.[40]

Ted Williams arrived early and announced that his feud with the press was over. In a game on March 17 he chipped a bone in his ankle and played little the rest of the camp or in the early weeks of the season. Jim Tabor also arrived early but was suspended for repeated violations of training rules. The Red Sox and Reds played a few games in Havana before heading north, playing exhibitions along the way. The Red Sox were ready to go.

There was more talk than usual that spring about Cronin's job being in jeopardy, though he still had four full years to go on his contract. The talk did not come from either Yawkey or Collins, who both supported Cronin, but from members of the press who thought he could not handle pitchers. Shirley Povich, speculating in April, could only point to the booing Cronin received in the annual city series with the Braves as evidence that a change might be coming. Yawkey again forcefully denied any dissatisfaction. "Never have I considered releasing Cronin and that fact could have been confirmed simply by putting the question to me."[41]

Nineteen forty-one was one of baseball's magical seasons, the subject of countless stories and books. Joe Cronin was not central to most of these events, though he played his small part. Joe DiMaggio hit in fifty-six straight games, one of baseball's enduring achievements. The Brooklyn Dodgers broke through for their first pennant in twenty-one years, the start of a generation-long run of success. The Yankees returned to the World Series to meet the Dodgers for the first time.

The Red Sox won their first five games but the race soon looked like 1940 all over again—a slow start by the Yankees and a bunch of teams staying close to the lead. In mid-June five teams were within five and a half games of first place, but beginning on June 7 the Yankees won forty of forty-six, effectively ending any pretense of a pennant race. The Red Sox were the best of the rest, finishing the season 84-70, seventeen games behind the New Yorkers. It was, to be sure, one of the more memorable second-place seasons in history.

Cronin was the early star of the season, hitting a home run in his first at bat of the season, and three in the first four games. On May 17 he was leading the league in hitting at .405, besting Washington's Cecil Travis, his old protégé hitting .398. After the hot start Tom Yawkey again took the opportunity to beat the drum for his manager. "There have been some things written about Joe in the past month," began the owner, "that are so far from the truth and so lacking in justice to one of the greatest fellows that ever wore a baseball uniform that they have got me to the point where I would like to start swinging on some of the wielders of the poison pen." Cronin was playing as well as he ever had, and was "doing everything as a player and manager that any owner could ask for."[42]

Criticizing Boston's press coverage in this era was useless—there were several papers in the city and many more in the suburbs, each trying to outdo the other in outrage and sensationalism, and there was never any consensus of opinion on anything or anyone. There were writers who thought Williams never did anything wrong, just as surely as there were those who thought he never did anything right. Cronin was a much more genial fellow and much more willing to charm the media when he thought it necessary. Nonetheless, there were always critics.

By the end of May Cronin was still hitting .372, though no longer leading the league. The new leader was Ted Williams, who had missed most of the first two weeks of the season with the ankle injury, but he had brought his average to .429. Once the Yankees started winning every day, all eyes in Boston shifted to Williams and stayed there.

Cronin had to be pleased with his 1941 pitching staff, as several of the newcomers helped. Dick Newsome won nineteen games in his delayed rookie year. Charlie Wagner, who had failed several earlier trials with the club, made good this time—12-8 with a fine 3.07 ERA. Mickey Harris, another rookie, was only 8-14, but his 3.25 ERA testified to his solid pitching. Joe Dobson won twelve games. Mike Ryba was the primary reliever, finishing 7-3 in forty games. All these hurlers were new to the club, and other than Dobson all were getting their first regular big league work. Lefty Grove won just seven times in his twenty-one starts, the final victory coming in Philadelphia on July 27, the three hundredth of his career.

Behind a fairly balanced offense, the club led the league in scoring for the first time in its history. Their weakest offensive position was catcher, but the combination of Frankie Pytlak (.271) and Johnny Peacock (.284) was an upgrade over recent seasons. Foxx, Tabor, and Williams drove in 100 runs, while DiMaggio scored 117 and played a stellar center field.

Cronin's .337 average at the All-Star break made him an easy selection to make his seventh All-Star start in the nine-year history of the affair. Williams (hitting .405) and Doerr also got starting nods, while Foxx and DiMaggio were selected as reserves for the game, one of history's most memorable. In what had begun as a dull, low-scoring affair at Tiger Stadium, Pittsburgh's Arky Vaughan hit two-run home runs in the seventh and eighth innings to give the Nationals a 5–2 lead.

After scoring a run in the eighth, the American trailed by 2 heading to the last of the ninth. The AL then rallied for 4 runs, capped by Ted Williams's game-ending three-run homer off Claude Passeau. Williams long remembered this as one of the greatest thrills of his baseball career.

When Williams hit his homer, Mildred was in the hospital to give birth to her second child. In fact, the excitement of Ted's home run caused Mildred to leap out of bed in a manner that disturbed her nurses. Despite this transgression, Mrs. Cronin successfully delivered Michael the following day, and both returned home in fine shape, ready to cheer on the Red Sox in the second half of the season.[43]

When Joe DiMaggio's hitting streak was stopped at fifty-six games on July 17, Ted Williams was batting .395. DiMaggio had received most of the attention for the previous several weeks, but now the focus shifted to Boston. Williams was hurt, and used only as a pinch hitter in the thirteen games between July 12 and July 20. Ted got back to .400 with a 2-for-3 day on July 25 and stayed over that magic number for eight weeks heading into the last weekend of the season in Philadelphia.

It had been eleven years since anyone had hit .400 (Bill Terry in 1930) and eighteen years since it had happened in the American League (Harry Heilmann). While it had been a fairly common occurrence in the 1920s, Williams attracted the attention of all of baseball late in the season. According to his roommate Charlie Wagner, Williams was obsessed with hitting .400.[44]

The final three games in Philadelphia consisted of a single contest on Saturday and a doubleheader on Sunday. All three Philadelphia starters had made their Major League debuts early that month and were unknown to Williams. This fact worried his manager. "Part of Ted's great success as a hitter was the way he studied pitchers," reasoned Cronin. "With new kids he never had faced or seen before he lost that edge."[45]

Sure enough, a 1-for-4 effort on Saturday against Roger Wolff dropped his average from .402 to .39955. Baseball tradition has always rounded batting averages to three digits, which would give Ted a .400

average if he chose not to play on Sunday. But it is hard to imagine that numerically obsessed baseball fans, especially in the decades ahead, would not have questioned an average that was obviously below a true .400. Nonetheless when Cronin saw Williams in the hotel late on Saturday night, he offered his slugger an out. "It was during this discussion that I asked him, 'How do you want to handle it?'" recalled Cronin. "He said, 'I want to play it out. I want to play it all the way.' As far as I was concerned that was it."[46]

Assuming Ted had his usual six at bats in the two games, he would need three hits to reach the milestone. In any event, Ted took the drama out of the pursuit fairly quickly. In the first game: single to right, home run to right, single up the middle, single to right, reached on an error. With nothing to play for, he took part in the second game anyway: single to right, double off a loudspeaker on top of the right-field wall, pop up. He finished the day 6 for 8 for a final average of .406, the highest since Rogers Hornsby batted .424 in 1924. "I never came closer to bawling right out loud on a baseball diamond than when Ted got that [first] hit," said Cronin. "I really filled right up. I was so happy that the Kid had done the trick without asking or getting any favors."[47]

Joe Cronin's .311 batting average and 62 extra-base hits helped him to a .508 slugging percentage, one of the highest totals of his career. On defense, however, he had slowed down sufficiently that Cronin replaced himself with Skeeter Newsome at the end of games. When Jim Tabor was hurt in August, Cronin shifted to third base for twenty-two games. Nonetheless, it was a surprise to most when on October 12 Cronin announced that he would not play shortstop in 1942 and that the position would be taken by either Johnny Pesky or Eddie Pellagrini. Pesky had hit .325 for Louisville and won the league's MVP award. Pellagrini had played for San Diego and batted .273.

In light of Cronin's supposed reluctance to keep Reese in the organization in 1939, his sudden decision to step aside two and a half years later is interesting. During that interval Cronin had had three great offensive seasons while gradually fading as a defensive player. Cronin's defense always received more criticism than it deserved—his large size gave him less range but a stronger arm than most smaller shortstops, and his fielding statistics were generally quite good. But by 1941 he had clearly slipped. Reese, meanwhile, had hit .227 in his first full season with the Dodgers. Replacing Cronin with Reese in 1940 or 1941 would have hurt the Red Sox, not helped them. In the voting for *The Sporting News'* Major League All-Star team, Cronin finished third among all shortstops, behind only Cecil Travis and Phil Rizzuto.[48]

Joe Williams commented on the matter in the *New York World-Telegram* after Cronin's announcement. "The story has been written that Cronin was envious of Reese. That's like saying Hemingway is jealous of us," wrote Williams. "And if we may put in our own two cents worth, we think it will turn out that he's right. Reese will always be pretty fair, but he's not going to make the customers forget about Hans Wagner—or even Joe Cronin."[49] Of course, Reese would turn out to be a good deal better than fair. On the other hand, during the next three years of Reese's career the Red Sox shortstop (Johnny Pesky) would average .330 and stroke 200 hits every season. In the three seasons after that, his replacement, Vern Stephens, would average over 145 runs batted in. The Red Sox would not have a "shortstop problem" until Pee Wee Reese was in his thirties.

When Cronin told the press he was stepping aside, he did not specify what he would do next. Most writers assumed that he would play third base, though the incumbent, Jim Tabor, was twenty-five years old and had driven in 101 runs in the season just past. Soon after his announcement, Cronin also suggested that Jimmie Foxx would be replaced, giving way to Tony Lupien, a Harvard graduate and Pesky's teammate at Louisville. "Pesky is our shortstop as long as he can hold the job and Lupien is our first baseman," Cronin explained. "If they fail to make good, Jimmy and I will take over our old positions."[50]

Tom Yawkey tried to persuade Cronin to stay on the field, perhaps at a different position. But Cronin believed then and later that he would be a much better manager if he did not have to play, that he could help the team more by directing from the bench. Yankee president and longtime baseball executive Ed Barrow had remarked that Cronin had already become one of the best managers in the game, but Cronin believed that playing hindered his ability to lead.[51]

In the meantime, the Red Sox asked waivers on Foxx in early December, looking for a trading partner for the once-great slugger.[52] Around the same time Lefty Grove, after some cajoling from Yawkey, announced his retirement from the game.[53] With the passing of Cronin, Foxx, and Grove—three of the greatest ever at their positions—the club was clearly entering a new era. Williams, Doerr, and DiMaggio were the new stars and would surely win the pennants that the old stars had not.

Cronin and his family spent about a month in San Francisco after the season, then returned east for winter meetings—first the Minor League confab in Jacksonville and then the Major League meeting in Chicago. When Cronin got to Jacksonville it was noted that he had again put on quite a bit of weight since the end of the season.[54]

On the morning of December 7, 1941, the Japanese navy launched a surprise aerial attack on the United States' naval base at Pearl Harbor, Hawaii, leading to America's total entrance into the war against Japan and Germany. The war changed the lives of every American, disrupting careers, educations, and personal dreams for tens of millions of people. Most dramatically, twelve million Americans served in the armed services over the thirty-two months of United States involvement, and 416,000 of them died in action.

Joe Cronin did not directly serve his country in the armed services. However, like all Americans, his life and career were affected by the war in very large ways. The job of a Major League baseball manager, in large part, is finding and fielding the best ballplayers. This job had suddenly become a great deal more difficult.

8 War

AMERICAN WAR MOBILIZATION HAD BEGUN
long before the attack on Pearl Harbor. There had been fewer than
two hundred thousand men in the regular army when the European
war started in September 1939, but a year of increasing hostilities,
culminating in the fall of France in June 1940, had led the United
States to begin drafting men in October 1940, for the first time during
peacetime in its history. The goal of the initial draft law was to raise
an army of nine hundred thousand men.

In order to avoid some of the disenchantment military drafts had
caused during the Civil War and the First World War, the new draft
was decentralized—controlled by 6,400 local draft boards. The process was theoretically democratic, with all men between the ages of
twenty-one and thirty-six required to register, although there were
deferments for fathers, husbands, workers in war-related industries,
and conscientious objectors among others. The classifications were
not always consistent among different local boards, but the largest
problem was that half of the men drafted were turned away for not
meeting army standards, many because they could not read at a fourth-
grade level. In 1940 sixteen million men registered for the draft, from
which the army needed about eight hundred thousand (5 percent) on
top of the volunteers already serving. However, if you were single
and healthy your odds of being drafted were much better than those
numbers might suggest.[1]

There were several Major League players drafted in 1941, most
famously Hank Greenberg. Greenberg was thirty years old, single,
and obviously physically fit, though initially rejected because of flat
feet. He was finally inducted in May and mustered out just prior
to the Japanese attack in December. Many other players—such as

Bob Feller and Phil Rizzuto—were classified 1-A, subject to immediate call-up. Several owners, including Clark Griffith and Brooklyn's Larry MacPhail, publicly suggested that ballplayers belonged to a special category, deserving of the deferments that scientists and doctors received. Such comments were unpopular with the public and soon faded away.

All classifications were determined locally, though there were national guidelines. Class 1-A was given to men who were available for immediate induction. Class 2 indicated some type of deferment, generally occupational. Class 3 contained people with dependents—usually a wife or children. Class 4 was used to designate men who were too old or physically incapable of service. The most common of these, 4-F, kept many ballplayers out of the service for an old knee injury or a bad elbow.

After December 7 the military began planning for an eight-million man army—and later a ten-million man army—which changed the math considerably. It was no longer a question of wondering if your number would be called—if you were a single, physically fit male between twenty (later eighteen) and forty (later forty-four)—occupational deferments aside—you were going to be called. It was just a matter of when. The army could not use eight million men immediately, because they had neither the training facilities nor the organizational infrastructure necessary to deal with all of them. But they soon would.[2]

Major League Baseball was and is a business that relies on the skills of healthy young men, precisely the people the military needed to fight the war. The idea that these men would be exempted was now ludicrous. On January 14 Commissioner Landis sent a letter, via Clark Griffith, to President Roosevelt asking if in the president's opinion baseball should shut down for the duration of the war. The next day the president responded in his Green Light letter, telling Landis, "I honestly feel that it would be best for the country to keep baseball going." The president stressed that all capable players should fight but that the players who remained would provide necessary entertainment to the hard-working labor force.[3]

So baseball would go on. Now baseball teams suddenly had another variable to consider when judging a player, a variable that trumped all others—his military classification. Before Pearl Harbor, Joe Cronin could confidently state that Johnny Pesky would be the team's short-stop in 1942, but now he could not be so sure. Pesky was twenty-two years old, unmarried, and about as healthy as one could be. He was 1-A. Counting on Johnny Pesky, or a dozen other guys on the roster, was now a dicey proposition.

Baseball's Major League meetings took place in Chicago during the week immediately following the attack on Pearl Harbor. On the tenth the Red Sox purchased thirty-two-year-old right hander Mace Brown, who would play a big part in the team's bullpen. Three days later Collins made one of his worst deals, trading outfielder Stan Spence to the Senators in a four-player swap that netted pitcher Ken Chase. Spence had had several fine seasons in the Minors but had been passed on the outfield depth chart by Williams and Dom DiMaggio. With Washington he would become one of the AL's better players during the 1940s. The Red Sox wanted the left-handed Chase because their top three southpaws from 1941 were either retired (Grove) or in the service (Mickey Harris and Earl Johnson), and management did not think Spence could field well enough to displace Lou Finney. Unfortunately, Chase won only nine more Major League games after the deal while Spence became a star.

Besides Harris and Johnson, by January the team had also lost first baseman Al Flair (a candidate to replace Foxx) and pitcher Larry Powell to the military. In addition, Pesky, DiMaggio, and Williams were likely to be called at any time. When asked about the situation, Cronin said the only thing he really could say: "Uncle Sam comes first now."[4] Cronin assumed that Pesky and Williams would not be with the team in 1942.

Cronin's relegation to the bench may have slackened his training regimen a bit after the season. "Joe is one of baseball's champion diners," wrote Shirley Povich that winter. "The only edible Cronin likes better than a 2-inch steak is a pair of the same."[5] Cronin began working out in a local gym, and in mid-January the family went to

Sarasota and rented a cottage, several weeks before the start of camp. Having escaped the winter, Cronin again played golf every day.[6]

Ted Williams had been classified as 3-A during the 1941 season, as the sole supporter of his mother back in San Diego. In early January 1942 his draft board in Minnesota, where Ted now made his home, reclassified him 1-A and ordered him to take his physical immediately. Ted took the physical, but lawyers on his behalf appealed his reclassification, and in late February President Roosevelt upheld his appeal. Ted made plans to go to spring training. "Naturally, I welcome him back with open arms," said Cronin from Sarasota. "I'm certain that his is a most worthy case and that Ted wouldn't hesitate an instant about jumping into the Army when and if he is called."[7]

Not surprisingly, this news created a tempest with some of the Boston sportswriters, who depicted Williams as a healthy young man who did not want to serve his country. Williams argued, and the appeals process agreed, that he needed to make money to support his mother, who was medically unable to work. Lots of ballplayers were 3-A, players like Joe DiMaggio and Stan Musial, and Williams could not understand why he was being singled out. Charlie Wagner, Ted's roommate, was 3-A just like Ted, because he supported his parents.

Joe Cronin, along with Tom Yawkey and Eddie Collins, privately advised Ted to join the service, fearing for his reputation. Williams remained firm, vowing to play the entire season and then enlist after he had drawn his salary and paid off annuities for his mother. The fans supported him, some members of the press began to support him, and the furor soon subsided. On May 22 Williams quietly enlisted in the Naval Aviation Service. The flight program allowed him to take classes during the summer, while still playing for the Red Sox, and enter the program in the fall. Johnny Pesky, his new teammate, entered the same program and took classes with Ted.[8]

Ultimately the 1942 Red Sox lost three significant players from their 1941 team—pitchers Harris and Johnson, called up right after Pearl Harbor, and starting catcher Frank Pytlak, who joined the navy in April. The Yankees lost only Johnny Sturm, who had had a very unproductive year as a rookie first baseman in 1941. The best AL players in the service were Cleveland's Bob Feller, who had enlisted on December 8, and Hank Greenberg, who after having been inducted the previous May and discharged on December 5, quickly re-enlisted after December 7.

As the Major Leagues prepared to play games in 1942, American personnel were landing in Great Britain at a pace of fifty thousand men per month. In the Pacific the United States was in full retreat—suffering a humiliating defeat to the Japanese in the Philippines that culminated in the forced march of one hundred thousand prisoners from the Bataan Peninsula. When the Major League season opened on April 14, the Bataan Death March was in progress.

With Johnny Pesky a civilian, for a while at least, Joe Cronin went through with his plan to ride the bench in 1942. "Joe gave me the job, and worked with me so that I could keep it," recalled Pesky. "He could not have supported me more."[9] The rest of the team loved working with the new shortstop, and the additional plays he was making. "He made a fabulous difference," recalled Dom DiMaggio. "Cronin had slowed down. He couldn't move around as friskily as he used to. Johnny used to get to balls that were just eluding Cronin."[10]

After Tony Lupien failed to hit in Sarasota, Jimmie Foxx began the season at first base. He started well, hitting .326 after the first week of May, but then slumped, and later suffered an injury when hit by a line drive while pitching batting practice. On June 1, hitting .270 with just five home runs, he was sold on waivers to the Chicago Cubs. "Jimmie was one of the greatest guys I was ever associated with," said Cronin, "and I regret that he will no longer be with the Sox. I wish him well."

Despite the niceties, there were always reports that the two had not gotten along, just like with Grove and Cramer, the other former Athletics stars who were drinking and hunting buddies with Yawkey.[11] Foxx said a few negative things about Cronin's managerial acumen on his way out the door, commenting that he made too many snap decisions and played too many hunches.[12] He also did not like the way his end in Boston had been handled: he had been replaced in the off-season, won his job back in the spring, and then lost it in June. In his decision regarding Foxx's future, Cronin would turn out to be right—Foxx was essentially finished.

Other than Foxx the Red Sox personnel remained stable during the 1942 season. Tony Lupien, the Harvard lad, took over at first and hit a steady .281, but without Foxx's power. Second baseman Doerr hit .290 and drove in 102 runs. Tabor hit just .252 with 12 home runs, the worst of his four seasons with the club. Rookie Pesky batted .331 and led the league with 205 hits. There was no Rookie of the Year award, but Pesky finished third in the MVP voting. Left fielder Williams turned in another great season, with a .356 average, 36 home runs, and 137 runs batted in, winning the Triple Crown, just the fifth in league history. Dom DiMaggio hit .286, with 58 extra-base hits and 110 runs scored. The team missed the right-handed power of Cronin and Foxx, but the Red Sox still featured one of the finer lineups in the game.

On the pitching side, the club posted a 3.44 team ERA, well below the league average of 3.66. The most impressive find was Cecil "Tex" Hughson, who had pitched twelve games for the club in 1941. He had showed up in Sarasota in 1942 with a sore arm and was sent to a doctor in Miami. Despite not making his first start until May 16, Hughson finished 22-6 with a 2.59 ERA in 281 innings. Charlie Wagner (14-10) and Joe Dobson (11-9) gave the club three effective starters for the first time in Cronin's tenure with the club.

Once again the Yankees started hot and had an eight-game lead by the end of May. The Red Sox played well for most of the year and cut the lead to three games in early July, but ultimately could not keep the pace. Boston finished 93-59, their best record since 1915, but still finished a full nine games behind the Yankees. This marked their sixth consecutive winning season, and the fourth time they had finished second in the past five years—each time trailing only the Yankees.

Not surprisingly Cronin had to deal with another Ted Williams outburst. On June 1 in the second game of a doubleheader in Boston, Ted became particularly upset by some of the fans out in left field and responded by yelling and gesturing at them on his way off the field.

When he came to the plate he very obviously just went through the motions with a few weak swings and a pop up. His next time up he deliberately hit foul balls toward the people who had booed him, hoping "to knock a few teeth out." On one attempt his aim was off—he hit a double off the wall. When he returned to the dugout, Cronin lit into him. "What's the matter, don't you want to play?" Cronin yelled. "Get out of here then!" Williams was typically repentant, even after his $250 fine.[13] One scribe figured that Williams would get his money back since Cronin was sympathetic to Williams's attitude about the hecklers.[14]

For Joe Cronin 1942 marked his first year as primarily a bench manager. He used himself as a pinch hitter twenty-eight times and filled in around the infield in another seventeen games. He could still hit—.304, with 4 home runs and 24 RBIs in just 79 at bats. His first start did not come until May 24 in relief of Pesky, when he came through with a double and home run. This fine performance did not impress his manager—Cronin never again played shortstop in the Major Leagues. His conditioning, a struggle for him in prior years, had gotten quite a bit worse sitting on the bench.[15]

Cronin enjoyed managing from the dugout. "You get time to think things out," he reasoned. "A playing-manager wonders whether the opposing team is going to sacrifice, or hit-and-run, or a plain steal. He has to think about the pitch. He worries about the pitcher throwing one in the groove. He has to think about all these things and his own position as well, and about everybody else's position. He has to place his infielders and outfielders. Bench managers reason things out. Playing-managers must be impulsive. They're too preoccupied to reason." What's more, Cronin felt it was awkward to have to helpfully critique what a player might be doing wrong at bat or in the field, especially when "you aren't going so well yourself."[16]

"There are still a couple of weak spots that we'll have to prop up," Cronin said of the team's future, "but we're a ballclub that's on the rise."[17] Since all of their best players—Williams, Pesky, DiMaggio, Doerr, Hughson, Wagner, Dobson—were very young, the future would have looked very bright in ordinary times. These were not ordinary times.

The slow trickle of talent off Major League rosters in 1942 became a deluge after the season, and no team felt the necessary sacrifice as much as the Red Sox. By December several players had joined the war effort, including stalwarts Williams, Pesky, and DiMaggio, who were all in the navy. Lou Finney, the third outfielder, retired to his family farm in Buffalo, Alabama, after his draft board told him he would be inducted if he did not—farmers were exempt from the draft at this point in the war.

Joe Cronin was thirty-six and classified as 3-A, but a potential recruit if the war went on long enough. In the meantime Cronin signed up as a director of the Red Cross recreation club. "I wanted to do anything I could to help out," said Cronin. "I think the Red Cross is a really worthwhile organization, one I am happy to be associated with." Cronin's initial effort was aborted—he was en route to London when the ship was halted for undisclosed reasons and routed back to the States via Bermuda. He was then released and sent home.

After Cronin spent the holidays at Newton Center, the Red Cross sent him to Hawaii for what turned out to be a six-week stay. His role was as a goodwill ambassador—mixing with the troops, helping organize baseball programs, and making numerous appearances in front of the soldiers. He visited hospitals, going from bed to bed and talking to the men about their favorite team or their hometowns. At one stop he told the troops, "The allied nations this year will win the World Series—the most important series anywhere." In early January he wrote a letter to J. G. Taylor Spink, editor of *The Sporting News*, asking that several issues be sent to him every week to spread around the barracks.[18]

Cronin created a bit of a stir when he told an interviewer in Honolulu that Joe DiMaggio was the "greatest all-around ballplayer of all-time," which he later clarified as "*one* of the greatest." As for Ted Williams, he was "a great hitter who needs a kick in the pants because of his moods." But mostly Cronin came away from this trip believing that the soldiers needed baseball to continue, that following the game from afar was important to all of them.[19]

More than that, all of the men joining the service made Cronin realize that he himself might need to get back in his uniform and play. He had spent much of the fall golfing, but apparently his long voyage and stay in Hawaii did not do him much good in the weight department. His reported weight was 220 pounds before the trip to Hawaii, meaning he was more than 30 pounds over his mid-career weight. He returned to Boston in mid-February, but still made several visits to local army bases and hospitals.[20]

Commissioner Landis told all Major League clubs to hold their spring training camps near their home cities in 1943 to save travel, so the Red Sox trained at Tufts University in nearby Medford, Massachusetts. Soon after camp opened Cronin marched thirty players to a local Red Cross center to donate blood. The team had some unusually favorable northeast weather after camp opened on March 22 but had to spend the last couple of weeks training indoors.[21]

In the spring of 1943 Americans were on the offensive in the Pacific, following the securing of Guadalcanal in February and a victory in the Bismarck Sea in March. American and British forces had joined up to fight the Germans in North Africa, culminating in the brutal but ultimately victorious Tunisian Campaign. Planning had begun for the invasion of Italy and of mainland Europe. Meanwhile, the Major Leagues were preparing for another baseball season, the second since Pearl Harbor.

For the fifth consecutive season, scoring decreased in the American League, dropping from 5.37 runs per game in 1938 to 3.89 in 1943, with more than half of the reduction taking place since the start of the war. The 1943 drop was largely blamed on dramatic changes in the ball—wartime restrictions had led to the unavailability of both horsehide (used for the cover) and cork (used in the center), so for most of 1943 balls had centers made of balata, a hard rubber-like material used to make golf balls. The Red Sox scored over 5 runs per game in

1942, but plummeted to 3.63 with the balata ball, a decrease much more dramatic than could be accounted for by leaguewide trends.

In the 1943 opener in Philadelphia, Tex Hughson shut out the Athletics, but this would prove to be the club's high-water mark of the season. Boston began the year 4-10, played well for six weeks to get to .500 in late June, then collapsed to finish 68-84, a drop of twenty-five wins from 1942. The Yankees lost Joe DiMaggio to the navy, but kept Charlie Keller, Joe Gordon, Bill Dickey, Spud Chandler, and several other stars, and did not miss a beat, finishing with ninety-eight wins and winning yet another pennant in a runaway.

The Red Sox who took the field in 1943 were nearly unrecognizable to the team's fans. The entire 1942 outfield was gone, and in their place were Pete Fox, Dee Miles, Tom McBride, Johnny Lazor, and Leon Culberson. In the team's only significant transaction of the year, in July the Red Sox bought George "Catfish" Metkovich from the San Francisco Seals to play right field. Roy Partee did most of the catching, while Skeeter Newsome replaced Pesky at shortstop. Only Lupien, Doerr, and Tabor remained from the 1942 lineup. Doerr played every inning of every game at second base and led the team with 16 home runs. On the pitching side, Tex Hughson and Joe Dobson were the key holdovers, with Dick Newsome, Yank Terry, and Oscar Judd getting the bulk of the remaining starts. Hughson had a fine 2.64 ERA, which earned him a mere 12-15 record.

Two other interesting pitchers on the club were Mace Brown and Mike Ryba. The thirty-four-year-old Brown, purchased from the Dodgers before the 1942 season, became the team's relief specialist. In his first year with the club he had pitched thirty-four games in relief, and finished 9-3 with a 3.43 ERA. In 1943 he pitched more often and better, forty-nine games and ninety-three innings with a 2.12 ERA. Ryba, who turned forty during the season, pitched in forty games including only eight starts, and posted a 3.26 ERA. Pitchers like Brown and Ryba were doubly valuable during the war—not only could they pitch a lot of games (in 1942 Ryba had even caught three games), but their advanced ages made them less likely to be drafted.

Cronin played just ten games in the field the entire season, all at third base, and nine of these were in May after a stretch of poor hitting by Jim Tabor. A badly sprained finger on his left hand sent Cronin to the bench for all but one game the rest of the season, and it was likely just as well. "Joe has packed weight on both front and rear," remarked writer Jack Malaney, "and doesn't move in the same lithesome manner as before."[22] Cronin's role was to pinch hit, a job he performed forty-nine times, often with memorable results.

Cronin did not hit well early in the season. By mid-June he was just 9 for 42 (.210) with no extra-base hits when Philadelphia came to Fenway for a five-game series. In the first game of a doubleheader on the fifteenth, Cronin pinch-hit a three-run homer in the seventh inning, though his club still lost, 7–4. Two days later, in another doubleheader, Cronin pinch-hit a three-run home run in each game.

After his three home runs, Cronin did not bat again for ten days, then he pinch-hit a double in New York. He hit his fourth pinch home run on July 9 off Bob Muncrief of the Browns and his fifth off Buck Ross of the White Sox, another three-run shot. The five pinch-hit home runs remain an American League record, and his 25 RBIs in that role are a Major League record for a season (since tied by Jerry Lynch and Rusty Staub). Cronin hit just 6 for 35 (.174) with no extra-base hits when he played a position, but 18-42 (.429) in the pinch.

This pinch hitting made Cronin more popular in Boston than he had ever been, more than when he had been the best shortstop in the game a few years earlier.[23] "Oh, my, Cronin is the best there is," said Connie Mack at the end of the season. "Joe is the best right now, or at any other time when a hit was badly needed." Red Sox coach Tom Daly explained, "Joe is never bothered by the count. He's a good hitter with two strikes." Cronin suggested that he might be able to pinch-hit for another two or three seasons.[24] He would only say, "I waited for the wind to be blowing out, pulled rank and sent myself to the plate."

Although the real battles raged thousands of miles away, the war was ever-present during Major League games. Each team hosted one regular-season game per year to benefit army and navy relief funds, in addition to several large-scale exhibitions. Some games required the purchase of a war bond as the price of admission; for others, fans had to bring cartons of cigarettes for the troops.[25] The Red Sox played exhibition games against the Quonset (Rhode Island) Naval Training Station, at least one versus the Great Lakes Training Station in 1944, and many others.[26] There were more doubleheaders, especially on Sunday. Fenway Park was one of the few remaining parks without lights, but there were more night games in other parks, better for the hard-working laborer in the defense plant.

At the end of the 1943 season, Major League Baseball announced that it would send two all-star teams to the Pacific Theatre to play a series of games for the troops. Cronin was named to manage the American League team, with Frank Frisch in charge of the Nationals. Hughson, Pete Fox, and Doerr were named to the eighteen-man AL squad. After several days of headlines and planning, the trip was abruptly postponed by the War Department because of the increasing transportation needs of the armed forces in the region. Although there was some hope that the trip would be rekindled later in the off-season, it never came off.[27] One lingering effect of the aborted trip was Yankee manager Joe McCarthy's feeling that he had again been snubbed, just as he had been passed over as manager for the 1940 All-Star Game.[28] It is likely that Cronin was chosen over McCarthy because of his familiarity with the region and personnel after the previous winter's trip for the Red Cross.

Meanwhile, Cronin took a job working at a defense plant in nearby Wakefield, Massachusetts. As many such workers could and did use a defense job as a way to avoid military service, Cronin had to deny rumors that he would quit baseball for the duration of the war. "I'll stay with the game until my draft number comes up," said Cronin. He stressed that he would not ask for a job-related deferment.[29]

During the first two wartime seasons, baseball retained some semblance of its prewar form in large part because of dependency deferments, with many players not called to the service because they were husbands or fathers. But the need for able-bodied men kept growing. In the summer of 1943, Paul McNutt, who served as the manpower commissioner for the War Department, urged local draft boards to consider a man's occupation more than his family status in classification, unless extreme hardship would ensue. Although there was not unanimity on this issue in the government or in the country, the need for men eventually won out.[30] There was a mounting feeling among ballplayers that baseball might have to shut down once fathers began being drafted, and that was now a certainty.[31]

The war did extend the careers of several older players who would have been forced out of the game under normal circumstances. Cronin's former teammates Jimmie Foxx, Paul Waner, and Lloyd Waner, along with many other greybeards, were suddenly in demand. The Red Sox signed forty-one-year-old Al Simmons before the 1943 season, but he hit just .203 in 133 at bats before drawing his release in October. "The spirit is willing," said Cronin, "but the flesh is weak."[32] Unlike the previous year when the Red Sox stood pat despite huge losses to the war, Cronin was now actively looking for players.[33]

The Red Sox found a good one in December when they purchased "Indian" Bob Johnson from the Washington Senators. Johnson, whose brother Roy had had a few quality seasons in the 1930s with the Red Sox and other teams, had overcome a late start to put together an excellent career. Raised in Tacoma, Washington, and one-quarter Cherokee, Johnson starred for the Portland Beavers in the Pacific Coast League before joining Connie Mack's Athletics in 1933, just as Mack had begun selling off his stars. Johnson drove in 90 or more runs in each of his first nine years in Philadelphia, hitting 20 or more home runs every year and making several All-Star teams. Now Johnson was thirty-eight years old, but still one of the better hitters in the league.

With the status of many of his players uncertain, Cronin continued to work out in preparation for more playing time in 1944. In his spare time Cronin had become a big fan of many of the local sports teams, going to the nearby Boston College football games in the fall, and Bruins hockey games as well. In April Mildred and Joe had their third child and first daughter, Maureen, with Joe on hand for the birth. His new daughter had Joe's striking blue eyes.

In March 1944 the Red Sox returned to Tufts University to train, mostly at their indoor cages and gymnasium. On the first day of camp only a handful of players were present, and Cronin was not always certain just who would show up and how long any of them could stay. His entire infield of Lupien, Doerr, Skeeter Newsome, and Tabor were now 1-A, so outfielders Leon Culberson and Johnny Lazor worked out in the infield. Lazor also played catcher in camp because there weren't enough catchers to warm up the pitchers.[34] For the second half of camp the Red Sox moved to Baltimore so they could play some exhibition games.

The 1944 Red Sox would be without the services of pitchers Joe Dobson, Dick Newsome, and Mace Brown, three of their better hurlers from 1943. Other than Hughson, Cronin was going to have to work out the starting pitching situation as the season went along, with Yank Terry and Pinky Woods among the more likely holdovers. Most of the offense returned intact, with Bob Johnson joining Leon Culberson and Pete Fox in the outfield. Just prior to the start of the season the Red Sox sold Tony Lupien to the Phillies, and installed Catfish Metkovich at first base, with Cronin his expected backup.

Meanwhile, in Europe the Allies were fighting the Germans northward through Italy, a trek that would take several months at the cost of tens of thousands of lives, while in the Pacific the Americans had taken the Marshall Islands and were preparing attacks on New Guinea and the Marianas. The Allies were preparing to invade France, an air and amphibious assault that would involve over one million men. Although the war was nearly five years old, and Americans had been fighting for more than two years, the toughest and deadliest days were ahead. Joe Cronin, a thirty-seven-year-old father of two, was classified as 1-A, just waiting for his number to be called.

The St. Louis Browns, who had not won a pennant in forty-three years of trying, startled everyone by winning their first nine games of the 1944 season. That said, there were no great teams in the league, and every club was in the race the entire summer. At the end of May the White Sox were in last place but only five and a half games out of first. The Red Sox started poorly but hung around long enough that a nine-game winning streak in June put them in second place for a while. Though Cronin was a very popular figure at a time when many of the players were largely unknown to most fans, he still came in for some good-natured ribbing about his weight. "Who's that other guy going around with you?" was in keeping with the spirit.[35]

After a slow start by the offense, Cronin inserted himself at first base on May 3 and came through with three hits, including an eighth-inning home run to help beat the Senators 11–10. The Red Sox seemed to play better with Cronin on the field, especially as he hit .368 (14 for 38) over the next two weeks. Cronin stayed in the lineup most of the first half of the season, with Metkovich moving to center field. Cronin's hot hitting did not continue—he was down to .250 by the All-Star break—and he mostly pinch-hit in the second half. Cronin's replacement at first base was Lou Finney, who had "retired" to his Alabama farm in the fall of 1942 but rejoined the team in June. "You don't get far out of shape when you get up at five o'clock in the morning and work until sundown on a farm," said Finney upon his return.

The Browns led the race for most of the summer, and the Red Sox were their closest pursuer much of that time, spending eighteen days in second place in July and twenty-four more in August. The keys to their season were the pitching of Tex Hughson and the hitting of Bobby Doerr, Pete Fox, and Bob Johnson—who had the three highest batting averages in the league at the end of August.

The Red Sox pennant hopes were ultimately derailed by a few more military call-ups. Tex Hughson pitched his last 1944 contest on August 9, a four hitter over the White Sox in Boston, which brought his record to 18–5 with a 2.26 ERA. "With Hughson," wrote Shirley Povich in September, "the Sox would probably be on top at this point, and with his workhorse qualities well known, they would probably have won the pennant."[36]

Bobby Doerr, classified as 4-F for most of the war because of a perforated ear drum, was reclassified 1-A in August and soon ordered to report. He played his last game on September 3, with the team two and a half games out of first place and his .325 batting average leading the league. In late August catcher Hal Wagner was inducted into the army. At the time, Wagner was hitting .332 (but without the necessary at bats to qualify for the batting title).

The Red Sox were just three games out as late as September 16, but the depleted club then lost ten games in a row. They finished 77-77, twelve games behind the Browns, who won their first (and only) pennant. The Red Sox improved by nine wins over 1943, although it might be more accurate to say that they declined less than most of the rest of the league. Other than the departed men, the team's best player was Bob Johnson, who hit .324, drove in 106 runs, and led the league with a .431 on-base percentage. Doerr and Johnson were overtaken for the batting title by Cleveland's Lou Boudreau (.327) in the season's final days. Cronin ended the season at .241 in 191 at bats, and in a reversal of 1943 he went just 4 for 26 (.153) as a pinch hitter.

In midsummer Cronin had to endure some criticism from an unlikely source—Jimmie Foxx, who had retired from baseball (though he would return in 1945). Foxx was quoted by *Yank* magazine about his years with the Red Sox. "Our hitting was good but the pitchers didn't hold up," said Double-X. He did not blame the pitchers but rather Cronin, who according to Foxx used poor judgment in both choosing his pitchers and how he used them. Soon after the issue appeared, Foxx claimed he had been misinterpreted, that he only meant that Connie Mack would have done better with the staff. He and Cronin were friends, Foxx insisted.[37] Cronin's bosses, both Yawkey and Collins, continued to support their manager. The end of the 1944 season marked ten years for Cronin as Boston's skipper and the end of his second five-year contract. In late August Cronin signed a three-year deal to continue as player-manager, reportedly for $100,000 in total.

As American troops were fighting deadly battles in the South Pacific and Europe in the winter of 1944–45, manpower needs accelerated. James F. Byrnes, director of War Mobilization and Reconstruction, turned his attention to the sports world. After shutting down all dog and horse tracks in January, he asked that all athletes who were classified as 4-F be re-examined. This edict led to the induction of many players who had been excused earlier because of flat feet, punctured eardrums, color blindness, or a trick elbow. "It is difficult for the public to understand," said Byrnes, "and it is certainly difficult for me to understand, how these men can be physically unfit for military service and yet be able to compete with the greatest athletes of the nation in games demanding physical fitness."[38]

Some officials wanted this policy to go further. Senator William A. Langer of North Dakota introduced a bill requiring that 10 percent of Major League rosters be men who had lost one or more limbs.[39] Although the bill went nowhere, the 1945 season did include the debuts of Pete Gray, an outfielder with the Browns who was missing most of his right arm, and Bert Shepard, a Senators pitcher who lost a leg after his plane was shot down in Germany.

Before draft boards took another look at 4-FS, they also called up many players who had avoided service through the luck of the draw. Stan Musial, for one, just happened to have registered with a draft board that was able to meet its quotas without calling fathers, while other draft boards had been calling fathers for a year or more.[40] In the fall of 1944 the Red Sox learned that third baseman Jim Tabor and catcher Roy Partee had joined the service, removing two of the best remaining players from their squad. In early January they lost Bill Conley, the third of their three 1944 catchers, to the navy. Finally, Lou Finney now said he had to return to his Alabama farm for the duration of the war.[41] As Shirley Povich observed, "The Boston Red Sox are kind of getting the idea that there's a war going on."[42]

After the 1944 season Cronin spent a few weeks in San Francisco with his father before returning home to his family. With Tabor in the service, the thirty-eight-year-old Cronin had to prepare for the likelihood of more playing time. After spending the holidays with the Griffiths in Washington, the Cronins headed south to Fort Lauderdale so that Cronin could work out in the warm weather between visits to several local USO camps. "Even I will probably be playing regularly," said Cronin in January, adding "and Leo Durocher too." Durocher was the Dodgers' player-manager, a year older than Cronin, who had played in just twenty-four games over the past four seasons.[43]

In 1945 the Red Sox moved their spring camp to Pleasantville, New Jersey, just outside of Atlantic City where the Yankees trained. When camp opened Cronin was expecting six pitchers and one catcher, but only three of the pitchers showed up, which cut short the practice until the next day.[44] Only thirteen players reported for the opening of the full training camp on March 19 reportedly because players were reluctant to leave war jobs without clearing matters with their local draft boards.[45] Having dropped eleven pounds over the winter, Cronin was hitting the ball well and playing some third base. In a game at New York's Polo Grounds on the way north, Cronin dropped a couple of high pop-ups near third base. "The pilot of the Red Sox received quite a ribbing from the fans," wrote one scribe, "but took it good-naturedly."[46] Before the start of the season, when asked how the Red Sox could win the pennant, Cronin quipped, "We're a cinch, if I'm up to my 1926 playing form."[47]

Before the start of the 1945 season Joe Cronin played a small role in a notorious historical event, an event more important than he or anyone else thought it would be at the time. On April 16, a Monday morning, the Red Sox conducted a tryout for three players from the Negro Leagues—Jackie Robinson of the Kansas City Monarchs, Sam Jethroe of the Cleveland Buckeyes, and Marvin Williams of the Philadelphia Stars. Robinson had just begun his first year with the Monarchs but was already famous as a college football star at UCLA before the war. There had not been an African American player in the Major Leagues in sixty years, though not because of any public or written policy.

The Red Sox's decision to hold the tryout was neither serious nor well intentioned. They were pressured into staging the tryout by Boston city councilman Isadore Muchnick, who had been pressing the issue for a few years. While there had been a few voices fighting for integrating baseball for many years, the cause began to gather momentum during the war, in which black men lost their lives fighting for the freedom of oppressed people in other nations. In 1944 Muchnick threatened action that would disallow the Red Sox and Braves from playing home games on Sundays unless the teams held tryouts for Negro Leaguers.

Eddie Collins was taken aback, claiming, "We have never had a single request for a try-out from a colored applicant."[48]

With the aid of Wendell Smith, a writer for the *Pittsburgh Courier* who was familiar with the players in the Negro Leagues, Muchnick spent a year working on his plan. In March 1945 Muchnick again threatened to revoke Sunday baseball in the city, and this time he had players ready and willing to try out. The Red Sox reluctantly agreed. The tryout was supposed to be on April 12, but it took four days and some additional prodding before it actually took place. The Red Sox were to open the season in New York on April 17, the following day.[49]

The proceedings lasted about ninety minutes. The three players first met briefly with Eddie Collins, then batted and fielded under the direction of coach Larry Woodall and scout Hugh Duffy. Joe Cronin watched from the stands and was particularly impressed with the play of Robinson. "He's good and fast—fast as, well, Jack Robinson," said Cronin, using an expression of the time.[50] All three men were thanked for their time and sent on their way. None of them ever heard from the Red Sox again. A few months later Robinson signed a contract with the Montreal Royals, the International League affiliate of the Brooklyn Dodgers.

Thirty-four years later, *Boston Globe* writer Clif Keane claimed that he had attended the tryout and that he had heard a booming voice yell out, "Get those niggers off the field." Keane did not identify the voice, although he suggested it belonged to one of three people: Yawkey, Collins, or Cronin. This stunning claim rejuvenated the story, and has led to thirty years of speculation as to the speaker.

There were reportedly several other people present that day, including a few white players who were also trying out, other reporters, coaches, and the three black players—none of whom ever mentioned hearing anything like what Keane reported. Jackie Robinson wrote about the tryout many times, and he was quite bitter about the Red Sox's actions for the rest of his life. One can be sure that Robinson would not have kept this story quiet, and the same could be said for many of the other people there.

And what of Clif Keane? Just prior to making his claim in 1979, Keane had referred to Red Sox first baseman George Scott as a "bush nigger" in the Red Sox clubhouse,[51] and had joked about Scott's diet of watermelon and fried chicken on a local radio show. Art Rust Jr. had recently written a book on black baseball, *Get That Nigger off the Field*, bringing to light a profane exclamation used by Cap Anson in 1888.[52] Keane's use of a strikingly similar phrase just a few years after Rust's book, in the midst of his own bigoted comments, should be enough to dismiss, or at least bring into doubt, his bold claims.

We know what Joe Cronin was doing during the tryout. He was sitting with Wendell Smith, who wrote about their lengthy interaction in his newspaper a few days later.[53] According to Smith, Cronin and Collins spoke cordially with the players when they arrived at Fenway Park, and the men were treated well by the team. Cronin sat with Smith while the players practiced and was particularly interested in Robinson. "I saw him play football at UCLA, and he was great," Cronin told the writer. Both Duffy and Cronin praised the players but Cronin would not say for certain that they were Major League ready. He cautioned Smith that the club's Minor League affiliates were mostly in the South (Scranton, Pennsylvania, was the lone exception) and would not allow black players. Smith did not mention, either then or later, anyone shouting racial invective.

In America's shameful history of segregation, this story is not particularly noteworthy. The tryout was largely a sham. The Red Sox, like the other fifteen Major League teams, and all big-time professional football and basketball teams, were all white and were content to stay that way. Recent historians have tried to present this story as a shocking display of racism on the part of the Red Sox, but there was nothing shocking about it. In the context of 1945 it would have taken an act of courage and moral leadership for the Red Sox to sign Jackie Robinson or one of the other applicants in 1945.

The ill-fated tryout took on a much larger significance in the years ahead, when the Red Sox dragged their feet on integration for many years beyond the point at which courage was necessary. But in April 1945 the Red Sox behaved as Major League baseball teams had been behaving for many years. They had the chance to right an egregious wrong, and they did not. This action, coupled with many unfortunate actions in the years ahead, haunted their franchise for decades.

Elsewhere, history was being made daily. In early March Americans crossed the Remagen Bridge over the Rhine and into Germany—within a few weeks the Third Reich was collapsing on all sides. In the Pacific, the United States had conquered Iwo Jima and then landed on Okinawa in preparation for an invasion of the Japanese home islands. Closer to home, President Roosevelt died suddenly on April 12 and was succeeded by Harry Truman, who had been vice president for less than three months. The new president could look forward to an imminent end to the war in Europe but likely a prolonged and horrific fight to conquer Japan.

Five days into Truman's presidency, the Red Sox opened their season in New York. Joe Cronin's efforts to get ready for the season had paid off, as he had gotten his weight down to 180 pounds and began the year as the club's starting third baseman. By way of comparison, Cronin had weighed as much as 220 pounds during the previous few years. Cronin was joined in the lineup by Catfish Metkovich, Ben Steiner in his big league debut, Skeeter Newsome, Bob Johnson, Leon Culberson, Pete Fox, and Fred Walters (also playing his first game), with Rex Cecil on the mound. There were no expectations that this unit would be winning any pennants.

In the opener, Cronin recorded two singles and a walk in four trips and made a few fine defensive plays, leading a Boston wag to joke that the Red Sox third baseman must be Cronin's son. "It was a lie, of course," wrote Arthur Daley in the *Times*. "This was the 38-year-old gaffer in person, twenty pounds lighter and still a whale of a player."[54] Cronin got another hit and fielded well on the eighteenth, though the Red Sox lost both ball games. On the nineteenth Cronin started the game 1 for 2 with another walk, but the crowd of just over five thousand watched Joe Cronin's playing career change in an instant. While sliding into second base in the seventh inning, Cronin fractured the fibula in his right leg.

Cronin went back to Boston and spent several days in the hospital, his managerial duties handled by coach Del Baker. Cronin returned to the bench on crutches on May 1 but did not wear his uniform again until June 8.[55] Although he took batting practice occasionally later in the season and would later prepare himself for a bench role in 1946, Joe Cronin would never again play in a Major League game. He had played in parts of twenty seasons—thirteen of those as his team's starting shortstop—and most of those as the best at his position in baseball.

The Red Sox began the season with eight straight losses before rallying into the pennant race. The team's big star was pitcher Dave "Boo" Ferriss, who joined the club after the season had begun. In early 1945 he received his discharge from the Air Force because of an asthmatic condition.[56] Ferriss had pitched for Boston's Greensboro affiliate in 1942 and trained with Louisville in 1945. Late in spring training he pitched well against the Reds, whose manager Bill Mc-Kechnie tipped off Cronin, who summoned Ferriss to the Red Sox. When Ferriss made his debut in Philadelphia on April 29, Cronin was in the hospital. Ferriss shut out the Athletics 2–0 and went on to win his first eight starts. He finished his rookie season 21-10.

Another noteworthy addition to the Red Sox that season was thirty-eight-year-old Dolph Camilli, who had played with Cronin on the San Francisco sandlots twenty-five years earlier. First base-man Camilli had starred in the National League for ten years, but when the Dodgers dealt him to the Giants in 1943, he had refused to report. Instead Camilli managed the Oakland Oaks for a year and a half before signing with the Red Sox in 1945, in large part because of his friendship with Cronin.[57] Unfortunately, he batted just .212 in sixty-three games.

The Red Sox fought their way back over .500 in June and stayed within a few games of the lead for a couple of months. Their high-water mark was two and a half back on July 15, before a 13-23 August knocked them out of the race. Boston finished 71-83, a truly forget-table season for the club and especially for their hobbled, soon-to-be retired player-manager.

Eclipsing everything, the war finally ended. Germany surrendered in May. After the United States dropped atomic bombs on the Japanese cities of Hiroshima and Nagasaki in early August, Japan also gave up. Six years of deadly combat, nearly four for the United States, had come to an end. For the Boston Red Sox, and for all the other baseball clubs, the ending of the war meant the return of most of their players. Frankie Pytlak, who had had a fine year as the team's catcher in 1941, returned in September after nearly four years away and played nine games. There would be more men returning.

For Joe Cronin, the off-season brought a good deal of hope but also some questions. Rather than scrambling to find players, Cronin would have too many players. How good would the returning players be? Would Ted Williams and Dom DiMaggio just show up in camp playing brilliantly again? What about the wartime players—would Dave Ferriss, winner of twenty-one games, succeed against higher quality competition? Eddie Lake had had a fine year in 1945 as the club's shortstop and had earned a chance to play. But what of Johnny Pesky, who had had such a promising rookie season three long years ago?

With all of these questions hanging in the air, one thing was certain. Life in America would get better in every way, and Major League baseball was no exception.

9 Bench Manager

THE END OF THE WAR HAD COME SUDDENLY, and plans for demobilizing twelve million men, most of them overseas, were nearly as complicated as sending them there had been. A few players got out quickly: Frankie Pytlak joined the Red Sox near the end of the season, Hal Wagner was discharged in September, and Mickey Harris in early October. Meanwhile, Joe Cronin went to the office every day awaiting word from the rest of his former charges. Whether some or all of them would be ready for spring training was not known. "The war isn't over yet as far as we're concerned, or as far as any ball club is concerned," said Cronin in early November. "We won't know until we reach Sarasota for the start of spring training."[1]

As it turned out, the American people began loudly demanding that all of their husbands and sons come home, and most of them soon did. By the end of the year, Charlie Wagner, Ted Williams, Johnny Pesky, Dom DiMaggio, Bobby Doerr, and Jim Tabor were stateside waiting for their discharges. All told there were 384 Major League players in the service during the 1945 season but only 22 in 1946, most of them fringe players.[2] The armed services would continue to affect baseball rosters, in real but less dramatic ways, until the draft finally ended in 1973.

Once baseball clubs knew that nearly all of their players would be returning for the 1946 season, they faced a new problem: how to merge their wartime players with returning veterans. Many of the incumbents had to adjust to a harsh new reality. Tony Cuccinello, who had finished second in the American League in batting average in 1945, was released by the White Sox in December and never again played in the Major Leagues. The younger wartime stars fared better. When the Yankees found themselves with two second basemen—prewar star

Joe Gordon and wartime standout Snuffy Stirnweiss—the Bombers moved Stirnweiss to third base.

The Red Sox's best position players from 1945 were left fielder Bob Johnson, who had led the team in home runs and runs batted in for two consecutive seasons; second baseman Skeeter Newsome, who had hit .290 to lead the club; and shortstop Eddie Lake, who had batted .279 and led the league with a .412 on base percentage. Despite their accomplishments, with Williams, Doerr, and Pesky returning to claim their positions, their job prospects were bleak.

In any event the Red Sox wasted little time in dealing with their excess bodies. Newsome was sold to the Phillies on December 12. Johnson was released on December 27, ending a fine thirteen-year Major League career. And in January the Red Sox dealt Lake to the Tigers for slugging first baseman Rudy York, who had starred before and during the war. By this time, Cronin had a free hand to make player deals himself and he later listed the York deal as the best one he ever made. "We'd spent years looking for a right-handed slugger to follow Ted Williams," Cronin said. "Bobby Doerr was great, but he felt the pressure [hitting fourth]."[3]

One surprising discard was Jim Tabor, the team's third baseman for several years before he entered the service in 1945. Tabor appeared to have a simple claim to his old job since the club had not been able to find a capable replacement, but his drinking and training problems may have contributed to the decision to sell him to the Phillies in January. The Red Sox hoped that Ernest Andres, who had played three years with Louisville before the war, would claim the position. An early inductee who had spent more than four years in the Navy, Andres now had a clear path to a starting position.[4]

Cronin spent the autumn in Boston with his family, going to the Red Sox offices every day during the week, waiting to hear from his returning players. On the weekends he watched a lot of football games—on Saturdays rooting for local college teams and heading to Fenway Park on Sundays to see the Boston Yankees, a short-lived NFL team.[5] Later that fall he and Eddie Collins traveled to the Minor League meetings in Columbus and the Major League sessions in

Chicago. After the holidays Joe and Mildred headed west to visit his father.[6] Mildred had a bout of pneumonia during the winter that sent her to the hospital for several days. "After I was past the worst," Mildred recalled, "his attitude was: 'You can't do this to me.' When I was ready to come home, he said: 'Mildred, you can take care of the kids. I'll take care of Ted Williams any day.'"[7]

Cronin had some unexpected business in San Francisco. Dom DiMaggio, back from naval duty in Australia, figured that after three years off he was now a free agent. "I might have written a letter to the Red Sox saying that I didn't belong to them anymore," recalled DiMaggio. "Joe Cronin came out to see me. He was really mad. The veins were popping out of his head." Cronin offered DiMaggio a salary of $11,000, citing the club's poor attendance during the war. DiMaggio negotiated the figure up to $16,000, plus an attendance clause giving him $500 for every 50,000 fans over 450,000. This clause netted the shrewd Dominic another $9,500 at the end of the season.[8]

Cronin also spent some time in Hollywood making a movie. Bert Dunne, a star outfielder for Notre Dame in 1924 and 1925, had played against Cronin in the Eastern League in 1926. As was typical for Cronin, he and Dunne had become lifelong friends, playing golf together and talking baseball. A bad arm caused Dunne to retire after the one season, but his scientific interest in the game led him to write a popular baseball instructional pamphlet, *Play Ball, Son!* Cronin wrote the introduction, praising Dunne's technical theories on the game and for making "the best technical book on baseball ever written for boys." The key to a boy's success in the game, wrote Cronin, was "his strength, his eyes, his courage—and how much he practices."[9]

Dunne's theories on hitting had led the Red Sox to film their own hitters. Ted Williams in particular spent a lot of time studying his stance and swing frame-by-frame. The success of the book led to the movie, directed by Herb Lamb, featuring high-school boys running, hitting, sliding, fielding, and pitching. Cronin appeared at the start of the film, which was shown to high schools and boys groups for many years all over the country. In 1947 Dunne put out a full-length book, *Play Ball*, an expanded version of the pamphlet, to which Cronin contributed an expanded foreword.[10]

After spending a few weeks back in Boston, Cronin headed for Florida on February 21. Boston was digging out from a serious snow storm, and Cronin might have been anxious to see some sunshine and baseball diamonds free of snow. It would be the Red Sox's first trip to Sarasota since 1942. The war was over, optimism reigned, and the Red Sox looked to be one of the better teams in the league. For the first time Cronin began the season as a bench manager, a status he likely would have achieved sooner had the war not taken away all his better players.

The returning veterans would have been enough to make baseball's 1946 spring training a compelling story, but a bizarre interlude threatened to overshadow the proceedings. Danny Gardella, an outfielder who starred for the New York Giants during the war, was frustrated when he found out he had to compete for a starting job and jumped his contract to play for a team in the Mexican League. The league had existed since 1925 but became an "outlaw circuit" in the 1940s when it was under the direction of Jorge Pasquel, a Mexican industrialist. The league included a lot of Cuban and American blacks in this period, and during the war attracted a few Latin players who wished to avoid military service.[11]

With Gardella in the fold, the emboldened Pasquel and his brother Bernardo offered large contracts and bonuses to many American players, including several stars. In addition to the larger salaries, the Mexican League players paid no taxes and had subsidized living expenses. Several Major League players took the bait, including Max Lanier, the Cardinals' pitching star, and Mickey Owen, the Dodgers' four-time All-Star catcher. "I am ready to compete with Organized Ball, dollar for dollar and peso for peso," said Jorge Pasquel. Happy Chandler, baseball's commissioner, responded to the threat by imposing a five-year ban on any defector who remained in Mexico when the Major League season began. Vern Stephens, star shortstop for the St. Louis Browns, signed with Monterrey but returned just prior to the commissioner's deadline.[12]

More relevant to the Red Sox, Ted Williams was offered $100,000 in a meeting with Jorge Pasquel, $60,000 more than his Red Sox salary. "Jeez, Pasquel had diamonds in his tie and diamonds on his watches, and diamonds on his wrists . . . and every time he talked he kind of splattered you a little bit. But I never really gave it a tumble." Early in the season Pasquel offered Johnny Pesky a five-year contract.[13] Fortunately for the Red Sox, and for the careers of both men, they chose to remain in Boston.

The fortified Red Sox were considered a prime contender for the American League flag in 1946, along with the Detroit Tigers, who had won the 1945 pennant, and the New York Yankees. The Red Sox's best position players were left fielder Ted Williams, center fielder Dom DiMaggio, shortstop Johnny Pesky, and second baseman Bobby Doerr. Rudy York at first, Catfish Metkovich in right field, and Hal Wagner behind the plate were solid Major Leaguers as well. The core of a fine pitching staff—Tex Hughson, Mickey Harris, Joe Dobson, Dave Ferriss, and Charlie Wagner, would be together for the first time and form the best group Joe Cronin had ever had.

The revelry of spring training was broken in late March by a story Harold Kaese wrote for *The Saturday Evening Post* titled "What's the Matter With the Red Sox?" Although Kaese presented a few possible answers to this question, his number one candidate was Joe Cronin. Kaese did not advance this opinion as his own, but instead assigned it to an unnamed "choir of critics" who believed that "there is nothing wrong with the Red Sox that a new manager wouldn't cure." Later he quotes "some Bostonians" as saying, "Cronin was a great player. He's a punk manager." Kaese hauled out a lot of well-told stories, including the difficulties with Grove and Ferrell and the quotes from Foxx in 1943 (later denied). He also advanced some newer criticisms—that Cronin favored California players over New Englanders; that his "rich Celtic personality" led to his being "impetuous, sensitive, and unpredictable"; and that his own disappointment during a team slump kept him from being able to lift his team out of it.

Kaese praised Cronin the player, calling him "a dauntless fighter, a man who swept over obstacles to make himself a dangerous hitter, and one of modern baseball's finest shortstops." He properly assigned Cronin's defensive struggles only to his first two years with the team and blamed the pressures of living up to Cronin's big sale price. Kaese also admitted that Cronin had many fans in the city and was friendly and supportive of the writers. For 1946 Kaese predicted pennant fever early in the season, while the critics confidently waited for the inevitable collapse and "the annual opportunity to turn the bonfire into a pyre for the game guy with the big chin, Joe Cronin."[14]

The article caused several observers to rally to Cronin's defense. Fred Lieb, in *The Sporting News*, thought the problem with the prewar Red Sox was obvious: "[Joe] McCarthy's Yankees. Even the genius of John McGraw, Connie Mack, Ned Hanlon and Miller Huggins could hardly have masterminded the Red Sox pitchers of those years ahead of the mighty Bronx Bombers."[15] Ed McCauley, of the *Cleveland News*, found a consensus among Boston writers in the press box one day in Sarasota. "Have you ever picked the Red Sox to win the pennant?" asked one writer. "Of course not," replied McCauley. "There's your answer to Kaese's story. No one who knows anything about baseball has ever expected them to win it."[16] Dan Parker of the *New York Mirror* wrote that "baseball needs more 'flops' of the Joe Cronin type."[17]

The writers were not the only ones to rally around Cronin. "I consider him a very smart manager," offered Connie Mack. "The fellow who wrote that article doesn't know his facts." Bobo Newsom, never shy about slamming Cronin over the years, claimed that his beef with the Red Sox was with Eddie Collins.[18] By early May Dan Daniel could write in baseball's premier newspaper that the Red Sox were the people's choice and that "millions of enthusiasts in this country and among our forces still overseas are pulling for Joe Cronin's club."[19]

The Red Sox entered the season with two question marks among eight positions: third base and right field. Ernie Andres started the season at third base, but after going 4 for 41 was farmed to Minneapolis. Rip Russell, purchased before the season from Los Angeles of the Pacific Coast League, took over but was also overmatched at the plate. Catfish Metkovich got most of the playing time in right field, but hit just .246. Cronin and Eddie Collins spent much of the season looking for better options at both positions.

The Red Sox's strengths easily compensated for the two under-manned positions, and the club dominated the 1946 American League race from the start. After winning six of their first nine games, they won fifteen games in a row to reach 21-3 on May 10. The club led the league by six and a half games at the end of May and eight and a half at the end of June, the latest they had led the race since 1918 (when Boston had won the pennant). Though he had hinted several times that his playing career was over, Cronin remained on the active list the first two months of the season. Finally on June 1 he formally retired. Tom Yawkey ripped up his contract and gave him a new one, reportedly for $40,000 per year, to manage through the 1947 season. The contract was seen as Yawkey's emphatic answer to Cronin's critics, most notably Harold Kaese.[20]

At the All-Star break, the Red Sox were 54-23, one game off the pace of the 1927 Yankees, considered the greatest of all baseball teams. Charlie Wagner, one of the club's pitchers, credited the team's spirit and looseness in the clubhouse for their success. "Of course," admitted Wagner, "when you're eight, nine, ten games out in front you can do those kinds of things."[21] Writer Ed Rumil credited Cronin, "who created the best team spirit and hustle Hub critics have seen in a local ball club since George Stallings ran the 1914 Braves."[22]

The Yankees played well for the first half of the season but couldn't keep up with Boston's blistering pace. Manager Joe McCarthy resigned as manager in late May for health reasons, and Bill Dickey took over. "We were playing almost .600 ball, and we still couldn't gain any ground on the Red Sox," remembered Tommy Henrich. "When you play that well and don't close the gap it kind of breaks your heart." Of course, this was new to the Yankees, who had grown accustomed to being the ones doing the heart breaking. The Red Sox stayed hot over the next two months and put the race away. The team's longest losing streak, six games, took place with the team on the verge of clinching the flag. They were sixteen and a half games in front and winners of eight straight on September 6 but were not able to pop the champagne corks for another week.

Finally, on September 13 in Cleveland, the Red Sox beat the Indians 1–0 behind Tex Hughson's three-hitter. Two months earlier the Indians had begun employing a radical shift on Ted Williams, with four infielders and two outfielders on the right side of the field, and only the left fielder to cover half of fair territory. In the pennant clincher, Williams foiled the tactic with a line drive to left-center that rolled to the wall at Cleveland's League Park. He scored easily, the only inside-the-park home run of his career. Later that afternoon the Yankees beat the Tigers—who had passed New York in the standings—to clinch the flag for Boston.[23]

No one was more elated than Tom Yawkey. "Having a perfect manager did the trick," said the owner. "I always said Joe Cronin was the best manager around and now I'm convinced of it. He's the best in the business, the best now and the best there ever was." Cronin must have loved hearing those words, but said, "I had the players. And I had the man who could get me those players."

Having clinched the pennant so early, Cronin wanted to get his best players some rest before the start of the World Series, which was twenty-three days away at the time of their victory in Cleveland. After the pennant was clinched on Friday, the Red Sox continued to Chicago to play a doubleheader on Sunday, to St. Louis for games on Wednesday and Thursday, and then to Washington for two over the weekend. Cronin took the unusual step of not just resting players, but allowing several of them to leave the club for several days. He gave many of his star players permission to skip the series in St. Louis, providing them five full days off. Williams, DiMaggio, Doerr, Pesky, Hughson, Ferriss, Harris and Wagner, along with Cronin himself, headed back to Boston, where Cronin held a few informal workouts.[24] The group watched the Cardinals play at Braves Field, scouting a possible Series opponent.

Not surprisingly, this action drew some fire. "Clubs with pennants clinched have rested some of their heroes in September," editorialized *The Sporting News*, "but nothing like the tremendous snub which

Joe Cronin tossed at customers in St. Louis ever had been recorded before, and something should be done to prevent a repetition."[25] In any event the second stringers split two games in St. Louis and were met in Washington by their more famous teammates on Saturday. The full squad won five of their final seven games.

The Red Sox finished the season 104-50, their best record since 1912 and still their second-best season performance. Many baseball people and press were delighted for Cronin, including Harold Kaese, who graciously sent a telegram that read, "Congratulations to a champ that made me a chump."[26] Remarkably, all of the team's returning stars had shaken off their accumulated rust. Johnny Pesky hit .335 in his second season, four long years after his first. Dom DiMaggio hit a career high .316, while Bobby Doerr batted .271 and drove in 116 runs. Ted Williams, who had lamented in May about being out of shape and not knowing the pitchers,[27] batted .342 with 38 home runs. Newcomer Rudy York drove in 119 runs from the cleanup spot.

But the key was the steady work of their four starting pitchers—Boo Ferriss, Tex Hughson, Mickey Harris, and Joe Dobson. Ferriss, who had starred in 1945 against lower-quality competition, won his first ten starts to quiet the doubters and finished the season 25-6. Tex Hughson went 20-11 with a 2.75 ERA, Harris 17-9, and Dobson 13-7. For the first time since his debut season in 1933, manager Cronin had four good starting pitchers who stayed healthy all season.

While the American League pennant race offered little drama, the Dodgers and Cardinals staged an epic battle in the NL, with Brooklyn catching their rivals at the wire to finish in a tie. Both leagues ended their season on Sunday the twenty-ninth, with the Series scheduled to begin on Wednesday. National League president Ford Frick, with no history to guide him—this being the first tie in Major League history—scheduled a three-game playoff for the pennant, delaying the start of the World Series until Sunday the sixth. Some suggested Frick scheduled three games rather than one in order to hurt the powerful Red Sox. "Why three games and not one?" complained Cronin. "Why not one game or toss a coin? Football's here, and hockey opens in three weeks."[28]

Wanting their club to stay sharp during the long layoff, Collins and Cronin scheduled a series of three exhibition games at Fenway Park, pitting the Red Sox club against a group of American League stars picked by league president Will Harridge.[29] Finding willing players proved remarkably easy; such stars as Joe DiMaggio, Hank Greenberg, and Hal Newhouser showed up to take part, promised only a share of ticket revenue.

As it turned out, the exhibitions were not a success, artistically, economically, or otherwise. The weather was unseasonably cold and damp, enough so to postpone a Boston Yankees football game at Braves Field. Furthermore, despite the lure of their favorite team and many of the world's greatest players, attendance was light—just 6,500 people showed up to watch the three games. The players gave less than their best, one scribe remarking that "it appeared the idea was to get it over with as soon as possible."[30] More importantly, Ted Williams got hit by a Mickey Haefner pitch in the first game, swelling his right elbow to twice its normal size and shutting him down until the Series. How this affected Williams's play later is unknown—he never used the injury as an excuse for his subpar performance. Joe Cronin didn't even bother attending the final two exhibitions, instead going to Brooklyn to watch the NL playoff.[31] The Dodgers had lost the first game in St. Louis on Tuesday, and their loss at home on Thursday ended the series.

If Williams's injury weren't enough of a distraction, on the eve of the Series a New York writer reported that Williams would be traded after the season, and the rumor naturally spread. Williams would, in various versions of the story, be dealt to the Yankees for Joe DiMaggio, to the Tigers for Hal Newhouser, or to the Indians for Bob Feller. Williams's critics in the Boston press happily reported the rumors, then suggested that the team's denials—including Cronin's emphatic "Ted Williams is not for sale," or Collins's "Nuts to that"—were half-hearted. Williams brooded over the story, telling friends that he did not want to play anywhere but Boston.[32]

On October 6 the 1946 World Series finally got underway in St. Louis's Sportsman Park. The Red Sox, after their dominant season, were heavy favorites to win the Series, perhaps in four or five games. Cronin's family joined him in St. Louis, including his father Jeremiah, who traveled from San Francisco. For Game 1, Cronin chose to bypass Ferriss, his twenty-five-game winner, in favor of Tex Hughson, his twenty-game winner. Hughson was brilliant, but the Red Sox found themselves down 2–1 heading into the top of the ninth inning. Singles by Mike Higgins, pinch hitter Rip Russell, and Tom McBride tied the score, and a home run by Rudy York in the tenth pulled it out. Cronin surprised many by pitching left-hander Mickey Harris, who had finished 17-9, in the second game. Harris pitched well, allowing just one earned run in seven innings, but Cardinals starter Harry Brecheen tossed a four-hit shutout, and St. Louis won 3–0 to even the Series.

Back in Boston, Cronin finally turned to Ferriss, who tossed a six-hit shutout, getting all the runs he needed when York hit a three-run home run in the first inning of a 4–0 victory. Hughson was back for the fourth game, but this time he could not get out of the third inning in a 12–3 drubbing. Red Munger, winner of just two games all year, pitched the complete game victory for the Cardinals. In Game 5, Joe Dobson hurled a gem for the Red Sox, allowing just four hits and three unearned runs in a 6–3 win. "There was consternation among the Bostonians in the press box when word came that Dobson would pitch," wrote Arthur Daley in the *Times*. "But all's well that ends well."[33] The teams then hopped the train back out to St. Louis, with the Red Sox clinging to a 3–2 Series lead.

Most observers felt that Cronin would pitch his two aces, Ferriss and Hughson, in the last two games to get the one victory he needed. Instead, he again called on Harris, a lefty to counter the Cardinals left-handed sluggers Stan Musial and Enos Slaughter. This time, Harris got rocked by the Cardinals in the third inning, allowing five hits and getting just two outs before being relieved. Down three runs, Cronin turned to Hughson, who threw four and a third shutout innings to keep his team in the game. Unfortunately, the Red Sox were again foiled by Brecheen, who allowed his first Series run in the seventh but little else, St. Louis holding on for a 4–1 victory to even the Series.

For Game 7, Cronin turned to Ferriss on five days rest, in a rematch with the Cardinals' Murry Dickson. Tied 1–1 after four, St. Louis chased Ferriss on four hits and two runs in the fifth. Joe Dobson held the Cards in check through the seventh, and the Red Sox tied the game in the eighth inning on a two-run double by DiMaggio. Dominic was thinking of a triple as he left the batter's box, but in what he later called his biggest disappointment in baseball,[34] he hurt his hamstring on his way to second base and barely hobbled into the bag. He was replaced as a runner and in center field by Leon Culberson. For the bottom of the eighth, Cronin turned to reliever Bob Klinger, who had had a fine regular season (2.37 ERA in fifty-seven innings) but had not pitched since September 19. Cronin hoped to get just one inning out of Klinger, then replace him with a pinch hitter in the top of the ninth.[35]

Enos Slaughter started the eighth for the Cardinals by singling up the middle. Whitey Kurowski attempted to sacrifice, but his weak pop-up was caught by Klinger. Del Rice hit a harmless fly to Williams in left field for the second out. Harry Walker then lined a hit to left centerfield, which Culberson ran down. He relayed the ball to Pesky, whose throw home was too late to catch the hard-charging Slaughter. This play—how Slaughter scored from first and whose fault it was—has been debated for six decades and counting. The consensus opinion seems to be that DiMaggio, had he been out there, would have cut the ball off quicker, and Slaughter would never have scored on Dominic—who had one of the best outfield arms in the game. In fact DiMaggio himself has always thought he could have thrown out Slaughter at *third* base.[36] Pesky has been blamed, probably unfairly, for hesitating before throwing home. No matter—the Cardinals led the game 4–3 heading to the ninth inning.

The Red Sox were not finished though as York and Doerr began the ninth with singles off Brecheen, who had entered in relief in the eighth inning. Higgins attempted to sacrifice, but his hard bunt forced Doerr at second base. Roy Partee fouled out to first base, and pinch hitter Tom McBride's ground ball forced Higgins at second. The Cardinals had won the World Series, four games to three. "We won the pennant too early," Cronin said after the final game, while also crediting the Cardinals for playing a great defensive Series.[37]

In the aftermath of any World Series, but especially one as close as this one, the losing manager inevitably comes in for a bit of criticism. For Joe Cronin the two biggest controversies were his starting of Harris in the sixth game, rather than pitching Ferriss and Hughson in the final two contests, and his use of Klinger in the finale. Harris was a seventeen-game-winner and pitched well all season, earning Cronin's confidence. In his two Series outings, matched against Brecheen, the Red Sox scored a total of one run. This was hardly Harris's fault.

The use of Klinger is a more compelling criticism. Earl Johnson, the club's top reliever, had pitched twice in the Series and was well rested. Moreover, he was left-handed and would theoretically have matched up better with lefty swingers Slaughter, who led off the eighth, and Walker, who smacked the fateful hit. Cronin felt that Klinger, who had pitched well for him throughout the season, could get through one inning. Unfortunately, Klinger allowed the run.

Returning home by train, the Red Sox gathered at Fenway Park on the sixteenth to clean out their lockers and say their goodbyes. The disappointed players presented their manager with a sterling silver cigarette case, a generous gift but not a useful one—Cronin loved cigars but did not smoke cigarettes. Tom Yawkey was even more generous, giving every player an undisclosed bonus in addition to their World Series shares.[38] Joe Cronin had lost the World Series for the second time, but he had every reason to be optimistic about the future of his team of stars.

Besides the Williams trade stories, another dramatic rumor surfaced on the eve of the World Series, one which later bore fruit. A story originating in New York in September suggested that Joe Cronin would soon move to the front office, with Joe McCarthy, recently deposed as manager of the Yankees, taking over the Red Sox job. Yawkey admitted to Joe Williams that part of this story was true. "For a family man, as Cronin is, managing a ball club is not always a desirable job. The day he decides to quit the dugout, that's the day we will welcome him into the front office." Yawkey was quick to add that Cronin would not replace Eddie Collins, but would work *with* Collins.[39] Dan Daniel wrote after the World Series that it was the loss to the Cardinals that quashed the plan. Cronin, according to his friends, wanted to quit managing only after winning a championship for the Red Sox.[40] Mildred Cronin admitted that she looked forward to the day that Cronin would take the uniform off. "I do wish a baseball team didn't have to travel so much," said Mildred. "It would be nice to have Joe home more. The children are getting to the age where they need Daddy around to keep them in check."[41]

During the summer of 1946 the Cronins bought a second house in Osterville, Massachusetts, on Cape Cod about eighty miles from their house in Newton Center. There had been an outbreak of polio in the Boston area after the war, and Mildred no longer wanted their children swimming in the lake that was directly across the street. For the next twenty years, Mildred and the children spent their summers on the Cape, and Joe would join them on most weekends when he was not traveling. A front-office job, where he would not have to travel with the team on road trips, would afford much more time with his family.[42]

Cronin's desires reflected his modest lifestyle. He and Mildred often entertained guests, held parties at their house, or went out to dinner or the theater with friends. Cronin loved to dance, and he loved to sing. He loved being around people and talking about current events, show business, and baseball. Cronin could talk baseball all day long.[43]

(The Cronins both had a love of theater, music, and show business. Over the years they had befriended George M. Cohan, Bob Hope, Bing Crosby, Joe E. Brown, and Harry Ruby. One time in Hollywood Ruby took the Cronins to dinner at Harpo Marx's house. When they arrived the door was wide open but the hosts did not answer the knocking. When they wandered into the house, they found Harpo and his wife playing catch. "I always like to make our guests feel at home," said Harpo.[44])

Just prior to Thanksgiving in 1946, Eddie Collins fell ill at his home near Boston. He was only fifty-nine years old and seemingly in fine health, and news of his illness (apparently the result of a heart condition) was kept from the public at the time. He skipped the baseball meetings that year and began showing up at Fenway less often and for shorter durations. In his absence, Joe Cronin began to handle more of the day-to-day duties of running the franchise.[45]

The joint meetings of the Major and Minor Leagues were held in Los Angeles in December, and for the first time Joe Cronin represented the Red Sox without Collins or Yawkey. The team's needs were the same as they had been in 1946—a third baseman and a right fielder. Nonetheless, the club acquired no new players, and during the off-season released several veterans—third baseman Mike Higgins and pitchers Mike Ryba, Charlie Wagner, and Mace Brown. All were given jobs in the organization—Ryba and Higgins became Minor League managers, Brown a scout, and Wagner assistant farm director.

Harold Kaese, whose article on the Red Sox had been part of the back story of 1946, wrote a less controversial essay for *Sport* in 1947 about Ted Williams and his relationship with children. The three Cronin children—Tommy, Michael (called Corky throughout his life), and Maureen—played starring roles. All three youngsters called Ted "meathead," evidence to Kaese that Ted was much more at ease with children than with reporters. The family went to spring training every year, and the boys worked with Williams on their hitting. Tommy, a left-handed batter, wanted to be Williams, and scolded his right-handed younger brother: "You'll have to be Rudy York." One day the boys were posing for pictures with Williams, when Corky asked for more time to adjust his elbow. "That Corky," said one wag in an undertone, "he's a better actor than his old man."[46]

The Red Sox who returned to Sarasota in February 1947 were a confident lot, and most observers considered them the favorite to win the pennant again, though perhaps with less ease than in 1946. The starting pitching and most of their best position players were still in their twenties and seemingly had a number of fine seasons ahead of them. Early in camp Cronin reportedly asked his pitchers to ease up on their workouts, remembering the sore arms the club had suffered through in recent spring trainings.[47] All four of his aces—Dave Ferriss,

Tex Hughson, Joe Dobson, and Mickey Harris—reported to camp healthy and took part in regular workouts. On March 26 Hughson raved about the Red Sox pitching, suggesting it would be even better than it had been in 1946. "This staff isn't going to wear out in a couple of seasons."

In light of Collins's illness, in early April Yawkey announced that he would be spending more time working in the office. Shirley Povich reported persistent rumors that Cronin would succeed Collins as general manager and be replaced by Joe McCarthy. The former Yankee manager had a chance to take over the Dodgers, for 1947 only, after Leo Durocher was suspended for the season. That McCarthy turned down this opportunity only amplified the rumors of his coming to Boston. Why take a one-year gig in Brooklyn if a full-time job awaited him with the AL champs?[48]

Once underway, the much anticipated 1947 season turned into a disaster for the Red Sox, mainly due to injuries suffered by their starting pitchers. The Red Sox were near first place through June, but the Yankees won nineteen consecutive games in July to put the race away. Harris came down with a sore left arm just as the team was breaking camp and did not make his first start until June 11. Tex Hughson had numbness in his middle finger early in the season, pitched through it, and then developed a sore elbow that persisted for most of the year.[49] Dave Ferriss also hurt his arm, though he continued to pitch. He and Hughson each finished 12-11, while Harris could manage only five wins. None of the three would ever again win more than seven games in a season.

Though no manager would use young pitchers today the way Joe Cronin used his in 1946, at the time it was not unusual. That year Hughson pitched 278 innings—third in the league behind Bob Feller's 371 and Hal Newhouser's 293. Both Feller and Newhouser had several more 200-inning seasons ahead of them, on their way to the Hall of Fame. Ferriss's 274 innings were fifth in the league, while Harris pitched 222. These pitchers worked a lot because they pitched so well, and established wisdom dictated that they stay in the game. Regardless of the cause, the injuries to the Red Sox pitching stars wrecked what had looked to be the beginnings of a long run of success.

Although the pitching injuries were the focus, many of the offensive players experienced down years as well. Bobby Doerr hit .258, DiMaggio .283, and Rudy York just .212 in forty-eight games before being dealt to the White Sox for first baseman Jake Jones. "The big Indian just isn't going to repeat," said Cronin just prior to making the deal.[50] On the positive side, Pesky hit .324 with a league-leading 207 hits, and Ted Williams won his second triple crown, leading the league in batting average, home runs, and runs batted in. Overall the offense scored 72 fewer runs than it had in 1946.

Cronin successfully addressed one of the two open positions—as rookie Sam Mele hit .302 and secured the right-field post—but could not adequately fill the third base hole. After beginning the season with Eddie Pellagrini at third base, in early May Cronin surprised many observers by swapping Pellagrini with shortstop Pesky. "Pellagrini is a great defensive shortstop," Cronin reasoned. "Pesky is both a top hitter and fielder. He can play any spot and I don't think the switch to third will affect him. If it works, we'll be a lot stronger defensively."[51] In the event the experiment was scrapped after a few weeks as Pellagrini hit just .203 for the season. The Red Sox most-used third baseman was rookie Sam Dente, who hit .232 in forty-six games.

The highlight of Cronin's season came in July, when (for the third time) he managed the American League in the All-Star Game, and directed his team to a 2–1 triumph. Bobby Doerr manufactured the winning run in the seventh by singling to left, stealing second, advancing to third when Johnny Sain's pickoff attempt went into center field, and scoring on a single by Stan Spence. Cronin received a bit of criticism for using five players—including Ted Williams, Joe DiMaggio, Lou Boudreau, George McQuinn, and catcher Buddy Rosar—for the entire game.[52]

Cronin's inevitable ascension to the front office was a story that never went away, especially once the Red Sox fell out of the race. Although Joe McCarthy was the usual rumored manager, there were other stories that summer stating that the new manager would be

Detroit catcher Birdie Tebbetts, or Detroit manager Steve O'Neill, or Cleveland shortstop-manager Lou Boudreau, or former National League manager Bill McKechnie, or even former pitching star Dizzy Dean.[53]

The Red Sox ended the 1947 season by losing in Washington on September 28, finishing in third place, fourteen games behind the Yankees and two behind the Tigers. The next day Cronin announced that the poorly kept secret was true: Joe McCarthy was the new manager, Cronin the new general manager, and Eddie Collins had been named to a new post as vice president. (The *Boston Post*'s Al Hirshberg, writing twenty-six years later in his history of the team, claimed that Yawkey had told a couple of writers after the 1946 season that McCarthy already had an agreement to take over in 1948.[54])

For fourteen years Yawkey had left the running of the club to his good friend Collins, but over the previous year had been obligated to spend more time in the office than he wanted. Yawkey's desire to be less directly involved with the day-to-day operations of the team, Collins's poor health, and Cronin's desire to travel less made the transition inevitable. As for McCarthy, he had been friends with both Yawkey and Cronin for many years.[55]

Joe Cronin, just shy of his forty-first birthday, would never again wear a baseball uniform in real competition. He had managed fifteen seasons and 2,315 games, winning 1,236, for a .540 percentage. He won two pennants and had only four losing seasons—two during the war. Cronin had problems with many of his temperamental stars in his early Boston years, but otherwise was well liked by nearly all of his charges. Most of the Boston press liked him personally, though his tenure as a manager—as part of the eighty-six-year championship draught—has largely come to be considered a failure by later fans and historians. The championship eluded him, and this fact has obscured whatever else he may have accomplished as Red Sox manager.

Although a manager's performance is very difficult to assess, especially decades later, the contemporary wisdom seems about right. After leading a motivated group in Washington, Cronin seemed shell-shocked by the surly brood that he faced in his early years in Boston, and he did not have the confidence or stature (or, to be fair, the support from his bosses) to keep his players motivated and working for the greater good. Once the veterans were replaced by youngsters who looked up to him, the drama lessened considerably, and Cronin's players and the press began to praise his managerial acumen.

Joe McCarthy's record as a big league manager was (and is) second to none. After five successful seasons with the Chicago Cubs, including the 1929 pennant, he took over the Yankees in 1931. While the Yankees had formed the beginning of a dynasty in the 1920s—winning three championships—McCarthy led them to eight pennants and seven World Series wins in his sixteen years at the helm. He was a quiet leader who rarely said much interesting to the press but was well respected by most of his players. He believed in discipline, hustle, playing the game the right way, and dressing and behaving professionally. He noticed everything that happened on the field and pulled players aside to teach them things he noticed that they might have missed. Bill James, among the many historians who consider Joe McCarthy the greatest manager in baseball history, credited his people skills—not because he got players to like him, but because he got players to do what they needed to do to win.[56]

The end of the McCarthy era in New York had not been pleasant. For his first fifteen years in New York he had worked for general manager Ed Barrow, who had hired him, found him players, and otherwise stayed out of his way.[57] In 1945 the Yankees were sold to a group that included Larry MacPhail, who took over from Barrow as team president. Unlike Barrow, a Hall of Famer who did most of his work behind the scenes, MacPhail was a self-promoter who loved to meddle in the affairs of the ballclub. Always a heavy drinker, McCarthy began to drink more.[58]

On July 20, 1945, with his team four and a half games out of first place, McCarthy left the club to deal with his "health" issues. He spent nearly three weeks at his home in Buffalo before returning to his team on August 9. McCarthy came back in 1946 only to see the Red Sox quickly pull away from the Yankees and every other team. After watching his team lose a tough game in Cleveland on May 20,

McCarthy did not go back to the ballpark for the series finale; the Yankees claimed he had a bad cold. When the team returned to the hotel, having lost again, McCarthy was clearly drunk. Over the next twenty-four hours, as the team moved on to Detroit, he suffered what might have been a nervous breakdown, publicly berating pitcher Joe Page on the airplane, ranting to coaches, belittling his team to reporters, and yelling at a cab driver. He spent another day in his hotel room before leaving the team again for Buffalo. The next day, May 24, he sent MacPhail a letter of resignation.[59]

"I came back," he said, a year and a half later, "because baseball is in my blood."[60] Many observers believed that McCarthy needed to straighten out all of the overly coddled Red Sox players. The press often criticized Yawkey for his excessive generosity, like his bonuses after the 1946 Series loss, and Cronin for allowing the players, especially Ted Williams, to set their own rules. McCarthy soon announced that he would "treat Ted Williams like any other player." The press, for the most part, was skeptical.[61]

10 General Manager

THE WORKING PRESS AROUND THE RED SOX was not surprised when Joe Cronin became general manager in October 1947. "Those of us who have traveled with the Red Sox during the last two seasons," wrote the local *Christian Science Monitor*, "have been aware of Joe's yearning to settle in the front office, where he could be near his family most of the summer instead of hopping around the American League on Pullmans and planes."[1] After attending the 1947 World Series with Mildred, Joe returned home and took a vacation—golf and fishing at his new home on Cape Cod.

Cronin's official title was "general manager," and after one year in that job he also took on the duties of team treasurer. For the previous fifteen years he had focused on managing a team on the field; now he was responsible for the farm system, the upkeep of Fenway Park, the spring training site, player contracts, the team's finances, and the club's radio and television contracts, among many other things. Besides manager Joe McCarthy, much of the front office reported to Cronin in his small and sparse office space in Fenway Park[2]: an assistant general manager, an assistant treasurer, a farm director, a secretary, and a road secretary.[3] Cronin loved to work and quickly dove into his new role.

During Cronin's tenure in the Red Sox front office, he usually followed one of two schedules. During his children's school year he spent the day at Fenway Park, going home to Newton at the end of the day or after the ballgame if there was a night game. During the summer months, June through August, while the rest of his family lived in their house on the Cape, Cronin would spend the week in Newton and go to Osterville for the weekend. If the team was on the road, Cronin would sit in his den at home smoking cigars and listening to the game on the radio. Never missing a pitch, he kept up a constant chatter with the radio, advising what the pitcher should throw or what the batter should do next. "You did not interrupt Dad during a baseball game," remembered his daughter Maureen.[4]

Upon hiring his new manager, Cronin declared that McCarthy would have complete control of all personnel matters, including trades.[5] In reality the two worked together, and then Cronin talked to other clubs to try to get the players McCarthy wanted. At any rate all trades were announced by Cronin, and McCarthy always gave his boss the credit when a trade was consummated. They had plenty of opportunity to talk in their first few months together, among the busiest periods of dealing in Red Sox history.

On November 17 Cronin made his first public appearance as Red Sox general manager, announcing a blockbuster deal with the St. Louis Browns. The Red Sox sent the Browns infielder Eddie Pellagrini, catcher Roy Partee, four Minor Leaguers, and $310,000. In return, the Red Sox received just two players—star shortstop Vern Stephens and pitcher Jack Kramer. The very next day Cronin announced another deal with the Browns, sending three Minor Leaguers and $65,000 for pitcher Ellis Kinder and infielder Billy Hitchcock. The Browns had finished dead last in the league in 1947 and also had lost a lot of money renovating Sportsman's Park. Richard Muckerman, the franchise's president, told a local paper, "One check alone from Tom Yawkey pulled the Browns out of the fire."[6]

The Browns may have been out of the fire, but they had just surrendered their two biggest winners from 1947—Kramer and Kinder—as well as their best player. Stephens, just twenty-seven, had played in four All-Star Games and led the league in runs batted in 1944 and in home runs in 1945. He was also outstanding defensively. "As a shortstop, I rate Stephens right up with Lou Boudreau of the Indians who is the best in our league," said Cronin, adding, "Kramer is one of the best pitchers in the American League."[7] The acquisition of Stephens was particularly interesting because the Red Sox already had All-Star shortstop Johnny Pesky. "Stephens, of course, will be the Red Sox 1948 third baseman," one writer allowed at the press conference announcing the deal. "Joe McCarthy will decide that," Cronin reminded him.[8] Nonetheless, most of the media wrote matter of factly about Stephens moving to third base throughout the winter.

"Stephens was the key man," Cronin recalled several years later. "We had tried several times to get him because he was a right-handed slugger who had the range of our left field fence. We'd wanted him for the same reason we'd wanted [Rudy] York two years before—as a power hitter to follow Williams."[9] Stephens had always hit well at Fenway Park, batting .324 with 13 home runs in only sixty-one games prior to the trade.[10]

In Boston there was much enthusiasm about the deals. "You fellows will have plenty to write about down in Florida," said McCarthy, "and Joe Cronin has certainly helped a situation [the pitching staff] that did not look too promising." Cronin's predecessor concurred. "I hope you appreciate what a whale of a job Joe did in putting over this deal," Eddie Collins said.[11] The other clubs in the league, especially New York and Cleveland, were less pleased. The Yankees had tried to acquire Kramer and Stephens in June for a package of players that included shortstop Phil Rizzuto.[12] The Indians had recently offered Boudreau for Stephens and others.[13]

Having consummated his first two trades, Cronin and his family spent the Thanksgiving holiday in Washington with the Griffith family. Now that he was running the franchise, it could be expected that Cronin and Griffith discussed trades during their family holiday. Rumors soon sprang up that Mickey Vernon, a first baseman the Red Sox undoubtedly coveted, could end up in Boston. After the holiday Cronin hooked up with McCarthy, and the two men, working together after fifteen years as opponents, headed to Miami for the Minor League meetings, then up to New York for the Major League meetings.

On December 10 Cronin announced another deal, and it was indeed with Griffith. Boston gave up outfielder Leon Culberson and Minor League second baseman Al Kozar for outfielder Stan Spence. Kozar, who had hit .339 for New Orleans in 1947, was considered a bright prospect. "If we didn't have Bobby Doerr at second base," said Cronin, "we'd never let Kozar get away from us." Culberson had started throughout the war for the Red Sox but had lost most of his playing time in the two years since. Spence was an underappreciated star—discarded by Boston in 1941, he had put together four All-Star seasons with Washington as a fine fielding center fielder who hit with power and patience at the plate.

Again, the rest of the league was not thrilled with the Spence deal. "I'm tired of the whole thing," complained Cleveland owner Bill Veeck. "For two years I've been trying to get Spence and every offer I made to Washington was considerably better than the one the Senators accepted from Boston today." Billy Evans, general manager of the Tigers, said he never even had a chance to make a bid on Spence. The Yankees were still licking their wounds from the Browns deals.[14]

Cronin shot back, especially at Veeck's charges of nepotism by Griffith. "Veeck is just talking for the Cleveland public. There's so much ham in him that he likes to bathe in the spotlight, like the Hollywood actors he emulates in the way he dresses. Griff isn't showing anybody favors—especially in the matter of deals. He's still in business himself."[15] The Senators were equally defensive. "If Kozar doesn't make it, I'll never believe in the opinion of baseball men again," said Washington manager Joe Kuhel.[16]

After the winter meetings Cronin returned home to Newton to bask in the glow of his improved ballclub and spend time with his family. Unfortunately, he soon had to deal with accidents to two of his three children. On December 14 Cronin was walking home from church with his son Tommy, when the child ran ahead into the road and was struck by a car. Tommy suffered cuts and bruises but no serious harm. The very next day, with Tommy still in the hospital, daughter Maureen fell down a flight of stairs at their home. Thankfully, all the Cronin children were in one piece in time to celebrate the holidays.[17]

Although many baseball men would chafe at all of the glad handing and personal appearances required of a general manager of a popular civic institution like the Red Sox, Joe Cronin was not one of them. Cronin had always done more than his share of appearances on behalf of the team, in addition to the rubber-chicken circuit of banquets and dinners that most baseball people deal with every winter. He reveled

1. The starting infield for the Sacred Heart club that won San Francisco's prep school championship in 1924. Cronin, second from left, was the shortstop and captain. National Baseball Hall of Fame Library, Cooperstown, New York.

2. Cronin spent three years in the Pittsburgh system
before being discarded in 1928. He was not yet good
enough to crack the strong Pirate lineups of this period.
National Baseball Hall of Fame Library, Cooperstown,
New York.

3. Clark Griffith was the greatest influence in Joe's life, on and off the field. National Baseball Hall of Fame Library, Cooperstown, New York.

4. (*Above*) Cronin was acquired by the Senators in 1928 mainly for his defense. National Baseball Hall of Fame Library, Cooperstown, New York.

5. (*Right*) By 1929 he was one of the better hitting shortstops in the league. The following year he was the league's Most Valuable Player. National Baseball Hall of Fame Library, Cooperstown, New York.

6. (*Left*) After the 1932 season, the twenty-six-year-old Cronin was named the Senators' manager, and he led them to a pennant in his first try. The Brace Collection.

7. (*Above*) Cronin scampers into third base at Griffith Stadium. Courtesy of the Boston Red Sox.

8. (*Above*) Cronin met Mildred Robertson, Griffith's niece, the day he reported for duty with the Senators in 1928. After a long courtship, they married after the 1934 season. National Baseball Hall of Fame Library, Cooperstown, New York.

9. (*Right*) While on his honeymoon, Cronin was sold for $250,000 to the Red Sox, whose young and wealthy owner Tom Yawkey was rebuilding a dying franchise. Cronin would play shortstop and manage the club. Courtesy of the Boston Red Sox.

10. Despite the great effort here, Cronin had defensive
difficulties in his early days with the Red Sox. Courtesy
of the Boston Red Sox.

11. Cronin is pictured here with Cleveland manager Walter Johnson, for whom Joe had played and starred for four years in Washington. Courtesy of the Boston Public Library, Print Department.

12. Cronin also regressed as a hitter in the mid-1930s.
The Brace Collection.

13. Joe Cronin at rest. The Brace Collection.

14. (*Above*) Johnny Marcum, Jimmie Foxx, Cronin, Wes
Ferrell, and Lefty Grove. Cronin had his difficulties in
Boston with several veteran players, especially Ferrell
and Grove. Courtesy of the Boston Red Sox.

15. (*Right*) Tom Yawkey and his manager in the early
days of their partnership. Courtesy of the Boston Red
Sox.

16. (*Above*) The Red Sox 1938 infield: Bobby Doerr, Cronin, Mike Higgins, and Jimmie Foxx. Cronin came back strong as a hitter in the late 1930s. Courtesy of the Boston Red Sox.

17. (*Right*) As the temperamental veterans were replaced by youngsters who respected their manager, Cronin's life became much easier. National Baseball Hall of Fame Library, Cooperstown, New York.

18. Cronin at Fenway Park with Yankee first baseman
Lou Gehrig. Courtesy of the Boston Public Library,
Print Department.

19. Friends and rivals: Cronin and Joe McCarthy. The
two would work together in the late 1940s, with mixed
results. Courtesy of the Boston Public Library, Print
Department.

20. (*Above*) Cronin's biggest frustration in the prewar years was the club's inability to develop young pitchers. Here Joe poses with Jake Wade and Denny Galehouse in 1939. Courtesy of the Boston Red Sox.

21. (*Right*) Ted Williams joined the club in 1939 and dominated the baseball scene in Boston for two decades. Courtesy of the Boston Public Library, Print Department.

22. Cronin teaches in Sarasota 1941. Bobby Doerr is in
the back row, second from left. Tex Hughson is in the
back row, far right. Courtesy of the Boston Red Sox.

23. Cronin with Philadelphia manager Connie Mack.
Mack thought Cronin the greatest clutch hitter he ever
saw. Courtesy of the Boston Red Sox.

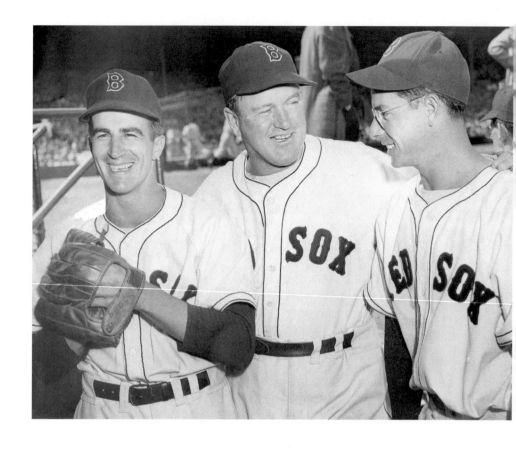

24. Cronin pictured with two of his young
stars—Johnny Pesky, who took Cronin's job, and
Dominic DiMaggio, who Cronin scouted and signed
himself. Courtesy of the Boston Red Sox.

25. In 1946, after the war, Cronin finally had himself a
pitching staff. Here he is with Dave "Boo" Ferriss and
Mickey Harris. Courtesy of the Boston Red Sox.

26. Cronin at Fenway Park talking with his wife,
Mildred, and Elise Yawkey, Tom's first wife. Courtesy of
the Boston Public Library, Print Department.

27. After the 1947 season Cronin took off the uniform
and became the club's general manager for eleven
years. Courtesy of the Boston Public Library, Print
Department.

28. (*Above*) In the 1950s the Red Sox held an annual camp for youngsters before spring training. At the 1952 camp, Jimmie Piersall (fourth from left) began the spiral that led to his famous breakdown that summer. Courtesy of the Boston Red Sox.

29. (*Right*) Cronin hired Mike Higgins to manage the club in 1955. Higgins remains a controversial figure in Boston. Courtesy of the Boston Public Library, Print Department.

30. (*Left*) Cronin spent much of twenty years with Ted Williams, and the two emerged as close friends despite numerous Williams incidents. Courtesy of the Boston Red Sox.

31. (*Above*) Joe participated in many Old-Timers games over the years. Here he is hitting off Lefty Grove in 1956. Courtesy of the Boston Red Sox.

32. (*Left*) In 1959 Cronin became the American League's president, a job he held for fifteen years. National Baseball Hall of Fame Library, Cooperstown, New York.

33. (*Above*) Cronin throwing out the first ball before a 1967 World Series game in Fenway Park. Also pictured are Gov. John A. Volpe (smiling to Cronin's right), Bobby Doerr (a coach with the Red Sox), Mildred Cronin, and Maureen Cronin (their daughter). Courtesy of the Boston Red Sox.

34. Joe loved giving out awards, something he did often
as league president. Here he hands some hardware to
Red Sox outfielder Reggie Smith in 1969. Courtesy of
the Boston Red Sox.

35. In retirement, Joe was a regular visitor to spring training camps. He poses in the late 1970s with old friend Ted Williams, Red Sox hitting instructor. Courtesy of the Boston Red Sox.

in this sort of thing and eagerly jumped into his new social duties his first winter. A glance at his January 1948 calendar shows that on the seventh, he spoke at a ceremony for the departure of a ship sailing from Boston to Glasgow, filled with food, clothing, and relief supplies for the people of Scotland. The next day he hosted the Boston press for a showing of a baseball promotional film. On the twenty-second he spoke at the Massachusetts State House against Robert Murphy, who was testifying to the unfairness of the baseball contract system. On January 26 Cronin received a gold key at a dinner in New Haven, Connecticut. On January 27 he hosted a lunch for the press at a local restaurant officially welcoming McCarthy as the new manager. On January 29 he accepted an award on behalf of the absent Ted Williams at the annual Boston baseball writers' dinner. There were undoubtedly additional dinners and appearances, including small press briefings every time a player signed his 1948 contract.[18]

Although Cronin had his critics in the Boston press concerning his skills as a manager and later as a general manager, he remained universally liked. As a manager Cronin did not mind sitting with the press and talking about his team as much as they wanted. He would make predictions about the season, talk about other clubs, muse on possible lineups, or speculate about potential rookies with his club. Whenever a local writer wanted to criticize one of Cronin's decisions, he invariably would begin by pointing out what a nice fellow Cronin was.

Joe McCarthy could not have been more different. He considered his dealings with the press to be a nuisance and didn't tell the writers anything he didn't have to. Ed Barrow, his long-time boss in New York, was always closed-mouthed with the press and wanted his manager to behave the same way. McCarthy was happy to oblige, and as the championships continued to pile up, the New York writers accepted the reticence of management as an unfortunate part of covering the club.

McCarthy's personality was a poor match for the Boston writers, who were antagonistic by nature but counted on Cronin to give them material for their papers. McCarthy, when asked about his lineup, might

say, "You will find out in plenty of time." He would answer questions
with "Yes" and "No," and if he wanted to speak to his players in the
clubhouse or on the practice field, he would ask the media to leave.
The writers, accustomed to Cronin's relaxed and open relationship
with them, were offended.[19] McCarthy discontinued the traditional
daily press briefings in the spring, instead getting the press together
only when he had something he felt he had to say. Ed Rumill, who
covered the Red Sox for Boston's *Christian Science Monitor* for forty
years, recalled that Cronin had allowed him to put on a uniform and
work out with team beginning in 1936—Rumill would feed balls to the
pitcher during batting practice. When Cronin became general manager,
he informed Rumill that his days in uniform must end—McCarthy
would not want a writer on the field.[20]

One of the ironies of the regime change was the relationship between
McCarthy and Ted Williams. The press hoped and assumed that
McCarthy would straighten out the incorrigible star. But the writers'
beef with Williams had little to do with how he performed his job—it
had to do with how he treated the writers. McCarthy, speaking years
later about Williams, recalled, "Williams was no problem. . . . He
played. He hustled; followed orders. He followed orders perfectly."[21]
This is consistent with Cronin's recollections of Williams. The difference is that McCarthy and Williams more or less agreed about
the press, and so McCarthy made no effort to help the press with
Williams. Williams spoke glowingly of Cronin his entire life, but this
is the one area where Williams did criticize his former manager—he
wished that Cronin had stood up for him more with the Boston writers in his early years.[22]

As a result of McCarthy's reticence with the media, the writers
went to Cronin to ask, for example, where Stan Spence was going
to play or who the third baseman would be. Cronin appropriately
deferred all such matters to McCarthy, but the manager would answer,
"You let me worry about that."[23] The relationship between the team
and the writers soon unraveled and did not recover until long after
McCarthy left.

Joe Cronin arrived in Sarasota a couple of weeks after training camp opened, allowing McCarthy the freedom to organize the players' routine. The change in managers, and all of the new players, created an air of excitement that had been missing during the disappointing 1947 season. Many observers, including Bill Veeck on his Cleveland radio show, had anointed the Red Sox as American League favorites. "The Red Sox will be 40% improved," said Veeck. "Joe McCarthy is 20% a better manager than any manager in the league. Last year Joe Cronin was 20% the worst manager. Twenty and 20 makes 40."[24] In a similar vein, old friend Bobo Newsom predicted a Boston pennant. "They've finally got Poppa Joe up in the business office where he belongs—if there," offered the always friendly Bobo.[25]

Observers noted that the Red Sox training camp was much more organized than in past years. Players were required to be at specific places at specific times, drills were run precisely and repeatedly until perfected, players had to run everywhere. Card playing and the telephone were banned in the clubhouse. So was shaving—if players wanted to shave, they could do so at home. The players had to adjust, and most of them did. Williams, Pesky, Doerr, DiMaggio—they all respected McCarthy and looked forward to playing for him. They wanted to win, and McCarthy's ways had worked in New York.[26]

Writer Arthur Daley noted some changes in the Joe Cronin of 1948. "Cronin now looks like an oil tycoon who hasn't taken a lick of exercise in twenty years," wrote Daley of the forty-one-year-old general manager. "He wears flashy sports clothes, a Panama hat, a big cigar and about twenty extra pounds of avoirdupois. He wears them all elegantly. But success hasn't turned his head. He's still the same genial and delightful character he always was. The former pilot knows a great deal more about the hired hands than the present one."[27]

Ever since the acquisition of Stephens, the writers had speculated about what McCarthy would do with his two star shortstops. Cronin said it was up to McCarthy, and McCarthy said he'd figure it out in the spring. In early March McCarthy decided to move Pesky to third base. Harold Kaese wrote that Stephens had "won the battle" for the position because he was one of the best fielding shortstops in baseball. Like Cronin Stephens did not look like a shortstop—he was a big powerful man, and he hit like a big man. He did not have the quickness of Pesky, but he made up for it by playing deep and using his great arm.[28] Cronin played this way himself, though Stephens was less erratic and never had to battle the weight problems that Cronin did. Pesky better fit the shortstop mold, but Cronin had moved him to third for a month in 1947 in favor of Eddie Pellagrini. Pesky had been out of shape in 1947 and had had a poor defensive season.[29]

When McCarthy announced the move he said only that Pesky had quick hands, and he thought he could handle third base—treating the shift as a promotion for Pesky, rather than a demotion. McCarthy also recalled, for the benefit of the gathered writers, moving Red Rolfe from shortstop to third base in New York, in deference to Frank Crosetti, and the Yankees subsequent four championships with the two players side-by-side. This recollection did not help matters, as the writers were already sensitive to McCarthy talking about the Yankees all the time. The press wanted to learn about who was pitching tomorrow, not how Red Ruffing used to throw his curveball. The tension continued.

Joe Cronin tried to stay out of the way as much as possible and spent a lot of the month at the Red Sox Minor League camp in Melbourne, across the state on the Atlantic Ocean.[30] Cronin's former players later recalled that they rarely saw Cronin after he became general manager, other than at contract time. In deference to McCarthy, he rarely came into the clubhouse or onto the field.[31] To cement the transition Cronin tried to get McCarthy to wear Cronin's old number 4 on his uniform, but McCarthy chose to wear no number, as he had done with the Yankees.

Cronin returned to Boston before spring training ended and was there to meet Ted Williams when the star returned to Boston with appendicitis. Cronin communicated with McCarthy every day, keeping his manager updated on Williams's daily workouts at Fenway Park. Rather than managing ballgames, Cronin was trying to work out a new television contract in cooperation with the Boston Braves.[32]

As the Red Sox prepared to play the 1948 season, many agreed that their new GM had put together an excellent team. With Stephens and

Spence joining Pesky, Doerr, Williams, and DiMaggio, the club had six recent All-Stars among their eight position players. Not to mention their new manager, winner of nine pennants and seven World Series. Most writers felt that the Red Sox had again passed the Yankees, the 1947 champions, in the race for supremacy of the American League.

The nagging concern was the pitching staff. Kramer and Kinder had had some success with the Browns, but they were by no means stars. Dobson was their best returning pitcher, and Ferriss appeared ready to start the season, but both Hughson and Harris were still hurt. Earl Johnson and Denny Galehouse were solid Major Leaguers, but neither was an ace. There were rumors in the spring that Cronin had offered Pesky to the Senators for Early Wynn, and Dom DiMaggio was also reportedly available.[33]

The season did not start well. After dropping their first three games at Fenway to the Philadelphia Athletics, the club finished April with a record of 3-6. At the end of May, the club was 14-23 and in seventh place in the eight-team league, trailing the surprising Athletics. Kramer and Kinder both started slowly, Ferriss seemed healthy but had lost his control, and Tex Hughson, the team's star just two seasons ago, was sent to a Class-B team in Austin, Texas. Cronin hoped that the warm weather would help Hughson's arm. When Hughson arrived in Austin, he jokingly wired Cronin: "Thanks for sending me to a winning club."[34]

In late May the *Boston Post* received a petition demanding the removal of McCarthy as manager and the return of Cronin to the dugout. "A state of emergency exists," cited the notice, and it would be in the best interests of all Red Sox fans if the switch was made. The *Boston Globe*'s Harold Kaese, who had blamed Cronin for the Red Sox problems before the war, now came to McCarthy's defense, blaming instead all of the stars—especially Stephens, Pesky, Doerr and Spence—who were not hitting. "The Red Sox are not as good as we thought they were," wrote Kaese.[35] Cronin himself conceded nothing. "You know we aren't as bad as we've looked," he said.[36]

Kaese did allow: "the only doubt over McCarthy's leadership concerns his ability to stand up to the pressure of defeat, mediocrity, and needling by the critics."[37] In fact, McCarthy was apparently on the verge of resigning. He had taken over a supposed juggernaut and was fighting to stay out of the cellar. During a long road trip in late May during which the Red Sox lost twelve of sixteen games, Cronin met the club in Washington and spent most of the next four days with McCarthy. Cronin came not to put pressure on his manager, but to relieve it. When McCarthy felt pressure, he drank. He was drinking now.

As uncomfortable as McCarthy's relationship with the press often was, the mores of the time kept his drinking out of the papers. "Even in his great days with the Yankees," Ed Linn later wrote, "he would disappear for days on end and be found in some seedy hotel lying in his own bodily wastes. To explain his absence, the Yankees would announce that he had gone to his farm near Buffalo to recover from an attack of bursitis." In fact, McCarthy had left the Yankees for the first several weeks of the 1944 season, supposedly with "polyneuritis,"[38] and again for three weeks in 1945 with "a stomach and nervous disorder."[39] Beginning about 1940, he occasionally left the team for shorter trips to Buffalo, generally because his "gall bladder was acting up again."[40]

In May 1948 in Washington, Joe Cronin apparently pulled McCarthy out of some similar illness. According to the *Post's* Al Hirshberg, "McCarthy was going crazy, and so was everyone else." Cronin soothed his friend's mood, gave him assurances about the club and his own abilities, and drove back to Boston.[41] The club continued its desultory trip for another few days, then returned home and turned its season around. After an 18-6 record in June the Red Sox had climbed to fourth, six and a half games behind the Philadelphia Athletics. They were still six and a half games back when they began their longest home stand of the season on July 15, a sixteen-game stand spread over just eleven days playing the four western clubs. Remarkably, they won fifteen of the sixteen games, including five doubleheader sweeps. After finishing a series sweep of the Indians on July 25, the Red Sox were in first place. They had made up more than ten games in six weeks.

Hirshberg credited Cronin for the turnaround. The GM had built the foundation of the team, hired McCarthy, and gone out and greatly improved the club. He had shepherded McCarthy around town to ease his transition with the public and press over the winter. Finally and critically, he had personally seen his manager through the crisis in May. "Joe Cronin loves McCarthy as a father and sometimes treats him as a son," wrote Hirshberg. "He took control not of the ball club, but of McCarthy."[42]

McCarthy continued to drink even when the team won. Linn described a game in September of 1948, during the heat of the pennant race, when McCarthy showed up to a game in St. Louis drunk out of his mind and spent the day flashing inappropriate signs, berating his players, and wandering aimlessly out of the dugout if not carefully guarded.[43] Looking back after several decades, one has to wonder how this affected his team.

Meanwhile, the Red Sox continued their blistering pace, finishing 25-9 in July, 19-10 in August, and 18-10 in September. They could not let up because the two teams who remained in the race—Cleveland and New York—stayed right with them in one of the greatest races in Major League history. In the end Boston beat the Yankees in the final two games of the season to eliminate New York and force a tie with the Indians. In the playoff at Fenway Park on October 4, the Indians beat the Red Sox, 8–3, with Indians player-manager Lou Boudreau getting four hits including two home runs. McCarthy famously started journeyman hurler Denny Galehouse in the playoff game, one of the more controversial decisions in team history. The Red Sox finished 96-59, playing well over .700 during the final four months, but the playoff loss was a heartbreaking way to end the season.

True to his word, whatever influence Cronin had on the 1948 team was off the field, and for the most part, Cronin's name was absent from the sports pages during the historic pennant race. He attended home games when he was in the city but did not go into the clubhouse or talk with the players. In late June he attended a game in Hartford to scout Scranton's Willard Nixon, who the Red Sox had just signed, and he visited other Minor League affiliates throughout the summer.[44] In August he attended a celebration in Washington honoring Clark Griffith for his sixty years in the game, joined by many players from the Senators' three pennant-winning teams as well as President Truman.[45]

Of Cronin's off-season acquisitions, Vern Stephens was a big success, driving in 137 runs while playing every inning of the season at shortstop. Stan Spence was a big disappointment, hitting just .235. He lost the first base job to Billy Goodman but later took over right field from Sam Mele. Jack Kramer finished 18-5, though his 4.35 ERA suggests he had a little help from his offense. Ellis Kinder started slowly but joined the rotation in midsummer and won ten games down the stretch.

Cronin did not need to fortify the team during the season, as most of the stars stayed healthy and productive. When Bobby Doerr suffered a charley horse and missed two weeks in early September, Billy Hitchcock filled in. When Hitchcock, too, got hurt, Cronin purchased Lou Stringer from Hollywood. Tom Yawkey was reportedly upset when he learned that his farm system did not contain a middle infielder who could fill in for a few days.[46]

Immediately after the season Cronin had to deny rumors that McCarthy would not return. "You can shout it from the rooftops that McCarthy is here to stay and did a grand job as leader of the Boston club this year," Cronin said.[47] He did call in all of his staff and Minor League managers and general managers for an organizational review. Cronin replaced farm director George Toporcer with Johnny Murphy, who had pitched for the team in 1947 before becoming Toporcer's assistant in 1948. McCarthy hired Kiki Cuyler and Johnny Shulte as coaches, replacing Del Baker and Larry Woodall. Cronin's top assistant, Phil Troy, was cashiered in favor of Dick O'Connell. For the next several years, Cronin focused much of his energy on directing the Minor League system and player development.

After the World Series, Cronin traveled to San Francisco for a three-week visit with his father and brother James (Raymond had passed away in 1940) and to see some old friends. Jeremiah had traveled East in 1946 for the World Series, but by 1948 had not been well for some time. Joe had returned to Boston by early November, but when his father took a turn for the worse, on February 5 Cronin boarded a train for the coast. Disembarking in Chicago to call his brother, he learned his father was failing quickly. Cronin caught the next plane to San Francisco and arrived just in time to see his father pass away on February 6.[48] Cronin had been close to both his parents but did not often return to San Francisco after his father died.

The Red Sox made very few changes to their Major League personnel that off-season. Yawkey felt that he had opened his wallet the previous year to secure the team's missing pieces and that the farm system now needed to produce its own players.[49] In actuality the team's system had been churning out prospects at a fairly impressive rate. Billy Goodman hit .310 as a rookie first baseman, while Mel Parnell, in his first full season after a trial in 1947, won fifteen games. Of the starting eight players in 1948, only Stephens and catcher Birdie Tebbetts had been developed by other teams. At any rate the Red Sox had another crop of young pitchers—Mickey McDermott, Chuck Stobbs, and Willard Nixon, among others—they hoped would supplement the rotation in 1949. Walt Dropo, the hulking six feet five, 220-pound first baseman from Moosup, Connecticut, had hit .359 for Birmingham in 1948 and seemed ready to take over at first base.

The Red Sox again made a pitch for Washington hurler Early Wynn in November, offering Johnny Pesky, but (despite Cronin's supposed advantage with Griffith) the Indians nabbed Wynn in a five-player swap. Another rumor had Cronin offering the Browns Pesky for third baseman Bob Dillinger, a deal many local fans supported.[50] In any event Cronin did not make a single player transaction the entire off-season. Instead, he mainly made news when announcing that a player had signed his contract, generally a formality in those reserve-clause days. Dom DiMaggio, often the toughest sign, was a brief holdout but came to terms at the start of spring camp. Ted Williams signed the first $100,000 contract, while suggesting he would retire after the 1951 season. At the brief photo session to formally announce Williams's signing, Cronin joked with his star, "You look like you could use a few steaks." Williams comeback: "You look like you had too many."[51] He likely had.

Although his front-office duties were keeping Cronin plenty busy, it was not the kind of work that keeps a man in fine physical condition. He had struggled with his weight for the last half of his playing career and was often said to be thirty pounds overweight heading into spring training. Without daily exercise, his weight continued to rise. In January *The Sporting News* told of a day that Cronin and Tom Dowd, the team's traveling secretary, had decided to walk part of the four-mile trip from the team's office to Newton, where both men lived. Dowd's wife would pick them up at some point en route, on Commonwealth Avenue. When Mrs. Dowd finally showed up, three miles into the trip, Cronin was so tired he had to be helped into her car. He was forty-two years old, and four years removed from being a professional athlete.[52]

Throughout Joe Cronin's eleven-year tenure as Red Sox GM, he took on more and more responsibility in league or baseballwide matters. His first role outside the Red Sox came as a member of baseball's Rules Committee in 1949. On this committee he joined fellow general managers Branch Rickey (Dodgers) and James Gallagher (Cubs); Commissioner Happy Chandler and Secretary-Treasurer Walter Mulbry; National Association president George Trautman (chairman); and umpires Bill Summers, Bill Stewart, and Tom Connolly. The function of this group was ostensibly to discuss and rule on possible changes to baseball's playing rules, something that often involved a get-together following baseball's winter meetings and a few meetings or conference calls during the year.[53]

In 1949, however, the playing rules were completely rewritten, the first extensive revamping since their creation in 1904. The effort was undertaken at the urging of Chandler, who formed a subcommittee consisting of Cronin, National League president Warren Giles, and International League president Frank Shaughnessy. These three men held several meetings in the spring and summer, reorganizing the rule book into more logical sections and rewording every rule. They submitted a proposal to the full committee in November, and the entire body again went over the book line by line until coming to an agreement in December.

Whereas the old rule book consisted of one list of seventy-two rules (Rule 1: "The Ball Ground must be enclosed . . .") with no sections or chapters, the new rule book logically arranged the rules into ten sections. Section 1 was the "Objectives of the Game, the Playing Field, and Equipment." Rule 1.02 stated, "The Object of each team is to win by scoring the most runs"—not a new idea surely, but one never formally placed in the rule book before. Each rule in the new book also listed the rules in the old book that the rule replaced.[54] The reorganization of the rule book, which occupied much of Cronin's time in 1949, largely remains in place at this writing.

Although the intent of the revision was to make the rules easier to understand, there were also new rules put in place governing the size of fielding gloves, the height of the pitcher's mound (fifteen inches), and the strike zone (the top of the knees to the armpits).[55] An attempt to add stricter penalties for take-out slides around second base was successfully rebutted by Cronin, a man who knew a thing or two about the subject. "The shortstop or second baseman who gets to the big leagues ought to know how to protect himself," said Cronin. "If they get hurt, it's their own fault. And anyway, the play at second base and the blocking at the plate are the only claims we have to being a contact sport."[56] The new rules, and the new rule book, were in place at the start of the 1950 season.

Once again, the star-laden Boston Red Sox were slow getting out of the gate to start the 1949 season. After losing their first two games in Philadelphia, the club stumbled through April, winning just five of eleven games. By June 16 they were 25-27, nine games behind the Yankees and in sixth place. Several players counted on to hit had struggled, and Cronin was forced to find reinforcements. Walt Dropo had broken camp as the first baseman, but he hit just .146 in eleven games. The club sent him to Sacramento and reinstated Goodman. Stan Spence, reacquired with some fanfare a year earlier, followed up a disappointing 1948 by starting just 3 for 20. In early May, Spence was traded to the Browns, along with some cash, for right fielder Al Zarilla. Sam Mele, never a favorite of McCarthy's, was hitting .196 in early June when he was dealt along with Mickey Harris for pitcher Walt Masterson.

Thus fortified, the club won ten of eleven games to get within five games of the Yankees, just in time for New York's visit to Fenway Park on June 28. The Yankees won all three contests, sending their rivals into an eventual eight-game losing streak. After sweeping the Red Sox in a July 4 doubleheader to widen the gap to twelve games, Yankee manager Casey Stengel suggested that the Red Sox were finished. "They'll never recover from this blow," opined the Professor.[57] But recover they did. Just six weeks later, the Red Sox, behind a 33-9 run, had cut the lead to two and a half games. Remarkably, the club maintained this blistering pace for six more weeks then beat the Yankees three straight times in late September to pull ahead by a game. The Red Sox still held this slim lead heading into the final weekend, but they lost their final two games in New York. The Red Sox had finished 61-22 in their final eighty-three games, which was one victory too few.

The Red Sox offense once again sported glittering statistics. Ted Williams came within one hit of winning his third triple crown, finishing with 43 home runs, 159 runs batted in, and a .343 average. Vern Stephens tied Williams for the RBI crown, while hitting 39 home runs, a record at the time for a shortstop. Doerr hit 18 homers and drove in 109; Dom DiMaggio scored 126 runs, Pesky 111. On the pitching side, the team was led by great performances from Ellis Kinder and Mel Parnell. Parnell finished 25-7 and Kinder 23-6, the latter not entering the rotation fully until midseason. These two hurlers went 31-4 after July 4 to help propel the Red Sox furious drive for the pennant. Alas, two of their four losses came on consecutive days in New York, those final two days of the season.

It is the nature of sports that second-place teams are analyzed for what went wrong rather than what went right, and the Red Sox of the late 1940s have been written about as much as any second-place team in baseball history. They became the first team to win ninety-six or more games two years in a row without winning a pennant (and then won ninety-four games in 1950, establishing another "record" for nonwinners). The previous best multiyear also-ran was the 1930–32 Senators, managed by Walter Johnson and starring Joe Cronin, who won ninety-four, ninety-two, and ninety-three games in successive years.

In David Halberstam's fine book about the season, Tommy Henrich (speaking to Bobby Doerr) theorized that the Yankees won because they were hungrier. "We needed the extra money from the World Series check," said Henrich. "That was our extra salary. You guys were making more money than us because of Yawkey."[58] Unfortunately for this theory, the Yankees almost certainly paid their players more than the Red Sox did. Although we don't have 1949 payrolls, we do have them for 1950 when the two rosters were largely unchanged. According to records released to a U.S. House Subcommittee in 1952, the Yankees' 1950 player payroll was $651,605, about 15 percent higher than the Red Sox's $561,482.[59]

In reality, the principal difference between the two clubs was much more mundane—the Red Sox had no useful bench or bullpen and a soft rotation after Parnell, Kinder, and Dobson.[60] Asked decades later for the reasons the Red Sox lost in 1949, Birdie Tebbetts was brief. "I'll give you the answer in two words," said Tebbetts. "Joe Page."[61] Page had thrown sixty games and 135 innings of relief for the New York Yankees, including 5 shutout innings in the penultimate game. The Red Sox did not have a reliable bullpen stopper, let alone someone as good as Page. Bobby Doerr thought the club would have won with Cronin at the helm. "I really do," said Doerr in 2007. "What we needed most in those years was a relief pitcher, and [Cronin] would have gotten one. McCarthy thought he could do without one and it cost us."[62]

As for roster depth, whereas the Yankees had Johnny Mize on their bench that final weekend, when Joe McCarthy needed someone to hit for Ellis Kinder on October 2, he turned to Tom Wright, who had just four previous Major League plate appearances. Although Cronin was the general manager and must be held somewhat accountable for the deficient roster, McCarthy apparently called the shots in this area. McCarthy had had success in New York with reliever Johnny Murphy and deep rosters, but for whatever reason did not have a deep team in Boston.

Despite persistent rumors throughout the 1949 season that Joe McCarthy was again on the verge of quitting,[63] he made it through the season. Based on the club's great play over the second half, Cronin and Yawkey both wanted McCarthy back, and he signed a new two-year deal on October 31. "Tom and I are very happy that Joe McCarthy decided to return to the baseball wars," said Cronin. "We both feel he has done an excellent job and will continue to do so.[64]

As for Cronin, he went back to work. He spent the winter coming to the office, meeting with scouts and Minor League officials, attending the Minor League and Major League meetings, and watching sports when he could. In October he sent infielder Billy Hitchcock to the Athletics for catcher Buddy Rosar but made no other changes of substance. The family spent the holidays at their home in Newton, and Cronin's best gift might have been a giant pennant he received from his five-year-old daughter Maureen, emblazoned with the words "1950 Red Sox Pennant."[65]

One of the more noteworthy events every off-season for the Red Sox was the signing of Ted Williams. Players in those days would usually get a contract in the mail and be asked to sign it and return it. The team would then alert the press every few days that a new batch of players had signed their contracts. Williams, the reigning Most Valuable Player, was different. He often was difficult to find in the off-season—he would be off fishing somewhere and not keep in touch with the team until just prior to reporting to Sarasota. Furthermore, his signing would usually require a small press conference, with much speculation as to the size of the contract.

In February 1950 Williams signed his contract, reportedly for as much as $125,000, the largest contract in history. "It's a better contract than I had last year," admitted Williams. "So much that I hope I'm good enough to deserve it." When asked for more details, he pointed at Cronin, and added, "That's all I can say about it. You'll have to ask the fat guy."[66]

Although Cronin expressed satisfaction with McCarthy and Williams, he apparently offered pay cuts to several of his star players, including Ellis Kinder, who had won twenty-three games, and Vern Stephens, who had driven in 159 runs. When it was time to report to training camp, Stephens remained in Long Beach, finally signing in early March, likely for a significant increase.[67] More important for Cronin was the birth of his third son and fourth child, Kevin, on March 10, completing the Cronin family. Mildred's final pregnancy kept her home for much of the winter and kept Cronin in Boston rather than in Sarasota for much of the spring.

Early in the 1950 season the Red Sox set off a firestorm when they announced that writers would not be allowed in the clubhouse before games and would be barred for thirty full minutes after the game. The writers blamed McCarthy, but the edict came at the instigation of the players, who voted overwhelmingly for the ban. The writers, as they often did, appealed to Cronin, who said he'd look into the matter. The players revoted in early May, reaffirming their decision, but on May 5 finally modified the ban to end fifteen minutes after the game.[68]

The Red Sox opened the season in Boston on April 18 and took a 9–0 lead after six innings over the Yankees, only to lose 15–10. "Quick season, wasn't it?" wrote one local scribe.[69] The tough loss notwithstanding, the club began the season playing better than they had in McCarthy's first two seasons, due mainly to historically great hitting. By June 8 the team was 30-19, having scored 10 or more runs twelve times (including 19–0, 20–4 and 29–4 victories). They were still four games behind the Yankees.

One of the season's lowlights came in a May 11 doubleheader loss to the Tigers at Fenway Park. After Ted Williams dropped a short fly ball in the first game, the fans in left field booed the star, who responded with a series of obscene gestures. When he bobbled a ground ball in the second game, the booing intensified, as did Williams's behavior—more vulgar motions with some spitting thrown in. The local press, whose relationship with the team was already at an all-time low, exploded in moral outrage. The *Boston American* was typical, opining that Williams had "removed himself from the ranks of decent sportsmen."[70] A talk with Yawkey and Cronin led to a half-hearted apology, followed by the usual rumored trade demands and denials by all concerned parties.

In mid-June the club slumped, and the mood worsened as they fell farther behind the Yankees and Tigers. The press was increasingly antagonistic, the players were ever more grouchy, and McCarthy was drinking. He skipped an exhibition in Scranton on June 12, instead going home to Buffalo, before joining the club in Cleveland the next day. After losing two of three to the Indians they dropped three more in Detroit. McCarthy was reportedly incapacitated for most of these games. Catcher Matt Batts later claimed that McCarthy was missing for days and found drunk in the street in Detroit, but this is almost certainly not true—he was in the dugout for each of the Tiger games. The club headed for Chicago, but McCarthy did not show up at the ballpark on June 20—reports differ as to whether his absence was voluntary. After the game he headed home to Buffalo, to recover from "an attack of pleurisy."[71] At first he told the press he'd be back in a week, but the next day he said he was through. When he managed his last game on June 18, the Red Sox were in fourth place, 31-28 and nine and a half games behind the first-place Tigers.

Joe Cronin's role in all this is unclear. Pitcher Tex Hughson, who was no longer on the team, later claimed that Cronin had told McCarthy he would be fired if he got drunk again on the job.[72] Cronin was not on the fateful road trip—he was in Hartford scouting Boston's Scranton affiliate, where he was contacted with the news by traveling secretary Tom Dowd. From Hartford he talked to McCarthy, perhaps suggesting his leave become permanent, and called Coach Steve O'Neill to ask him to take over. O'Neill had earlier managed the Indians and Tigers, winning the 1945 World Series with Detroit.

One must pause to consider the role McCarthy played in the ulti-

mately disappointing two and one-half seasons he led the Red Sox.
Most of his Red Sox players—including Williams, Pesky, and Dom
DiMaggio—respected and admired McCarthy and spoke well of him
decades later. A few have criticized him on the record—including
Hughson, Batts, and Jack Kramer. The question for historians is this:
is it possible, or even likely, that a manager who was repeatedly drunk
on the job would cost a team a game somewhere along the line—a
game that would have won them either the 1948 or 1949 pennant?
Doerr later suggested that the Red Sox would have won those pennants
had Cronin been on the bench, though he was thinking more of how
the two men would have managed their rosters. Joe McCarthy won
seven championships with the Yankees and has to be considered one
of history's great managers. But his most serious "health" issues came
after his final championship in 1943. The McCarthy that managed
those final years with the Yankees, or with the Red Sox, might not
have been the same leader who had won all the titles.

McCarthy's team won a lot of games—ninety-six in 1948 and 1949,
and they were over .500 when he quit in 1950. But to observers of
the time the teams were massive underachievers. The first two teams
dug themselves huge holes and came within a whisker of digging
themselves out, though their manager (especially in 1948) seemed
overwhelmed by the pressures of the job. If Cronin indeed acted on
that fateful road trip in 1950, he might have acted too late.

The 1950 club began playing better under Steve O'Neill. Ted
Williams broke his arm when he crashed into the wall in the All-Star
Game, but in his absence the team got even hotter, winning eleven
straight in August to get back in the race. Billy Goodman, who had
chipped a bone in his ankle and subsequently lost his first base job to
Walt Dropo, replaced Williams in left field. Dropo drove in 144 runs
in his first full season, while Goodman, filling in as different players
got hurt, batted .354 and won the batting title.

Williams returned in late September, but the Red Sox could get no
closer than a half game behind the Yankees and ended up four back.
The Red Sox finished a blistering 63-32 under O'Neill but could not
make up the deficit he inherited. They scored 1,027 runs, the last team

to log 1,000 until 1999. Dropo and Stephens each knocked in 144 runs, while Doerr drove in 120 and Williams 97 in just eighty-nine games. After three straight near misses, the core of young stars on the 1946 Red Sox was no longer so young.

Writer Ed Rumill spoke for many when he wrote of the state of the Red Sox after the 1950 season. "They have missed and disappointed again, these expensive, colorful, and generally favored Red Sox," wrote Rumill. "Missed when this time, more than ever before, the crowd thought they would surely break down the intangible and seemingly perennial barrier that has stood between them and the blue ribbon classic of October."[73]

11 Opportunity Lost

IN THE GENERATION BEFORE ITS FIRST AMA-
teur-player draft in 1965, organized baseball made several attempts to
reduce the size of bonus payments to amateur players. Several sizeable bonuses were handed out in the 1930s, arguably beginning with
the $20,000 the Yankees gave to pitcher Charlie Devens in 1932. In
a preview of misspent bonuses to come, Devens won just five games
in his big league career. But the most spectacular bonus contract
before the war was given to Dick Wakefield, a University of Michigan
outfielder to whom the Detroit Tigers gave $52,000 and a new car in
1941. Wakefield had a great year and a half for the Tigers, hitting .316
and .355 in 1943 and 1944, but he entered the service in mid-1944
and never returned to stardom.

The Red Sox had not been particularly active in the early bonus
market. In what was probably their first sizeable outlay, the club gave
$15,000 to Holy Cross pitcher Dick Callahan in 1944. Callahan had
won seventeen consecutive games for the Crusaders, including two
no-hitters. Despite the high hopes and big contract, Callahan never
reached the Majors. The following summer the Red Sox signed Irv
Medlinger, a left-handed pitcher from Chicago, and Ted Del Guercio,
a pitcher from Newark, New Jersey, who reportedly received $20,000.
Medlinger made the Majors, though not with the Red Sox, and he
never won a game. They had better luck with outfielder Sam Mele
from New York University, signed for $20,000 in early 1946—Mele
had a long career in the game as a player, manager, and scout.[1]

During the 1940s Major League owners grew increasingly uncomfortable with the notion of bidding five-figure bonuses for untried
youths, and at the 1946 winter meetings enacted a new rule in an
attempt to slow such bonuses. Put into effect in February 1947, the

rule provided that any player who received a bonus of more than $6,000 from a Major League team (lesser limits applied for each level of the Minor Leagues) could not be optioned to a lower level without clearing waivers, which could not be withdrawn. Soon afterwards, the rule was amended to modify the bonus limits and to allow a one-time option to the Minors. This rule was in effect when Joe Cronin took charge of the Red Sox organization in 1947.[2]

The bonus rule had the effect of limiting the number of bonuses a team would give out, especially teams who were contending and did not want to devote a roster spot to an untested youngster. In June 1948 the Red Sox signed Yale pitcher Frank Quinn for a large outlay, reportedly $75,000. He spent the remainder of the year in Birmingham, before necessarily joining the Red Sox in 1949. Quinn's contribution was twenty-two innings pitched over eight games. In May 1950 having thrown only two innings, Quinn was placed on waivers and picked up by the Senators, who optioned him to Chattanooga. He never returned to the Major Leagues.[3]

The club had better luck with its other bonus player in this period, Virginia high-school pitcher Chuck Stobbs, who received $50,000 in 1947. After a great partial season (9-2, 1.72) with the Lynn Red Sox in 1947, Stobbs spent all of 1948 with the big club, pitching just seven innings for a team that lost the pennant in a one-game playoff. With Quinn joining him in 1949, Stobbs entered the starting rotation as a nineteen-year-old, pitched well, and stayed in the Majors until 1961.

Although there were a few successful bonus players in this period, including the Phillies' standout pitching tandem of Robin Roberts and Curt Simmons, both Major and Minor League officials began agitating to eliminate the rule soon after it was enacted. In July 1948 both Connie Mack and Clark Griffith threw their weight and experience behind abolishing the rule, though Cronin took a more cautious approach. "I have read a great deal regarding it," he said, "but feel we must delve into it pro and con before making any decisions."[4] The Major Leagues voted to repeal the rule at their 1949 meetings but could not get the Minor Leagues to agree.

A major impetus for changing the rule was the resentment by the established players of the young untried kids who were getting more money than the Major Leaguers. The Red Sox veteran players understandably resented Stobbs, whose $30,000 bonus was more than the annual salary of all but a few players on the team. The cause accelerated in 1950 after Paul Pettit, a high-school southpaw from Los Angeles, signed with the Pirates for $100,000.[5] At the next fall's meetings the Majors were even more opposed, now including Joe Cronin. "The Red Sox have been against the bonus rule since its inception as we feel the boys are handicapped by it," said Cronin, employing a bit of revisionism. The rule was finally eliminated in December 1950 after nearly four years.[6]

Though the Red Sox signed just two bonus players (Stobbs and Quinn) during the four years the rule was in effect, the club continued to bring talented players into the organization. Over this same period the Red Sox signed amateurs Walt Dropo, Frank Malzone, Charlie Maxwell, Jimmy Piersall, and Frank Sullivan, all of whom were future All-Stars, plus several other players who would become Major League regulars.

Most teams had been willing to sign one or two bonus players, but the rule created a buyer's market for the clubs. With a practical limit on the number of bonus contracts that could be offered, the amateur players were effectively competing for those bonuses. Beginning in December 1950, with the shackles of the bonus rule set aside, the Major League clubs had a sort of feeding frenzy, signing a succession of unknown players to five-figure bonuses. No team was more enthusiastic than the Red Sox. After nearly fifteen years of aggressively spending money on Major League–ready players—either big leaguers or players from the high Minors—the Red Sox of the early 1950s aimed Tom Yawkey's bankroll at amateurs.

Not long after the elimination of the bonus rule the Red Sox landed New Jersey pitcher Dick Brodowski for a reported $17,000. Late in the spring the team signed several other unknown players for $20,000 or more, and then gave a spectacular seventy-five thousand to third baseman Dick Pedrotti of Pasadena City College. The scout who signed Pedrotti, Tom Downey, was in the employ of the Cleveland Indians but resigned when general manager Hank Greenberg would not spring for the big bonus for Pedrotti. Upon hearing this news, Cronin contacted Downey, hired him over the phone, and told him to sign Pedrotti for whatever it took.[7]

The Red Sox were just warming up. In 1952 the club inked seventeen bonus players for a total of more than $700,000. Pitcher Frank Baumann, from St. Louis, received $100,000, as did outfielder Marty Keough of Pomona, California. In the space of a single month they signed three amateur catchers—Haywood Sullivan of the University of Florida, Larry Isbell from Baylor University, and Jerry Zimmerman of Milwaukie, Oregon—for a total outlay of $150,000. Both Sullivan and Isbell were well-known college quarterbacks.

The most famous signees were Dave Sisler, son of Hall of Famer George and brother of first baseman Dick, and Harry Agganis, a football and baseball standout at Boston University, each of whom received $40,000. Cronin claimed that all of the bonuses did not represent a change in policy. "We always have been seeking the best players available to put through our farm system," he said. "We can only hope a fair share of them make the grade."[8] When the Red Sox signed Al Antinelli, a sophomore pitcher from Colgate, an official at the school accused the team of being "ruthless." "They may be more professional than we are," replied Cronin. "We've never interfered with a boy's education."[9]

The Red Sox were by no means the only team bidding for all of these players, and they lost out on a few of them. One source estimated that the Major Leagues spent upwards of $4.5 million on signing bonuses in 1952.[10] When the inevitable crusade arose to put a stop to the free spending, the Red Sox were one of the teams calling for new prohibitions. "Sure you're for a change now," said Pirates general manager Branch Rickey at the 1952 All-Star Game, "after you've tied up the cream of the crop."[11] In August Commissioner Ford Frick appointed an eight-person committee, chaired by Rickey and including Cronin, to study the issue and make a recommendation. The group met several times that fall.

Although the Red Sox were one of the major reasons that teams were clamoring for a change, Cronin did not like the current system. "The old bonus rule didn't do the job and wasn't fair, either to the kids or the ball clubs," he said in June. "But we've got to have some kind of bonus rule." Although there were occasional calls for an actual amateur draft, Cronin was not ready to go that far. "Pro football has a draft, and that cuts down bonus payments. [But] we want to encourage free enterprise on the part of everyone, including, of course, the kids themselves."[12]

Not surprisingly, the committee recommended a new bonus rule, which was approved easily at the winter meetings in December 1952. A "bonus player" was now any amateur who received a bonus of $4,000 or more. Such a player was required to remain on the active Major League roster for two full seasons.[13] Since each team would not want to use more than two or three roster spots on bonus players, the rule had the intended effect of reducing the number of bonus players, especially for the better clubs, and therefore the number of bidders for each player.

The Red Sox had spent close to $1 million on amateur players in the two years of deregulation. The players they signed, men like Keough and Baumann and Eddie Urness, were expected to be stars in the middle and late 1950s, for a team that had contended for more than a decade. Complicating matters, many of the players would likely have to perform military service before they would ever be Major League ready. Haywood Sullivan was drafted in March 1953 and missed two full seasons. Frank Baumann started 10-1 at Louisville in 1953, before joining the army and not returning until mid-1955. Eddie Urness, an Oregon pitcher who received $86,000 in 1952, missed two full years, as did Dave Sisler. This was commonplace for single men in the 1950s and made the large outlays of bonuses all the more risky.

In a related development, after the 1952 season the Red Sox dropped their Birmingham affiliation, leaving them without a Double-A club. The reason, according to Cronin, was that the organization did not have enough players to stock the club. "We have about 100 minor league players in the service and we have them coming and going all the time, but the ones coming out probably aren't ready for Double-A ball."[14] Despite all of their high-priced bonuses, the Red Sox had just six Minor League affiliates, fewest in the Major Leagues (matched by Washington). Although the Red Sox were spending more money on high-priced bonus players, they did not have as deep a system as most teams had.

Nonetheless, most observers believed the Red Sox were loaded. "I would be willing to bet," said Branch Rickey Jr., Pittsburgh Pirates farm director, "that from 1956 through the following five or six years, the Boston Red Sox will be taking the place of the Yankees in the American League. By that time they will have more good players than any team in either league. I know because we tried to sign the same players that they have obtained the last two years. The Red Sox made sure they signed every player in whom other clubs were interested. Money meant nothing."[15]

With the bonus restrictions back in force, in January 1953 the Red Sox signed Billy Consolo, a high-school infielder considered one of the greatest prospects ever to come out of Los Angeles, for $60,000. Cronin himself, in town for the Major League meetings, had paid Consolo's family a visit in December to talk terms, and the Red Sox beat out several clubs to sign him the day after he graduated from high school. Under the terms of the new rules, Consolo had to spend two years with the Red Sox. He played rarely in 1953 (.215 in 65 at bats), much more the next year (.227 in 242 at bats) before being optioned to Oakland, where he turned in a fine year in Triple-A as a twenty-year-old in 1955.

Cronin later told the story of his visit to see Consolo in 1952. He and Mildred were invited by the family for dinner, and Cronin mentioned the large Italian population in Boston that would love Billy. Mrs. Consolo replied, "Just the same as Cleveland," suggesting that the Indians had already tried this tactic. Then Cronin mentioned Leonardi's, a fine Italian restaurant where he would take Billy to dinner. Again, Mrs. Consolo countered, "It must be like Cavoli's in

Cleveland." After a few attempts at boosting his city met the same resistance, Cronin finally praised Mrs. Consolo's cooking. "That did it," recalled Cronin.[16]

The bonus rule had the intended effect on the Red Sox, who signed no other bonus players while Consolo was on the team. In 1955 with Consolo in the Minors, Boston signed Jim Pagliaroni, a catcher from Long Beach, for $85,000. Pagliaroni played in just one game for the club, after which Cronin talked him into joining the army to get his commitment out of the way. (By the time he left the service in 1958 the rule had been overturned, and he went to the Minor Leagues. Both Consolo and Pagliaroni later said that they felt animosity from their teammates because of all the money they had received without contributing.)

The new bonus rule was controversial from the moment it was enacted and calls to modify or repeal it were constant. Most GMs disliked the regulation, but they could think of no other way to solve the problem of high bonuses. Chuck Dressen, manager of the Senators, had an alternative: he suggested that teams be allowed to farm out the bonus players, who would still count against the team's twenty-five-man roster. In effect it would punish the team, but not the player. This plan had supporters, including Chicago's Frank Lane and Baltimore's Paul Richards, but the hard liners—notably Cleveland's Hank Greenberg and Cincinnati's Gabe Paul—resisted any modifications.[17]

After five years of grumbling, the Major Leagues voted to repeal the rule at their meetings in Colorado Springs in December 1957. Joe Cronin spoke for many when he said, "With the bonus players on the rosters, fans were deprived of seeing baseball at its best." One of the many reasons teams desired a change was the belief that some teams were cheating by making under-the-table payments to players. In the five years of the regulation there were fifty-nine bonus players, twenty-one of whom had not fulfilled their two-year commitment at the time the rule ended. Among the fifty-nine were three eventual Hall of Famers—Detroit's Al Kaline, Brooklyn's Sandy Koufax, and Washington's Harmon Killebrew.[18]

With the restrictions removed, bonus payments predictably increased, with the Red Sox outspending most teams. In December 1957 the Red Sox signed pitcher Don Schwall, a basketball star at the University of Oklahoma, to a bonus exceeding $50,000. Late the same month they gave another $50,000 to infielder Al Moran, a freshman at Michigan State. Bob Tillman, catcher and basketball star at Middle Tennessee State, joined up in January, followed by Wake Forest right-handed pitcher Ben Tench, Rutgers catcher Bob Hoffer, Stanford outfielder Bill Jensen, third baseman Ken Knutson of Iowa, Missouri right fielder Bo Toft, and shortstop Ed Coleman from San Francisco.[19]

This latest crop, like all of the Red Sox bonus players of the 1950s, failed to justify the team's investment in them. Of all the players to whom the Red Sox gave bonuses from 1950 through the end of the 1958 season, the best payback came from Tillman, who was their regular catcher for a few years in the 1960s. Although Rickey Jr. and others feared that the Red Sox had cornered the market on the stars of the late 1950s, they had not. Given that most other teams had also tried to sign these players, it is difficult to blame the Red Sox scouts for signing the wrong players. Most likely the blame lies either with baseball's inability to project the futures of raw young talent or with the Red Sox farm system that failed to turn any of these young players into stars.

Al Hirshberg, in a story for the *Saturday Evening Post* in 1960, quoted an unnamed rival scout about the plight of the Red Sox system. "The Red Sox are always looking for the big star," he said. "They won't for settle for anything else. You can't run a farm system that way. You never know when one might surprise you and unexpectedly develop into a star."[20] Indeed, the Red Sox had just six Minor League teams by 1956, while the Yankees had twelve, the Dodgers fourteen, and the Cardinals fifteen. Tom Yawkey's money was used to buy bonus players, but not to build a deep Minor League system. The best player the Red Sox developed in the 1950s, third baseman Frank Malzone, received no bonus when he signed in 1947, then spent nine years inching his way through the system before breaking through.

Finally, in November 1958 the Red Sox signed Long Island outfielder Carl Yastrzemski for $125,000. Yastrzemski went on to a Major League career that justified the outlay in a way that all of the other bonus players did not. Cronin would leave the Red Sox a few weeks later, having never seen a Red Sox bonus player become a star.

The price the Red Sox paid for the obsession with bonus players ran deeper than dollars and cents. For while the organization spent a decade leading the ill-begotten charge to overpay high-school and college boys, a much more productive source of talent was being mined right under their noses. Throughout the 1950s Red Sox scouts were traveling the country to watch high-school games, and Joe Cronin was personally visiting the homes of untried amateurs, vigilantly on the lookout for the next superstar. All of these bonus players had one thing in common. They had white skin.

A few months after his tryout with the Red Sox in April 1945, Jackie Robinson signed a contract with the Montreal Royals, the top farm club of the Brooklyn Dodgers. In 1946 Robinson became the first black player to play for a Major League organization in the twentieth century and led the Royals to the International League championship. The following season Robinson starred for the Dodgers and was joined in the big leagues that same season by four other black players: outfielder Larry Doby with the Cleveland Indians, infielders Hank Thompson and Willard Brown with the St. Louis Browns, and pitcher Dan Bankhead with the Dodgers.

At the conclusion of that historic 1947 season, Joe Cronin became the general manager of the Boston Red Sox. This was an extraordinary time in baseball history, for the game would soon benefit from the greatest crop of new talent ever available. There were five black Major Leaguers in 1947, and soon there would be ten, and then fifty, and then two hundred. And not just any players but some of the greatest players to ever play the game, available to the first willing suitor: Willie Mays, Henry Aaron, Ernie Banks, Frank Robinson, and many more top-flight stars. Within a generation more than 20 percent of Major League players would be either African Americans or dark-skinned Latinos, and the All-Star Game rosters would be 40 percent black.[21]

Regrettably, Joe Cronin and the Red Sox sat this revolution out. There has been much historical debate about just who in the Red Sox organization was responsible for the club's foot dragging on integration in the 1950s, but there can be no doubt about how much it hurt the team. In the short run, it hurt them because the club was missing out on the chance to sign many great players, players who might have helped them win pennants and championships. In the longer run the franchise was forever branded as the last to integrate, which, coupled with several racial problems in the 1960s and later, secured the team's reputation for antipathy to black players and fans.

They had their chances, even after the Robinson fiasco. In his 1973 book *What's the Matter with the Red Sox*, Al Hirshberg told a story (which he heard at least second-hand) that the Red Sox could have signed Willie Mays in 1949. Mays was an eighteen-year-old outfielder for the Birmingham Black Barons, who played in a park owned by the Birmingham Barons, a Red Sox affiliate in the Southern Association. According to Hirshberg's story ("which I have never been able to check," he wrote) the Red Sox had a tip on Mays and sent scout Larry Woodall to take a look at him. It rained for a couple of days and Woodall never bothered to hang around and see him play.[22] In Jules Tygiel's definitive 1982 book on baseball's integration, he reports Hirshberg's story, calling it an "unconfirmed tale."[23] Years later George Digby, who had been the Red Sox area scout when Mays played in Birmingham, first told the story that *he* scouted Mays for the Red Sox, worked out a deal with the Black Barons to sign him, but was rebuffed by the front office, presumably Cronin.[24]

In 2002 Willie Mays told Howard Bryant that he had thought he was on his way to Boston and had told all his friends back home that he was headed to the Red Sox. That may be true, though Mays did not mention this in either his 1966 autobiography (when he mentioned the Dodgers having an early shot at him) or in his 1988 autobiography.[25] But the Red Sox not signing Willie Mays would not have been particularly remarkable at the time. At the end of the 1949 season, only four of the sixteen Major League teams had been integrated, and a total of eleven black players had made the Majors.

In late 1949 Cronin went to Montreal to scout the Royals club, reportedly to see Sam Jethroe, one of the players he had seen try out at Fenway Park in 1945. Jethroe was Dodger property but available because the Dodgers had no place for him. While in Montreal, Cronin was asked if Jethroe was good enough to play in the Major Leagues. "On his record I suppose Jethroe can play anywhere."[26] In any event, Jethroe finished the year hitting .326, scored 154 runs and led the league with 154 runs scored and 89 stolen bases. After the season he was acquired by the Boston Braves.

The Red Sox signed their first black player for 1950, and ironically it was Mays's player-manager at Birmingham, thirty-two-year-old infielder Piper Davis. A former Harlem Globetrotter, Davis was a five-time All-Star in the Negro American League, and became the Blacks Barons' manager in 1948. After the 1949 season the Red Sox purchased Davis's contract and sent him to play at Scranton in the Single-A Eastern League.[27] "He's a fine kid," said Cronin. "If he makes good, I'm going to waste no time in moving him to Boston."[28] The Red Sox paid a small price up-front and the balance (the total was not disclosed) if Davis lasted until May 15. Recent sources have suggested the total was as low as $15,000, but it may have been higher.[29]

Setting aside the issue of race, the signing did not make much sense. The Red Sox already had three All-Star infielders (Johnny Pesky, Vern Stephens, and Bobby Doerr), each of whom were younger than Davis. The incumbent at first base was Billy Goodman, who had hit .298 as a twenty-three-year-old in 1949. What's more, they had to send Davis to Scranton because their two higher Minor League affiliates, Louisville and Birmingham, would not have allowed black players. Predictably Davis had no trouble in the Eastern League, three rungs below the Major Leagues, hitting .333 in 63 at bats. He was released just prior to the deadline for making the final payment. According to Davis decades later, he ran into Cronin changing trains in Washington and was told he was let go for economic reasons.[30]

The fact that the Red Sox's top two farm clubs, both of which they owned outright, were in the South was certainly a handicap for any attempt to integrate, though an easily rectified one. Although Davis was hitting well for Scranton, a thirty-two-year-old veteran of the Negro Leagues had no business in the Eastern League, and his hitting .333 was not necessarily evidence that he could play in the Major Leagues. The team could have logically concluded that he was too good for Scranton but not good enough for Boston, where there were no openings in the infield anyway.

This episode was an embarrassment to the Red Sox and to Cronin, although mostly one that manifested itself decades later. Davis might not have been the right player, but it seems foolish to have signed him to a contract, watched him succeed for a month in a Minor League well below his ability, and then released him. If the Red Sox wanted Davis in February, surely he had done nothing to change their minds. Walt Dropo had taken over at first base in Boston in 1950, creating a new obstacle for Davis, but that does not explain why Davis was signed in the first place.

One defense offered for the Red Sox's dawdling on integration: the city of Boston was uniquely unready for a black player. The heavily Irish city had only thirty-two thousand black residents in 1950, just 3 percent of its population. This theory was tested in 1950 when Jethroe, who had tried out at Fenway Park with Jackie Robinson in 1945, joined the Boston Braves. A speedy centerfielder who had starred for several years for the Cleveland Buckeyes of the Negro American League, Jethroe was believed to be twenty-eight at the time (but was actually thirty-two). By all accounts he experienced no problems with the Boston fans, and Jethroe rewarded them by hitting 18 home runs, scoring 100 runs, leading the league with 35 stolen bases, and winning the Rookie of the Year Award. Within two years the Braves had fielded four different black players and signed several more, including Henry Aaron. The Braves were owned by three local contractors—Lou Perini and Guido Rugo, both Italians, and the Irish Joe Maney—who presumably had a better grasp on the social dynamics of their native city than Tom Yawkey and Joe Cronin.

In 1953 the Braves moved to Milwaukee, intensifying pressure on the Red Sox to integrate.

That same year Al Hirshberg wrote a story for *Our Sports*, a magazine about black athletes for a predominantly black audience, titled "Boston Needs a Negro Big-Leaguer." Before the 1953 season twenty-seven black players had played in the Majors, though for only six different clubs. In Hirshberg's account the Red Sox were "desperately looking for a Negro star." After recalling the release of Davis, Cronin told Hirshberg, "We've bid for Negro players who were free agents and claimed those whose names we found on the waiver list."[31] Cronin had met with the Indians during the 1952 World Series and made a big offer to acquire Larry Doby but would not meet Cleveland's price. Later that fall the Red Sox tried to acquire black pitcher Bill Greason from Oklahoma City of the Texas League. Greason had begun his career with the Black Barons in 1948 and 1949 and then spent two years in the Marines. With Oklahoma City in 1952, Gleason went 9-1 in eleven games. Despite bids from the Red Sox (reportedly $60,000) and the Yankees (who had also yet to integrate), Greason stayed in Oklahoma for one more year before being dealt to the St. Louis Cardinals.[32]

Trying to get either an established star (Doby) or a Major League–ready player (Greason) was typical of the Red Sox approach to building their team in these years. They were always more comfortable paying the huge sums for the big stars or the big bonuses to the hot young prospects. What they did not do often enough, with either black or white players, was sign large quantities of raw talent and patiently wait for some of them to develop into Major Leaguers.

In 1953 the Red Sox finally signed two young black players: nineteen-year-old infielder Elijah "Pumpsie" Green, purchased from his hometown Oakland Oaks before he had played a professional game; and eighteen-year-old catcher Earl Wilson from Ponchatoula, Louisiana. Wilson was described in Tom Downey's scouting report as "a well-mannered colored boy, not too black" who "conducts himself like a gentleman."[33] Green began his career in Wenatchee, Washington, in the Single-A Western International League, while Wilson played for Bisbee-Douglas, Arizona, in the Arizona-Texas League. A spiking to his nonthrowing hand early in the season sidelined Wilson, and during his recuperation he became a pitcher. His success soon made the switch permanent. Nonetheless, neither player was close to the Major Leagues.

Elsewhere, integration was accelerating. Six more teams integrated in 1953 and 1954, leaving just four all-white clubs: the Yankees, Red Sox, Tigers, and Phillies. Fifty-two black players had played in the Major Leagues since 1947, including several future Hall of Famers. While it is true that the Red Sox missed out on Willie Mays, the greater truth is that they missed out on *all of them*—Henry Aaron, Ernie Banks, Roberto Clemente, and dozens of other good or great players. They were all available, and the Red Sox had the wherewithal to sign or acquire all of them. For the price they paid for Frank Baumann, they could have signed all of these players and more.

After the 1954 season the Red Sox hired forty-five-year-old Mike Higgins to manage the club. Higgins, a Texan, has received more than a little blame for the Red Sox's all-white team in this era. Al Hirshberg, writing the first postintegration team history in 1973, reported that Higgins had once told him, "There'll be no niggers on this ball club as long as I have anything to say about it."[34] Larry Claflin, another Boston sportswriter, later recalled Higgins calling him a "nigger-lover" after the writer questioned the manager about the race issue.[35] Unfortunately, none of this was reported at a time when it could have done any good—or when Higgins was still alive to defend himself. This theme runs throughout this story—the blame tends to be placed on the people after they have died, when they can no longer tell their side of the story.

In late 1954 the Red Sox offered $100,000 to the Brooklyn Dodgers for Charlie Neal, a star second baseman for their St. Paul affiliate in the American Association. "It was a substantial bona fide made just before we brought Charlie up to the Brooklyn roster" admitted Dodger vice president Fresco Thompson. "The only reason we didn't accept it is that Neal figures in our plans for next season."[36] In any event, Neal spent another year in the Minors before joining the Dodgers in 1956. In that same year the Red Sox tried to buy star outfielder Al Smith from the Indians.[37]

Those bids foiled, the Red Sox were back to waiting for Pumpsie Green and Earl Wilson, as they signed no other black players for several years. Green spent two seasons with Wenatchee, hitting .244 and .297, then batted .310 for Stockton in the Class-A California League. In 1956 he moved up to Albany of the Eastern League, where he batted a solid .274 and was named the league's All-Star shortstop. It was at Albany that he and Wilson finally became teammates, the pitcher having passed through Bisbee-Douglas, El Paso, San Jose, and Montgomery. At Albany, Wilson finished 13-9 with a 3.12 ERA, placing him on the cusp of the Major Leagues.

By the end of the 1956 season, eighty-one black players had played in the big leagues, though three of the sixteen teams—the Red Sox, the Tigers, and the Phillies—had yet to integrate. During spring training of 1957 the Red Sox traveled to San Francisco to play the Seals, their top Minor League affiliate. In their first game the Red Sox faced Earl Wilson, who beat them 5–2. It looked like Wilson might be good enough to join the team right then. As fate would have it, a few weeks later Wilson had to join the Marines and served a full two-year hitch. Before his discharge after the 1958 season, the Phillies and Tigers had integrated, giving the Red Sox the dubious distinction of being the only remaining lily-white Major League team.

In June 1958 the Red Sox signed Larry Plenty, a catcher and star fullback from Boston College and assigned him to their Waterloo, Iowa, team in the Midwest League.[38] By 1959 they reportedly had seven black players playing in the Minor Leagues.[39] Finally, in July of that year both Green and Wilson joined the Red Sox, but Joe Cronin was no longer the club's general manager. Pumpsie Green was the 120th black player in the Major Leagues.

Most of the histories of the team in subsequent decades have attempted to assign blame for the Red Sox delayed integration. Hirshberg, writing in 1973, absolved Yawkey and Cronin of responsibility, saying that it was the Red Sox scouts who failed by not finding black players or by turning in false reports on the ones they did find.[40] Jules

Tygiel, the preeminent scholar on the subject of baseball integration, wrote that it was the men at the top who hired the scouts and who did not have a presence in the Caribbean until 1960 nor a black scout on the payroll until 1964.[41]

In a correspondence with Tygiel just before his untimely death in 2008, he suggested that the Red Sox lacked the imagination necessary to find black players. It was not enough to simply claim that they were open to black players—they had to hire scouts to watch black players play, and steer them to games involving black players.[42] The club made a few attempts to buy ready-made talent (notably Doby and Neal) but missed out on all of the great Negro League players and the young black amateurs who came later. Wilson and Green took six years to get to Boston, not an unusual delay for a teenager starting in the low Minor Leagues.

As for Cronin, there is no direct evidence in his private or public life that would suggest he was a racist. Cronin was a prominent member of the Massachusetts Committee of Catholics, Protestants and Jews, a group formed to foster better relations between different faiths and races. After many years with the organization he became an executive director and in 1952 began hosting a Junior Goodwill Dinner every winter at Fenway Park for a selected group of 150 to 200 high-school boys of different backgrounds. The children heard several speakers each year, including the mayor, clergymen, and many prominent people from the sports world, promoting brotherhood and tolerance. After the 1954 dinner, *The Sporting News* printed two letters from boys who had attended the dinner. One was from a boy who had been born in China and had been taught that Americans were intolerant toward people of different races. "True, Mr. Cronin, it will be years before the struggle against this racial and religious prejudice is over, but achievements and organizations such as the Massachusetts Committee of Catholics, Protestants and Jews will no doubt expedite the attainment of this goal."[43] The group honored his long service at a special banquet in January 1958. A year earlier Cronin was honored by the Brotherhood of Temple Ohabei Shalom in neighboring Brookline for his good works in the community.[44]

The strongest evidence against the Red Sox, and against Cronin, is circumstantial yet undeniable—the Red Sox very obviously did not have any black players. This fact, whether due to policy or simply incompetence, did untold damage to the Red Sox of the 1950s and beyond.

12 Youth Movement

AFTER THE RED SOX THIRD NEAR MISS IN 1950, Joe Cronin made a few attempts to bolster his club. The most talked-about news was the signing in November of shortstop Lou Boudreau, who had been released as manager and player by the Indians. Tom Yawkey had not forgotten how Boudreau had beaten the Red Sox in 1948. He had slowed considerably as a player since then, and the Red Sox clearly did not need a shortstop—they already employed Vern Stephens (who had led the league in RBI in 1950 while fielding well), and Johnny Pesky (a .312 hitter who had spent the last three seasons at third base). Boudreau, thirty-three, was older than both Stephens and Pesky and in 1950 had played in just eighty-one games. Boudreau reportedly chose the Red Sox over the Yankees because of his friendship with manager Steve O'Neill, who had managed Boudreau in the Minors and coached under him in 1949. Speculation that Boudreau would someday replace O'Neill as manager began almost immediately.

At the winter meetings in St. Petersburg, Cronin dealt outfielders Al Zarilla and Dick Littlefield and pitcher Joe Dobson to the White Sox for pitchers Bill Wight and Ray Scarborough, workhorses who had losing records for poor clubs (Scarborough had been traded from the Senators to the White Sox in late May). Cronin had tried to get Scarborough the year before, perhaps because Scarborough had beat the Red Sox five times (total) between 1948 and 1949, including crucial victories in the last week of each season. Recently deposed White Sox manager Jack Onslow was stunned by the deal, suggesting that Wight alone was worth more than the three players Chicago received. "I'm convinced Tom Yawkey, Joe Cronin and Steve O'Neill hit Frank Lane (Chicago general manager) over the head, got his signature while he was semi-conscious and told him about the deal when he woke up."[1] The trade also opened a spot in right field for Billy Goodman, the .354 hitting utility player from 1950. For the left side of the infield, O'Neill ended up moving Stephens to third base and split the shortstop job between Boudreau and Pesky.

Ted Williams created a bit of a stir when he told a writer in Miami (Williams was on his way to the Keys to fish) that he would take it easier in the spring than he had in the past. "I'm not going to go through another spring training like last year," said Williams, claiming he had played in thirty-seven of the thirty-eight exhibition games. "It's okay with me for Joe Cronin to read about it in the papers."[2] As usual when word got to the Boston press Williams was not reachable, leaving management to deal with the story. Although trade rumors involving Williams were an off-season staple, they were more prevalent than usual after the 1950 season. A few prominent national articles suggested that Williams should be dealt for the good of the club.[3] "I guess I'll have to get a record made [denying the rumors]," said Cronin, "and when the telephone calls come, I can just switch it on and roll over and go back to sleep."[4]

Cronin typically spent his off-season around Boston while also attending the Minor and Major League meetings. Mildred almost always accompanied Joe on his winter travels, leaving the children at home with nannies. The family often went to Washington to visit the Griffiths and Robertsons, and in early December all were present for Clark and Anne's fiftieth wedding anniversary. In the spring, Joe, Mildred, and the children went to Sarasota for a few weeks. The older boys—Tommy and Corky, each an aspiring ballplayer—worked out in uniform with some of the players.[5]

The Red Sox family was dealt a blow in early April 1951 with the death of Eddie Collins. Collins had cut back considerably on his workload since relinquishing his general manager's duties but still came into the office most days for a few hours. He had suffered a severe stroke in August 1950 and another in March as he was preparing for the season. He died on March 25 at Peter Bent Brigham Hospital in Boston, just sixty-three years old.[6] Joe Cronin was visibly stunned when given the news. "He will be missed by all. He was a great contributor to baseball," Cronin managed to say. Cronin and Ted Williams, who was also very close to Collins, tried but failed to get a flight from Sarasota to Boston. Tom Yawkey flew up from South Carolina and was joined by hundreds of baseball dignitaries.

The 1951 Red Sox started much better than they had in previous years, and played fairly consistently all season. In early May the Red Sox again reached into Tom Yawkey's bank account, sending two players and $100,000 to the Browns for catcher Les Moss. This deal was hardly helpful—Moss hit .198 after the deal and was dealt back to the Browns after the season. Still the Red Sox were three games out of first place at the end of May, and three back at the end of June.

Another personnel change in 1951 was brought on by the collapse of first baseman Walt Dropo. After hitting 34 home runs with 144 RBI in his rookie season in 1950, by July 4 Dropo had just four homers in 172 at bats. The Red Sox optioned him to San Diego, moved Goodman to first base, and put Clyde Vollmer in right field. Vollmer promptly had the month of his life, with 13 home runs and 40 RBI in July. The Red Sox hung on and were still just two and a half games behind the first-place Yankees on September 17. But they dropped twelve of their last thirteen games and finished in third place, eleven games out.

Once it became clear that the Red Sox were not going to win the 1951 pennant, speculation began that O'Neill would be fired. Many people had thought the team would win, ignoring the advancing age of their best players and overrating their new pitchers—Scarborough and Wight—who both pitched poorly. As Shirley Povich later wrote of O'Neill, "All he had to do, it was presumed, was take the daily lineups to the umpires and retire to a sitting position." In fact, continued Povich, the club was "miscast as pennant favorites last spring." O'Neill paid for this overestimation and was fired after the season.[7]

The core players were showing their age. Vern Stephens hit well, but a knee injury limited him to 109 games. Johnny Pesky hit .313 but missed twenty-three games. Ted Williams batted just .318, his career low to this point. And Bobby Doerr missed several weeks with a back injury. In fact after consulting with doctors in September, Doerr was informed that he would need surgery to continue his career. Instead, he retired. Cronin told the press that Doerr would have a job with the Red Sox whenever he wanted it. When asked if that included managing the team, Cronin replied, "That includes everything."[8] But Doerr left baseball and bought a ranch in Oregon. He already owned two hundred acres and a small home on the Rogue River, to which he added a farm near Eugene, 175 miles away. He and his family split their time between the two homes for many years.[9]

Besides Doerr, another reported candidate for O'Neill's job was Lefty O'Doul, Cronin's friend from San Francisco, who had lost his managerial position with the Seals.[10] Finally, after nearly a year of rumors, Cronin announced that Lou Boudreau would manage the club. By all accounts, the decision to hire Boudreau was made by Tom Yawkey and not Cronin, who preferred Mike Higgins, now managing in the club's farm system. Boudreau caused a bit of a stir after he was hired, saying, "Everybody, including Ted [Williams], will be traded if necessary to give us the strength we need."[11] Cronin publicly backed his new manager. "It is the Red Sox policy to give the manager full authority on player deals," said Cronin.[12]

After the annual round of trade rumors, including a swap of Williams for Tiger third baseman George Kell, and one sending Williams to Cleveland for catcher Jim Hegan and pitcher Bob Lemon, Williams stayed in Boston. Cronin made two minor deals in November, notably sending Chuck Stobbs, their bonus player from 1948, to the White Sox in a four-player swap. As was often the case with the Red Sox in this era, they failed to understand how much hitter-friendly Fenway Park affected their players' statistics—Stobbs was a pretty decent pitcher for several years with other clubs.

Outside events soon ended any thought of trading Williams, who was recalled to the Marine Corps on January 9. He was ordered to take his physical on April 2 and serve for seventeen months. When Williams was discharged in 1945 he had signed up for the Marine Reserves, and had been classified as "inactive" for more than six years. With the Korean War in high gear, the Marines needed pilots, including, apparently, a thirty-three-year-old man with a wife, a daughter, and a bad elbow, who had not flown an airplane in six years. "In my heart, I was bitter about it," Williams later wrote. "But I kept thinking one of those gutless politicians somewhere along the line would see that it wasn't right and do something."[13] The orders stood, and Williams remained publicly diplomatic. "If Uncle Sam wants me, I'm ready. I'm no different from the next fellow," he said.[14]

The loss of Williams effectively ended whatever hopes the Red Sox may have harbored about 1952 or for the foreseeable future. "His loss will have a tremendous effect on our ballclub," Cronin said. "It would be silly to say we can replace him."[15] In fact, many assumed that Williams career was over. In due course Williams received a reporting date of May 2 and went to spring training with the Red Sox. The loss of both Doerr and Williams clearly spelled the end of the postwar Red Sox, a consistently excellent team despite their lack of championships. This transition only hastened the club's investments in the amateur market discussed in the previous chapter.

In early 1952 the Red Sox instituted a winter instructional school for youngsters in Sarasota, beginning a month before spring training. The club invited thirty-five prospects, among them Jimmy Piersall, Dick Gernert, Ted Lepcio, Faye Throneberry, and Tom Umphlett. Boudreau and his staff, in addition to Cronin, farm director Johnny Murphy, and a few Minor League managers, ran the camp. The players practiced running bases, playing each position, sliding, pitching, and hitting. "It's up to the kids themselves now," said Cronin after the camp concluded. "If they practice what we showed them and keep working on it, some great kids will come out of our school."[16] Although he grew to understand the importance of innate natural ability, Cronin always believed that a good player could become a great player by outworking everyone else—as he himself had done.

One of the bigger stories to emerge from the camp involved Jimmie Piersall, an outfield prospect from Waterbury, Connecticut. An all–New England basketball player, Piersall spurned several college offers when he signed with the Red Sox in 1947. In the Minor Leagues he had developed a reputation as an extraordinary defensive player. Steve O'Neill in 1951 had called him the Red Sox center fielder of the future. Dom DiMaggio, one of the best ever at the position, was also full of praise for the kid who might someday take his job. "Piersall is the best center-fielder in the American League right now," said Dominic.[17] Piersall's bat was less impressive—.271 and .255 in two seasons at Triple-A Louisville, although he rebounded to hit .346 after being demoted to Birmingham in 1951. With left fielder Williams entering the service and journeyman Clyde Vollmer the incumbent in right, there appeared to an opportunity for Piersall.

It therefore came as a surprise at the rookie school when Boudreau played Piersall at shortstop. Cronin called the experiment an "organizational idea," one he and Boudreau conceived at their staff meetings after the season. Cronin and Boudreau, each a former All-Star shortstop, worked with Piersall and were excited by what they saw. At the team's regular training camp, Piersall played both infield and outfield, as Boudreau experimented with several people at new positions. Johnny Pesky, the incumbent shortstop who had hit .313 as a nearly full-time player, played at several positions that spring.

On Opening Day in Washington, Piersall played shortstop, rookie Ted Lepcio manned second base, and rookie Faye Throneberry was in right field, while Vern Stephens, Billy Goodman, and Clyde Vollmer were on the bench. If that was not enough experimentation, Boudreau also hit pitcher Mel Parnell seventh in the order, ahead of Lepcio and catcher Gus Niarhos. The general manager blessed the strategies and the youth movement. "That school served a wonderful purpose," said Cronin. "We had to teach some of the kid outfielders to wear sunglasses. In some of those leagues they didn't play a dozen daylight games all year. The boy we had in right field opening day, Faye Throneberry, saw nothing but night games in two years in the minors."[18]

(This issue—night baseball in the Minor Leagues—concerned Cronin greatly at the time. In 1950 he had tried to get the Major Leagues to pay for better lighting for Minor League clubs in the interests of player development. In March 1952 he proposed that the

Majors instead subsidize the Minors to play day games. "It would not cost more than $25,000 per Major League club," he claimed. He felt the Minor League lights were atrocious and that night games reduced a player's likelihood of taking extra batting practice before games, as he had done.[19])

A national story written about Piersall's shortstop switch in early 1952 referred to the rookie as "high strung," "spirited," and "voluble," and as someone who tended to "press too hard."[20] Prophetic words it would turn out. Piersall was a sensation with the fans, for he clowned with them, made goofy gestures, ran in circles, and imitated opposing players. For a while it was comical. The behavior first turned problematic on May 24 in a fight with Yankees infielder Billy Martin, at whom he had been screaming insults. Later that same day he scuffled with teammate Mickey McDermott, who had apparently been teasing him about his earlier fight. Piersall battled with umpires constantly, three times being ejected from games early in the season. In mid-May, hitting .255 and fielding erratically, Piersall was benched. Vern Stephens's hot hitting kept Piersall out of the lineup, though his antics continued.

On June 5 Piersall was given a chance as the right fielder, and responded by hitting .368 between June 6 and June 15 and playing great defense. But his clowning grew more outrageous. He let opposing infielders know he was bunting by pantomiming bunt attempts. When the bullpen cart would drive by him in the outfield he would stick out his thumb to hitch a ride. He laughed with fans, made fun of his own mistakes, and those of others. In the ninth inning of a game against the St. Louis Browns, Piersall imitated legendary pitcher Satchel Paige's every move, finally resorting to flapping his arms like a chicken and squealing like a pig. (The Red Sox rallied for five runs, including a walk-off grand slam by Sammy White, to beat the rattled Paige.) Perhaps most outrageously, when returning to the dugout from right field he ran directly behind center fielder Dom DiMaggio, imitating the gait and mannerisms of his revered teammate. Not surprisingly, his teammates thought he was "bush" and did not want to play with him. Boudreau benched Piersall again on June 15, claiming, incorrectly, that he wasn't hitting. Such a move was not without its own risk, since an earlier benching had caused Piersall to break down in tears.

On June 28 Piersall was sent back to Birmingham. At first glance it was a shocking move, as Piersall was a fan favorite and playing well. Cronin defended the move to the press. "I've never seen Lou so nervous," said Cronin. "After he sat shaking in my office for some time, he finally told me Piersall had to go for the good of the club. Lou said, time and again he had begged Piersall to behave himself but that he just got worse and worse every day."[21] Cronin told another writer, "Apparently everyone on this club is against him."[22]

In Birmingham, Piersall's behavior grew worse. Among his antics, he stole the game ball from the pitcher's mound on his way to his position and refused to give it up, joined his manager in an argument with an umpire only to mimic his skipper's mannerisms, and dropped his bat to mock the pitcher from the batter's box. During a three-day break for the Southern League All-Star Game, Piersall flew back to Boston to see his family. While back home he came to see Cronin, begging to be brought back to the Red Sox. Cronin told him, "Go back to Birmingham and behave and perhaps something will turn up later." Piersall went back, but his six ejections and four suspensions indicate he did not follow Cronin's advice. After one ejection for arguing balls and strikes, he pulled out a water pistol and sprayed home plate. "Now maybe you can see it," he told the umpire. This action drew Piersall his fourth suspension. He again flew back to Boston.[23]

Cronin had decided that Piersall should be seen by a psychiatrist, but it took some time to get his player to agree. He spent most of July 18 with Piersall, driving around the city and talking. The next day Cronin drove Piersall and his wife Mary to see a doctor, who described the patient as "very nervous, very tense, a very sick boy."[24] He advised that Piersall check into a private sanitarium for a prolonged rest. "I have this to say and its going to be brief," Cronin told the press before that evening's game. "After consulting with, and on the advice of, doctors, Piersall is to take a rest. The ballclub is primarily interested in Jim Piersall, not where, how or what position he is going to play. I think you people will acquiesce in that decision. I'm sorry I can't elaborate."[25] Piersall checked into Baldpate, a private facility in Georgetown, Massachusetts.

After a couple of "escapes" and at least one violent episode, Piersall was moved to a state mental hospital in Danvers and subsequently to a facility in Westborough, which was closer to his wife and children. Piersall's official diagnosis was manic depression, what we today call bipolar disorder. Strapped to a bed, he received shock treatments and drifted in and out of coherence. Electroshock therapy was not uncommon in the 1950s as a way to reduce immediate symptoms (including paranoia and severe mania) but at the risk of memory loss. At the end of his hospital stay, in early September, Piersall could remember very little of what had happened after reporting to Sarasota in mid-January. He did not remember he had made the Red Sox club, let alone the sequence of events that led to his hospitalization.[26] Piersall was prescribed medication to stabilize his mood swings and control his condition, and fifty years later was still taking lithium.[27]

Cronin visited Piersall several times in the hospital but did not speak with the press about the situation again until Piersall was released, when Cronin reported that his player was "much improved and may play ball again."[28] Piersall spent a few evenings at Cronin's house listening to the team when they were on the road. Cronin was shocked to discover that Piersall had no memory of having played for the Red Sox earlier that season.[29] The Red Sox rented a five-room house in Sarasota for Piersall and his family to spend the winter. The doctors approved, on the condition that Piersall not pick up a baseball until the start of spring training. Piersall played golf, fished, and relaxed by the pool for four months.[30]

With the help of Al Hirshberg, in 1955 Piersall wrote his autobiography, *Fear Strikes Out*, which went through many printings and was made into a 1957 movie starring Anthony Perkins. In the film, the Joe Cronin character was the manager and played by Bart Burns. Cronin claimed that he would not watch the film. "I lived through that nightmare once. That was enough."

Beyond the Piersall saga, the Red Sox 1952 season had a few eventful moments. Ted Williams played parts of six games in April before leaving for Korea, his career presumed to be over. The team and fans gave him a big sendoff in his last home game on April 30. Williams missed the worst of the Piersall breakdown, and one wonders how he would have reacted had Piersall mimicked Williams's mannerisms as he had with DiMaggio.

On June 3 Cronin pulled off a big trade, dealing six players including Johnny Pesky and Walt Dropo, to the Detroit Tigers. In exchange the Red Sox received third baseman George Kell, left fielder Hoot Evers, and shortstop Johnny Lipon—all of whom immediately joined the starting lineup—and pitcher Dizzy Trout, who turned in four fine months in the rotation. Among the players of Boudreau's vaunted youth movement, catcher Sammy White and first baseman Dick Gernert kept their jobs all year. Despite (or possibly because of) all the experimentation, the Red Sox stayed in the first division most of the summer. The club was just three and a half games out of first as late as August 27, at which point they finally ran out of steam, winning just eight of their last thirty-two games and finishing 76-78.

The Cronins were typically busy travelers in the off-season. The family went to the Griffiths around the Thanksgiving holiday, which always coincided with Clark's birthday—he celebrated his eighty-third on November 20. The guests at the birthday celebration included his very large family, Baseball commissioner Ford Frick, many former players, and Supreme Court chief justice Fred Vinson. The Senators had not competed for twenty years, but Griffith was still in charge, trying to improve the team, hoping for one last pennant. After this trip, Joe and Mildred went to the winter meetings in Phoenix in early December and then headed north to San Francisco to visit old friends.

At the 1952 winter meetings the Red Sox virtually put up a sign announcing that they were open for business, but their position was not as strong as it had once been. The old guard was fading fast, and the expensive bonus kids were not ready. Dom DiMaggio had slowed in centerfield, though he hit .294. Vern Stephens had never really recovered from his leg injury in 1951. Doerr, Pesky, and Williams were gone. The club that had scored 1,027 runs in 1950 could manage only 668 two years later. Most teams, wrote Al Hirshberg, wanted Goodman, Kell, White, or Parnell in any deals, players the Red Sox could not afford to give up. "Now, all they have left is money, and who wants money?" wrote Hirshberg.[31]

After the holidays Cronin attended his usual junket of baseball banquets, gatherings that combined two of his favorite things—baseball talk, and food. Tommy Rich, the president of the Eastern League, frequented many of the same banquets and often told a story about Cronin. In the tale Rich goes to St. Patrick's Cathedral one day with Joe McCarthy, in his Yankee days, to take their devotions. They noticed Joe Cronin, in town with the Red Sox, walk in and light two candles at the nave. McCarthy waited for Cronin to leave, then went up and lit three candles of his own. Later that day, said Rich, the Yankees beat the Red Sox 3–2.[32]

In March 1953 Jimmy Piersall arrived at spring camp, ready to play baseball. According to his autobiography, Piersall was treated splendidly by his teammates, opponents, umpires, and fans. He joked with Mickey McDermott and Billy Martin, his combatants in 1952. He won the right-field job and quickly lived up to all the reviews from the previous spring, making a series of game-saving catches. On May 9 he made a catch in Boston in deep right field that Phil Rizzuto called "the greatest catch I've ever seen." A New York writer called him "the greatest outfielder who ever lived."[33] To Casey Stengel, Piersall was the "best defensive right fielder" in history.

Piersall has blamed his 1952 breakdown at least partially on Boudreau's moving him to shortstop. In 2008 Piersall told a reporter, "Boudreau was a jerk. I was an all-star center fielder, but he wanted to make a shortstop out of me."[34] On the other hand, many observers thought he was doing a fine job at short when a batting slump caused him to lose his job in early May 1952. His worst behavior actually began when he started playing the outfield in June. Boudreau's move was bold and perhaps wrong, but many men have been asked to switch positions early in their career without experiencing a nervous breakdown. Furthermore, Piersall's illness—bipolar disorder—was genetic and not caused by any outside event. His breakdown did not have to happen in 1952, but it almost certainly would have happened sometime.

Meanwhile, all of baseball was wrestling with a new and vexing issue—the sudden and dramatic reality of television. Although a baseball game had been first televised in 1939, the first regular local baseball telecasts began in 1947, when ten of the sixteen Major League teams showed some home games. In 1948 the Red Sox and Braves both allowed their home games to be telecast for free. By the early 1950s both the Red Sox and Braves were televising every home game.[35]

In these early days baseball played a large role in popularizing television, as the game afforded a cheap way to fill air time. Baseball had nothing to lose—in 1949, only 2.3 percent of homes had a television (although this number was higher in metropolitan areas), and there were only seventy-seven stations in the country (thirty-one of which televised baseball). But by 1952 there were TVs in one-third of American homes. Major League attendance had dropped 30 percent in four years, while the Minor Leagues were also suffering. Whether these facts were related was the subject of much debate in the 1950s.

Joe Cronin believed that they were: that Major League telecasts were hurting baseball attendance, especially in the Minors. In 1950 baseball first began broadcasting Major League games outside their local market, using "networks" of radio or television stations. "The Red Sox are fearful of the harm that extensive broadcasting of major league games might have on minor league ball," he warned. Cronin announced that the Red Sox would not contract with radio or television stations outside of New England.[36] Nonetheless, the telecasts of the Red Sox and Braves might have had some effect on the New England League, a Class-B circuit that re-formed in 1946. The league included a team in Lynn, which played its games just ten miles from Fenway Park and Braves Field, and therefore had to compete, like the entire league, with televised games from both clubs. Half of the eight clubs, including Lynn, failed to finish the 1949 season, after which the league folded.

Grantland Rice examined the television dilemma in the April 1951 issue of *Sport* and presented a contrary view from an unnamed insider: "The chief danger to minor-league baseball, and also to many major league teams, is not the televising of major league games, but television itself." A growing number of people owned televisions, and these people were staying home and watching Milton Berle, Sid Caesar, prizefights, and roller derby—all at no cost. Television represented a revolutionary shift in how Americans spent their leisure time, and both the Major Leagues and the Minor Leagues (who played most of their games at night) were victims of that shift.[37]

Although the Red Sox had to compete with television, beginning in 1953 they no longer had to compete with the Braves. The Braves had finished behind the Red Sox in attendance every season since Fenway Park was rebuilt in 1934, although more recently the National League club had fielded some quality teams and received good support, peaking with almost 1.5 million fans in their 1948 pennant winning season. Four years later, however, the club was under 300,000, averaging just 3,677 fans per game. Owner Lou Perini determined that Boston was no longer a two-team city and gained permission to move to Milwaukee in March 1953, just weeks before the start of the season. Thus ended seventy-seven years of National League baseball in Boston.

The biggest direct effect of the departure for the Red Sox was the end to their long-standing City Series, annual exhibition games the clubs played just prior to the start of the regular season. In 1953 the clubs held the event one last time, with the Red Sox joining the Braves for their debut in Milwaukee on April 9, which was rained out after just two innings. The two clubs then returned to Boston for a pair of games in Fenway Park, just two weeks after the local fans had learned the Braves were leaving town. Yawkey and Cronin invited Lou Perini to join them in the owner's box away from the crowd, but the proud Perini sat in a seat near his team's dugout. There was some booing of the Braves players, but overall Perini thought he and his team were treated well.[38] The Braves departed Boston for their new home, and spent thirteen years in Milwaukee before moving to Atlanta in 1966.

The franchise shift also had a direct impact on the Jimmy Fund, the Braves' official team charity. Founded in 1948 by the Braves and the Variety Club of New England, the Jimmy Fund directed money to support cancer research and treatment at the Children's Cancer Research Foundation (later the Dana-Farber Cancer Institute) in Boston. With the departure of the Braves, the Red Sox took over as a cosponsor on April 10 and have supported the charity ever since with events, telethons, and billboards at the ballpark. Joe Cronin was named general cochairman, became chair of the executive committee of the foundation in 1954, and continued to serve the organization until the end of his life, receiving its Good Heart Award in 1959. By 2006 the Jimmy Fund had raised over $500 million for cancer research and was closely intertwined with the Red Sox brand in New England.[39]

Meanwhile, the Red Sox's youth movement, for better or worse, picked up steam in 1953. Sophomores Sammy White and Dick Gernert held their jobs at catcher and first base. Milt Bolling won the shortstop job, an opening created when Vern Stephens was dealt to the White Sox in February. Piersall took over in right field. And most alarmingly, Boudreau replaced Dom DiMaggio in center field with Tom Umphlett. DiMaggio had had some eye problems in the spring which gave Umphlett an opening, and when Dom recovered in mid-April, he stayed on the bench. On May 12 having yet to play a single inning in the Red Sox's twenty-one games, DiMaggio announced his retirement from baseball. He had gone to Cronin a couple of weeks earlier and asked to be traded or released. Cronin did not oblige, hoping to change DiMaggio's mind.

"I want to make it perfectly understood," said DiMaggio in his statement, "that there is nothing wrong with my right eye, which recently underwent treatment. I believe I could have played at least one more year of good baseball, but under the present circumstances I prefer to turn my interests elsewhere rather than be a hanger-on." DiMaggio described Tom Yawkey as "a grand sportsman" who all of New England should be proud of. "And the same holds true for General Manager Joe Cronin."[40] DiMaggio pointedly did not mention Boudreau, at whom he remained bitter for many years. Years later DiMaggio told Peter Golenbock, "[Boudreau] hurt the parent club and destroyed the minor league system. He set the Red Sox back thirteen years."[41] Cronin said of DiMaggio, "He's always given the best he's had and I know he'll be a success at whatever he goes into."[42]

The most dramatic news for the 1953 Red Sox was the return of Ted Williams from Korea. Due to finish his tour in October, Williams got an early discharge because of a recurrent ear infection that bothered him when he flew. The Marine captain arrived in San Francisco on July 9, having flown thirty-nine combat missions, including one in which he crash landed his F9F-5 fighter. His first public appearance took place at the All-Star Game in Cincinnati on July 14. He met with Cronin and Yawkey before the game, held court in the American League dugout for an hour, and later threw out the ceremonial first pitch. Afterwards, AL manager Casey Stengel said he would have played Williams had he had his uniform.[43]

Ted was coy about returning to baseball. "I don't even know whether Yawkey, Cronin, and Boudreau want me around. They're building a new team with kids. They may not want an old man around. I'm 35 [in a few weeks]." In fact Cronin talked Williams into returning immediately rather than waiting until the spring.[44] The Red Sox players, many of whom were unfamiliar to Williams, welcomed the star back when he reported the day after his official discharge. He and Cronin quickly agreed to a contract for the remainder of the season.[45] Much had changed since Williams was last in Boston—Pesky, DiMaggio, and Stephens were gone, and their most popular player, Piersall, had been learning to play shortstop when Williams last saw him.

Williams first pinch-hit on August 6, popping out against the Browns, and then hit a pinch homer off the Indians' Mike Garcia on the ninth. In the remaining weeks of the season Williams played thirty-seven games (twenty-six in left field) and hit .407 with 13 home runs. Youth movement or no, Williams was by far the best hitter on the team. A dinner honoring Williams's return on August 17 at the Hotel Statler raised $150,000 for the Jimmy Fund, including a $50,000 check from the young Edward M. Kennedy, future U.S. senator, on behalf of the Joseph P. Kennedy, Jr., Foundation.[46]

At first glance the rebuilding seemed to work in 1953, as the team played well all season and finished 84-69, an improvement of eight wins from 1952. Cronin expressed his excitement early in the season, saying, "I'm delighted the players are doing so well and getting this experience. They're learning what it means to be in the majors, facing good pitching and meeting strong opposition." He reiterated that Boudreau was running the club and was in charge of who played and who did not. "I'm glad he's giving these youngsters a chance."[47]

In fact the offense remained one of the worst in the league. What the Red Sox would discover, though not quite learn, is that a youth movement requires a fair amount of patience. Replacing Dom DiMaggio, still a good player, with a promising youngster like Tom Umphlett is almost certainly going to make the team worse in the short term, and the likelihood of Umphlett, or any similar young player, becoming a star was quite low. (In fact, Umphlett hit .283 his rookie year, but never as well again.) What the Red Sox were trying to do—replace several stars in a brief period with untried prospects—was not a strategy likely to pay off for some time.

The improvement of the 1953 team was almost solely due to its great pitching, notably Mel Parnell (21-8, 3.06 ERA), Mickey McDermott (18-10, 3.01), and thirty-eight-year-old relief ace Ellis Kinder, affectionately known as "Old Folks." Kinder pitched in sixty-nine games, breaking the league record set by Ed Walsh in 1908, and finished 10-6 with a 1.85 ERA. When Boudreau came to the mound to bring in Kinder, he motioned to the bullpen by putting his hand on top of his head, signifying a crown. Kinder won the team's Most Valuable Player award (an honor he'd also won in 1951).

Although the Red Sox were never in the pennant race, their surprising fourth-place finish led Yawkey and Cronin to give Boudreau a new two-year contract after the season. Boudreau, in fact, thought the team could have competed were it not for injuries to Goodman and Bolling (though their sixteen-game deficit to the Yankees casts some doubt on Boudreau's contention).

Cronin spent his winter attending meetings and banquets. And not just the big ones: in December 1953 he attended a ceremony naming a school gymnasium in nearby Medford for sports cartoonist Gene Mack; in January he was given the first annual Sportsmanship Award by the Mt. Pleasant Council of the Knights of Columbus in Roxbury.[48] That winter Cronin also instituted weekly luncheons with the press,[49] which might have been as much a way for him to be around baseball talk as it was for the media.

In addition to Cronin's duties with the team—working with employees, advertisers, radio and television stations, and park-maintenance officials—he also served on a growing number of league- or baseball-wide committees. The Rules Committee conversed throughout the year and met occasionally in New York. In 1953 the committee reinstated the sacrifice-fly rule, not charging a time at bat on a run-scoring fly ball. Cronin had proposed this change, saying that such a player's batting average "should not suffer." Another new rule prohibited players from leaving their gloves on the playing field while their team was batting. "In these days," said Cronin, "infielders and outfielders wear glasses and they leave them in their gloves. This could be dangerous." A new rule also disallowed players "tagging up" with a running start on a fly ball. Many other proposals, from the legalization of the spitball to awarding two bases on an intentional base on balls, were rejected by the committee.[50]

Inactive in the trading market in recent off-seasons, on December 9 Cronin made what might have been his best deal as general manager, trading Umphlett and pitcher Mickey McDermott to Washington for outfielder Jackie Jensen. At the time, many observers thought the Red Sox had overpaid for Jensen—Umphlett, after all, had been promising enough to unseat Dom DiMaggio in April, and southpaw McDermott, for years considered a promising prospect, had finally broken through with eighteen wins and was still just twenty-four years old. But McDermott was also a heavy drinker and carouser whose off-field antics had grown tiresome to the Red Sox—in 1953 he had punched a Boston sportswriter and cursed at Tom Yawkey's wife.

In fact, Clark Griffith almost nixed the deal when he heard about McDermott's nightclub act.[51]

Twenty-six-year-old Jensen, a former All-American football and baseball player at the University of California, was a good right fielder, base runner, and hitter, whose right-handed power swing seemed ideally suited for Fenway Park's short-left field dimensions. At the time of the deal, Jensen was considering retiring—he was frustrated with the way his career was evolving and did not feel he would ever make enough money in the game to justify the time away from his wife and children back in Oakland. Cronin telephoned him and made the case that Boston and Fenway Park were made for him and that he would be a star there.[52] This proved to be true—over the next six years Jensen led the league in RBI three times and won the 1958 Most Valuable Player Award. McDermott never again put together a season like he had in 1953, and Umphlett hit .219 and .217 in his next two seasons, before dropping from the Majors.

The most promising feature of the 1954 Red Sox, observers agreed, was the outfield of Williams, Jensen, and Piersall. Billy Goodman was solid at second base, as was George Kell at third. Catcher Sammy White, first baseman Dick Gernert, and shortstop Milt Bolling were the best products of the youth movement thus far. Lou Boudreau began to talk openly of winning the 1954 pennant, but his left fielder was having none of it. "To say that the Red Sox are going to win the pennant is silly talk," said Williams in February. He thought the White Sox and the Yankees, five-time defending champs, were the class of the league, but allowed that the Red Sox could finish third.[53]

For the Red Sox 1954 marked the arrival of Harry Agganis, a name already well known to most everyone in the region. The son of Greek immigrants, Arisotle George Agganis (Harry was a derivation of his family nickname, "Ari") was a legendary three-sport athlete at Lynn Classical High School, about ten miles north of Boston. He starred as a ball-handling center in basketball and won championships and state player of the year honors in baseball. As a left-handed T-formation quarterback, Agganis directed Classical to the national high-school football championship in Miami as a junior, earning All-American honors. His school declined an invitation to return to the championship in 1947 when they were told they had to leave their two black players at home. Frank Leahy, football coach at Notre Dame, called Agganis "the greatest prospect I have ever seen."

By the time he left high school in 1948, he had played football in Miami's Orange Bowl, baseball at Chicago's Wrigley Field and New York's Polo Grounds, and had won countless awards and honors. Agganis declined several offers from Major League teams and from dozens of major-college football programs to attend nearby Boston University. There were rumors that he had a deal with the Red Sox to stay in Boston, but more certainly he wanted to stay near his widowed mother, with whom he was very close.

Agganis played baseball and football at BU, extending his fame throughout the country. As a sophomore in 1949, he set a school record for touchdown passes and then spent a year in the Marine Corps—mainly playing baseball and football for Camp Lejeune in North Carolina, matching up against many professional players who were in the service. After one year he earned a dependency discharge to care for his mother.

Returning to college for his final two years, he garnered All-American honors and set school records for interceptions, punting average, touchdown passes, and total yards. Twice appearing on the cover of *Sport* magazine, after his junior year Agganis was selected in the first round of the National Football League draft by coach Paul Brown of the Cleveland Browns, who wanted Agganis to succeed legendary quarterback Otto Graham. Instead, Agganis returned for his senior season. In late November he ended heated speculation about his future when he signed with the Red Sox for a reported $40,000 bonus, just prior to the new bonus rule that would have required he spend two years in the Major Leagues. Joe Cronin granted Agganis special permission to play one final college game—in the all-star Senior Bowl in Mobile, Alabama, where he won the game's MVP award.[54]

In 1953 Agganis, a left-handed hitting and throwing first baseman, went to Sarasota with the Red Sox, but was soon optioned to Louisville.

He had a fine year in the American Association, with 23 home runs and 108 RBI, finishing second in the voting for league MVP. In 1954 he came to camp to battle Dick Gernert for the first base job. Agganis won most of the battle, earning the left-handed half of a platoon. He also found himself in the unusual situation of being a rookie who was more famous than most of his teammates and who had played in front of larger crowds than he saw at Fenway Park. Agganis started well and was hitting .300 in early June, before slumping and finishing the season at .251 with 11 home runs. His best day was on June 6—he homered to help the Red Sox beat the Tigers 7–4, and then headed over to Boston University for commencement exercises, where he was awarded his bachelor's degree in education.

Cronin had likely seen a lot of Agganis before he joined the Red Sox, both in Lynn, where the Red Sox had a farm club, and at Boston University, which was just a few miles away. In midsummer, Gernert was sent to Louisville, as the team further cemented Agganis's place on the club. "I hope he can make the grade," said Cronin. "He's colorful. He's a good competitor. And being a local boy, he can be a great drawing card."[55] This last was no trivial matter—the Red Sox's attendance had peaked in 1949 at nearly 1.6 million, but 1954 would mark their fifth consecutive decline, down to 930,000. The club organized a Fill Fenway campaign for the home opener, getting support from the mayor's office, but drew only 17,000 fans.

On June 21 the Red Sox held their annual Mayor's Field Day at Fenway Park, celebrating the team's place in the city. Archbishop Richard J. Cushing took the opportunity to praise Yawkey and Cronin ("one of the finest men I have known"). In particular, Cushing said, "There is no worthwhile charity in Boston that hasn't had the support of Joe Cronin and the Red Sox." Mayor John B. Hynes presented Cronin with a citation, praising him as "one of baseball's immortal stars and one of our outstanding adopted citizens." The men urged support for the Red Sox, who were in the midst of a disappointing season.[56]

The Red Sox's youth movement hit a rough patch in 1954 and Boudreau began to lose patience with the plan. As Cronin still wanted to play the youngsters, the relationship between the two men deteriorated. The offense improved, mainly because of Williams, who broke his collarbone in the spring but returned to hit .345 in 117 games, and Jensen, who drove in 117 runs. Cronin dealt Kell in late May to the White Sox for $100,000 and infielder Grady Hatton, supposedly to force his manager to play bonus baby Billy Consolo at third base, but instead Boudreau played the thirty-two-year-old Hatton.[57] Many of the young players did play—Agganis, Ted Lepcio, Milt Bolling, Sammy White, Karl Olson—but none of them hit much. The pitching fell off quite a bit from 1953. Ace Mel Parnell broke his wrist in April when he was hit by a pitch from old teammate Mickey McDermott and won only three games.

The Red Sox concluded their dreary season with a 69-85 mark, their worst record of the Yawkey era other than 1943. In October the Red Sox fired Boudreau, replacing him with Mike Higgins, who had played for Cronin in the late 1930s and again in 1946. Higgins had managed in the Red Sox system for eight successful seasons, culminating with Louisville's victory over Syracuse in the just completed Junior World Series (an annual matchup pitting the champions of the American Association and the International League). Cronin had gone to Louisville to watch the series and alerted Yawkey that Higgins was considering offers from other Major League teams. So informed, Yawkey agreed to make the change. "I got a call on Sunday (October 10)," said Cronin. "It was from Mr. Yawkey. He told me he decided to make Higgins the manager." Ironically, it had been Yawkey who insisted on hiring Boudreau three years earlier, when Cronin wanted to hire Higgins.[58] As usual, it was difficult to sort out who was in charge in Boston in the 1950s, and things would get no better. Higgins would help run the Red Sox for the next eleven seasons.

13 Power and Glory

THROUGHOUT THE 1950S JOE CRONIN TOOK on increasing responsibilities in the larger affairs of baseball. As discussed earlier, in 1949 he was named to the Rules Committee, which completely rewrote the rule book and subsequently enacted many important changes to the playing rules. He was part of the committee that wrote the new bonus rule in 1952, and he joined the Major Leagues' Scheduling Committee the next year. In 1956 he was named to baseball's Pension Committee and also its Revision Committee—a group charged with updating the agreement between the Major and Minor Leagues—and the next year he helped write a disaster plan for the American League. Cronin was later named a member of baseball's Executive Council, which worked with Commissioner Frick to govern the sport.

Along Cronin's path from well-loved player-manager to powerful league executive, 1955 would be an important year. Besides his usual service to the game, he also began to speak out on behalf of the downtrodden owners, something that surely made him more popular in baseball's board rooms. In early March Cronin talked with *The Sporting News* about the rising player salaries. "Major league salaries and expenses have reached the saturation point," said Cronin. "A club like ours has a real tough time of it because of the size of our park. We have to fill our park every night to make money." (The Red Sox averaged only about twelve thousand fans per game in 1954.) Nonetheless, it was time, Cronin felt, to "seek the players' co-operation. I believe the players are living all right."[1]

In May he went after the players more directly, again using the platform of *The Sporting News*. "The players have become too commercial," Cronin said. "They think too much of the ways they have of making more money [via] outside interests they develop through baseball. Some of them are driving away fans with their attitude towards the game." He criticized players who endorsed products they didn't use, players charging appearance fees to speak to kids, and players using agents. He thought many players were more concerned with selling products than with selling baseball. He named no names but instead employed a broad brush to directly challenge ballplayers. The illustration of Cronin accompanying the piece reminds one of Lionel Barrymore's turn as Mr. Potter in *It's a Wonderful Life*—a heavyset man wearing an expensive suit and smoking a big cigar.[2]

Not surprisingly, the players disagreed. Bob Feller, the American League player representative and a well-respected veteran, answered Cronin (his "good friend") in the next week's issue. "I don't recall Joe, as a player, going out and hustling customers into the ballpark," said Feller. He admitted that players had an obligation to speak in the community to schools and churches and to help promote the game. But for commercial groups or to events that require travel and time away from home, a player ought to charge a fee. "I go to a stage show and see an entertainer I enjoy. Next week my lodge has a party, so I call up this fellow and say to him, 'I'm your fan. Now I want you to come to our lodge and put on a show for free.'" According to Feller, this is what Cronin was asking the players to do. Feller was polite but took apart Cronin's criticisms one by one.[3]

Early Wynn was more blunt in a column he wrote for the *Cleveland News*, blasting both *The Sporting News* (for its sensationalism) and Cronin (for his critique). "By the time a few pleasure-bent executives get through, there isn't too much in sight for the player," said Wynn. Both Cronin and the newspaper (in an unsigned editorial) took Wynn to task for his "misreading" of the story and his "intemperate blast." Cronin complimented Feller's reply and even agreed with much of what the great pitcher said.[4] In the coming battles between baseball players and owners, there would never be a doubt as to which side Joe Cronin was on.

Cronin spent the weeks between the 1954 World Series and the winter meetings working on organizational matters with farm director

Johnny Murphy, the managers of each of the Minor League affiliates, and the scouting staff. With the club committed to their high-priced bonus players, no one knew the team's youngsters better than new manager Mike Higgins, who had spent the past eight years managing in the system. When asked about moves the club might make over the winter, Higgins expressed satisfaction with the solutions on hand. "We have some promising youngsters on the roster now and we're anxious to watch their play next spring," said Higgins.[5]

Meanwhile, the Rules Committee took up the problem of the ever-increasing length of games. Cronin thought the only complaints were from the press box. "I've never heard a single complaint from a fan over the longer games," said Cronin. "Maybe they're getting more for their money." Nonetheless, the committee asked the umpires to enforce a rule requiring the pitcher to deliver the ball within twenty seconds. The third base umpire was designated to clock the pitcher from the time he got the ball back from the catcher. Cal Hubbard, the supervisor of American League umpires, spent the spring clocking pitchers and never timed anyone over eleven seconds.[6]

Cronin arrived in Sarasota in late February 1955 but spent most of the next five weeks fielding questions about Ted Williams. At the end of the previous season Williams had told the press his career was over, a story he had first broke in the *Saturday Evening Post*. He had missed the first month of 1954 with a broken collarbone but hit as well as ever upon his return—so well, that most observers assumed he would reconsider his decision. Cronin did not really believe the story, mainly because Ted had never told the team he was quitting. "It's a long time between now and spring training," Cronin had said. In fact, there was speculation that the decision to replace Boudreau with Mike Higgins was partly to help lure Williams back.[7] Williams had played with Higgins in 1946 and had not taken to Boudreau as he had to Cronin and McCarthy.

Williams initially appeared to follow through on his plan and did not show up in Sarasota. The press asked about Williams every day, and Cronin would say he hadn't heard from his star but thought he'd be around soon. In early March the real story began to emerge—

Williams was going through a difficult divorce, and his "retirement" would help his financial settlement. Whether Cronin was in on the ruse is not known. The deliberations dragged through the spring and well into the season, finalizing on May 9. Four days later Williams was in Boston taking batting practice.[8]

Joe Cronin and Mike Higgins did not make any major roster moves prior to the start of the season, preferring to allow the young players to develop. The biggest position battle in the spring involved Harry Agganis, who was challenged at first base by rookie Norm Zauchin. A big right-handed hitter, Zauchin had fared well for Higgins in Louisville in 1954, while Agganis had slumped in the second half of his rookie campaign. Zauchin out hit Agganis in spring training and earned the position to start the season. But Zauchin went hitless in the season's first three games, Agganis played for a week, and when Zauchin continued to slump, Agganis got the job for good. With Williams still absent, Agganis began hitting in Ted's customary third slot in the batting order. On May 15 in a home doubleheader against the Detroit Tigers, Agganis went 5 for 10 with two doubles and a triple, boosting his average to .307, tenth highest in the league. For the many local observers accustomed to Agganis's extraordinary athletic achievements, he was merely on his expected path to greatness.

After Agganis complained of pain in his side, on May 16 the Red Sox sent him to Sancta Maria Hospital in Cambridge, where he was diagnosed with pneumonia. After missing two weeks, he returned to action on June 2 in Chicago. With Williams back in the lineup, Agganis batted fourth behind his star teammate, and hit 3 for 8 in two games to bring his average to .313. But his coughing and fever returned, and Agganis was sent back to Boston. Cronin met his plane and drove him back to Sancta Maria. On the thirteenth doctors reported that Agganis's pneumonia was abating, but the Red Sox soon announced he would be out for at least two months. On June 27 a blood clot broke free from his calf and moved to his lung, causing a pulmonary embolism. Shockingly, the great Harry Agganis was dead at twenty-six.

"Everyone connected with the Red Sox is grieved and shocked," a stunned Cronin said. "Harry was a great athlete, a grand boy, and a credit to sports."[9] Cronin's family recalls this time as the saddest they ever saw their father.[10] Agganis's death devastated the greater-Boston area, and people who lived through the period can still tell you where they were when they first heard the news. His body lay in a bier at his church in Lynn for a day and a half, and more than 10,000 mourners passed by. The funeral took place on June 30. Cronin tried to get the Red Sox game in Washington cancelled, but as it was a benefit for the Red Cross, the Senators insisted it be played. Of the players, only pitcher Frank Sullivan attended the funeral, along with Cronin, Higgins, and most of the employees from the front office. St. George Greek Orthodox Church was packed, and 20,000 more people lined the route from the church to Pine Grove Cemetery, far more than the 8,400 who attended the Red Sox-Senators game in DC. The Red Sox wore black arm bands for the next thirty days.

For the grieving Red Sox, the season went on. In fact, the club surprised many observers with their 84-70, fourth-place showing. Boston's success was largely due to their fine pitching, including youngsters Frank Sullivan (18-13, 2.91), Willard Nixon, and Tom Brewer. Williams did not join the club until the end of May but still hit .356 with 28 home runs. Jensen and Piersall had fine years, and Zauchin took over at first base and hit 27 home runs. Mike Higgins was named manager of the year in his debut, and his contract was extended through 1958. Though the season was tragic, there were promising signs on the field.

In late October the Cronins headed to Washington to be at the bedside of Clark Griffith. The eighty-five-year-old Senators president entered the hospital on October 19 to be treated for neuritis, but within a few days he began hemorrhaging in his stomach and developed congestion in his lungs.[11] He passed away on October 27, ending his forty-four-year association with the Senators and more than six decades in baseball. Griffith was a member of Cronin's family, and also a close friend, role model, and mentor. Like Griffith Cronin spent his adult lifetime in baseball and loved nothing more than being with baseball people and talking the game. Their respect was mutual.

"Determination, humility and guts made Joe Cronin the man he is today," Griffith once said of his young friend.[12]

In late November 1955 Cronin completed the purchase, on behalf of the Red Sox, of the San Francisco Seals. The deal was announced on the twenty-eighth at the Minor League meetings in Columbus, Ohio. The Seals played in the Triple-A Pacific Coast league—there were as yet no Major League teams on the West Coast. After fifty years of stability in the Major Leagues, three teams had moved in the mid-1950s—the Boston Braves to Milwaukee, the St. Louis Browns to Baltimore, and the Philadelphia Athletics to Kansas City. "The Coast League is the top league in the minors, beyond question," said Cronin. "I can't tell you how pleased I am to be connected with San Francisco baseball, after so many years."[13]

Might the Red Sox have been entertaining the notion of moving to San Francisco, Joe Cronin's native city?[14] "Don't underestimate the significance of a franchise on the Coast being owned by the wealthiest man in the baseball, Yawkey," wrote Arthur Daley in the *Times*. "New Englanders, meanwhile, will be biting their finger nails in unashamed anxiety."[15] Cronin did what he could to dispel the rumors. "Our chief interest is baseball in Boston," he said.[16] The Pacific Coast League had spent several years operating somewhat independently of the Major Leagues, but the Seals franchise in particular was in dire straits. The Red Sox intended to straighten it out, while also claiming the territory in case the American League wanted either to move or create a franchise there.

Along with the Boston to San Francisco rumors, there was also a report that Cronin was going to take over the Senators and move *them* to San Francisco. Cronin hastened to point out that he could not afford to buy a baseball team and furthermore that he no longer considered San Francisco his home. Joe and Mildred had lived near Boston for fifteen years and had four children who had never known another home. Still, the rumors persisted.

Within a few days Cronin appointed Jerry Donovan, a long time San Franciscan and friend, as Seals' president and general manager and Eddie Joost, another local who had played with the Red Sox in

1955, as manager. On December 9 Cronin landed in his native city, greeted by two hundred people who escorted him to his hotel via motorcade. He promised the press that the Seals would be given good veteran players, not only youngsters, and that they would play mainly day games other than Fridays.[17]

In the meantime, Cronin's off-season was filled with the usual business. On November 8 Cronin made a nine-player swap with the Senators, who were now being run by Calvin Griffith, Cronin's brother-in-law. The Red Sox dealt five prospects—Karl Olson, Tex Clevenger, Dick Brodowski, Neil Chrisley, and Al Curtis—for four veterans—first baseman Mickey Vernon, pitchers Bob Porterfield and Johnny Schmitz, and outfielder Tom Umphlett. Cronin believed he had a surplus of young players and that his team was on the verge of contending for a pennant. "We have so many young players that we could afford to trade off youth for experience," he said.[18] As it turned out, Vernon had one very good year in Boston, but none of the other eight players in the deal would help their new teams.

On January 25 Cronin learned that he had been elected by the baseball writers to the Baseball Hall of Fame. He had been receiving votes for a few years but a large backlog of deserving players kept most players waiting. When he heard the news, he was driving home from the office. "I was high-tailing it home to help make supper for the family," said Cronin. "My wife, Mildred, has been ill and I was more concerned about the supper than about being elected to the Hall of Fame."[19]

Cronin was very happy ("a thrill you can't lose," he said) and doubly so because he would enter the Hall with Hank Greenberg, his long-time rival as a player and of late as an executive—Greenberg had been the general manager of the Cleveland Indians for the previous eight years. "This is *Abie's Irish Rose* all over again—a Jewish kid from the sidewalks of New York and an Irish kid from the sidewalks of San Francisco making the shrine together," Cronin said.[20] Stories of their election depicted each of them as players who had made themselves great by outworking everyone else. "They didn't have the natural talents of the supermen who preceded them into the Hall," wrote Arthur Daley. "They crawled through those portals by dint of the hardest kind of work."[21]

The Red Sox staged a celebration for Cronin in a ceremony before their game on July 20. Commissioner Ford Frick, Gov. Christian Herter, Mayor John Hynes, and many baseball dignitaries spoke in praise of Cronin, as did sportswriters and current players. Cronin asked the crowd for a moment of silence for many of his departed friends, including Clark Griffith, Connie Mack, and Eddie Collins. He received a few plaques, several checks that he turned over to the Jimmy Fund, and a new Cadillac (with the license plate HF-56). An indication of the respect he had in Boston was the parade of groups who honored him that night—the Boston Police Department, Little Leaguers, all the branches of the armed services, park vendors, and the Catholic Youth Organization, among others.[22]

Three days later, in Cooperstown, New York, Greenberg and Cronin were officially inducted to the Hall. Tom Yawkey, surprisingly, had never visited the Hall of Fame prior to Cronin's induction, but the occasion prompted him to arrange for two train cars from Boston and accommodations for thirty-four people—including the Cronin family, several of Cronin's closest friends, the entire front office, Eddie Collins's widow, and six Boston newspaper editors.[23] Prior to the ceremony, Cronin told the press, "If all the thrills I've known in baseball were packaged together—this would be it—this moment."

The ceremony itself was brief when compared with the pomp to come decades later. Lydall Smith of the *Detroit Free Press*, president of the Baseball Writers Association of America, was the master of ceremonies. After introducing the dignitaries present, including Yawkey, three members of the Hall of Fame—Tris Speaker, Ray Schalk, and Frank Baker—and a few other former players, Smith turned the program over to Commissioner Ford Frick, who introduced Cronin and Greenberg. Greenberg praised Cronin, who was a star when Greenberg was breaking in but had made Greenberg feel welcome by tipping him off about what the pitchers were throwing. "But sometimes he made a mistake," said Greenberg.

Cronin spoke for about five minutes. "This is indeed the greatest thrill of my career," he said. He called out Joe McCarthy, who was present, for being responsible for so much heartache as manager of the Yankees. He mentioned Herb Pennock and Walter Johnson, two deceased inductees with whom Cronin had worked. He congratulated Greenberg, who had performed "great deeds on the ball field." He concluded by expressing his good fortune for being associated with "two of the greatest men in the history of baseball for a great number of years, Clark Griffith and Tom Yawkey." He was quite emotional throughout his speech, as was Yawkey, who could hardly speak afterwards. The next day the entire entourage headed back to Boston to continue the season.

In 1956 the Red Sox played about as well as they had in 1955—finishing with the same record (84-70) and again in fourth place, thirteen games behind the Yankees. Though the club enjoyed a few fine offensive performances, notably by Williams (.345) and Jensen (.315 with 97 RBI), the squad was again led by an underappreciated group of young starting pitchers: Tom Brewer, (18-9), Frank Sullivan (14-7), and Willard Nixon (9-8). The youth movement had yet to affect the club's offense, but the pitching staff was usually among the league's best throughout the 1950s.

Much of Cronin's energy that season was occupied by a crisis with his star player. Although generally well behaved since his return from Korea three years earlier, Ted Williams had become increasingly upset about the booing he received at Fenway Park. Both the fans and the media had become more hostile throughout the decade as a series of uninspiring teams failed to contend. Williams was not the only target—Jackie Jensen was booed for hitting into double plays, rookie Don Buddin for his erratic play at shortstop—but Williams was the most sensitive. On July 17 he hit his four-hundredth career home run in a 1–0 victory over the Athletics in Fenway Park. While crossing home plate he appeared to spit in the direction of the press box and admitted after the game that the gesture was directed at a few of the local sportswriters.[24] Three days later, on the night Joe Cronin was being honored at the park, Williams repeated his gesture while returning to the dugout after he misjudged, then caught, a routine fly ball to end an inning. "Nobody's going to stop me spitting," said Williams. "The newspaper guys in this town are bush and some of the fans are the worst in the world."[25] Cronin, preoccupied with his own night and his trip to Cooperstown the next day, stayed quiet.

The big explosion came on August 7, the Red Sox having spent most of the intervening time on the road. Before a packed crowd of over thirty-six thousand for a weekday game, the Red Sox and Yankees waged a scoreless pitcher's duel through ten innings. In the top of the eleventh, in drizzling rain, Mickey Mantle hit a high pop fly to Williams, who dropped the ball for a two-base error. Boos rained down on Williams. On the very next play, he made a nice running catch of a liner hit by Yogi Berra, ending the inning. The fans cheered, an act of hypocrisy that pushed Williams over the edge. On the way to the dugout he spit three times, the booing growing after each transgression, with the final act directed at a fan yelling on top of the dugout. In the bottom of the inning, the Yankees loaded the bases and brought in Tommy Byrne to face Williams, who walked to end the game. Williams threw his bat in the air, steaming over not getting a chance to hit. The Red Sox celebrated their victory in a hailstorm of boos from their own fans.[26]

Tom Yawkey listened to the game on the radio in New York. After the game he called Cronin and the two agreed to fine Williams $5,000. "Why the man does these things is something I can't figure out," said Yawkey. "I can't, I can't, I can't." Cronin added, "We couldn't condone such actions. And it was too bad it had to happen after a great catch he made in the 11th inning."[27] According to Hy Hurwitz in *The Sporting News*, Cronin had wanted to discipline Williams for years, but Yawkey had always restrained him. This time, Yawkey had had enough.[28]

The local press, many of whom had long felt that the Red Sox pampered their immature star, eviscerated Williams in the papers the next day. The *Globe*'s Harold Kaese thought Williams should just quit. "He is getting too old for the game—old physically and old mentally," Kaese wrote.[29] Williams expressed no regrets, other than for being fined, and blamed the writers for inflaming the fans in the first place. The next night, against the Orioles, everyone wondered how the fans would treat Williams after all they had read in the papers. In fact, the people cheered from the moment Williams stepped on the field until the end of the game, a chorus amplified when he hit a go-ahead home run in the sixth inning.

Williams later claimed that he turned a corner that night—he would never forgive the writers, but he realized that the fans were behind him, and he never again expressed anything other than great appreciation for them.[30] In return the Boston fans took Williams's side in the feud with the writers. Williams claimed in his autobiography that Yawkey never took the $5,000 from his pay, though Yawkey, Cronin, and Williams himself repeatedly said otherwise in the months after the incidents of 1956.

One impact of Williams's spitting was Cronin's decision to ban the sale of beer in the stands at Fenway Park. Patrons now had to leave their seats and go under the stands to buy their beer, a step Cronin hoped would improve fan behavior. Though he obviously felt that drunken fans were responsible for some of Williams's problems, he claimed that the people were on his side. "More than 90% praised us for this move," he reported.[31]

Other than the controversies with Williams, Cronin devoted much of his time to his increasing responsibility within baseball's governance. On August 2 Ford Frick announced the formation of the Revision Committee, informally called the Save the Minors Committee. The National Association, the formal name given to the Minor Leagues, had been suffering for several years. While there had been fifty-nine Minor Leagues as recently as 1950, six years later there were only twenty-eight. Every year several teams were forced to either move or disband, and many times entire leagues dissolved in midseason. The biggest problem, according to the Minors, was television, but the Majors had been thwarted in their attempts to restrict their broadcast into Minor League territories by the threat of antitrust action by the U.S. Congress.

Cronin was one of six members of the Revision Committee, along with Kansas City's Arnold Johnson (chair), Cleveland's George Medinger, Cincinnati's Gabe Paul, the Giants' Horace Stoneham, and Philadelphia's Bob Carpenter. The group originally proposed that a series of twelve Major League All-Star Games be played in various Minor League cities in 1957, with all proceeds going to the Minor Leagues. The group ultimately suggested the creation of a fund, and the owners agreed to contribute $500,000. In addition the Major Leagues agreed to reduce their roster limit at the start of the season to twenty-eight, rather than forty.[32]

Cronin also joined baseball's Pension Committee in 1956 and helped iron out a new agreement with the player's union. The old plan provided a pension, beginning at age fifty, of $50 per month for five-year players, $60 for six-year players, up to $100 for players with ten or more years of service. Cronin's fellow committee members included Pittsburgh owner John Galbreath, along with players Bob Feller and Robin Roberts. The new plan, which included different benefit levels depending on when the player began drawing his pension, started at $88 for a five-year player taking benefits at age fifty, and increased to $550 for a twenty-year man who waited until age sixty-five. The new plan also included medical benefits, hospitalization, and benefits for widows.[33] The plan represented one of the first big successes of the Major League Players Association, formed in 1956. Cronin would be dealing with the association often in the coming years.

Later in 1956 Cronin was named to a committee to formulate a disaster plan for baseball. With the increase in air travel, the prospect of an accident incapacitating most or all of a team was an unspoken fear within the game. The two leagues came up with the outlines of a plan, but agreed that the each league would develop a plan independently. The AL plan, worked out by a committee of Cronin, Greenberg, and the Yankees' George Weiss, determined that a "disaster" would take place if, after a plane crash or similar event, a team lost the services of seven or more players. If this occurred, each of the seven other league clubs would submit a list of twelve players from their Major League roster to the affected club, which would have the right to purchase as many players as it lost for $75,000 each. The money would come from a leaguewide insurance policy.

The months following the 1956 season were typically eventful for the Cronins. The start of school year brought the entire family back to Newton Center, filling Joe's evenings and weekends. The two oldest boys were in high school and had their father's love of competition: Tommy in hockey and baseball and Michael in baseball and football. Twelve-year-old Maureen rode horses, and even six-year-old Kevin had started throwing a ball around.

Meanwhile, rumors that Cronin would eventually move west continued. Jerry Nason, the *Globe's* sports editor, wrote in September that Cronin was heading to San Francisco "to do the spade work" that would lead to an American League team in the city. Larry Claflin, in the *Boston Evening American*, wrote that the Cronin move was definite, and that Bucky Harris, currently the Tigers manager, would move to Boston to take Cronin's old job. Tom Yawkey, contacted in South Carolina, called the reports "harebrained."[34] In October Cronin hired Harris to be his assistant, a move that strengthened the swirling rumors.

The first year of the affiliation with the Seals had not gone as planned. Cronin had promised a winning team, but the Red Sox had stocked the club mostly with prospects who could not compete with some of the veteran-laden clubs in the Coast League. Cronin had visited the city in May to calm the natives, but the Seals still limped home at 77-88, twenty-eight and a half games behind first-place Los Angeles. Eddie Joost, Cronin's hand-picked manager, had been fired in midseason and replaced with Joe Gordon. In September Seals GM Jerry Donovan said, "We can't possibly come back next season with the same ballclub. Cronin was mighty discouraged about our finishing far off the pace."[35]

Meanwhile, at the 1956 Major League meetings Cronin made a startling proposal to combat the Yankees. "I honestly feel that for the best interests of the league," he suggested, "Cleveland, Chicago, Detroit, and our own club should try to work out some equitable deals whereby we would make a better showing next season." The Red Sox, he felt, had an excess of outfielders and catchers, and were willing to make deals with contenders who possessed surpluses in other areas. His apparently sincere idea was not well-received. "I am only interested in having Chicago beat the Yankees," said White Sox manager Al Lopez. "I don't want to strengthen Boston or anyone else." Charlie Dressen, manager of the Senators, chimed in: "What's the matter with the Red Sox? Don't they want to trade with Washington?"[36] Despite Cronin's scheme, the Red Sox made no significant deals during the 1956–57 off-season.

Cronin left for Sarasota in mid-February 1957, spending a week at John Galbreath's home for additional meetings on the pension plan. Back with the Red Sox in early March, he was still frustrated by his inability to make any deals. On March 18 came the shocking revelation that Cronin had offered the Indians a sum of $1 million for pitcher Herb Score and was turned down. The twenty-three-year-old Score had won thirty-six games in his two big league seasons, twice leading the league in strikeouts. Many writers were skeptical that the offer was serious, though Greenberg insisted it was "a valid cash offer."[37] The greatest sales price on record remained the $250,000 the Red Sox had paid for Cronin in 1934. (Just a few weeks into the 1957 season Score was hit by a line drive off the bat of New York's Gil McDougald, ending his season and seriously derailing his career. He came back in 1958, hurt his arm, and was never again a star.)

In March 1957 the Red Sox left Sarasota for an extended spring road trip to the West Coast, starting with three games in San Francisco against the Seals. The series drew capacity crowds for all three games, including standing room only for the opener on March 22. "It was one of the most incredible things that ever happened in baseball," said Cronin. "This amazing attendance should convince every club owner in both the National and American Leagues that San Francisco is ready for the majors."[38]

On the day of the first game, a Friday, Cronin spent some time driving around the city with Mike Higgins, Barbara Tyler (Cronin's secretary), and Tommy McCarthy (the club's press steward). Cronin was showing off his old neighborhood and the areas of the city damaged by the 1906 earthquake and fire. At 11:45 a.m., with Cronin at the wheel, another earthquake hit. The epicenter was a few miles south in Daly City, and it measured a 5.3 on the Richter scale in San Francisco, the largest quake since the big one in 1906. The city received only minimal damage, but it surely enlivened Joe Cronin's tour that morning. That evening Cronin was extensively honored before the game. Among the tributes was a lifetime membership to the Columbia Park Sports Club, for whom he had played sandlot ball in his youth, and a scroll from Sacred Heart High School.[39]

From San Francisco the club headed south to play single games against the Hollywood Stars and the Los Angeles Angels, both members of the Coast League. Writer Ed Rumill, who accompanied the club on their western trip, was impressed by the popular reception Cronin received there. "Joe must have a million friends on the West Coast, even though he never played for his home town of San Francisco," wrote Rumill. "Folks out that way never forgot him as a kid on the sandlots and closely followed his playing, managerial and now front-office careers in the East."[40] The Red Sox left California for Arizona, where they played a few exhibitions against clubs who trained there—the Giants in Phoenix, the Cubs in Mesa, and the Indians in Tucson—then played a game in New Orleans, before finally heading back to Sarasota. The players loved the trip, as it broke up the usual monotony of five weeks in a Sarasota motel. Cronin said he favored more like it.[41]

After winning eighty-four games for two straight seasons, the Red Sox won eighty-two in 1957 without threatening the Yankees. In fact, the Red Sox settled into third place on July 5 and stayed there the rest of the season, ending a full sixteen games out of first place. The club got fine contributions from third baseman Frank Malzone, who hit .292 and drove in 103 runs in his first full season, Jackie Jensen, with 103 RBI, and Jimmy Piersall, who hit 19 home runs to go along with his great defense. Ted Williams battled his demons and a few injuries to have one of his greatest seasons, hitting .388 with 38 home runs, and winning his fifth batting title at age thirty-nine.

The twenty-seven-year-old Malzone had spent seven years in the

Minors, plus two more in the military. He had put together three good season of Triple-A ball but was seemingly not taken seriously in an organization that had many high-priced bonus babies. In a book published more than thirty years later, pitcher Jerry Casale claimed that the Red Sox were run by bigoted Irishmen—Cronin, Higgins, and farm director Johnny Murphy—who did not like Italians. Casale claimed that he, Malzone, Consolo, Ken Aspromonte, and others were good players who never got the chances they deserved.[42] Although such a claim cannot be definitively refuted, Malzone had failed a trial in 1956, Consolo had been given $85,000 to sign (suggestive that his ethnicity did not alarm the club), and the player that Aspromonte was demoted in favor of—Ted Lepcio—was also Italian. Furthermore, Cronin had grown up in a very Italian city and had recruited and purchased Dom DiMaggio, who became a lifelong friend.

At the end of the 1957 season Major League Baseball did come to California, with the transfers of the Brooklyn Dodgers and New York Giants to Los Angeles and San Francisco. In late May the National League granted permission for the moves, and the decision was finalized late in the season. While the Dodgers had purchased the Los Angeles territory the previous winter, both Cronin and Yawkey had claimed on multiple occasions that the Red Sox had purchased the Seals in part to claim the San Francisco territory for the American League. Although Cronin talked publicly about the value of the territory—"The Giants must feel that San Francisco is the best city to put their ball club," he said in early October—in the end the Red Sox amicably swapped the San Francisco club for the Giants' Triple-A team in Minneapolis.[43]

In the meantime the Red Sox's second and final year of affiliation with the Seals was a rousing success. Along with providing the club top prospects, the Red Sox also came through with several Major League veterans, such as Bill Renna, Grady Hatton, and Harry Dorish, who helped drive the club to the top of the league in midsummer. The team's best player was left-hander Leo Kiely, who had spent four seasons with the Red Sox mainly as a reliever. For the Seals, Kiely finished 21-6, including a remarkable 20-4 in relief. The Seals clinched the pennant on a Friday evening, September 13, after which general manager Jerry Donovan called Cronin at home to give him the good news. Of course, it was 3:00 a.m. in Boston when Cronin got the call, but he was awake enough to authorize a celebratory banquet. Thus ended the fifty-five-year history of the San Francisco Seals.

A few days after Joe and Mildred Cronin had returned home from the World Series, the Cronins learned of the death of Clark Griffith's widow—Mildred's aunt—the former Anne Robertson. While in Washington for the funeral, Joe learned that his brother Raymond had died in San Francisco. Ray was just sixty-one and living alone when his body was discovered on October 15, likely several days after he had died. Joe headed for the airport immediately following Mrs. Griffith's service, but a long delay caused him to miss Raymond's funeral. Raymond was the last of Cronin's family in San Francisco—both of his brothers, along with his parents, were now gone.[44]

Cronin returned home to his busy off-season routine. In early November he oversaw the replacement of the dirt and grass at Fenway Park—the first renovation of the field since the park was rebuilt in 1934. In mid-November he headed to Minneapolis to meet with Tommy Thomas, the new general manager of the Millers, now the Red Sox's Triple-A affiliate. In early December the Cronins traveled to Colorado Springs for the winter meetings. While there Cronin was named American League representative to the Executive Council, replacing Yawkey.

Back home, on December 15 he was the special guest on a local television show hosted by broadcaster Curt Gowdy, modeled after *Meet the Press*. Cronin answered questions from local writers about whether the club would be better off without Williams ("That's so silly, I won't dignify it with an answer"), a new stadium for the team (Yawkey would be interested if the state builds it), and why the team had not made any recent deals (they did not want to give up their young talent). Most pointedly he was asked why the Red Sox had lagged so far behind the Yankees despite all of their high-priced young players. "The Yankees have had superior scouts," Cronin said. "One man alone—Joe Devine—picked up three players who were regulars in the Yankee infield—Gil McDougald, Jerry Coleman, and Andy Carey." He could also have mentioned that Devine had signed Cronin himself years earlier, along with many other stars.

After the holidays Cronin managed to pull off a big trade with the Washington Senators, dealing Minor League outfielder Albie Pearson and first baseman Norm Zauchin for veteran infielder Pete Runnels. Pearson would win the Rookie of the Year Award in 1958 and enjoy a few other good seasons, but Runnels would win two batting titles and star for the Red Sox for five years. Cronin's dealings with the Senators had drawn comment even at the very start of his tenure as general manager, but the chiding became especially pointed once brother-in-law Calvin Griffith took over the club after Clark's death. "We always have to offset the advantages the Red Sox have through their marital relations," said Cleveland GM Frank Lane later that year.[45]

When Joe Cronin sought to make a trade he had only seven possible trading partners—interleague trading was not permitted until 1959—unless each player cleared waivers in his league. During Cronin's eleven years running the Red Sox, he made twenty-seven Major League deals (excluding trades in which money was a major component) with the seven AL teams, and twelve were with the Senators. The vast majority of his twenty-seven deals had little impact on either team. In fact, not once did Cronin give up a player the Red Sox later regretted losing. Setting aside the 1947 deals with the Browns—when money was the primary factor in landing Vern Stephens, Jack Kramer, and Ellis Kinder—Cronin's best two trades were with the Senators: the acquisitions of Jackie Jensen in 1953 and Runnels in 1958.

On the other hand, doling out credit or blame for baseball trades is a difficult business, particularly with the Red Sox. When asked late in his Red Sox tenure about the best deal he ever made, Cronin claimed that it was his deal for Rudy York in 1946.[46] Eddie Collins was the Red Sox GM at the time, but by then Cronin made most of the trades. Similarly, Red Sox managers in the 1950s provided a lot of input on the deals that Cronin made.

When he was not trading with the Senators, Cronin's work with the Rules Committee continued. Before the 1956 season Cronin had sponsored and passed a rule limiting a manager or coach to one trip to the mound to visit a pitcher per inning. A year later the committee changed the requirement for batting championship qualifiers from 400 at bats to 477 plate appearances—Ted Williams had missed the 1954 batting title in large part because he walked so often that he did not reach the at bat requirement. In 1958 the committee set minimum outfield distances for all future Major League parks: 325 feet at each foul line and 400 to straightaway center. This rule would have outlawed many existing Major League parks, including Fenway Park and Yankee Stadium, had those parks not been "grandfathered."[47]

An interesting controversy arose in 1958 when the AL passed a rule requiring that all hitters wear batting helmets. The vote was 7–1, with Cronin dissenting. "I have to vote 'no' because Ted Williams won't wear a helmet no matter what the rule says." When Williams continued to insist that he would not, Cronin clarified the club's position: "The rule merely states a player must wear protective headgear. Well, as far as the Red Sox are concerned, the ordinary ballcap will constitute enough protection around the head." Later, Williams began to wear a plastic lining in his cap, which the umpires chose to allow. Shirley Povich sarcastically suggested that Williams place "two layers of cigarette papers" inside his cap.[48]

That January the Boston baseball writers invited Jimmie Foxx to be the main speaker at their banquet. The fifty-year-old Foxx, living in Miami, confessed that he was ill, broke, out of work, and unable to make it to the dinner. When word of his plight reached Boston, several people sent money, and the writers sent the air fare. Within a week Foxx had been on several national television shows talking about his situation. He spoke at the banquet on January 22, telling the audience, "My life is a new book from here on." Two days later Cronin announced that he had hired Foxx as a hitting coach with the Minneapolis club at a salary of $8,000. "It is with great personal pleasure to Tom Yawkey and myself to have Jim back in baseball where he belongs." Unfortunately, Foxx's comeback was short lived. Foxx spent the season in and out of bed with various ailments, and Cronin fired him after the season. Minneapolis manager Gene Mauch, who idolized Foxx, later recalled the story. "By then, Jim had a bad drinking problem, and was seldom at the park on time to be of help," said Mauch, who had kept his friend's problems from the press. Foxx would never work in baseball again and would die broke in 1967 at age fifty-nine.[49]

Cronin skipped most of spring camp in Sarasota in 1958, not arriving until late March and staying only a week. While there he expressed optimism about the coming season: "We have more depth, and our pitching and hitting look better."[50] As it turned out, the year was like most of the 1950s—a 79-75 record (three games worse than 1957) and a third-place finish. In the first nine seasons of the decade, the Red Sox finished either third or fourth eight times. Once again, many of their players had fine seasons. Pete Runnels hit .322 in his first season with the club, and Jensen led the league with 122 RBI and captured the MVP award. Williams won the batting title despite a 60-point drop to .328. Tom Brewer (12 wins) and Frank Sullivan (13) had their usual solid seasons, and Ike Delock (14-8) had a nice year as a starter and reliever. But just as many mediocre performances prevented the club from contending.

Though it had been many years since he had put the uniform on, Cronin still took a personal interest in the young players coming to the Red Sox, playing father figure to kids who were making their way in the big city for the first time. "Joe Cronin always made sure you contacted your parents," recalled pitcher Bill Monbouquette, "and if you didn't have money, he said the Red Sox would pay for the telephone call. That's the way he was. I loved Joe Cronin." Monbouquette also recalled Cronin sending for him after he had charged an umpire during a game. "He said, 'Frenchy, you're the worst S.O.B. I've ever seen in my life. You can't charge an umpire like that. Do you want to go back to Minneapolis?'"[51] Having dealt with his fair share of personalities in his career, Cronin never lost the belief that he could sit a man down and appeal to his better angels.

Williams nearly made it through the season without any controversies, but his luck ran out on September 21. In a game at Fenway against the Senators, Williams took a third strike in the third inning against Bill Fischer and then, angry at himself, hurled his bat. Unfortunately, the bat traveled seventy-five feet in the air into the box seats and struck a sixty-nine-year-old woman on the head, fortunately a glancing blow. The woman, Gladys Heffernan, was Joe Cronin's housekeeper. As the fans booed, Williams ran over to Mrs. Heffernan, reportedly with tears in his eyes. She insisted she was fine but was helped under the stands and spent one night in a local hospital, where Williams visited her again. Cronin was shaken by the affair but stuck up for his star. "The guy feels bad enough as it is. He feels terrible," said Cronin. Heffernan also bore no grudges, saying the boos were unjustified. "Ted is a wonderful person," she said.[52]

Meanwhile, the biggest problem confronting the American League in 1958 was the plight of the Washington Senators. Calvin Griffith had wanted to move the franchise ever since inheriting it in 1955 and was eyeing Minneapolis, Montreal, Houston, and Dallas–Fort Worth. Five Major League clubs had moved in the 1950s, and all five had seen large increases in attendance. Cronin was named to the league's realignment committee, which discussed proposals for franchise shifts as well as expansion. The league turned the Senators down, with the Red Sox being adamantly opposed. Of important consideration, Yawkey and other the baseball magnates feared antitrust hearings in Congress if there was no team in Washington.[53]

After the season Cronin visited Scottsdale, Arizona, where the Red Sox would hold spring training in 1959. Cronin had apparently enjoyed his visit on the club's 1957 exhibition trip and announced the transfer the next summer. "It's great to be part of the West," said Cronin. "I'm sure I'll never be sorry the Red Sox decided to be a part of the great western boom."[54] (The Red Sox spent just seven years in Arizona before returning to Florida in 1966, where they have trained ever since.)

Cronin's off-season was interrupted on December 3 with the announcement that American League president Will Harridge had decided to step down. "I feel the American League should have the opportunity of bringing in a younger and more energetic man to handle the problems," said the seventy-five-year-old Harridge, while also insisting he was in fine health. Speculation about his successor immediately centered on two men—Cronin and the Yankees' George Weiss—both of whom had been involved in league and baseball affairs for years. Apparently Weiss was approached about the position but declined to be considered. Cronin had been mentioned as a possible successor to Harridge several times over the years, when rumors of Harridge's retirement cropped up. Now that the job was open, he was not coy. "I would be honored and would accept if asked to serve," he said.[55]

The league organized a committee to find a successor, naming Tom Yawkey as the chairman. The committee met a few times but never really considered any other candidate once Weiss withdrew. The committee recommended Cronin on January 14, and he was unanimously approved by the league on January 31, signing a seven-year contract at $60,000 per year. "I don't know of anyone I'd rather have succeed me than Joe Cronin," said Harridge. "Joe is going to do a top-notch job for the league."[56] To replace Cronin, the Red Sox promoted three people to fill portions of his former role—Bucky Harris to general manager, Dick O'Connell to business manager, and Hiram Mason to treasurer. No Red Sox executive would ever again wield the power Joe Cronin did in the 1950s.

Joe Cronin's twenty-four years with the team, including eleven as general manager, were over. His legacy as GM is decidedly mixed. The Red Sox's longtime reputation as a "country club" run by cronies who presided over an undisciplined bunch of underachievers began in the 1950s, although it intensified after Cronin left. Much of this can be laid at the club's terrible relationship with the press, the men who wrote the history in later years. That said, all of the people hired within the organization—assistants in the front office, managers and coaches at all levels, scouts—seemed to be friends of either Cronin or Yawkey or both, and there was apparently very little accountability.

On the field, the Red Sox had continued to field good, though unspectacular, teams. During Cronin's GM years, the club finished in the first division (the top half of the eight team league) ten of eleven years, and won more than half their games nine times. But the farm system he left was nearly bare, and the Red Sox would pay the price with eight consecutive losing seasons beginning in 1959. The primary job of the GM is to find, develop, and retain good ballplayers, and the talent in the organization seeped away throughout the 1950s. Cronin failed to build a strong farm system, over-relying on a group of high-priced bonus players who did not pan out, and—most egregiously—not aggressively pursuing the initial wave of African American players who revolutionized the game. Management, led by the undeniably likeable Joe Cronin, squandered the advantage that Tom Yawkey's money gave them and instead found itself drifting towards the bottom of the American League.

14 Mr. President

WHEN JOE CRONIN ASSUMED HIS NEW POST in January 1959, he became only the fourth president in the fifty-nine-year history of the American League. The original, Ban Johnson, had turned his circuit into a major league in 1901, and then presided over the league's successful battles with the National League, becoming the dominant executive in baseball for two decades. After baseball hired Judge Kenesaw Mountain Landis to serve as its first commissioner in 1921, the league presidents were stripped of much of their authority, and never again would the positions afford any sort of power outside of their own league. Johnson held on for six more years before his forced resignation in 1927. Ernest Barnard of Cleveland replaced Johnson and held the office until his sudden death in March 1931.

Bernard's replacement, William Harridge, took an unusual road to the presidency. Born in 1883 on Chicago's south side, Harridge parlayed a high-school education and a few stenography classes into a position as a clerk for the Wabash Railroad in Chicago. One of his clerical duties was scheduling the transportation for the American League umpires. Harridge's fine job impressed Ban Johnson enough that he hired him away as his private secretary in 1911. After Johnson resigned in 1927, Harridge was promoted to league secretary. And after Barnard's death he became president.

During his twenty-eight years heading the AL, Harridge concentrated on (1) administering the business of the league, and (2) avoiding publicity for either himself or his office. The president's duties included hiring and managing the umpires, disciplining players and managers, approving contracts and intraleague trades, and making the league's regular-season schedule. Harridge made rare news in 1951 when he ruled that Eddie Gaedel, a dwarf the St. Louis Browns employed (as a stunt) in a single game as a pinch hitter, would no longer be eligible to play. Many fans likely did not know the name of the AL president at the time of his ruling. When issues of larger import came up, such as franchise shifts or possible league expansion, Harridge calmly presided over the appropriate meetings and let the teams work things out. The club owners wielded the real power and became the public face of the league. As one writer humorously observed, "a league president has been something like the popular conception of the Vice President of the United States—someone to send out for cigars and ice during a party."[1]

When Cronin took the reins in 1959, the American League had been lagging behind the National League in many important ways. The NL had outmaneuvered its counterpart in relocations to Milwaukee, Los Angeles, and San Francisco, all huge successes, while the AL experienced more modest benefits from their moves to Baltimore and Kansas City. The New York Yankees had nearly monopolized the American League's pennant—four straight and nine in the previous ten seasons—and generally by large margins, while the NL enjoyed several fine pennant races. The National League had also been far more aggressive in signing black talent, including superstars like Willie Mays, Henry Aaron, Ernie Banks, and Frank Robinson.

After six decades in Chicago, the league offices were moved to Boston to accommodate the new president, Joe Cronin. (This decision reflected the standard practice—when Warren Giles replaced Ford Frick as National League president in 1951, the NL office relocated from New York to Giles's hometown of Cincinnati.) In his first weeks on the job Cronin focused on locating and setting up new offices. The chosen space was in the IBM Building at 520 Boylston Street, near Copley Place in the heart of the city. IBM used most of the building and rented part of the top floor to the American League. It took about a month to ready the space, during which time Cronin used his office at Fenway Park.

Cronin brought two Red Sox employees to the American League staff—Joseph W. McKenney as director of public relations and Barbara Tyler as his personal secretary. Tyler had been Cronin's secretary for all his years as general manager—in fact, she had been Eddie Collins's secretary before that. "I watched Joe grow into his job," said Tyler. "He's not a fault finder and always maintained an open door policy. He's the typical self-made man who has never lost the common touch."[2] The rest of the staff included William S. Cutler, the office manager, and Cal Hubbard, a former umpire who served as the league's supervisor of umpires. Will Harridge, the new chairman of the board, a largely ceremonial position, maintained his office in Chicago and continued coming to work, reviewing league memoranda, and offering advice as needed.

Compared to Harridge, Cronin would be much more accessible to the press and public. He had spent a few decades talking openly with the media, and he would not stop in his new position. He could sit in the stands with a writer in spring training and give his opinions of the players they were watching—something Harridge could not have done.[3] As one writer put it, "Cronin probably could have become a newspaper man himself. He has the inquisitiveness for it. 'What's new?' is his favorite greeting."[4] His friends in the press were happy for him, and perhaps a bit happy for themselves as well. "He'll make a fine head of the American League," wrote Arthur Daley in the *Times*. "His sportswriting buddies can hardly wait for his first press conference so that the dean of the correspondents can say, 'Thank you, Mr. President.'"[5]

Speaking to the National Press Club in Washington on April 8, Cronin was typically forthright when discussing his league and its future plans. "I'd like to see the Yankees drop to third place," he said, realizing the effect the ever-dominant Yankees had on league attendance. He also offered the opinion that perhaps the American League should move a team into Brooklyn to create a rivalry with the Yankees.[6] For the writers Cronin's comments were a welcome change from Harridge's caution. With the security of a seven-year contract at $60,000 per year, Cronin had no reason to change the way he dealt with the press.

Baseball's most pressing concern in Cronin's early months on the job was the possibility of expansion. After five decades of a stable

Major League map, five clubs (all of whom had shared their cities with other teams) had relocated in the middle of the decade. By the time Cronin became president, people in the game realized that there weren't enough teams to satisfy all of the cities that wanted and could support one, although rumors of teams moving were still common. Almost immediately after the Giants and Dodgers abandoned New York in 1958, efforts were launched to lure another team to America's biggest city. Attorney William Shea, appointed to lead the effort by New York mayor Robert Wagner, first tried to coax another NL team to New York. When these efforts failed, Shea and his allies instead proposed the formation of a new Major League, the first serious such attempt since the demise of the Federal League in 1915. Shea enlisted the support of several political allies who represented their own cities, plus longtime executive Branch Rickey, at the time semiretired. The Continental League sought the blessing and cooperation of the two established Major Leagues.[7]

Commissioner Ford Frick appointed a seven-member group, including league presidents Cronin and Giles, who drew up a list of conditions for the new league. Among the stipulations were that all cities be at least as large as the smallest current Major League city (Kansas City) and have stadiums that could seat at least thirty-five thousand people, and that all current major and Minor League agreements be adhered to (specifically, protecting the rights of existing teams to all the players under their control). On July 27, 1959, the Continental League announced that it would open play in 1961, naming five of its eight cities: New York, Denver, Toronto, Houston, and Minneapolis-St. Paul. (Later, ownership groups were created in Atlanta, Dallas, and Buffalo.) Cronin urged caution. "Just branding a league 'major' doesn't make it one," he said. "They have to come up with major league talent."[8] Rickey, the new league's president, met with Cronin and Giles to work on just this issue.

Another actor in this story was the U.S. Congress, which held hearings that summer to evaluate baseball's adherence to antitrust law, threatening, among other things, to reduce the number of players a Major League team could hold under contract from four hundred to eighty.[9] One of the weapons used to placate Congress was a promise to eventually create more Major League teams—lawmakers, especially those who represented the affected cities, were especially receptive to the promise of a new league. Complicating matters considerably, in October 1959 the Washington Senators announced plans to move to Minneapolis, one of the Continental League cities. By abandoning the nation's capital, the Major Leagues would anger both the new league and Congress. The American League voted down the Senators' move, at least temporarily.

On October 22 Cronin announced the formation of a committee to consider expanding his league. Shea accused the AL of using this as a tactic to block his new circuit, but Cronin denied this. "I can assure Mr. Shea and anyone else," he said, "that our plans for expansion are not mere idle talk."[10] What Cronin had in mind was adding Minneapolis to his league, with New York returning to the NL. This plan—two nine-team leagues—would necessitate interleague play, something Cronin and most of the AL owners supported. The National League rejected the idea in early December, though it was revived the next year. "I am sorry that Mr. Giles opposes interleague play," said Cronin. "Frankly, I am for it."[11]

All three of these stories—the hearings on Capitol Hill, the organization of the Continental League, and league expansion plans—continued to fester throughout 1960. Although the AL did not abandon its desire for the nine-team leagues, they ultimately began looking for a suitable tenth city. With the expansion of both Major Leagues inevitable, the Continental League disbanded in July with the hope that four of its ownership groups would be granted expansion franchises. Without consulting its rival, the National League acted first—announcing plans to expand in 1962 to New York and Houston—homes of the two most attractive Continental League groups. It was now assumed that the AL would consider which of the remaining six cities to accept.[12]

Cronin wanted a different solution. "We've let the National League get too far out ahead of our league," he said. "They've been grabbing the big population centers, and now they are re-entering New York. We can't go into the wrong towns when we expand, because we already have ground to make up." Cronin proposed that the league instead invade Los Angeles, a city that had not even applied for membership. "We may have a responsibility to the Continental, but the American League welfare has to come first in anything we do."[13]

On October 26, 1960, the AL announced its plans: the Senators would finally move to Minneapolis, becoming the Twins, and new franchises would be formed in Washington (the Senators) and Los Angeles (the Angels), both beginning play in 1961. Alarmingly, neither team as yet had an owner, let alone players, and they would be heading to spring training in just four months. Understandably, most observers felt that Cronin and the owners had acted hastily. "I do think the American League would have used better judgment," said Commissioner Frick, "were it to delay its expansion plans until 1962, as the National League is doing." Frick later met with Giles and Cronin to work out procedures to better cooperate in future expansions.[14]

Despite Cronin's bold announcement, the AL's proposed move into Los Angeles immediately hit a roadblock. Walter O'Malley, who owned the Dodgers, believed that he had a right to the territory he had spent so much to establish. Among other things, O'Malley had paid damages to the Pacific Coast League, had paid for the existing Minor League team and park, and was now building a new ballpark in Chavez Ravine. Del Webb, one of the Yankee owners, insisted on a new club in Los Angeles as the price for the NL invading New York (and he may also have been angered that his construction company did not get the contract to build Dodger Stadium). Cronin backed Webb's contention entirely.[15] Commissioner Frick, perhaps angered at Cronin's chutzpah, disagreed, maintaining that the NL had the right to New York, having recently lost two teams there, but that the AL needed approval of the NL to move into Los Angeles.

In November the frontman of the Washington ownership group was identified—Gen. Elwood P. Quesada, the head of the Federal Aviation Agency. Many observers noticed that the fans of Washington had gotten a raw deal with the franchise swap. The 1960 Senators had finished in fifth place with a team filled with young players and posted their highest attendance since 1949. Yet despite being a charter member of the American League, Washington would get a brand-new expansion team, while Minneapolis would get a promising and established club that would compete for the pennant in just two years. Frank Lane, for one, felt the league had given Calvin Griffith, Cronin's brother-in-law, too much. "What our leaders should have done," said Lane, "was given [Griffith] the Minneapolis franchise and made him start from the bottom. But then, of course, he had Joe Cronin on his side."[16]

A month later the Los Angeles situation was finally straightened out. Hank Greenberg had been considered the frontrunner to secure the team but changed his mind when informed he had to compensate the Dodgers. Gene Autry, who owned a string of radio stations in California, attended the league meeting hoping to secure the rights to broadcast the new club's games. When Greenberg backed out, Autry decided to buy the franchise himself. To appease O'Malley, Autry agreed to play the 1961 season at Wrigley Field (and not the Coliseum, where the Dodgers played) and then beginning in 1962 to be O'Malley's tenant in Dodger Stadium for at least four more years.

In early December Cronin presided over the first expansion draft in baseball history, with the two new clubs each drafting twenty-eight players from the eight established teams. "It wasn't a bad lot of players," said Cronin. "They'll be in the fight for eighth place, maybe seventh place."[17] As it turned out, the Angels finished in eighth place in their first season, while the Senators tied for ninth (last). The new clubs had trouble drawing fans, about six hundred thousand apiece, lending credence to the suggestion that the expansion of the league had been rushed.

For Cronin, another important development came out of the first expansion draft. Washington's first general manager, Ed Doherty, had worked for the Red Sox for many years in publicity and had been close to the Cronin family. When Doherty was in Boston for the draft he had dinner at the Cronin house. Tom Cronin picked Doherty up at his hotel, and on the ride to dinner Doherty offered young Cronin a job as assistant farm director. Tom had spent two years at Arizona State, but once he realized he would not be a Major League player, he left college for a job in the insurance business. He had been at it for only a few months when he received the Senators' offer.[18]

Joe and Mildred, both of whom had spent their lives in and around the game, were delighted that their oldest son was embarking on his own baseball career. Joe's advice to his son was not to rely on the family name. "Bear in mind that it was your father, and not you, who was a pretty good ballplayer. If anybody wants your advice on how to play ball, remember to tell them, 'that's not my department.'"[19] Within a few months, Doherty would report, "He works and he wants to learn, just like he used to when he was in uniform working out with the Red Sox as a kid." With Tom out in the world, the remaining Cronin children were not far behind. Corky was a sophomore at Harvard, a few miles from home. Maureen went to Sacred Heart High School, and ten-year-old Kevin was an aspiring ballplayer.

One area in which the league president could exercise true authority, beyond mere consensus building or persuasion, was with the league's umpires, who were hired and fired at the discretion of the league office. In the era of eight-team leagues, the American League employed sixteen full-time umps who worked in crews of four. The league often hired one or two additional umpires and optioned them out to the Minor Leagues for recall if needed. Typically there would be one or two openings on the staff each year, and Cronin would work with Cal Hubbard on deciding who to hire. The two men would receive recommendations from the top Minor Leagues, and Hubbard often scouted the umpires under consideration.

Each off-season Cronin and Hubbard met with the umpiring staff for two days to review the rule book and any new rules or league regulations and to revisit the controversies of the previous year. Occasionally Cronin wanted the umpires to pay particular attention to certain rules. In 1959 Cronin and Giles asked them to report any pitcher they believed had deliberately thrown a ball at a batter's head—each infraction would result in a $50 fine.[20] On other occasions Cronin might be concerned about pitchers balking, taking too long to throw pitches, or applying saliva to the baseball. Although the two leagues used the same rule book, the umpires received different instructions on how to call the game. In the American League, for example, the second base umpire positioned himself behind second base, while his NL counterpart stood on the infield grass. The AL home plate umpires held a balloon chest protector, while the NL ump wore a protector inside his shirt, and they had different policies on discarding balls that hit the dirt and how many players could congregate on the mound during a conference with the pitcher.[21]

Throughout the regular season, whenever an umpiring crew came through Boston the umpires were expected to drop by to meet with Cronin and Hubbard. John Rice, an AL umpire for nineteen years beginning in 1955, remembers the games in Boston because Cronin and Hubbard would attend and tell the umps what they had done wrong. Rice thought Hubbard, as an ex-umpire, sympathetic and friendly, but Cronin was often insulting and dismissive of the umpires and their struggles. In those preunion days, the umps would confide in Hubbard if there was a problem with their paycheck or if the facilities at a park were substandard.[22]

Cronin's office also had to discipline players or managers after on-field altercations or ejections, based largely (in those days before video was available for every game) on reports filed by the umpires. The first significant incident in the 1959 season took place on May 3 in Cleveland. Old friend Jimmy Piersall, now playing for the Indians, brandished a bat at Washington pitcher Pedro Ramos after the hurler had thrown a fastball close to Piersall's head. After both teams charged the field, Indians manager Joe Gordon began jawing with Ramos, who fired the ball at him. Cronin fined Gordon $100, and both Piersall and Ramos $50.[23] Two months later Cronin suspended Gordon and Cleveland's Minnie Minoso after their repeated arguing over an interference call during a game in Boston. Both Gordon and Minoso were angry, as was Frank Lane, Cleveland's general manager, who scoffed that Cronin was just a "rookie president." Moreover, he was "a Monday-to-Thursday president. He takes Friday, Saturday and Sunday off," likely referring to Cronin's habit of heading to his family's home on Cape Cod for the weekend.[24]

In 1960 Piersall caused his former boss additional trouble. On May 30 in Chicago, Piersall was on second base when he began loudly arguing balls and strikes, before finally being ejected by second base umpire Cal Drummond. In the violent argument that followed, Piersall had to be restrained from going after the umpire. Finally coaxed off the field, Piersall threw bats, helmets, and gloves out of the dugout. Cronin fined him $250. On July 23 in Boston, Piersall was ejected for going into a "war dance" in center field to try to distract Ted Williams at bat, drawing another $100 fine. After more umpire baiting at Fenway Park on the twenty-fifth, Cronin summoned Piersall and his wife Mary to his office on July 26 for a "fatherly talk," an event that recalled a meeting the couple had with Cronin during Piersall's difficulties in 1952. This time Piersall pledged to give up his antics and concentrate on baseball. In the meantime the Indians players had scheduled their own meeting to discuss Piersall's behavior but cancelled it when Piersall gave them the same pledge.[25] His ejection in Boston was his sixth of the season, but he was thumbed just one more time that year. Still, Piersall's seven ejections remain the highest known total for a player in Major League history, matched only by the Braves' Johnny Evers in 1914.[26]

Later in the 1960 season Cronin was faced with an unusual scandal involving two of his better umpires, Ed Runge and Bill McKinley. After working a game in Washington on August 28, the two arbiters visited the Gaiety Supper Club, a strip joint in Baltimore and then took two strippers to a motel in Hyattsville, Maryland. The four had just settled in when two men burst into the room and took a photograph, later demanding $5,000 to keep them from sending the picture to the press and to Cronin. When the umpires refused, the men asked that the umps instead conspire to influence the outcome of a ballgame. Runge and McKinley called the police, and authorities set a trap for the men at the Baltimore airport. Preparing for the encounter, one detective said to the umpires, "When you meet them, I want you to act scared, and act broke." Runge responded, "I am scared, and I am broke." Two men and one of the dancers were arrested and charged in the case.

Runge and McKinley were granted leaves of absence for the balance of the 1960 season, vowing to assist the authorities in the investigation. "Joe Cronin acted wisely and well," wrote *The Sporting News* in an editorial. Both umpires returned the next season. McKinley worked five more seasons, Runge ten. "They don't come any better than Ed," said Mrs. Runge at the time of the incident in 1960. "He's never done anything to be ashamed of in his life."[27]

Along with his official duties, Cronin had to make many ceremonial appearances in his role as league president. He made a point to attend as many opening days as he could, including the annual league opener in Washington and a few others spread over the first couple of weeks of every season. Although he lived and worked near Fenway Park and went to Red Sox games whenever he and they were home, he tried to visit every team's ballpark at least once per year. He never missed the opening of a new park, or an important on-field ceremony. In 1960 Cronin visited each of the AL training camps in the spring then headed to San Francisco for the opening of Candlestick Park.

One of the duties he most enjoyed was handing out trophies to the league's award winners, a role that helped map out his travel schedule. On June 17, 1960, he was in Cleveland to present a silver bat to Harvey Kuenn, 1959 batting titlist, as well as a Gold Glove to first baseman Vic Power. Coincidentally, the Red Sox were in town that evening, and Cronin witnessed Ted Williams's five-hundredth career home run.[28] Cronin bragged that he had likely seen more of Williams's home runs than anyone else.

Ceremony aside, Cronin used his bully pulpit as the situation demanded. In early 1959 he ordered all clubs to fly into cities the day before a scheduled game rather than waiting until the morning. Back in the days when teams traveled exclusively by train they did not have the luxury of this choice. Nonetheless, Cronin was concerned about frequent travel difficulties—he warned clubs of heavy fines if flight delays caused them to miss a ballgame.[29] On a less serious note, the next year he chastised Chicago owner Bill Veeck for using his electronic scoreboard to lampoon the umpires. In 1963 Cronin urged all teams to put players' names of the backs of uniforms, something only the White Sox had done in the league.[30] He also began a campaign to stop players and managers from smoking in the dugout or within sight of the patrons.[31]

Soon after he attained his new post, Cronin also began lobbying for a second All-Star Game, an event he considered one of the highlights of the season. He elicited the support of Warren Giles, and the two won the approval of the players and owners for two games played four weeks apart in 1959.[32] The leagues continued to play two contests for four years, returning to the single game in 1963. Baseball also had its first interleague trading period in 1959—for only twenty-five days, November 21 to December 15. There were a number of interleague deals that first year, involving such prominent names as Bobby Thomson, Johnny Callison, Johnny Temple, and Billy Martin. Though Cronin was against the move when first proposed that summer,[33] he later admitted that it had gone off well. "The experiment created considerable interest in baseball during the off-season," said Cronin. "So far as I can determine, it did no harm."[34]

The expansion of the AL to ten teams in 1961 also extended the season from 154 to 162 games. Even before the season, there were concerns about baseball's hallowed records, and what would happen if a player used the longer season to break a longstanding mark. As fate would have it, in 1961 Yankee sluggers Roger Maris and Mickey Mantle engaged in an historic chase after the most revered record of all—Babe Ruth's sixty home runs. Commissioner Ford Frick suggested that Ruth's record would not be erased unless it was passed within 154 games, otherwise both records would be listed with notation describing the different circumstances. Cronin disagreed, insisting "a season is a season, regardless." The *New York Times* surveyed the mythical "man on the street" and determined that a clear majority of fans sided with Frick, saying that Ruth's record could not be broken unless done in 154 games. In any event, Maris tied Ruth in the Yankees' 155th game, before hitting his 61st in the 162nd contest. Cronin congratulated Maris while side-stepping further controversy with Frick.[35]

One of the personal highlights of Cronin's years as league president took place after the 1962 season when he and Mildred, along with Frick and his wife, embarked on a trip that took the two couples around the world. The original excuse for the voyage was to accompany the Detroit Tigers on a goodwill tour to Hawaii, Japan, and South Korea in October. The Cronins and Fricks further planned a much longer trip. As it turned out, several weather-related delays in that fall's World Series caused the foursome to miss their original departure date, as the Yankees did not defeat the Giants in the seventh game until October 16, four days after the Tigers had left for Honolulu.[36]

The executives finally met up with the Detroit club on the twenty-first in Tokyo. There was a business aspect to the trip (Frick met with his Japanese counterpart on the issue of Japanese teams signing American players to contracts), and Cronin rarely did anything without promoting baseball. But most of the trip was pure pleasure for the Cronins, including, of course, several formal dinners. Still, Joe had his eye on the future. "The greatest thing for Japanese baseball," he said after returning home, "would be to have one of their players make it in the majors in our country. The boy who does that will be the biggest man in Japan." In order for that to happen, Cronin felt, Japanese baseball would have to improve to the caliber of the Pacific Coast League, and it was not yet there.[37]

The Cronins and Fricks left the Tigers in Tokyo on October 29 for Hong Kong. From there the group traveled on to Bangkok, Singapore, Cairo, Athens, Rome, Paris, and London. (Mildred Cronin later would tell the story of walking down a Cairo street and having someone yell to her husband, "Hey Joe, what do you hear from Pesky?"[38]) The Cronins had spent their adult lives traveling to baseball games or meetings, but this was their first extensive vacation since their honeymoon journey through the Panama Canal in 1934. It was a trip of a lifetime, one the Cronins would reminisce about for many years.

Upon returning stateside in late November, Cronin was asked about the swirling rumors that he would soon succeed the sixty-seven-year-old Frick as commissioner. Frick's term expired in September 1965, but many stories suggested that the round-the-world trip was an elaborate briefing session for the inevitable transition. Cronin denied any knowledge of such a plan, instead reporting that Frick was "in fine health, full of pep and vitality." In any event, Frick did not reveal any retirement plans, delaying baseball's decision for the time being. The issue would come up again very soon.

Meanwhile, the sudden home-run surge in 1961 led to discussions about whether baseball needed to help the beleaguered pitchers. The debate was fueled by big home run years by several players, notably the Yankees duo of Roger Maris (61 home runs) and Mickey Mantle (54), but also lesser figures like Jim Gentile (46) and Norm Cash (41). The Yankees hit 240 home runs as a team, shattering the league record of 193 they had set the year before. "To the best of my knowledge," said Ford Frick, "the ball has not been hopped up."[39] When asked about the baseballs in his league, Cronin concurred: "The Spalding people would not make a change in the ball without an order from me. I have made no such directive."[40]

In order to quell some of the suspicion, the two leagues arranged to have their baseballs tested by an "unidentified professor" from MIT. The 1961 balls were compared to a box of balls from 1956.[41] Not to be outdone, a few newspapers hired testing laboratories to cut up old and new baseballs and perform their own comparisons. All of the testing came to the same conclusions: the balls had not been changed.[42]

Partly in response to the home-run barrage, Cronin became an advocate for the legalization of the spitball, which had been outlawed in 1920. "There's nothing dangerous or bad about the spitter," Cronin said. "I had to bat against both and I'll tell you a good knuckleball is much harder to hit than a spitball." Commissioner Frick was Cronin's ally in this cause. The reasoning was partly to help the pitchers, but mostly to help the umpires, who were spending an increasing amount of time trying and (and often failing) to enforce the prohibition. Many pitchers were believed to be throwing it, but none of them were getting caught. In late 1961 Cal Hubbard, acting on Cronin's behalf, introduced a resolution with the Rules Committee to effect this change. It was voted down, 8–1.[43]

After a second straight season of seemingly high offense in 1962,

Frick reconvened the Rules Committee to consider ways to help the pitchers and speed up the game. "Take a look at the batting, home run and slugging records for the recent seasons," said Frick, "and you become convinced that the pitchers need help urgently." Accordingly, on January 26, 1963, at a meeting in the Roosevelt Hotel in New York, the committee voted to dramatically enlarge the strike zone. In reality the definition was simply a restoration of what had been in the rulebook for decades prior to its revision in 1950: the area over the plate between the bottom of the knees and the top of the shoulders. Since 1950 the zone had extended from the top of the knees to the armpits.

Both league presidents were ordered to ensure that the umpires called the new zone, and Cronin sent Cal Hubbard to spring training to be certain the umps understood and complied with the new definition. In the end motivating the umpires to call the strike zone is at least as important as simply changing the rule book. "The new ruling will definitely put an end to all the talk that the umpires in the National League give pitchers [the low strike] and in the American League the umpires call [the high strike]," said Cronin.[44] "I think the high hard pitches will come back to baseball. The pitchers with good hard ones will be successful."[45]

In fact, the increase in offense in the early 1960s was largely misunderstood. Although there was a noticeable, though slight, increase in home runs in 1961, to a record 0.96 per game, the effect on scoring was less apparent. AL teams scored 4.53 runs per game in 1961, while the NL scored 4.52 — increases from 1960, but not particularly large. The AL had scored more runs as recently as 1956 and had bested their 1961 rate every year from 1920 through 1941. The NL story was similar — run scoring was not historically high in the early 1960s.

Having overreacted to the symptoms, baseball soon had a much larger problem. With a new strike zone in place and umpires determined to enforce it, run scoring plummeted to levels not seen in decades. Home runs held steady in the AL for a couple of years before ratcheting down to .68 per game by 1968. More importantly, run scoring dropped for seven straight seasons, reaching a paltry 3.42 per game in the Major Leagues in 1968. "The next sound you hear," wrote Jim Murray as early as 1963, "will be the fans snoring. After that they won't even bother to come to the ballpark to sleep."[46]

If the fans were staying away, they mainly confined their apathy to the American League. While the NL saw its per-game attendance increase 18 percent between 1962 and 1965, over the same period the AL attendance declined by 13 percent. The American League was starting out behind their rivals, so by the mid-1960s the NL was drawing a startling 50 percent more fans per game. And the media continued to drive the narrative in the 1960s that the American League was suffering in every way when compared with the National.

Al Hirshberg laid out the case in the March 1964 issue of *Sport* in an article titled, alarmingly, "Is the American League Really *That* Bad?"[47] Besides two struggling expansion teams in Los Angeles and Washington, the league had a revolt on its hands in Kansas City, and a team in Cleveland that drew 562,000 fans in 1963, just fifteen years after it had drawn more than 2.6 million. Cronin blamed most of his league's attendance problems on the Yankees running away with the 1963 pennant, but the league would draw essentially the same number of fans in 1964 with a great pennant race.

Cronin also believed that the AL was still paying for the NL putting the Dodgers and Giants in California in 1958. By relocating two established teams with a ready-made rivalry, the league had created a "gold mine" in Cronin's view. Cronin's essential argument was correct—the Dodgers and Giants drew over 4.1 million fans in 1963, and the NL's other eight teams averaged 11,205 fans per game, slightly fewer than the ten American League teams. "Give us a rivalry like that," said Cronin, "and our league will do just as well." Instead the AL had placed an expansion team in Los Angeles—with no established stars, and with the closest team half a continent away.

Cronin put no stock in the Dodgers' sweep of New York in the World Series—he called the Yankees "a sounder team than the Dodgers"—or his league's poor record in the All-Star Game, which he now called "an exhibition." As for the AL's lack of star players when compared with the National League, Cronin credited the NL's "getting the jump" on his league in signing black players. "In the early days," felt Cronin, "the Negro ballplayers wanted to follow Jackie Robinson. Not only that, but the Giants, the Dodgers, and the Braves did fine scouting jobs which paid off later." This would change soon, Cronin said, as the American League had just as many young black players in the Minor Leagues. In sum, Cronin said, "We are not worried." If Cronin was not worried, others were. "Any practical baseball man will tell you the American League is sick, sick, sick," wrote Harry Grayson in mid-1964. "The saddest thing about the outlook is that nobody is doing anything about it."[48]

"We have stars comparable to theirs at every position," Cronin protested in 1962, answering a question being asked more and more.[49] As much as Cronin resisted the notion that his league consisted of the Yankees and nine also-rans, New York had won four of the five pennants since Cronin took office. "Naturally I am disappointed in the standings," he said in August 1963 about the annual Yankees runaway.[50]

While Cronin chafed at the criticism directed at his league, it drove him to an occasional act of defiance against what he saw as the arrogance of the National League. The most significant example was the accelerated 1961 expansion, which he pushed in order to gain ground against the Nationals. In Cronin's first year in office, he had made a less important stand on the playing schedule. When the NL announced its 1960 schedule, Cronin refused to go along with their opening date and countered with a schedule that began a full week later. "I see no point in letting the National League dictate the opening date," he said. "I don't want our clubs to play under unfavorable conditions for a week."[51]

Nonetheless, Cronin's repeated calls for interleague play, along with the NL's constant refusal, added to the perception that the superior Nationals were calling the shots within the game. The National League drew more fans, won the All-Star Game every year, and had most of the game's top stars.

15 New Order

Joe Cronin's most constant and color-ful antagonist during his tenure as league president was undoubtedly Kansas City Athletics' owner Charles Oscar Finley. Having made millions in the insurance business, Finley spent the 1950s, in his words, "chasing ball teams," losing out on bids for the Philadelphia Athletics and Detroit Tigers among others. He was also a serious bidder in the fall of 1960 for the expansion Angels, which were secured by Gene Autry. Finally, that December he purchased controlling interest in the Athletics from the estate of Arnold Johnson and bought out the team's minority interests over the next year.

Finley did not walk onto the stage quietly. On the contrary he soon made it clear that he believed all other baseball owners were dinosaurs who needed to be taught how to run their businesses. Finley tried anything and everything to interest people in his team: cow-milking contests, greased pig contests, a sheep pasture (with a shepherd) beyond right field, a zoo beyond left. He installed a mechanical rabbit named Harvey behind home plate to pop up and hand the umpire new baseballs and Little Blowhard, a compressed air device inside of home plate that blew dirt away. He hired Miss USA to be the team's batgirl and installed a yellow cab to transport relief pitchers from the bullpen.[1]

Although most of Finley's promotions were harmless attempts at energizing his local fan base, occasionally they rose to a level that required action from the league office. To allow the fans to see the players and managers discussing strategy, Finley installed bright fluorescent lights in each dugout. The New York Yankees, visiting Kansas City for the first time in early May, were bothered by the bright lights and shut them off. Undeterred, Finley had a lock installed on the switch so it could only be turned on or off with a key. The Yankees protested to Cronin, who ruled that teams must be allowed to switch off the lights.[2]

In the meantime, Finley was full of bright ideas to improve the game's management. He wanted interleague play and realignment to promote geographic rivalries, and pushed for World Series and All-Star Games to be played at night. He wanted the season shortened. He argued for the adoption of a designated hitter for the pitcher and a designated runner who could freely pinch-run for a player without replacing him in the lineup. He pushed to have active players eligible for the Hall of Fame. He installed a clock in the scoreboard to enforce a long-ignored rule that limited a pitcher to twenty seconds between pitches. Some of this caught on, some of it did not, but Finley publicly seethed at the ignorance of his fellow magnates. He once offered the following advice to a hypothetical man thinking of becoming a baseball owner: "Do not go into any league meeting looking alert and awake; slump down like you've been out all night and keep your eyes half closed, and when it is your turn to vote you ask to pass. Then you wait and see how the others vote, and you vote the same way. Suggest no innovations. Make no efforts at change. That way you will be very popular with your fellow owners."[3]

Finley tried to convince Cronin to do something about the somber clothes worn by the umpires, suggesting striped shirts like those worn by football referees. "Why not have them wear top hats," continued Finley. "Give 'em collapsible chairs to sit on. Let's make them comfortable." Cronin countered that some of the umpires were rather portly, to which Finley replied, "Why do they have to look like they are having triplets? Let's get some who have some pride in their appearance."[4] Finley failed with the umpires, but he did get permission to outfit his own team in yellow with green trim in 1963, and added numbers to their sleeves in 1964. He failed to get baseball to approve colored bases and base paths. He also asked that his team be able to use yellow and green bats for a one-night promotion; when rebuffed, he called the rules committee "a pack of simple-minded fools."[5]

More importantly, Finley spent the first four years of his ownership complaining about the city and Municipal Stadium (which Finley leased from the city) or trying to move his team (which had just arrived in Kansas City in 1955). Despite his continual promotions, the Athletics attendance decreased from 775,000 in 1960 to 684,000 in 1961, and Finley responded as if the fans were ingrates. In August 1961, only eight months into his tenure, Finley visited Dallas looking for a ballpark, and formally applied for permission to move at the league meetings in May 1962. After the league turned down his application in September ("The American League does not wish to revise its circuit," said Cronin), Finley returned to Kansas City and suggested that the locals "let bygones be bygones."

Shifting gears, something Finley could do with rapidity, he asked the city council to build him a fifty-thousand-seat stadium. "I am convinced that without a new stadium," Finley reasoned, "Kansas City cannot much longer have major league baseball." On September 27 in Boston, Cronin met with Finley and representatives of the KC city council but failed to work out a lease agreement. The Kansas City media, with whom Finley publicly feuded, believed Finley did little to promote the team and was principally to blame for the sagging local interest.[6]

Finley spent much of 1963 negotiating for a more favorable ballpark lease, though the city claimed he was not acting in good faith. In May after a public courting of Atlanta, Finley disclosed that he now wanted to move his team to Oakland, claiming that he had lost $1.4 million in two years. Cronin was amenable to putting an AL team into his native region—scheduling had proven difficult and costly with only one team (Los Angeles) on the West Coast—but he was not amenable to Finley's constant public pronouncements, which only served to harm the Athletics' relationship with Kansas City. In late December KC mayor Ilus Davis asked Cronin to intervene in the lease negotiations.

Tiring of rejections from the American League, on January 6, 1964, Finley forced the issue, signing a two-year lease to use Fairgrounds Stadium in Louisville, Kentucky. Cronin was furious at Finley, who had ignored his repeated requests to stop negotiating with other cities and keep his demands out of the press. Finley shot back: "This is

America! I'm no loudmouth, but when I get ready to speak, I'll speak." Furthermore, Finley sent Cronin a telegram telling him to keep their conversations private unless Finley gave his "personal approval." Shirley Povich wrote that Finley had flushed Cronin out of his ivory tower. "They have been peaceful times for Cronin during his five-year term but he is being confronted with the biggest question ever asked of a league president."[7]

In this battle Cronin had the support of the other nine club owners. "I think it's a distinct possibility that Cronin could take over the franchise," said White Sox owner Arthur Allyn. "I don't think [Finley] has the foggiest chance of getting approval." Accordingly, on January 16 the league voted nine to one against the Louisville shift and gave Finley until February 1, later extended to February 16, to conclude a lease in Kansas City. If he did not, he would be expelled from the league.[8] Although the owners had no love for Charlie Finley, they also had a legitimate political concern—baseball had yet to vacate a one-team city, and U.S. senator Stuart Symington of Missouri had taken a keen interest in the Athletics' situation.

Undeterred Finley threatened to sue the American League. In late January Finley announced that he would seek approval to move to Oakland rather than Louisville. In mid-February, Symington sent Cronin a telegram asking that the league follow through on its threat to expel Finley, who had done "substantial damage" to the city and to the sport. Cronin called an emergency league meeting for February 21, at which the other owners took the unprecedented step of reviewing Kansas City's latest lease offer. By a vote of 9–1, the league ruled the city's offer "fair and reasonable" and that Finley had failed to comply with their edict at their January 16 meeting. Cronin called another meeting to formally vote on expelling Finley. On February 23 Finley finally capitulated, wiring Cronin that he would accept the city's terms, an iron-clad four-year lease that would keep the franchise in place through 1967. "I sincerely hope the citizens of Kansas City will come out and watch the A's fight for the first division," Finley told the press, a variation of his "bygones be bygones" request of 1962.[9]

Temporarily thwarted in attempts to move his team, Finley continued to be a thorn in Cronin's side. Just prior to the 1964 season, Finley got the bright idea that the Yankees owed their success not to great talent, but to the unusual dimensions of their playing field: deep fences in most of left and center fields, but with very short distances in right field. Finley decided to make his right field configuration identical to that of Yankee Stadium. "I feel that in revamping my ball park to go along with the Yankees," said Finley, "I will be, for the first time, able to compete with them on an equal basis."

Unfortunately, in 1958 the Rules Committee had decreed a minimum distance of 325 feet down the foul lines, allowing exceptions only for existing ballparks. Accordingly, Cronin refused Finley's request for a league meeting to reconsider the rule. Always one step ahead of the law, Finley simply ordered his fence to precisely conform to the Yankee Stadium distance from center field to right field until it reached a point just a few feet from the foul line and 296 feet from home plate, the distance used in New York. From there, the fence angled sharply back out so that it was exactly 325 feet away on the foul line. He thus neatly skirted the rule.

Finley then painted "KC Pennant Porch" on the new fence (which was forty-four inches high, just as in New York). "I'm out to win at Kansas City," said Finley. "If it means copying Yankee tactics, that's not beneath my dignity." Asked about Finley's plans at a press conference on April 5, Cronin said only, "I understand he is a very successful insurance man." After spending the winter answering questions about Finley, Cronin was weary. "I don't want any 'iffy' questions on him. Every question has got to be black and white, or I can't get into it."[10] In the meantime, Cronin sent Cal Hubbard to Kansas City to look at Finley's new fence.

After two exhibition games, Frick and Cronin sent telegrams to Finley ordering him to remove the fence. "These two men must be living in the dark ages and do not know we have telephones," said Finley. "They didn't even give me the courtesy of a telephone call." Although threatened with forfeiting games if the fence was still in place for the home opener on April 21, Finley said, "You can say for me that the fence will be here when the season opens." The next day Finley backed down but only because of "the great respect and admiration I have always had for" Cronin and Frick.[11] Still hanging on to his cause, he warned that the Yankees' unfair advantage was killing the game. Finley moved the right-field fence back to 325 feet, changed the sign to read "One-Half Pennant Porch," and painted a line on the field that represented Yankee Stadium's dimensions. He then ordered the public address announcer to call out, "That would have been a home run at Yankee Stadium!" for every fly ball that went past this line.[12] After his pitchers allowed a Major League record 220 home runs, the next year Finley moved the fence further back, to its 1963 location, and put a forty-foot screen above it. But for Finley, there was always a new battle to fight, and he would be slowed by neither defeat nor public approbation.

Joe Cronin's problems with Charlie Finley were not over—the two had many battles ahead in the remaining decade of Cronin's tenure—but Cronin had survived the first great crisis of his presidency. The two men could not help but clash. Finley believed that baseball was losing ground to football among the sporting public (a contention that was undeniably true) and needed to change to attract younger fans. To Finley Cronin symbolized the establishment—a man afraid to try new ideas. Actually, Cronin advocated many changes in the game, including interleague play and the return of the spitball and was usually ahead of the league's owners (who had the true authority) on such matters. But Cronin was primarily concerned with protecting the game on the field. When Cronin spoke against putting numbers on a player's sleeve, it was not because he was afraid of change, as Finley charged—it was because he thought the pitcher's number would distract the hitter. Finley wanted change for the sake of change as a way of keeping the fans interested and cared little for what the players might want. When Cronin considered Finley's orange baseball, he thought not just of the fan but also of the player trying to hit or field a very different ball.

Their personalities were also no match. Though Cronin could show anger on occasion, he made great efforts to get along with people. Finley had no friends in the game and cared little for anyone but himself. Bowie Kuhn later wrote of being in Cronin's office once while Cronin was on the phone with Finley. The owner was loud, abusive, and obscene. When the call was over and Kuhn expressed shock, Cronin said, "Oh, that's Charlie, you have to let him run on."[13] Although Cronin rarely spoke ill of anyone in public, John Harrington, who worked for Cronin in the AL office in the early 1970s, admitted, "Joe did not like Charlie at all."[14]

Meanwhile, on August 5, 1964, Ford Frick announced that he would not seek re-election when his term as baseball's commissioner expired in September of 1965. Frick's announcement was not a surprise—he would soon be seventy years old, and speculation about his replacement had been bandied about for a couple of years. Frick served as commissioner for fourteen seasons, and his tenure was marked by the lack of central authority within the game. The assorted and futile attempts to curb bonuses, the lack of cooperation between the leagues to relocate or expand, haphazard television contracts—all were problems that led to an erosion of the game's popularity at a time when professional football's strong leadership had allowed it to succeed in these same battles. The National Football League first held a draft of amateur players in 1936, began sharing revenue in the 1950s, and signed a lucrative television contract in 1961 that distributed the windfall to all its teams. By 1964 when baseball conceived of a national Monday night television game that would do the same, no network was interested.

To succeed Ford Frick no person was mentioned more often than Cronin, who many considered a virtual certainty. "Cronin is their man," wrote Ed Rumill. "They need look no further." Bob Addie spoke for many when he wrote, "It would be a real upset if anybody but Joe Cronin gets it."[15] Cronin's supporters felt that the job required an experienced baseball man. Frick, previously the president of the National League, had been the game's first commissioner with experience in the game. He wanted a baseball man as his successor. "All things being equal," said Frick in 1964, "I believe the new commissioner should come from inside baseball."[16]

There were other voices, a minority at first, who wanted an outsider—a respected man of stature who could help baseball deal with Congress and the Justice Department. Baseball's first two commissioners had been outsiders—Kenesaw Landis had been a federal judge and Happy Chandler a governor and U.S. senator. Larry MacPhail, a former baseball executive who had helped boost Chandler in 1945, believed the situation again called for a well-known outsider. "The next commissioner absolutely must be a man of national prominence and an executive," said MacPhail. His favorite: Milton Eisenhower, president of Johns Hopkins University and the ex-president's younger brother.[17] Other names mentioned were high on stature and low on baseball knowledge: Supreme Court Justice Byron White, Gen. Maxwell Taylor, and Senator Kenneth Keating.

A more immediate problem for Cronin in the late summer of 1964 involved his role in the sale of the New York Yankees to the Columbia Broadcasting System, announced in August. Under the terms of the deal, CBS would pay Yankee owners Del Webb and Dan Topping $11.2 million for 80 percent of the team, with each man retaining 10 percent and staying to run the operation. The Yankees would become a CBS subsidiary.[18]

The sale was revealed by of all people Charlie Finley, who recounted for the press the unusual story of how it came to pass. On August 13 Finley received a letter from Cronin outlining the deal and asking for approval (all team sales had to be approved by eight of the league's ten franchises). Before he had a chance to respond, Finley received a telegram from Cronin telling him that he had the eight votes he needed, though he still wanted Finley's vote just to complete the record. Arthur Allyn, the owner of the White Sox, told the same story—the other eight owners, including the Yankees, had voted yes before Finley and Allyn even knew of the deal. Cronin apparently got most of the votes by telephone and put off contacting the two owners most likely to disapprove of the deal.

Finley and Allyn were enraged at how this had been handled, especially as there had been a league meeting just three days earlier in which the topic was never broached. Allyn and Finley telegrammed their negative votes to Cronin, and Finley released his angry wire to the press. It read, in part: "This is another sad chapter in your nonadministration as president of the American League, and further evidence as to the reason why the National League is so far out in front of the American League. The AL is suffering badly from lack of leadership." Both Allyn and Finley demanded a league meeting. Cronin responded that no meeting was necessary as the sale had been ratified by the league, approved by the league's lawyer, and was therefore final. "Any details of such a transaction must come from the Yankees," he said.[19]

Opposition to the sale from the press mounted quickly, as various conflicts of interest were revealed, including that baseball had television contracts in place with NBC and CBS for regular season and World Series games; all Major League teams had their own contracts with local stations, many of which were owned by CBS; the Yankees telecast their games on WPIX, an independent station in New York that competed with a CBS affiliate; Joe Iglehart, majority owner of the Baltimore Orioles, owned forty thousand shares of CBS stock; and Lee MacPhail, who cast the Orioles' vote, was the brother of the sports director at CBS. Roy Hofheinz, president of the Houston Colt .45s of the National League, called it "the darkest day for baseball since the Black Sox scandal." Cronin scoffed at the opponents. "No communications organization will ever dictate to us, formulate our policy, or influence our decisions," he said. The opposition was due to a "lack of knowledge," he claimed, ignoring the fact that the biggest protests, from Finley and Allyn, came from people who wanted to have a meeting where they might gain some of that knowledge.[20]

Cronin's claims, wrote Shirley Povich, were "sheer effrontery. If not, Cronin is more naïve than has been suspected. The unvarnished fact is that both CBS and NBC have been dictating to the major leagues for years." In 1964, at the time of the sale, CBS was televising a game of the week pitting the Yankees against another league opponent. The Yankees received $600,000 for the season, and their opponent $25,000 per game. The deal did not even involve the league—CBS contracted with the individual teams directly.[21]

Cronin's handling of this matter was heavily criticized in the media. Several legislators, including New York congressman Emmanuel Cellar, thought baseball's antitrust exemption should be re-examined. Further, the sale drew interest from the Justice Department, which began by contacting both Allyn and Finley. This ominous threat angered Finley further, causing another broadside at the "unqualified" Cronin, who was "jeopardizing [Finley's] investment thru his shenanigans." Faced with extensive criticism from the press, as well as pressure from the suddenly concerned CBS, on August 27 Cronin scheduled a league meeting in Boston on September 9 to discuss the matter.

Prior to the meeting, Finley announced that he would leave baseball if the sale was approved. Besides Cronin and the owners, appearing at the meeting was Frank Stanton, president of CBS. Cronin finally explained the procedure that led to the rushed sale. Although he had known about the negotiations several days before the announcement and discussed them with Topping at the league meeting on August 10, he felt it would be harmful to tell the other owners until it was finalized. Once the deal was agreed to on August 12, CBS wanted it approved and announced quickly, in keeping with their standard business practice.[22]

Once all the arguments had been heard and Finley and Allyn had had their say, the league approved the sale 8–2, the same vote that had been cast a month earlier. Two days later Allyn demanded another meeting, claiming that Cronin had suppressed a vital piece of information: the opinion of a Justice Department official that the sale might affect baseball's antitrust status. "Withholding from the September 9 meeting of such crucially material information obviously invalidates the vote approving the transaction," said the White Sox owner. Finley mildly disagreed with Allyn, saying that Cronin had mentioned this point briefly and off-handedly, but that "the other owners could not care less about any discussion."[23]

Though the sale was finalized by baseball on November 2, the Senate Antitrust and Monopoly Committee held hearings in February to look into the matter further. The head of the committee, Philip

Hart (D-Michigan) was friendly with the Tigers, and accepted the testimony of Cronin and Frick that baseball would not allow cbs to meddle in its internal affairs. Frick agreed that several Major League owners who held stock in cbs must divest themselves of their holding.[24] The sale was final.

If Cronin's ascension to baseball's commissionership had seemed inevitable in mid-1964, by the end of the year there were growing doubts. To begin with Cronin's handling of the cbs matter had drawn heated criticism in and out of the game. More important, the controversy had further bolstered the argument that the game needed someone better able to work with the federal government. The situation remained fluid, however. After Cronin's impressive appearance in front of the Senate in February, Bob Addie thought he had reassured some of the doubters and had regained his status as the favorite.[25]

As when he was a candidate for the al presidency in 1959, Cronin made it clear that he would accept the job if it was offered. "Not that Cronin is campaigning strongly," wryly suggested writer Dave Condon. "He covets the commissionership no more than L.B.J. coveted the presidency."[26] His most brazen attempt to promote his chances was an exclusive interview he gave to *Sport* magazine under the headline "Joe Cronin: If He Were Commissioner." Far from promising a revolution, Cronin deflected several questions (concerning local television contracts, franchise shifts, and the spitball, among others) as being outside the powers of the commissioner, supported the independence of the two leagues, and refused to talk about the sale of the Yankees. Cronin did allow that the national game of the week should be moved to Monday so as to interfere with fewer Minor and Major League games and that the players should be encouraged to be more "colorful." He thought interleague play was the answer to sagging attendance but admitted that it did not have the support of the National League.[27] For observers who felt the game needed a strong and active commissioner, Cronin's interview would not have helped his case, as Cronin advocated a commissioner who deferred to the leagues and owners whenever possible. Cronin's main qualifications were that he knew the business, loved the game, and worked well with nearly everyone in management.

In *Sport's* very next issue, Leonard Koppett explored the state of the game in a story titled "Baseball's Biggest Crisis," where he suggested that the sport was at its most critical crossroads since the Black Sox scandal of the early 1920s. Koppett presented a list of nine important problems baseball must deal with:

the altered conditions of American life;
new competition, especially from football;
the procurement of players and the health of the Minor Leagues;
    central administration, including the commissioner;
further expansion;
modern financing;
legal issues, including congressional antitrust legislation;
public image;
and television.

In Koppett's view, baseball needed fresh ideas and leadership to handle all of these matters, and the choice of the new commissioner would suggest how seriously the sport took its current predicament. Koppett believed that baseball needed a commissioner who would overlook the needs of individual teams in favor of the long-term interests of the sport itself.[28]

In early 1965 the owners named John Fetzer of the Tigers and John Galbreath of the Pirates as a two-man screening committee to vet possible candidates. Each of the twenty clubs was asked to submit recommendations, which produced an initial list of 156 names. Fetzer and Galbreath presented 50 names at an owners meeting in July, and the list was further whittled to about 15. Ford Frick commented further on the desired candidate: "Baseball's problems are now more manifest and manifold. Today, the commissioner's office deals with corporate problems—moving franchises, ownership by large corporations, laws before Congress, financial arrangements, things like that."[29]

On November 16, 1965, baseball owners caught everyone by surprise when they named retired Air Force lieutenant general William

"Spike" Eckert as baseball's fourth commissioner. Although speculation had been divided about whether the choice would be a baseball man or a prominent outsider, Eckert was neither—a military bureaucrat who had worked on defense contracts and procurement matters, a man who had never been mentioned in the press in connection with the job and someone not believed to have been on any of the lists being considered. "Good God!" crowed Larry Fox of the *New York World-Telegram*. "They've named the Unknown Soldier." The owners had hired a dignified man who would appease governmental agencies but would otherwise do little to govern the game. To help the novice commissioner, the owners created two new positions: Lee MacPhail, general manager of the Baltimore Orioles, was named Eckert's assistant, and writer Joe Reichler became public-relations director.[30] In reality the game would be run by the owners.

The very same day, Cronin signed a new seven-year contract to continue as American League president. He had wanted the commissioner's job and had had the support of at least Tom Yawkey and Calvin Griffith, but the selected candidate needed seven votes in each league, which no insider was able to get.[31] One writer thought Cronin's shortcoming was that his genial disposition would have kept him from "riding herd" on the club owners. Others remained supportive. "Most of us wondered—and are still wondering—why Joe Cronin was bypassed," said writer Bill Lee in the *Hartford Courant*. Nonetheless, Cronin had plenty of adventures ahead in the job he had.[32]

The big news in the American League in 1965 was the sudden collapse of the New York Yankees after five consecutive pennants. This turn of events delighted the league president, who had annually predicted that the Yankees would have a much more difficult time than they had in previous years. Cronin's bias was not malicious, but his league was continually derided because of the Yankees' dominance, and as league president he knew the health of the league depended on greater parity. In March Cronin had once again predicted a tight pennant race, pointing out that several teams had improved when compared with the Yankees.[33]

Cronin's most public difficulty during the season came after an incident in Minnesota on July 18. In the first game of a Sunday double-header with the Angels, an infield single by Jim Fregosi caused Twins manager Sam Mele to rush out of the dugout to protest the safe call by umpire Bill Valentine. The ensuing argument escalated to some incidental bumping, and then the mild-mannered Mele appeared to throw a punch at Valentine, grazing his jaw. Several players were required to separate the two men. Cronin happened to be at the game, and the next day he fined Mele $500 and suspended him for five days. Mele was appalled at the suspension and denied the punch (though photographs in the newspaper did not help his cause). Not everyone was sympathetic. "It baffles me, however, that Mele thought his fine and suspension excessive punishment," wrote Bill Lee in the *Hartford Courant*. "It struck me that Mele was lucky to get off so lightly."[34] Mele had begun his career in 1947 playing for Joe Cronin in Boston, and the men had remained friends. In 1965 there was no method of formally protesting such a decision—Cronin's decision was final.

Mele's suspension was particularly noteworthy because the Twins were then in first place, three and a half games ahead of Cleveland. In fact Minnesota won 102 games and the pennant going away, while the Yankees finished 25 games behind. Though he would have preferred a tight race, Cronin was delighted at the Twins' victory—this was Mildred's family's team, a club that had left Washington for greener pastures and found them. The Cronins traveled to Minneapolis and Los Angeles to watch an excellent seven-game World Series, ultimately won by the Dodgers.

During the following offseason, Cronin made news with some changes to the league's umpiring crew. Although the National League umpires had organized into a union in 1963 (and had nearly struck over pension demands in 1964), thus far the AL arbiters had not taken that step. Arthur Daley, writing in the *New York Times*, credited Cronin's umpire-in-chief Cal Hubbard, who listened to and understood the concerns of his umpires—the NL did not employ an umpiring supervisor, and the umps did not feel Warren Giles cared about them. In 1964 Major League umpires made between $7,000 and $18,000 per year, amounts that had not been increased in years.[35] Umpires were sent contracts every winter, and they had little choice but to sign them.

In 1965 the American League increased their umpires' pensions from $250 to $300 per year for each year of service, while also lowering the retirement age from sixty to fifty-five. This latter action was Cronin's decision and led to the immediate retirement of three veteran umpires: Ed Hurley, Bill McKinley, and Joe Paparella. Paparella had told Cronin a year earlier that he was quitting after the season, so the new policy only cemented his decision. McKinley and Hurley were angry. "I received a letter from the front office and I thought it was my contract," Hurley said. "I opened it and overnight I became old, a has-been. If I hadn't been sitting down I'd have had a heart attack." According to Hurley the league umpires were not aware of the new policy—they were told it was the age at which an umpire *could* retire and start drawing a pension, not that he must. Cronin's view was that the umpires had asked for a lower retirement age, and now they had it.

McKinley was certain why this had happened. "We knew the National League umpires were organizing, and Ed Hurley in particular kept hounding [Cronin] for more money. So the five senior men went to [Cronin's] office to carry the ball. Cronin took it upon himself to present our requests [to the owners] rather than giving us a chance to see the club owners. The result of the meeting was that I got a letter saying that I had been retired." McKinley believed that the retirement age was just a convenient excuse. "There was no warning. Just a letter, an eight-cent letter, saying I was through."[36]

Hurley lived in Holyoke, Massachusetts, and his letter from Cronin arrived just after he had paid a social visit to the league office, when not a word had been spoken about his impending forced retirement. When he went to see Cronin again, he was advised to get a job to supplement his new pension, $4,850 per year. Ironically, Hurley was two years younger than Cronin, who had just signed a seven-year contract, and Hurley had nineteen years of service with the American League. In a fantastic bit of hyperbole, Hurley suggested, "It's things like this that start wars, that make it possible for Hitlers." There was nothing he could do short of taking expensive legal action, which neither he or McKinley did. Cronin and the owners held the cards and were not swayed by the support the umpires got in the press.[37] As it happened, one of the three men hired to replace the retired umps soon became a much larger story and quickly pushed the plight of the retired umpires off the sports pages.

In 1951 Emmett Ashford took a leave of absence from his Post Office job for a two-month umpiring trial in the Southwestern International League, becoming the first black umpire in organized baseball. Offered a full-season position after the season, Ashford resigned from the Postal Service, leaving behind fifteen years of pension. He moved up to the Western International League in 1953 then to the Pacific Coast League in 1954.[38]

During his twelve years in the PCL, Ashford became the best-known umpire in the Minor Leagues. "He was a showman, exuberant, strong, alert, loud and expressive," recalled Paul Wysard of Ashford's days in the PCL. "He was constantly in motion, full of nervous energy and obviously delighted to be out there in front of everybody." Between innings he often sprinted down the right field line to keep his legs loose. He enthusiastically played to the crowd, doffing his cap and making impromptu speeches. In 1963 Ashford became the league's umpire-in-chief, taking responsibility for the organization and training of the crews, and advising the league on disputed games or rules.[39]

By the early 1960s, writers on the West Coast began clamoring for Ashford's promotion to the Major Leagues. A. S. Young took up the cause in the *Chicago Defender*, suggesting of league presidents Cronin and Giles, "whereas they hire, and approve the hiring of Caucasian umpires solely on the basis of qualifications, they refuse to act on the Ashford case—and probably won't until the Ashford campaign, which should be unnecessary, becomes embarrassing." In 1965 while Cronin was a leading contender to be baseball's commissioner, Jim Murray supported Bill Veeck for the top job, with Ashford as his umpire-in-chief. Both endorsements were due to Cronin's supposed foot dragging on Ashford.[40]

In September of 1965 the American League bought Ashford's contract from the PCL. "It was the last thing I remember for several days," recalled Ashford. The nation's press was thrilled. Melvin Durslag, writing in the *Los Angeles Herald-Examiner*, figured that Ashford was "bound to raise the game to his refined level." Bill Slocum, in the *New York Journal-American* wondered, "If corporate Baseball has joined the 20th Century, can Mississippi be far behind?"[41]

Ashford's regular season debut took place on April 11, 1966, in the traditional American League opener at Washington's D.C. Stadium. His first Major League hurdle was getting into the ballpark. Vice President Hubert Humphrey was there to throw out the ceremonial first ball, and the Secret Service at the player's gate needed to be convinced that a black man was there to umpire the game. Humphrey later kidded Ashford, who had worked at third base, that he hadn't had any plays to call. "No plays, no boots," responded Ashford, "but it was the greatest day of my life." Joe Cronin told his new employee, "Emmett, you made history today. I'm proud of you."[42]

Ashford's style, well known on the west coast, took the conservative Major Leagues by a storm. The stocky (five feet seven, 185 pounds) Ashford sprinted to his position between innings, stepping on the bases or leaping over the pitcher's mound, and raced around the field after foul balls or plays on the bases. *The Sporting News* was impressed enough to claim, "For the first time in the history of the grand old American game, baseball fans may buy a ticket to watch an umpire perform." The fans did not always need to watch Ashford, they could just listen to his high-pitched cannon of a voice, as he called out a batter or runner.[43]

On a strike call, Ashford jerked his right arm first to the side, then up, then down like a karate chop. That completed, he would reach either up as if twice yanking a train whistle, or to the right as if opening a car door. Even while dusting the plate he knew every eye in the house was on him, and he behaved accordingly, pirouetting on one foot and hopping back to his position. Emmett would say, "I didn't go to umpiring school because they weren't taking blacks in those days, so I evolved my own style." Ashford was also known for his natty attire on and off the field. While umpiring he wore polished shoes, a freshly pressed uniform, cufflinks, and a handkerchief in his suit pocket.[44] Ashford toned down some of his mannerisms as his big-league career progressed. "Sure, I was a showboat," he told the writer Ray Fitzgerald. "For 12 years, that was my routine in the Coast League. I couldn't change overnight, but I'm different now. I've toned myself way down." But still, "I'm not exactly without color," he said, using a favorite double entendre.[45]

Although Cronin did not condone Ashford's showmanship, he approved of his overall work. Ashford came to the park prepared to umpire, and he took his duties and his decisions on the field very seriously. Cronin and Ashford developed a friendship that lasted beyond either of their careers in the game.[46]

Ashford was fifty-one when he began his Major League career, meaning he had just four years before he would have to retire. Ashford turned fifty-five in November 1969, but Cronin granted him one additional season. After the 1970 season Ashford announced his retirement. He had been one of the officials in the World Series, but as the junior umpire in a five-game Series, he had not had the opportunity to work home plate. "Maybe it's just as well it didn't happen," he said. "The World Series would never have been the same." He later told writer Larry Gerlach: "I am grateful to those who supported me, especially Joe Cronin, who took the bull by the horns and had the guts to call me up when it wasn't the popular thing to do. Jackie Robinson had his Branch Rickey; I had my Joe Cronin."[47]

The 1961 American League expansion, the first experiment of its kind, had not been as successful as hoped—other than the Angels surprising third place showing in 1962, the new teams had performed poorly, and neither had drawn many fans. The National League, which had expanded in 1962, felt compelled to hold a dispersal draft after the 1963 season to help their two new teams (New York and Houston) with new players. Cronin rejected this idea for his league, calling it "another garbage draft from a selected list."[48]

Nevertheless, baseball remained under pressure to expand further—

from Congress and from several local leaders who thought a Major League club would help lend credibility to their cities. In mid-1965, a group of six U.S. congressmen sent a letter to Frick (in his final months on the job), Cronin, and Giles, suggesting that baseball expand in 1966 by adding franchises in Milwaukee, Buffalo, and Dallas-Ft. Worth. Frick politely pointed out that "nobody outside baseball knows what is involved in expansion." Cronin was more expansive. "There are many problems involved," he said. "There's no doubt that expansion will come some day. The last expansion went off fine, but we're still building up the farm clubs which is one of the problems involved."[49]

Many cities were actively attempting to lure existing franchises—Oakland almost landed the Athletics in 1964, Seattle had a deal with the Cleveland Indians that fell through late in the process, and a few teams were rumored to be considering Dallas-Ft. Worth. In 1966 the National League's Milwaukee Braves moved to Atlanta, marking the first time in more than sixty years that Major League Baseball had abandoned a one-team city. This moved Milwaukee to the head of the line when expansion or franchise movement was speculated upon in the press. "We have no plans to expand at this time," Cronin said in early 1966, "but when we do make the move we'll have to place another team on the West Coast. Travel costs are simply too great when the trip has to be made for only a single series with the Angels."[50]

On July 24, 1967, Milwaukee's County Stadium hosted an exhibition game between the Minnesota Twins and Chicago White Sox, an event largely seen as a trial for the city's baseball-starved fans. Both Cronin and Commissioner Eckert attended, among a crowd of more than fifty-one thousand people—well beyond the seating capacity of about forty-four thousand. Cronin praised the fans but was noncommittal about his league's plans for the city. He still believed the question was years away.

Not surprisingly, Charlie Finley unwittingly acted to loosen the log jam. The four-year lease he had reluctantly signed with Kansas City in early 1964 would expire at the end of the 1967 season. In mid-September

Finley told Cronin that he intended to formally request permission to move to either Seattle or Oakland at the league's October meeting. Seattle voters were considering a bond measure for a new stadium, and if it passed, Seattle might be Finley's first choice. Oakland, which already had a new stadium but would share a market with the San Francisco Giants, was his backup plan.[51] Eventually Finley decided he could not wait for Seattle's February vote, so he settled on Oakland.

Also attending the meeting on October 18 in Chicago was a Kansas City delegation, including Mayor Ilus W. Davis and Senator Stuart Symington. The group did not try to dissuade Finley, who had thoroughly destroyed his relationship with the city, as much as they sought a new expansion club in conjunction with losing the Athletics. In particular Davis insisted that some team, regardless of the owner, must play in Kansas City in 1968. The AL's 1961 expansion had come together in just a few months, so there was precedent for an accelerated schedule.[52] At the eventful meeting, owners approved the immediate transfer of the Athletics to Oakland and also voted to expand "no later than 1971" by adding franchises in Kansas City and (probably) Seattle.

Before making the announcement to the press, Cronin called the Kansas City delegation at a neighboring hotel. Cronin assumed they would be pleased. He was mistaken. A furious Symington told Cronin he would introduce antitrust legislation, while Mayor Davis said he would file an injunction in Kansas City to stop Finley from moving. Besides the political problem attached to the city losing baseball for three years, there was a practical matter: Kansas City's voters had approved the construction of a new baseball stadium, but the project would not proceed unless a long-term lease was signed prior to March 1, 1968.

Although it was nearly midnight, Cronin reconvened the league meeting, claiming that the previous meeting had never been adjourned. Apparently only five owners were present, the rest having scattered toward their homes or hotel rooms. An hour later Cronin re-emerged to announce that expansion would take place in 1969 and that the new Kansas City owner would be in place by March 1968. Symington returned to Washington and blasted Finley from the floor of the Senate. "The loss of the A's is more than recompensed by the pleasure of getting rid of Mr. Finley," said Symington. "He is one of the most disreputable characters ever to enter the American sports scene. Oakland is the luckiest city since Hiroshima."[53]

As he had been in 1960, Cronin was criticized for his league's hasty move. After the earlier expansion, Ford Frick had demanded that in the future the two leagues act in concert. Warren Giles was understandably upset that this had not happened and hoped that the league would reopen the matter to involve the National League. Giles was not merely concerned with protocol; he also did not like the AL grabbing the Seattle territory while also entering the Bay Area to compete with the Giants. He knew the AL needed to add a team on the West Coast, but he had not expected two. After the NL had gotten the better of their rivals with their profitable franchise shifts in the 1950s and again in the first expansion in 1961–62, this time the AL had acted fast to get a new and growing market in Seattle and a brand new stadium in the big city of Oakland. His league may have stumbled into the solution, but Cronin appeared to have won this round.[54] The National League waited until the following spring to announce its own expansion plans, adding teams in San Diego and Montreal.

The American League's official offer to Seattle contained a few conditions, including the passage of the domed-stadium measure in February. To help out many former and current baseball stars traveled to Seattle to promote the stadium—including Cronin, Joe DiMaggio, Carl Yastrzemski, and Mickey Mantle. Cronin spent a lot of time in the area, even commissioning polls to gauge local support. "He came in," recalled Max Soriano, one of the principal owners of the new franchise, "and he said, 'Max, you've got to do a little better.' He says 'you're up around 55, 56 percent, but you've got to do something more to get up to over 60 percent.'"[55] Passage of the measure required 60 percent of the vote, and in the end it garnered 62.3 percent. "It will mean so much to the community," said Cronin. "I'm so happy about it."[56] The city hoped to have the domed stadium ready for the new team, the Pilots, by 1971.

One highlight for Cronin in these years came in 1967, when the Red Sox won the American League pennant for the first time since 1946. Better still, the league waged a memorable four-team pennant race, with Minnesota, Detroit, and Boston all in contention on the final day of the season. The entire Cronin family attended the final two game series at Fenway Park, pitting the Twins and Red Sox. The Cronins sat with several of Mildred's brothers and sisters who owned or otherwise worked for the Twins. Joe was supposedly neutral, but understandably thrilled with the excitement of that final weekend, which he later recalled as a highlight of his presidency.

In the midst of this particularly tumultuous period for baseball, Cronin's life was more consumed by baseball than it had been when he was a player-manager. There was no off-season for the league president, and he and Mildred no longer had children to raise. Michael had graduated from Harvard in 1963 and married a few days later. Tommy married in 1966 and soon left his post with the Senators to take a promotions job with the Twins (joining most of his mother's family). Maureen had graduated from Marymount College and married in 1967. Kevin, the baby of the family, entered Stanford in 1968. With the children living their own lives, Joe and Mildred had more time to live theirs. More often than not, they chose socializing with friends, going to baseball games, and traveling to promote the sport they both loved. It was the life they knew.

16 Unrest

"BASEBALL," WROTE ARNOLD HANO IN 1968, "reminds me of a guy with an ice pick in his inner ear. His equilibrium is shot. He walks like a punch-drunk pug. Any minute you expect him to fall on his face. And when baseball finally does fall, do not weep. Just throw some dirt over the body. Take the dirt from the pitcher's mound. That'll be appropriate. Pitching is the name of the guy who stuck the ice pick in baseball's ear. Though the pitchers have had their accessories. Lots of them."[1]

Hano was not alone in thinking that baseball had gotten dull, though he expressed his thoughts more colorfully than most. After the strike zone was enlarged in 1963, scoring had plummeted to about 4 runs per game (per team) and held steady for a few years. In 1967, for no discernible reason, offense dropped to 3.77 runs per game, then fell further to 3.42 in 1968, lowest in the Majors since 1908. The American League batted .230, an all-time low for any Major League. A full 21 percent of all games in the Majors were shutouts. In August Warren Giles, the NL president, sent a directive to his league's managers and general managers asking for help in resolving this "obvious imbalance."

Despite adding four new teams, building several new stadiums, and reaching new markets in Minneapolis, Houston, Atlanta, and Oakland, attendance in the Major Leagues had fallen 11 percent during the decade, from 16,109 per game in 1960 to 14,217 in 1968. What was particularly alarming was that baseball's malaise coincided precisely with the rise in popularity of professional football. In a poll asking people what their favorite sport was, baseball led football 39 percent to 32 percent, but the gap was closing, and football led strongly among fans under thirty-five.[2] As Hano pointed out, "pro football knows how to deal with imbalance." Hano felt that if pro football were in a similar rut, it would tinker with the rules of the game, which baseball needed to do now: a lower mound, smaller strike zone, longer pitching distances, restrictions to eight pitchers per team, a permanent pinch hitter for the pitcher, stricter penalties for the spitball. "But whatever the solutions," Hano concluded, "they must come forth."

As bad as the problems were, they were especially bad in the less popular American League. Nonetheless, its president did not think the situation warranted any changes. "It's a funny thing," said Cronin. "When I was playing and we had big-score games, the cry was 'Give us back the good old days of good pitching, stolen bases, bunting, and the hit and run.' Well, now that type of game is back and everybody is complaining. I don't think anything radical should be done. I might be in favor of lowering the mound to ten or twelve inches. But that's about all."[3]

In May 1968 when only two hitters in his league were batting .300, Cronin said, "I don't see why we should get disturbed. When it gets warmer, the hitters are going to catch up with the pitchers and in the end all of the .300 hitters are going to hit .300 as usual." As only four AL hitters had managed a .300 average in 1967 and two in 1966, Cronin's words were hardly reassuring. On August 30 the leading AL batter was hitting an alarming .288, causing Shirley Povich to write, "In the American League, the hitting has lapsed from the inept to the incredible." The problem was not merely a statistical anomaly—the game was losing the battle for the hearts and minds of American sports fans. "The majors are caught in a kind of pincer movement," thought Povich, "comprised of its own aspects of boredom on the one hand, and the challenges of pro football, with all its thunk, on the other. No brave statements from the commissioner's office can hide some of the truths."[4] In the end, Carl Yastrzemski's late surge brought his average to .301, sparing the league the embarrassment of not having a .300 hitter.

With growing criticism from the press, baseball's general managers met in October and requested two rule changes: the return of the pre-1963 strike zone (from the top of the knees to the armpits) and the lowering of the mound from fifteen inches to ten inches. Both of these revisions were enacted by the Rules Committee in December and took effect in 1969. Major League run scoring increased from 3.42 to 4.07 runs per game, but the American League would revisit this issue again in just a few short years.

The late 1960s saw many changes around the game of baseball, most dramatically with the increasing independence of the players, both individually and collectively. Although the Major League Players Association had formed in 1953 and made small gains in their pension plan in ensuing years, the group did not begin to flex its muscles until the hiring in 1966 of Marvin Miller as its chief. An experienced labor economist, most recently with the United Steelworkers, Miller's early months were spent educating the players about their rights and what benefits they might earn if they banded together and held firm.

Baseball management had a Player Relations Committee, chaired by Joe Cronin and also including Warren Giles and the two league attorneys. Before Miller the purpose of this committee was to meet occasionally with player representatives, hear what the players wanted, relay these requests to the owners, and then tell the players what had been decided. The minimum salary, a common player grievance, had been raised only once in twenty years—from five to $6,000 per year. When Miller met with the PRC in 1966, he was struck by how little the members knew about labor law. "It was difficult," Miller told me in 2007, "dealing with so much inexperience. They had no idea what they could and couldn't do."[5]

Cronin, Miller thought, "could have been a metropolitan politician." While Giles was driving management crazy by talking frankly and honestly, Cronin was slicker. "He was always trying to figure out the best way to get what he wanted," recalled Miller. The other men, including Miller, respected Cronin's long service to the game and the insights that he brought to the conversation. But Cronin believed that he was protecting the game from people who were trying to change it—including the new generation of players and their representative. After the 1966 World Series Miller ran into Cronin at the airport in

Los Angeles and the two men had a drink. "Young man," Cronin told the forty-nine-year-old Miller, "I've got some advice for you that I want you to remember. The players come and go, but the owners stay on forever."[6]

Miller liked Cronin, recalling him as "a very personable man." But he felt Cronin's attitude to be typical of baseball management. "The league presidency was a nothing job," he later wrote. "Other than staying on the right side of the right owners, Cronin's biggest challenge was choosing between a pitching wedge and a nine-iron." In one meeting early in his tenure, Miller pointed out that the playing schedule for the upcoming season had a long stretch of games for one team with no days off, wondering whether this might be fixed. Cronin, generally calm and collected, angrily responded that the league president had absolute authority over the schedule.

In August 1967 the owners hired John Gaherin, who would act as the counterpart to Miller. Cronin remained the chairman of the PRC and continued to deal with the players union, but the job of enlightening baseball management on labor law was now Gaherin's instead of Miller's. Cronin often joked with Miller during pension negotiations that he was a beneficiary of the pension plan and had a lot at stake.[7]

While Cronin fretted over the growing power of the players, he still held control over twenty umpires, a role he took very seriously. Unfortunately, his work in this area led to the most controversial act of his presidency. On September 15, 1968, Al Salerno and Bill Valentine were at Cleveland Stadium, umpiring at second base and third base respectively, in the Indians' 2–0 victory over the Orioles. The next morning, shortly after Salerno awoke, he received a phone call from Cronin. "I thought he was calling to tell me about a World Series appointment," said Salerno. Instead, Cronin told the umpire he was fired—he would get ten days severance pay and should go home. The stunned Salerno went to see Valentine, who was staying at the same hotel. Valentine was just hanging up from his own conversation with Cronin. He, too, had been fired, effective immediately. Both men were told they were being let go because they were incompetent. "They're just bad umpires, that's all," Cronin told the press.[8]

Salerno and Valentine had a different story to tell. Both men had been involved in trying to organize their fellow American League umpires, as their National League counterparts had done in 1963. By 1968 the compensation levels for the two staffs had separated dramatically. The AL salary range was between $6,500 and $17,000 per year, compared with $9,000 and $25,750 in the National League. The AL pension vested at ten years, versus five in the NL, and paid smaller benefits.[9] Salerno had attended a meeting with the National League Umpires Association on September 12 in Chicago, where he was told that the AL umps could join their union if all twenty of them agreed to sign on. The next day Salerno wrote letters to the other league umpires, most of whom were already aware of and approved Salerno's mission. Three days later he and Valentine were unemployed.[10]

Salerno had worked in the league since the end of the 1961 season, when his contract had been acquired from the Pacific Coast League. Valentine arrived in 1963, also from the PCL, meaning that the two men had seven and six years of service, respectively. According to the umpires, they had earned annual raises as their careers progressed and had never received a negative performance review. Each had been chosen to work in an All-Star Game. In the final crucial game of the 1967 season, when a Detroit win in California would have meant a tied pennant race, Valentine worked home plate—something supporters claimed would never have been allowed had he been a bad umpire. Furthermore, it stretched credulity to think that the American League would place its two worst umpires on the same crew for the 1968 season.

In the ensuing firestorm everyone other than Cronin's loyalists or employees lined up behind the umpires. Shirley Povich, like many observers, noted the irony of Cronin's explanation of incompetence. "To Cronin's credit," wrote Povich, "this was not a snap judgment. In Salerno's case it took the AL President seven years to arrive at it; in Valentine's case, six years." Sounding the same theme, Red Smith wrote that Cronin "has to be one of the least perceptive or most indulgent employers this side of Utopia." But most writers were more direct. "Today Cronin looks foolish," observed Bob August in the *Cleveland*

News, "a baseball dinosaur lumbering through the 1960's. He made a mistake and it was a beaut."[11]

The story also added to the American League's sagging image. For one thing the press and public became aware of the large differences in compensation and benefits for the umps in the two leagues. Plus, the NL union had made its gains without any public rancor or turmoil with the league office. Cronin's suggestion that the two veteran umpires had never been good at their jobs only added to the ridicule. When asked about the different pay scales, Cronin said that he had no idea how much money the NL umps made, adding feebly that the NL's higher attendance allowed for higher salaries.

If Cronin's intention was to pressure his umpires not to organize, his efforts backfired decisively. The day after the regular season, the remaining Major League umpires met in Chicago. The NL umpires voted unanimously to admit the AL umps into their group, to be renamed the Major League Umpires Association. The arbiters also considered striking the 1968 World Series to protest the firings. Salerno and Valentine attended the meeting and urged the umps to work, which they did. In the off-season the union's lawyer met with Cronin to begin the process of working out a relationship, but Cronin would not agree to reinstate the fired umpires.[12]

In early January, the new union filed an unfair labor practice charge with the National Labor Relations Board concerning the firings. In a separate action, in September 1969 Salerno and Valentine filed a $4 million suit in federal court against Major League Baseball, Joe Cronin, and the American League for unlawful dismissal and defamation of character. The suit was quickly dismissed by the court on the grounds of jurisdiction—prior Supreme Court cases had upheld baseball's exemption from antitrust laws (including its labor provisions). The attorneys for the umpires immediately appealed. In December 1969 the NLRB agreed to assume jurisdiction on the union's charge, a strong indication that the board did not hold baseball immune to the labor portions of antitrust.[13]

A loss in either court action—the labor charge with the NLRB, or the lawsuit—would have a disconcerting effect on baseball's tenuous status with respect to antitrust law. In the spring of 1970 the American League negotiated a confidential settlement with the new union, which required that both actions be dropped. In exchange the umpires would receive full reinstatement at a salary of $20,000 per year—the current rate for their experience level, but eight thousand more than they made at the time of their dismissal. The umpires would begin the 1970 season in the Minor Leagues—Salerno in the International League, Valentine in the Texas League—and would be "reviewed" after two months by Cronin's office. This review was clearly designed as a face-saving gesture by Cronin.[14]

While Valentine was willing to accept the deal, Salerno was not, claiming he had gone into debt fighting the case. Just days before the scheduled NLRB hearing, the AL sweetened the deal considerably, offering the umpires $20,000 in back pay and credit toward the pension plan for their time away—both would be fully vested if they signed. Salerno again balked. Valentine drove from his home in Little Rock to see Salerno in Utica, New York. So desperate was Valentine to get back into baseball that he offered Salerno $10,000 of his own share of the settlement. Alternatively the league offered Salerno $37,500 without reinstatement. Salerno, on the advice of his attorney, declined all offers. He was advised he would win the case with the NLRB and wanted at least $100,000 to drop the suit. He also did not believe the league would follow through on its promise to promote the umps from the Minor Leagues. Valentine saw it the way the media saw it—full reinstatement with back pay and benefits. His lawyer tried to get the AL to deal with him separately, even at lesser terms. They would not.[15]

The NLRB hearings took place over nine days in July 1970. Testifying for Salerno and Valentine were three present or former American League managers—Alvin Dark, Dick Williams, and Eddie Stanky—as well as John Flaherty, a veteran AL umpire. All testified that Salerno and Valentine were good umpires, in the top half of the umps in the league. Valentine broke down on the stand when recalling the fateful conversation with Cronin, when he was called a "bad umpire." Salerno spoke for two hours about his efforts to organize, which he said were not a secret to anyone around the league.[16]

In his defense Cronin stated that he had no knowledge of plans to unionize the umpires. Further, he related that Valentine and Salerno were hot-headed and arrogant, and he recalled a few situations that the two umps had handled poorly. Cronin claimed that he had heard several complaints about the two umpires at the 1968 All-Star Game. His testimony was later refuted by former Pacific Coast League president Dewey Soriano, who had spoken with Cronin at that same All-Star Game, in Houston. According to a sworn affidavit prepared too late for the hearing, Soriano had asked Cronin specifically about several umpires who had worked in the PCL during Soriano's tenure and were sold to the American League. "Mr. Cronin replied that Salerno had done an outstanding job," said Soriano, "and that he would like to have more umpires like Salerno, who was one of his top umpires." Soriano had seen Cronin at the expansion draft in October and asked what had changed with the two umpires. "Let's just say they were involved in politics," Cronin told Soriano.[17]

In November the NLRB ruled that the umpires had not adequately proven that they were fired for their union activities. As for the lawsuit the Court of Appeals upheld the lower court's dismissal, and the Supreme Court declined to hear the case. The two umpires had bet everything on a victory in one of two actions, but won neither. "I really believed," said Valentine later, "until the hearing, that we would be reinstated." Just like that, it was all over.

In the intervening years the two umpires dealt with their fate quite differently. Valentine, who had begged Salerno to make the deal with the AL and wept at the NLRB hearing, held several jobs in Little Rock, working on the radio and directing the local Republican Party for a few years. In 1976 he was named the general manager of his hometown Arkansas Travelers of the Texas League, a job he held for more than three decades. He won the league's executive of the year award several times and has been named to the Texas League Hall of Fame and the Arkansas Sports Hall of Fame, among many honors. When he won an award for service to the Minor Leagues in 1983, he used the occasion to thank Cronin, who "gave me my start on the executive side of baseball at a very early age."[18] When he spoke with me in 2007, he remarked that he could not imagine a more rewarding life in baseball than the one he has lived. When asked about Cronin he just laughed—Cronin had done a terrible thing, he felt, but things had worked out all right. In a similar position, Valentine thought, perhaps he would have done what Cronin did, wrong as it was.[19]

Salerno, who had refused reinstatement in the hopes of greater riches, did not fare so well. In the ensuing years Salerno worked at a number of odd jobs, none of which lasted long. He had a heart attack in 1979 at just forty-eight years old and suffered many health setbacks after that. His marriage ended in the mid-1980s, his wife having grown tired of his complaining about what baseball had taken away from him. When we spoke in 2007, he was still fighting the case, still writing letters to the commissioner's office, politicians, and Supreme Court justices. "Cronin wrecked my life, my marriage. I am just waiting to crawl in my hole." A few weeks later he died, at age seventy-six.

Meanwhile, it did not take long for the owners to realize they had made a mistake in hiring General Eckert, who had proven to be indecisive and unfamiliar with the game. In December 1968 only three years into his seven-year contract, Eckert was fired, though everyone kindly treated it as a resignation. Leonard Koppett, writing in the *Times*, thought Eckert was set up to fail. "He could not give the illusion of vigorous leadership—the illusion the owners wanted—and when he did involve himself in a few problems of substance, the owners considered his honest efforts to be meddling." The biggest problem the commissioner faced, according to many, was the independence of the two leagues, which often acted without concern for the game as a whole.[20] The AL's latest expansion—a hasty arrangement that forced the NL to move quicker than it wanted—was just the latest example.

The machinations to name a new commissioner moved quite a bit quicker than they had three years earlier, though it did take several meetings over a few months. Joe Cronin had some support—notably from brother-in-law Calvin Griffith and Tom Yawkey—but his advancing age (sixty-two) and the recent umpire firings were reason enough to look elsewhere. None of the leading candidates—San Francisco's Chub Feeney, the Yankees' Mike Burke, or Montreal's John McHale—could gather enough support, and in the end the owners chose another unknown candidate. Bowie Kuhn was no Spike Eckert, however. Kuhn had been the National League attorney for several years, knew the game well, and, at just forty-two, promised to be an energetic hands-on commissioner. "I promise to be where the action is," Kuhn told reporters.[21] Kuhn had grown up in Washington and attended the 1933 World Series as a six-year-old, cheering on Joe Cronin and his Senators.[22]

The presence of a publicly active commissioner like Kuhn inevitably served to marginalize the role of the league presidents, Cronin and Giles. Commissioner Frick, a former league president, had deferred to the individual leagues as much as he could—on umpires, rules, scheduling, and franchise shifts. The messy AL expansion of the early 1960s, which Frick had deplored but did not stop, had been followed by an equally messy AL expansion under Eckert. Kuhn took the opposite view—any matter that he felt involved the interests of baseball as a whole would demand the new commissioner's attention.

In April 1969 the Boston Red Sox and Cleveland Indians made a six-player swap that sent star outfielder Ken Harrelson to Cleveland. The immensely popular "Hawk" had made as much news for his "mod" off-field lifestyle and fashion (including long hair, beads, and colorful clothing ensembles) as he had for his fine 1968 season. (Cronin had reportedly appealed to Dick O'Connell, Boston's general manager, about Harrelson's hair. "As long as Harrelson hits, he can wear his hair as long as he likes," responded O'Connell.[23]) Deciding that he could not leave his many business interests in Boston, Harrelson announced that he would retire from baseball. His lawyer told the press that Harrelson could make $750,000 a year in Boston off the field. Cronin ordered the two teams not to play their new players, saying the deal would be negated if Harrelson did not report or if the two teams could not work out a revised deal. The next move was up to the clubs.[24]

Had Frick or Eckert been commissioner, the two teams, and perhaps Harrelson, would have tried to work things out. Cronin would not have interfered with the two general managers, his good friends Dick O'Connell and Gabe Paul. Kuhn, on the other hand, felt that "the commissioner had more clout than anyone else and ought to use it."[25] He ordered all parties to New York, where he lectured Harrelson about how much he would miss the game and how much he owed the fans. Harrelson agreed to go to the Indians, aided by a new two-year contract at $100,000 per year, double his previous salary. Although Kuhn received some criticism for allowing Harrelson to be rewarded (Dick Young, in the *Daily News*, felt Kuhn had made the problem worse), others were pleased that someone finally seemed to be in charge. In just his first two months on the job, Kuhn was credited with averting a player strike (over the pension plan, in March), saving the Harrelson deal, and salvaging a deal in the National League involving Rusty Staub and Donn Clendenon.[26] In all cases Kuhn involved himself in a way that no recent commissioner or league president would have. Kuhn became the vigorously active face of baseball management, partly at the expense of the league presidents.

As part of a year-long publicity campaign to celebrate the game's 1969 centennial (it had been one hundred years since the first openly professional team, the Cincinnati Red Stockings), the fans of each Major League city selected an all-time team. Cronin was named the shortstop for both the Red Sox and Senators teams and took part in ceremonies at each team's ballpark. (Although Cronin's Senators had moved to Minnesota, he and baseball considered the expansion Senators to be a continuation of the old Senators and the Twins to be a new team.) The culmination of the game's campaign was a spectacular reception hosted by President Nixon at the White House, the night before the All-Star Game in Washington's RFK Stadium. Over five hundred baseball notables were present, including the two All-Star teams, all of the all-time teams that had been announced the previous day at a banquet, members of the press and other dignitaries. "Those who have been mourning the death of baseball," wrote the *New York Times*, "must have been shocked by the glittering scene in Washington a few nights ago.[27] The successful event was considered another coup in the short reign of Commissioner Kuhn.

Once the National League finally revealed its own expansion plans for 1969, the American League took things a step further in early 1968 by announcing that they would split into two six-team divisions and play a championship playoff series in 1969. The NL balked, claiming a playoff series would reduce the glamour of the World Series and divisions would separate some historic rivalries. Nonsense, said Joe Cronin. "You can't sell a 12th-place club," he said. "It goes back to the old theory of having too many second division clubs. We're not looking for trouble. We are a peaceful and quiet league. We're just a little progressive."[28] In the event, the NL did adopt the two-division set up a few months later.

The new alignment led to immediate difficulties for the American League. Unlike the NL, whose two California teams had been among its most popular and successful franchises, the strong AL teams were almost all in the northeast. Among the six teams in the new Eastern Division were the league's top five finishers in 1968 (Detroit, Baltimore, Cleveland, Boston, and New York), plus Washington. The Western Division included both expansion teams (Kansas City and Seattle), three teams that had been in their markets for less than a decade (California, Minnesota, and Oakland), plus the Chicago White Sox. Not surprisingly, Chicago owner Arthur Allyn did not like the new arrangement, as his team would play just seventy-two games against all of their long-standing rivals to the east, but twenty-seven games in the Pacific Time Zone, making it difficult for local fans to watch or listen to the games.[29]

While the National League's per-game attendance increased by 7 percent in 1969 and another 10 percent the next year (to 17,160), the AL's decreased in 1969 by more than 10 percent (to 12,471) and stayed at that level for several years. The NL got lucky with the great story of the 1969 Mets and a fine race in the West, while the AL had no close races in the first three years of divisional play. Worse, the AL had several problem franchises. The White Sox, a charter member of the league, drew only 589,546 fans, and even that figure was misleadingly high. The team played eleven games in Milwaukee that season, drawing over 18,000 fans per game—in their seventy games in Chicago, they averaged fewer than 6,000. The next season, playing all of their games in Comiskey Park, their attendance fell under 500,000.

While many observers felt that the AL had outmaneuvered the NL in gaining a franchise in Seattle, the reality would turn out less rosy. The Pilots were owned by a group consisting of William Daley of Cleveland, who held the majority stake, and Seattle brothers Dewey, Max, and Milton Soriano. Dewey Soriano, who had been president of the Pacific Coast League, ran the club operations. It soon became obvious that the group was woefully underfunded and had developed a hostile relationship with the business and political communities. The club played in Sicks' Stadium, an old Minor League park that, even after a hasty expansion (about which the team squabbled with the city), seated only twenty-three thousand at the start of the season. "I remember Joe Cronin coming out," recalled Max Soriano in 1994, "and saying, 'You know, really, this franchise should start once the domed stadium is built.'"[30]

Perhaps more importantly, the Pilots could not get a local television contract, depriving the club of both money and promotion. In September the team missed a few lease payments on the ballpark and the city threatened to evict them. By the end of the 1969 season, Daley had an offer to sell the franchise to interests in Milwaukee, and Seattle was fighting to save its team. Although some AL owners were ready to abandon Seattle and had expressed frustration that the city had made no progress on its new stadium, as a potential reprieve the league gave the city a list of demands: find a local ownership group to take over, upgrade the existing park to Major League standards, and begin work on the new one.

Cronin visited Seattle in January to meet with Fred Danz, a local man willing but ultimately unable to take over the club. Meanwhile, the Bank of California was demanding immediate payment of a $3.5 million debt. Cronin told the local press that the club's financial issues were the city's problem. "The American League is not in the banking business," said Cronin.[31] Nonetheless, in February the league voted to loan the Daley-Soriano group $650,000 to keep them afloat, which Daley said would help them get to 1972, when the new stadium would be ready.[32] A few weeks later it was clear that $650,000 was not going to be nearly enough. Meanwhile, ownership had negotiated a sale to a Milwaukee group (fronted by Allan "Bud" Selig), and the league gave in to the move. As the shift became a reality, both the city and Washington state sued the league, and a judge issued an injunction.

The Pilots subsequently began bankruptcy proceedings, and on March 31 a bankruptcy court cleared the way for the club to be sold and transferred. On April 7 the club played its home opener in Milwaukee, with Cronin in attendance. In May the league voted to grant another franchise to Seattle once it had proper ownership and had built its promised stadium.

Just eighteen months after the loss of Seattle, the league was faced with the loss of its Washington club. Bob Short, who had purchased the Senators just three years earlier, was losing money and wanted to move to Arlington, Texas. Both Bowie Kuhn, a Washington native, and Joe Cronin, who had spent many years there, worked to find a buyer that would keep the team in the city. (Kuhn later wrote that Cronin was divided on the issue, since the majority of his league's owners were sympathetic to Short's predicament.[33]) In the end, no buyer was willing to meet the requested price, and the league approved the transfer. This was the fourth franchise shift during Cronin's tenure as league president, including two of the league's four expansion franchises (Washington and Seattle). (After a total of eleven relocations in just twenty years, the Major Leagues would not again move a team again until 2005, when the Montreal Expos resettled Washington.)

While Joe Cronin was working to keep his clubs in place, he still had to deal with the growing power of the Major League players. The most significant issue baseball faced in the early 1970s was the lawsuit brought by Curt Flood. A brilliant center fielder for twelve years with the St. Louis Cardinals, Flood was traded to Philadelphia in October 1969 in a seven-player deal. Unwilling to give up the life he had built for himself in St. Louis, Flood announced his retirement—as Ken Harrelson had done in April—before ultimately deciding he would challenge the legality of the trade. In January 1970 Flood, backed by the union, alleged that baseball's reserve clause violated federal antitrust laws and sued Commissioner Kuhn, league presidents Cronin and Chub Feeney (who had recently replaced Warren Giles), and Major League Baseball for $1 million.

Flood brought his action just four months after Salerno and Valentine had filed their lawsuit on related (antitrust) grounds. Cronin's views on the matter were predictable—in a joint statement issued with Feeney (almost certainly at the direction of Kuhn), the supposed consequences of Flood winning his suit were laid out. According to the presidents the rich clubs would sign all the best players, players could negotiate with one club while playing for another, teams would no longer be able to support player development—destroying the Minor Leagues—and player trades would cease. In conclusion, felt Cronin and Giles, "Professional baseball would cease to exist."[34] Marvin Miller shot back, accusing Cronin and Giles of libel by suggesting the player's union was not acting in the interests of the game.

The case divided the media, and ballplayers, into pro-Flood and anti-Flood factions. Carl Yastrzemski, one of the game's biggest stars, criticized Flood, saying his suit would ruin the game. Most players might not have appreciated the ramifications of Flood's action, but they generally supported the suit. Ed Kranepool of the Mets called Yastrzemski "nothing but a yo-yo for American League president Joe Cronin."[35] Notably, Yastrzemski had also spoken against the players' stance in negotiations the previous spring.

Flood's case was heard in June 1970, with Cronin in court as a defense witness. He called the reserve clause essential to baseball, and answered "No" when asked if players had a weaker negotiating position than the clubs in contract negotiations.[36] On the stand Cronin spoke at length about his long career, including his 1934 sale by the Senators to the Red Sox. Cronin called Clark Griffith, the man who sold him, "one of the finest baseball talents (and one of the finest human beings) I have ever known." One of Flood's lawyers asked

Cronin: "Didn't he [Griffith] attain some fame by jumping his reserve clause?" Cronin answered that he knew nothing about this. In fact, as the court was told, Griffith had jumped his contract in 1901 to join the new American League, which did not honor the reserve clause of National League players.[37]

In the end Flood lost his case, and the federal judge suggested that the reserve clause should be negotiated in collective bargaining. On appeal the suit reached the U.S. Supreme Court, which ruled for Major League Baseball, 5–3, upholding a 1922 case that placed organized baseball outside of antitrust law. Although Cronin and his fellow executives cheered the decision, during the more than two years that the suit was active baseball lost ground with the players and the media, who had seen the inequities of the reserve clause laid bare. Although most of the press was outraged by the suit when it was first filed, and many players were wary, by the time of the Supreme Court decision the tide had turned considerably.[38]

In 1971 Cronin had to deal with a different sort of player difficulty, this one involving talented and enigmatic outfielder Alex Johnson. An eight-year veteran, Johnson's uneven effort had led to numerous fines and had caused three teams to discard him. With his fourth, the California Angels, he had won the 1970 batting title without appreciably altering the rest of his behavior—not running out ground balls, screaming obscenities at teammates, and ignoring instructions from his managers and coaches. Things deteriorated further still in 1971, when he was fined twenty-nine times before midseason. "He did things differently last year," said manager Lefty Phillips. "He gave about 65 percent. Now it's down to about 40 percent."[39] In early June Johnson failed to run out a ground ball in a game in Boston, with Cronin in attendance. Cronin met with Phillips after the game, concerned that Johnson's behavior was not just affecting the Angels, but the image of the entire league. Philips sat Johnson out for four games, but nothing changed when he returned. On June 26 the Angels suspended Johnson indefinitely without pay.

On June 30 Marvin Miller announced that the Player's Association would file a grievance on Johnson's behalf—a surprising development, as most players had been outraged by Johnson's behavior as well. After Miller interviewed Johnson extensively, he concluded that the player had "serious emotional problems" and should have been placed on the disabled list just as if he had broken a bone. Miller contacted Cronin in Boston in hopes of avoiding a hearing and asked Cronin to show some tolerance as he had with Jimmy Piersall in 1952. Cronin replied that the cases were altogether different, a stance Miller considered to possess "more than a tint of racism."[40]

In late August Johnson's case was presented to binding arbitration, a new procedure the players had won in collective bargaining a year earlier. After two psychiatrists, one hired by the Angels and the other by the union, agreed that Johnson was emotionally disabled, the arbitrator ruled for Johnson, a decision he later characterized as "easy." He reversed the suspension and ordered the Angels to give Johnson his back pay. Although Miller had made few friends in his five years as union head, this case brought his reputation to a new low. "The man is killing the sport," exclaimed Angels owner Gene Autry. "The next time I have a player who doesn't hustle I'll close down the ballpark."[41] In the hearing management had tried to make the case that a reversal of the suspension would set a precedent whereby other players who did not hustle would claim emotional illness.[42] In reality Johnson suffered quite a bit of humiliation in 1971, and the two experts had publicly concluded he was mentally unbalanced. Not surprisingly, no player has attempted to use this avenue to escape suspension in the intervening years.

Cronin became involved in a couple more player and contract squabbles the following season. When Oakland pitcher Vida Blue had a contentious salary standoff with Charlie Finley, Kuhn swooped in to try to resolve the situation, with Cronin his ally. John Harrington, who worked for Cronin as league treasurer, later recalled that Blue visited Cronin's office during his holdout, and Cronin helped convince the player that he had little choice but to sign.[43] A few months later, during the second game of the AL playoffs, Oakland's Bert Campaneris threw his bat at Detroit pitcher Lerrin LaGrow, prompting Cronin to suspend Campaneris for the remainder of the series. When Kuhn told Cronin he thought the incident warranted a longer punishment, Cronin reminded Kuhn that he had suspended him for as long as he could—the World Series was beyond the league president's reach. Kuhn agreed but imposed his own will by further suspending Campaneris for the first week of the 1973 season. (Kuhn said that he felt suspending Campaneris for the World Series would unduly punish his teammates.)

"Cronin always came down solidly in favor of what was best for the game and worked the system to that end," wrote Kuhn in his memoirs. "By contrast, National League presidents Warren Giles and Chub Feeney after him tended to be more protective of their league, more reluctant to see the commissioner get involved."[44] John Harrington made a similar point while also recalling how much Giles and Feeney both used to tease Cronin about the differences between the two leagues. Cronin cheered when the American League won the 1971 All-Star Game, its first win after eight straight losses. Cronin, as he normally did, had gone into the dressing room before the game to tell the managers and players how much the game meant for all of them.

Though Joe Cronin's power had receded with the ascension of Bowie Kuhn, he continued to thoroughly enjoy the trappings and obligations of his job. As he approached his sixty-fifth birthday in October 1971, his pleasures remained simple. Cronin enjoyed watching baseball games, eating fine meals, golfing with friends, gathering socially with baseball people, good conversation, a glass of scotch. As president of the American League, his life was filled with all of this—he flew around the country to meet baseball people, make speeches, watch baseball games, and talk to old friends. It was an idyllic job for someone like Joe Cronin.

When he wasn't traveling, he spent his weekdays in Boston while Mildred was at their house on the Cape. Their four children were off on their own, so Joe had the big house to himself. If the Red Sox were at home, he went to the game and had dinner in the pressroom. Otherwise he found a friend to join him for dinner, later watching or listening to whatever ballgame might be on. His favorite restaurant in the city was Jacob Wirth, less than a mile from his office—a German restaurant that has been located at the same site on Stuart Street since 1878. Cronin would sometimes lunch there with members of his staff—John Harrington, Dick Butler, or Bob Holbrook—and would also get a sandwich to go so that he could eat it at home later while watching or listening to a ballgame. He often attended Mass during the week, sometimes bringing along fellow Catholic Harrington. He never missed a Holy Day of Obligation.

He spent every weekend with Mildred, whether the Red Sox were home or away, making the eighty-mile drive on Friday afternoon, returning Monday morning. In Osterville baseball was constantly on television or the radio if possible—Joe did not like to go to bed if there were AL games still going on that he could hear. If he had to travel somewhere for the league, Mildred often joined him, and she knew as many people in baseball as Joe did. When I conducted interviews with men who had known Joe Cronin, they almost invariably wanted to talk about Mildred as well, as she was a constant presence in his public life.

Cronin also loved the work and never stopped trying to improve the game. The American League continued to provide him with his fair share of challenges in this era. By 1972 the AL's lesser position with respect to the National League had surfaced once again. The attendance disparity between the leagues had grown from 4 percent in 1968 to 45 percent by 1971. Besides the imbalanced divisions and the struggling franchises, the American League had once again stopped scoring runs. In 1972 the league scored just 3.47 runs per game, not appreciably different than the 3.41 they scored in 1968 (the so-called Year of the Pitcher). The increased offense brought on by the 1969 rule changes had been temporary, at least in the American League.

Cronin convened a league meeting in New York in December 1972 at which the AL owners voted to "exert every effort" to achieve three innovations by the start of the 1973 season: interleague play, a designated pinch hitter for the pitcher, and a designated pinch runner who could be used multiple times in a game. Cronin announced that the National League's continuing refusal to consider any of these changes was not acceptable, and he asked Bowie Kuhn to hold a joint meeting of the two leagues, with Kuhn casting the deciding vote. Kuhn, who reputedly supported all three initiatives, announced a meeting for January 11 and 12 in Chicago.

The designated hitter rule had been advocated by baseball men off and on since the nineteenth century, but the recent offensive malaise had increased the number of voices. In spring training in 1969 both leagues experimented with the designated hitter, and the AL used a designated pinch runner. The rules were in use only if both teams agreed before the game. Subsequently four Minor Leagues approved the DH rule for the 1969 season: the International League, Eastern League, New York-Penn League, and Texas League.[45] Although the two Major Leagues set the rules aside for a few years, Joe Cronin and many of the American League owners kept lobbying to adopt them for the regular season.

At the January 1973 meeting the AL owners forced a showdown with their NL counterparts. As it turned out, the AL was unable to get the NL to adopt any of the rules, nor to get Bowie Kuhn to break the impasse between the two leagues. The two leagues agreed to form a committee to study interleague play, considered a victory for the American League and raising hopes that it could be adopted in 1974. The NL did, however, grant the American League permission to use the DH rule for three years, 1973 through 1975, as an experiment. At the time many people assumed that the NL would adopt the rule in a year or two.[46]

Cronin returned from the meeting with mixed emotions. He was happy to have won the right to use the designated hitter, and the specifics of the rule—what happened when a DH was pinch-hit for or took the field himself—were written in the AL office by Cronin and Dick Butler, the league's supervisor of umpires. On the other hand, Cronin was disappointed he could not get Kuhn to use his vote to force interleague play.[47]

The designated hitter rule served its purpose—in 1973, offense in the American League rose to 4.28 runs per game, the most since

1962, and attendance increased 12 percent. The press was generally sympathetic, with *The Sporting News* leading the way in a series of editorials. The rule remains one of the more controversial and debated changes in baseball history—many fans still deplore the impurity of the DH nearly four decades later, even as the rule is used in nearly every professional league in the world . . . with the exception, still, of the National League.

After enjoying the introduction of the designated hitter, Cronin spent much of the 1973 season dealing with a series of spitball controversies. Cronin had been an advocate of the legalization of the pitch for many years, partly because of the difficulties his umpires had in enforcing its prohibition. While many pitchers were suspected of throwing the spitball, the most notorious was Gaylord Perry, whose 1972 move from the Giants to the Indians brought him to the American League for the first time. In June 1973 after Perry had defeated the Yankees in New York, center fielder Bobby Murcer called Cronin and Bowie Kuhn "gutless" for not cracking down on the spitter, comments that earned Murcer a $250 fine.[48]

In a separate incident, in late August Texas pitcher Jim Merritt bragged of throwing spitballs (calling them "Gaylord Perry fastballs") after he threw a shutout to defeat Perry and the Indians. He later claimed he was joking, but Cronin still assessed a small fine.[49] Red Sox pitcher Bill Lee thought the punishment was ridiculous. "Tell Joe Cronin this: I threw a spitter in Detroit a while back," said Lee. "It was to Tony Taylor. Of course, he hit it into the upper deck, but if Cronin's going to act like an idiot and fine Merritt, he'd better fine everyone who throws it." For good measure, he added, "If K-Y jelly went off the market, the whole California Angels pitching staff would be out of baseball."[50] Cronin laughed when told of the comments. "Lee has the kind of color we need," he said.[51]

The most serious incident began in Detroit on August 30, when Perry pitched a six-hitter to defeat the Tigers. Perry's success so unnerved Tigers manager Billy Martin that he ordered his pitchers Joe Coleman and Fred Scherman to throw obvious spitballs in the eighth and ninth innings, goading home-plate umpire Red Flaherty to stop them from throwing it. After the game Martin admitted what he had done, suggesting that he wanted to bring attention to Perry's obvious cheating. Cronin suspended Martin for three games. "Your blatant actions and your endorsement of such tactics cannot be tolerated," Cronin wired Martin. Before Martin was due to return from his suspension, the Tigers fired him, "for the good of the organization."[52]

Joe Cronin's second seven-year contract was due to expire at the end of the 1972 season. In December 1971 the issue of its renewal was raised at a league meeting, and a few owners—notably Charlie Finley, Texas's Bob Short, and Baltimore's Jerry Hoffberger—expressed some caution about making any hasty decisions. Cronin was sixty-five years old, after all. In addition, there was increasing pressure from Kuhn, supported by some league owners, to move both league offices to New York where the commissioner's office was. Cronin had no intention of relocating at this stage of his life. In the end Cronin was rewarded with a three-year extension, through 1975. "Joe knew after that meeting that he would not be in the job much longer," recalled Harrington.[53]

In any event in October 1973 Cronin announced that he was stepping down in favor of Yankees general manager Lee MacPhail. Cronin would assume the largely ceremonial position of chairman of the board, a role Harridge had held from 1959 until his death in 1971. Cronin revealed that he had signed the three-year extension with the understanding that he would step aside if the league found a suitable replacement.[54] Although the decision had been made by the league owners, Cronin appeared satisfied to step aside and remained on good terms with MacPhail and the league. The transition from Cronin to MacPhail would become official on January 1, 1974.

In the mean time Cronin had one last league controversy to unravel, something that would occupy him nearly to the end of his term. On September 30, Ralph Houk resigned as manager of the Yankees after thirty-five years with the organization, including eleven as manager. Although he had two years remaining on his contract, he said he thought the players and team needed a fresh start. Less than two weeks later he signed to manage the Detroit Tigers. So far, everything was pretty routine.[55]

Shortly thereafter, Oakland Athletics' manager Dick Williams, who also had two years left on his deal, dramatically announced his own resignation on national television just moments after his team had won their second straight World Series. Williams had spent three years dealing with Charlie Finley and had finally had enough. He and Finley actually thanked each other on television and wished one another luck. In the ensuing press conference, Williams said that he still wanted to manage and in fact might be interested in the vacated Yankees job. Everyone assumed that the Yankees would hire him within a week.

A few days later, Finley announced that Williams still had a contract with the A's, the Yankees could not sign his manager without adequate compensation and that he would lodge a protest with the league if any team tampered with Williams. The shaken Williams claimed he had been told by Finley that he would not stand in his way. The move also stunned the Yankees, whose general manager Gabe Paul then contacted the Tigers to request compensation for Houk. Finley assured the press that he was not standing in Williams's way—he was merely asking to be compensated, something that had happened several times in recent history. When the Mets hired Gil Hodges in 1968, they had given the Senators, his previous employer, $100,000 plus a player. The Yankees saw the strength of Finley's position and attempted to negotiate a deal, but they could not reach terms. Undeterred, the Yankees went ahead and signed Williams anyway. Finley filed an injunction in federal court, which was upheld.

Joe Cronin held two days of hearings at his office in Boston, reviewing the complaints of the Tigers, Yankees, and A's. On December 20 he announced his final decisions as league president, ruling against the Yankees in both cases. The difference, Cronin explained, was that the Yankees had accepted Houk's resignation and had begun the paperwork process with the league office. They had protested only when Finley had done so. Finley, on the other hand, had done nothing to formally indicate that he had accepted Williams's resignation. "A man can't divorce his wife by making a statement on television," Cronin said. "He must go through the judicial process." Gabe Paul was understandably upset, but the Yankees did not really protest the particulars of the ruling.

On December 31, 1973, Cronin's tenure as American League president ended after fifteen years. The game had changed dramatically over that period, and he had been at the center of many of those changes. His league had grown from eight to twelve teams, four franchises had moved, and the league had split into divisions and added a round of playoffs. He had led the drive for the most significant rule change of the twentieth century and served long enough to see it succeed. His league was very obviously the weaker of the two during his entire term, though that disparity began before he took office. The keys to the NL's dominance were moves made in the 1950s—the signing of black players and the relocations to Los Angeles and San Francisco. Cronin spent most of his tenure trying to catch the National League.

He made missteps. The one true power he had—control of the league's umpires—had been mishandled a few times, most notably in the firings of Salerno and Valentine. Deference to the league's owners, many of them good friends to whom he owed his job, limited his ability to push his league forward. His handling of the two expansions and the sale of the Yankees to CBS could have gone more smoothly. The ill-defined role of league president was certainly as much the problem as his ability to fill it. The league owners did not want him to tell them what to do—he was their employee, after all.

With his retirement, Cronin's active career in baseball came to a close. It had been forty-nine years since he signed his first contract with the Pirates, and he had spent forty of those years in some form of baseball management. When asked how the Williams-Houk case ranked among his toughest decisions in baseball, Cronin laughed: "I still think the most difficult thing I faced was trying to hit Lefty Grove's fastball and Bob Feller's curve," he said.[56]

17 At Rest

AFTER FORTY-NINE YEARS IN PROFESSIONAL baseball, beginning in 1974 Joe Cronin held the largely ceremonial post of American League chairman of the board. In this role he could attend all of the league meetings, represent the league at social functions, make promotional speeches, and watch lots of baseball games, without having to make any authoritative decisions. In short it was a perfect job for an older Joe Cronin, who loved being around people and talking baseball.

He continued his yearly turn on the winter banquet circuit, acting as guest of honor at the annual writer's dinner in Boston in 1974. At one banquet that same winter, Dick Williams grimly sidled over to Cronin. "Mr. Cronin," said Williams, "I hope you're enjoying your retirement as much as I am enjoying the one you made me take."[1] As always both Joe and Mildred went to as many of these affairs as they could and often as not found themselves at the head table. In January 1975 Cronin was honored by the New York writers with the William J. Slocum award for "long and meritorious" service.[2]

After the 1974 season, Joe and Mildred sold their big house in Newton Center, their primary home for thirty-five years. They now resided full-time in Osterville on the Cape, where Mildred had long summered, and also bought a condominium on a golf course in Apopka, Florida, about twelve miles from Orlando. The Cronins thus joined the thousands of older New Englanders who spent the frigid winter months in sunny Florida, where Joe could golf regularly with his legion of friends.

Once spring training began, Cronin made the rounds at all the ballparks in Florida (Calvin Griffith's Twins were just twelve miles from Cronin's new winter home). Cronin remained active during the season, visiting many Major League ballparks and handing out awards, a role he had relished as AL president. Moreover, the American League created the Joe Cronin Award, to be given to a league player for an outstanding achievement or milestone. The first post-1900 award went to Angels pitcher Nolan Ryan, who broke the all-time single-season strikeout record in 1973. Cronin handed out the first plaque himself before a game in Anaheim in April. Just as often the award was given to someone for a career milestone—the second winner was Al Kaline, who made his three-thousandth hit in 1974. The award was given out almost annually over the next twenty-five years.

Cronin was not content in a mere ceremonial role however. "I'm attending just as many meetings," he told Bob Addie two years into his new job. "And it seems there is always quite a bit to do. Baseball has become very complex like everything else and its problems can't be solved by an off-the-cuff decision."[3] He was appointed to the Rules Committee, a group he had served on in the 1950s before his ascension to the league presidency. In his first year as league chairman, he was part of a group that negotiated a new contract for the Major League umpires, whose union he had inadvertently helped form in 1968.[4] In 1978 Kuhn appointed Cronin to the Umpire Study Committee, formed to look into the pay scale and hardships of Minor League umpires.

One of Cronin's passions in the last twenty-five years of his life was the National Baseball Hall of Fame, which had inducted him in 1956. He rarely missed the annual summer ceremony, spending time at the Otesega Hotel with his fellow legends, holding court, signing autographs, and swapping stories. Cronin became a member of the Hall's board of directors in 1959, and eventually its chairman. In addition, for many years Cronin was a member of the Hall of Fame's Committee on Veterans, a group that selected managers, executives, and umpires to the Hall, as well as players who had been passed over by the writers. For Cronin this was yet another opportunity to be around baseball people while also recognizing some of the old-timers who were likely as not his friends. In 1975 he helped elect Bucky Harris, who had played Cronin in 1928 over the objections of Clark

Griffith and was later Cronin's assistant general manager in Boston. The next year saw the induction of Cal Hubbard, a longtime umpire who had worked as AL supervisor for eighteen years, reporting to Cronin for the last ten. In 1979 upon the death of Warren Giles, Cronin became the chairman of the committee. The following winter, the committee elected Tom Yawkey, who had been Cronin's boss for twenty-five years.

In 1977 Cronin testified in the civil lawsuit brought by Charlie Finley against Bowie Kuhn and Major League Baseball. The previous June commissioner Kuhn had made one of the most controversial decisions of his tenure, disallowing Finley's sales of three of his top players—Joe Rudi and Rollie Fingers to Boston for $1 million each and Vida Blue to New York for $1.5 million. Finley made the deals because the three players were going to be free agents in the fall, and he did not wish to lose them without being compensated. He intended to use the cash to acquire new players. Though Kuhn ruled that Finley was wrecking his team, Kuhn's decision did even more damage. Finley lost several free agents in 1976, and by 1979 his team would lose one hundred games. Had Finley attempted similar sales ten years earlier, before Kuhn, Cronin would not have interfered with his owners, and the commissioner (Frick or Eckert) would have considered it a league matter.

At the trial in January 1977, Cronin testified that baseball needed competitive balance in order to survive. (In 1970 Cronin had suggested that baseball could not survive if the reserve clause was tampered with. By 1977 the reserve clause was essentially moot, putting Cronin's prediction to the test.) Finley's lawyer pointed out that Cronin's Red Sox had repeatedly bought players from other clubs, including a big haul from the lowly St. Louis Browns in 1947.[5] The lawyer could have mentioned that Cronin himself had been purchased for $250,000 in 1934—a much larger price, relative to contemporary salaries, than the Finley sales. In any event Finley lost his case, and with it his ability to compete in the era of free agency.

By the late 1970s Cronin was spending more and more time at his home on Cape Cod. He was operated on for a hernia in 1978, and while recovering lost thirty pounds—weight he needed to lose. From his summer home in Osterville, a now mostly retired Cronin could sit and watch the sailboats off Narragansett Bay, while answering his correspondence—numbering seventy or eighty letters per week. He still attended Little League games and games in the Cape Cod League, a competitive summer league for college-age players. He annually threw out the first ball to begin the Cape season. He was still an eighteen-handicap golfer well past his seventieth birthday. But he most loved spending time with his family. "The kids and [nine] grandchildren drop in for a meal, and stay for weeks," reported Cronin.[6] When he had time to himself, and even when he didn't, he still listened to any baseball game that he could—broadcasts from Boston, New York, Detroit, and Baltimore wafted throughout the house, with Joe often listening intently to every pitch.[7]

Even in retirement, the honors kept coming his way. He was inducted into the Washington Hall of Stars at halftime of a Washington Redskins football game at RFK Stadium. In March 1981 he was one of thirty-two Hall of Famers to attend a banquet at the White House hosted by President Ronald Reagan. Cronin had been to the White House many times in his roles as Senators manager and league president, but this time many of the men listened to the president tell his own baseball stories—Reagan had broadcast games for the Cubs in the 1930s.

In 1983 baseball celebrated the fiftieth anniversary of the first All-Star Game, which returned to Chicago's Comiskey Park to mark the occasion. Joe Cronin was named the American League's honorary captain. Most men in Cronin's position would have accepted this honor and proudly walked on the field to tip their cap during the pregame introductions. Joe Cronin, seventy-six years old, fifty pounds over his playing weight, and not in the best of health, relished the chance to be back in the American League dugout. Roland Hemond, the general manager of the host White Sox, remembers how happy Cronin was that day: "He arrived early, got in his uniform [1933 vintage Senators, with his old number 4], talked with whoever he could find, and did not stop smiling the whole evening." Many of the living players from the

1933 game were honored on the field before the game. The suitably inspired American Leaguers romped to a 13–3 victory, breaking an eleven-game losing streak.[8]

On November 18, 1983, Cronin was the guest of honor for a celebration in the main ballroom of the Sheraton Hotel in Boston, with all proceeds from the night going to the Jimmy Fund. Eighteen Hall of Famers were in attendance, the largest such gathering ever in the city. Ted Williams, Joe DiMaggio, Mickey Mantle, Willie Mays, Charlie Gehringer—all gathered to pay homage to Joe Cronin, swap stories, and praise each other. That same evening, the Red Sox announced that they would retire Cronin's number 4, with a formal ceremony at Fenway Park the next spring.

Williams, whose presence drew the most attention (he rarely bothered to attend events like this), admitted that his years in Boston were not always easy. "I was a loner with a pretty lousy sense of humor," he recalled, "and I've never been the most fun-loving guy in the world." But he would give up none of it, he said, the missed batting titles or the heartbreaking losses, because of the joy he had playing for Joe Cronin. "He could have been governor if he had wanted, he was that well liked. I owe as much to him as anybody I know. He was like a father to me. I love that man."

Cronin, tearing up at the outpouring of love in the room, allowed that he would do well managing the players gathered there. "I won't need any relief pitchers with [Bob] Feller and [Sandy] Koufax as my starters. What an outfield . . . but who's going to be my designated hitter?" Cronin praised many of the people individually, calling Bill Dickey the greatest clutch hitter he'd ever seen, and DiMaggio the best "for all-around play." At these words, Joe stepped back from the microphone, walked over to DiMaggio and the old rivals embraced warmly. While he had everyone's attention, he reminded the room that DiMaggio had grown up in San Francisco's North Beach, just like Ping Bodie, Cronin's old hero. As much of the room had likely not heard of Bodie, Cronin proceeded to tell them about his home-run hitting exploits with the Yankees, and how much he had meant to Cronin and his boyhood friends.

By this time his close friends and family knew the terrible truth of the cancer that was ravaging Cronin's body. He had been ill several times in the past year, and one could not help but notice how much weight he had lost, and how he hunched over. His was a very painful cancer, attacking his prostate and his bones, but only those very close to him ever heard him complain. He told his daughter that he felt as if his bones were breaking inside his body. He failed badly that winter in Florida and was given the last rites of the Catholic Church in late December. He recovered, hanging on long enough to get back to Massachusetts in the spring. Although hospitalized again in May, he made it to Fenway Park on May 29, when the Red Sox retired his and Williams's uniform numbers. The event thrilled Cronin's friends and family, who saw how Cronin loved every minute of his final visit to Fenway Park.

John Harrington, who had worked for Cronin in the early 1970s, visited him many times in his final months and recalled how sharp and alert he remained. Cronin would talk for hours, as if he wanted to talk forever, afraid of what would happen if he stopped talking. They talked of friends they had in common, things they had gone through in the league office in the early 1970s, or just baseball. Harrington was working with the Red Sox then, and Joe wanted to know about the current team, who the up-and-coming players were, what the team needed to do to improve.[9]

Cronin apparently made a "brief, guarded visit" to the All-Star Game held on July 10 in San Francisco.[10] His appearance was not publicized. He was admitted to Massachusetts General Hospital in Boston on July 21, with the family releasing no information about his condition. When he was discharged on August 16, he went back home to Osterville for the last time. He hung on for several more weeks but died on September 7, 1984, at his home, surrounded by his family. Joe and Mildred would have celebrated their fiftieth anniversary on September 27.

Upon the news of Cronin's death, the testimonials poured in. "I am deeply saddened," said Ted Williams. "I always admired Joe as a great family man with a wonderful wife. I really grieve for them and I send my sincerest condolences to them." The Red Sox released their own statement: "Joe will be missed by all of baseball, but especially by the Red Sox. He was a Hall of Famer not only as a player, but as a man." Calvin Griffith, Cronin's brother-in-law and long-time league rival, said of Cronin: "He was the greatest thing I ever saw in uniform or in a man. He was just incomparable. He was just one great guy and our family particularly is going to miss him dearly."

Commissioner Bowie Kuhn spoke not just for baseball but for himself in his own statement. "He obviously was a great Hall of Famer, a superior field manager and an outstanding league president and club general manager. My personal recollection of him always will be of a wonderful, kind, thoughtful, decent beautiful man for whom I have as much affection as anyone I have ever known in this game."[11] Writer Dick Young, who did not lightly give praise, dished out plenty upon Cronin's passing. "Now there was a prince," wrote Young. "I speak not of his Hall of Fame credentials. The *Baseball Encyclopedia* handles that well. When I think of Joe Cronin, I think of the kindly Irishman with the wonderful smile and beautiful soul. I cannot remember one time I met him, and there were hundreds, when his greeting was not friendly, upbeat. Seeing Joe Cronin on any given day made that day so much better."[12]

The funeral mass was held in Hyannis on September 10. More than 1,200 people packed St. Francis Xavier Church, while a large crowd of spectators stood outside and lined the streets. Many of the mourners were friends from his long baseball life, going all the way back to Socko McCarey, who threw batting practice to Cronin when he played for the Pirates in 1927. Pesky and Dom DiMaggio were there, though Doerr and Williams could not attend. Most of the high baseball brass was in attendance, including Kuhn and AL president Bobby Brown, as were many past and present employees of the Red Sox, including Jean Yawkey, Haywood Sullivan, and manager Ralph Houk. Tip O'Neill, the speaker of the U.S. House of Representatives, sat in a pew.

"Doctors said that Joe's heart had failed," said Rev. Joseph Scannell in his eulogy, "but his heart never failed." Scannell told a story of Joe happening upon a shivering newsboy in San Francisco one day: "'Cold day, isn't it?' said Joe. 'It was cold, sir, until you came by,' responded the boy. How many of us can say that? Give God thanks that Joe came by, that he came into our lives." Cronin's body was interred at St. Francis Xavier Cemetery in Centerville.

On October 30, a memorial mass was held at St. Mary's Cathedral in San Francisco, the city that Cronin never forgot, even if circumstances moved him to the East Coast for most of his life. "He loved the city," recalled Eddie Montague, who had traveled with Cronin to their first spring training with the Pirates in 1925. "He had numerous fast friends there. Buzz O'Leary, the legendary bar owner, used to ship Joe loaves of sourdough bread, which he loved."[13] Many of these friends, including Dolph Camilli, Dick Bartell, Dario Lodigiani, and Charlie Rivera, were among the hundreds of people who came to pay tribute, along with Dom DiMaggio, who had been on hand for his funeral in Hyannis just a few weeks before.

Sportswriter Will McDonough had befriended Cronin years earlier and remained close to the family. He had spoken with the dying Cronin and remarked how much the ill man loved life to the very end. "You know," Cronin told McDonough, "I have had a wonderful life. I wouldn't change a thing. I'm the luckiest guy I know. How many people ever get to do just what they wanted to do their whole life?" McDonough described Cronin's typical routine of a summer evening, first watching a ballgame, then lying in bed with a radio tuned to another faraway game. "What a picture," wrote McDonough, "this legend of a man, nodding off to sleep, radio resting on his stomach, like a little boy romancing his first love. There will never be another like him."[14]

Joe Cronin's love affair with baseball lasted a lifetime. He had hundreds, perhaps thousands, of friends who loved him throughout his life, many of whom he met along the baseball trail. He had a wife and family who shared his passion for the game and allowed him to spend his off-days listening to ballgames into the wee hours of the morning. His path took him from the sandlots of San Francisco to stardom in the Major Leagues, and continued until he sat with the power brokers of the sport. But he never left a doubt where his heart lay. "You know," he told a writer late in his life, "when it's said and done, all the fun is on the field."[15]

Notes

Although I have used endnotes throughout the text, a general note on the sources might be of use. Many sources were consulted so frequently that citing them each time I used them would be overly repetitive. For the playing statistics of Joe Cronin and dozens of other people, I used both Baseball-Reference.com and Retrosheet .org, the two most valuable baseball sites on the Web. I also used Retrosheet for game logs, umpire registers, ejection data, and transaction data, all of which was of much value throughout the book.

I accessed most newspapers via Proquest (*New York Times, Washington Post, Chicago Tribune, Los Angeles Times, Chicago Daily Defender, Hartford Courant,* and *Christian Science Monitor*) or Paper of Record (*The Sporting News*). As Joe Cronin was a national figure for most of his life, these sources often were all I needed. For stories for which I wanted more detail, I consulted additional papers in San Francisco or Boston, often enlisting others to get copies for me. Cronin's huge clipping file at the Baseball Hall of Fame Library was also helpful.

Prologue

1. Peter Gammons, "Numbers That Count," *Boston Globe*, May 30, 1984.

2. John Harrington (September 11, 2007) and Dick Bresciani (April 29, 2008), interviews by author.

3. Milton Richman, "Cronin Recalls Ted As Sox' Best Ever," *Boston Daily News*, June 1, 1984.

4. Joe Giuliotti, "Hub's Winning Numbers," *Boston Herald*, May 30, 1984; Tommy Cronin, interview by author, March 7, 2008.

5. Joe Giuliotti, "A Night for Past Glory," *Boston Herald*, May 30, 1984.

6. Richman, "Cronin Recalls Ted."

1. San Francisco

1. Dan Kurzman, *Disaster! The Great San Francisco Earthquake of 1906* (New York: William Morrow, 2001), 248.

2. U.S. Census figures at www.census.gov.

3. Kurzman, *Disaster!* 251.

4. Editors, "San Francisco Earthquake, 1906," *The Literary Encyclopedia*, January 1, 2001, http://www.litencyc.com/php/stopics.php?rec=true&UID=1522 (accessed February 24, 2007).

5. Oakland Museum of California, "Aftershock!—Voices from the 1906 Earthquake and Fire," http://www.museumca.org/exhibit/exhi_aftershock.html.

6. Al Hirshberg, *From Sandlots to League President* (New York: Messner, 1962), 18.

7. John Drohan, "No Rockin' Chair for Cronin," *Baseball*, March 1941, 449.

8. Harry T. Brundage, "Friday, the Thirteenth, Lucky for Joe Cronin," *The Sporting News*, December 31, 1931, 8.

9. Carl Haas, interview by author, September 11, 2007.

10. Brundage, "Friday, the Thirteenth," 8.

11. Walter G. Jebe Sr., *San Francisco's Excelsior District* (Charleston SC: Arcardia, 2004).

12. Maureen Cronin, interview by author, February 2, 2007.

13. Haas, interview.

14. Anthony J. Connor, *Voices from Cooperstown* (New York: Gallahad Books, 1982).

15. J. G. Taylor Spink, interview with Joe Cronin, *The Sporting News*, April 27, 1960.

16. Joe Williams, *New York World-Telegram*, March 19, 1935.

17. Hirshberg, *From Sandlots*, 21.

18. Connor, *Voices*.

19. Connor, *Voices*.

20. Brundage, "Friday, the Thirteenth," 8.

21. Ed Linn, "Joe Cronin—The Irishman Who Made His Own Luck," *Sport*, April 1956, 57.

22. *The Sporting News*, July 30, 1936.

23. John Kieran, "Sports of the *Times*," *New York Times*, August 12, 1941.

24. *The Sporting News*, April 27, 1960.

25. Hirshberg, *From Sandlots*, 23–26.

26. Spink, interview with Joe Cronin.

27. *Oakland Tribune*, December 3, 1924, 16.

28. SABR Scouts Database, http://members.sabr.org.

29. Hirshberg, *From Sandlots*, 31.

30. Hirshberg, *From Sandlots*, 31.

2. PITTSBURGH AND OTHER PLACES

1. Bill Weiss and Marshall Wright, "Top 100 Teams," MiLB.com, http://web.minorleaguebaseball.com/milb/history/top100.

2. Dick Beverage, PCL historian, suggests this as the likely scenario (e-mail message to author).

3. Dan Levitt, *Ed Barrow: The Bulldog Who Built the Yankees' First Dynasty* (Lincoln: University of Nebraska Press, 2008); David L. Porter, ed., *The Biographical Dictionary of American Sports: Baseball* (Westport NC: Greenwood Press, 2000).

4. Cliff Blau, "The Major League Draft," http://mysite.verizon.net/brak2.o/ml_draft.htm.

5. Haas, interview.

6. Hirshberg, *From Sandlots*, 33–34.

7. *Los Angeles Times*, March 11, 1925.

8. *Washington Post*, March 29, 1925.

9. *Washington Post*, March 20, 1925.

10. Cliff Blau, "Roster Limits," http://mysite.verizon.net/brak2.o/rosters.htm.

11. David McCullough, *The Johnstown Flood* (New York: Simon and Schuster, 1987).

12. Lloyd Johnson and Miles Wolff, *Encyclopedia of Minor League Baseball* (Durham NC: Baseball America, 2007).

13. Hirshberg, *From Sandlots*, 35.

14. *The Sporting News*, January 1, 1947.

15. Johnson and Wolff, *Encyclopedia*.

16. *Indiana Evening Gazette*, May 10, 1926, 5.

17. U.S. census figures at http://www.census.gov/population/documentation/twps0027/tab15.txt.

18. Jim McCulley, "Cronin Beat Out Bartell for Early Weiss Berth," *New York Daily News*, February 3, 1959.

19. Bill Lee, *Hartford Courant*, January 22, 1948.

20. Joe Cronin's file at the National Baseball Hall of Fame.

21. *Chicago Tribune*, July 20, 1926; *The Sporting News*, February 8, 1956, 7.

22. Clipping in Cronin's Hall of Fame file, unknown source, bylined New Haven, June 2, 1932.

23. *Hartford Courant*, July 19, 1926.

24. Hirshberg, *From Sandlots*, 40.

25. Ralph S. Davis, "Buc Pitchers Need but Surprise Fans," *The Sporting News*, February 17, 1927, 2.

26. Ralph S. Davis, "Pirates Put It Over in Spite of Weather," *The Sporting News*, March 24, 1927, 2.

27. *The Sporting News*, February 8, 1956, 7.

28. Hirshberg, *From Sandlots*, 40.

29. Dick Bartell, with Norman Macht, *Rowdy Richard* (Berkeley CA: North Atlantic Books, 1987).

30. Hirshberg, *From Sandlots*, 40.

31. Clipping in Cronin's Hall of Fame file, unknown source, bylined Los Angeles, April 1, 1928.

32. *The Sporting News*, February 8, 1956, 7; Hirshberg, *From Sandlots*.

33. Linn, "Joe Cronin."

34. Hirshberg, *From Sandlots*, 49.

35. Frederick G. Lieb, "The P. T. Barnum of the Bushes: Jester Joe Engel—Chattanooga Club Chief," *Sporting News Baseball Register 1953*.

36. *Washington Post*, January 11, 1931.

37. Letter from Kansas City business manager John Savage to Baseball Commissioner Kenesaw Mountain Landis, August 20, 1928, Joe Cronin's file at the National Baseball Hall of Fame, Cooperstown NY.

38. "Howley Accepts Defi of Nats to Pitch Crowder on Monday," *Washington Post*, July 15, 1928, 19.

39. Linn, "Joe Cronin."

40. Mark Armour, "Bobby Reeves," SABR's Biography Project, http://bioproj .sabr.org/.

41. Mrs. Joe Cronin, "The Private Life of a Baseball Wife," *Liberty*, May 2, 1936.

3. Washington

1. Shirley Povich, *The Washington Senators* (New York: Putnam, 1954), 74–75.

2. Michael Lenehan, "The Last of the Pure Baseball Men," *Atlantic Monthly*, August 1981.

3. Mike Grahek, "Clark Griffith," in *Deadball Stars of the American League*, ed. David Jones (Dulles VA: Potomac, 2006).

4. Mark Armour and Daniel R. Levitt, *Paths to Glory: How Great Baseball Teams Got That Way* (Washington DC: Brassey's, 2003).

5. Jon Kerr, *Calvin—Baseball's Last Dinosaur* (New York: Wm. C. Brown, 1990), 7–10.

6. *Washington Post*, October 24, 1925.

7. Kerr, *Calvin*, 7–10.

8. Kerr, *Calvin*, 8.

9. Kerr, *Calvin*, 15–16.

10. Frank H. Young, "Browns Face Braxton Today," *Washington Post*, July 17, 1928.

11. Frank H. Young, "Harris Trust Hopes with Rookies," *Washington Post*, July 19, 1928.

12. *Washington Post*, September 20, 1928.

13. Bill Cunningham, "Brains at Bat," *Colliers*, April 13, 1935, 28.

14. *Washington Post*, August 12, 1928.

15. *Washington Post*, October 16, 1927.

16. Henry W. Thomas, *Walter Johnson—Baseball's Big Train* (Washington DC: Phenom Press, 1995), 303–10.

17. Hirshberg, *From Sandlots*, 55.

18. *The Sporting News*, December 20, 1928.

19. Several letters in Cronin's file at the National Baseball Hall of Fame Library.

20. Cronin's contract card at the Baseball Hall of Fame Library.

21. *Washington Post*, March 3, 1929.

22. *Washington Post*, March 20, 1929.

23. *Washington Post*, April 1, 1929.

24. *Washington Post*, May 18, 1929.

25. *Washington Post*, June 16, 1929.

26. *Washington Post*, July 23, 1929.

27. Bill Nowlin, *Red Sox Threads* (Boston: Rounder Books, 2008).

28. Courtesy David Vincent, caretaker of SABR's Home Run Log.

29. *The Sporting News*, February 8, 1956, 8.

30. Hirshberg, *From Sandlots*, 57.

31. Linn, "Joe Cronin."

32. Thomas, *Walter Johnson*, 312–13.

33. Cronin's contract card.

34. Quoted in Thomas, *Walter Johnson*, 314, original source unknown.

35. *Washington Post*, May 27, 1930.

36. *Washington Post*, July 4, 1930.

37. *Washington Post*, September 21, 1930.

38. *Washington Post*, May 31, 1930.

39. *The Sporting News*, January 19, 1933.

40. Thomas, *Walter Johnson*, 318.

41. *New York Times*, October 11, 1930.

42. *Washington Post*, January 11, 1931.

43. Mrs. Joe Cronin, "My Husband Manages the Red Sox," *Look*, July 22, 1947, 50.

44. Mrs. Joe Cronin, "My Husband Manages," 50.

45. Mrs. Joe Cronin, "My Husband Manages," 50.

46. Fred Lieb, *The Pittsburgh Pirates* (New York: Putnam, 1948), 239.

47. *Washington Post*, December 20, 1930.

48. Telegram from Joe Devine to Kenesaw Mountain Landis, January 13, 1931.

49. *Washington Post*, March 10, 1931.

50. *Washington Post*, May 17, 1931.

51. *The Sporting News*, May 28, 1931.

52. *Washington Post*, June 12, 1931.

53. *Washington Post*, July 10, 1931.

54. *Washington Post*, September 9, 1931.

55. *Washington Post*, April 6, 1932.

56. *Washington Post*, March 8, 1942.

57. "Cronin, Ill, May Miss Opener," *Washington Post*, April 8, 1932.

58. "This Morning with Shirley Povich," *Washington Post*, May 27, 1932.

59. "This Morning with Shirley Povich," *Washington Post*, June 3, 1932.

60. Povich, *The Washington Senators*.

4. PLAYER-MANAGER

1. The longest pair is now the Tigers' Lou Whitaker and Alan Trammell (1977–95). See *The SABR List and Record Book* (New York: Scribner, 2007), 368.

2. *New York Times*, October 6, 1932.

3. Frank H. Young, "See Judge and Cronin as Best Fitted for Manager's Post," *Washington Post*, October 5, 1932.

4. *Washington Post*, October 7, 1932.

5. *Washington Post*, October 8, 1932.

6. Frank H. Young, "26-Year-Old Shortstop Appointed by Griffith to Succeed Johnson," *Washington Post*, October 9, 1932.

7. William Ivory, "Harris, Stanley," in *Biographical Dictionary of American Sports—Baseball*, ed. David L Porter (Westport CT: Greenwood Press, 2000).

8. Heywood Broun, "It Seems to Me," *New York World-Telegram*, September 23, 1933.

9. Young, "26-Year-Old Shortstop."

10. Fred Stein, *And the Skipper Batted Cleanup* (Jefferson NC: McFarland, 2002).

11. *Washington Post*, December 11, 1932.

12. *Washington Post*, January 1, 1933.

13. "Cronin Elated at Trades of Nats," *Washington Post*, December 16, 1932.

14. *New York Times*, January 15, 1933; *Washington Post*, January 6, 1933; *Washington Post*, January 15, 1933; *Washington Post*, February 24, 1933.

15. "'Band' Greets Cronin on Arrival at Biloxi," *Washington Post*, February 21, 1933.

16. Dan Daniel, *The Sporting News*, March 4, 1933.

17. "Mack Discovered Cronin Is Smart," *Atlanta Constitution*, December 21, 1932.

18. *Washington Post*, October 11, 1932.

19. *Washington Post*, February 25, 1933.

20. Bob Addie, "The Last Time Washington Won a World Series," *Washington Post*, September 7, 1975.

21. Rob Kirkpatrick, *Cecil Travis*.

22. *Washington Post*, April 6, 1933.

23. Nicholas Dawidoff, *The Catcher Was a Spy* (New York: Pantheon, 1994).

24. *Washington Post*, April 6, 1933.

25. Frank Young, "Owner Sees Added Punch, Sees Prospect for a Pennant," *Washington Post*, April 12, 1933.

26. *The Sporting News*, April 13, 1933.

27. Westbrook Pegler, "Cheers Greet Roosevelt's Presence," *New York Times*, April 13, 1933.

28. Tom Deveaux, *The Washington Senators* (Jefferson NC: McFarland, 2001), 115.

29. "Baseball Fight," *Time*, May 8, 1933.

30. Shirley Povich, *The Washington Post*, July 5, 1933.

31. David Vincent, Lyle Spatz, and David W. Smith, *The Midsummer Classic* (Lincoln: University of Nebraska Press, 2001).

32. Stoney McLinn, *Philadelphia Record*, reprinted in *The Sporting News*, July 20, 1933.

33. Shirley Povich, *Washington Post*, July 29, 1933.

34. *The Sporting News*, August 3, 1933.

35. Edward Burns, *Chicago Daily Tribune*, September 14, 1933.

36. Bill Braucher, "Cronin Permits Senators to Do As They Please," undated and unsourced clipping from Cronin's Hall of Fame file.

37. John Drebinger, "Sports of the *Times*," *New York Times*, September 24, 1933.

38. Shirley Povich, *The Washington Post*, July 8, 1933.

39. Kirkpatrick, *Cecil Travis*.

40. Joe Vila, *The Sporting News*, August 10, 1933.

41. Bill Corwin, *New York Journal*, reprinted in *The Sporting News*, August 24, 1933.

42. Shirley Povich, *Washington Post*, September 22, 1933.

43. Saves were not figured at the time but were retroactively determined in 1969.

44. *Los Angeles Times*, September 24, 1933.

45. Deveaux, *The Washington Senators*, 120.

46. Associated Press, "Mack Backs Cronin for Picking Bolton," unsourced clipping from Cronin's Hall of Fame file, October 12, 1933.

47. Dan Daniel, "Daniel's Dope," *New York World-Telegram*, October 17, 1933.

48. *The Sporting News*, October 19, 1933; contract card from the Hall of Fame library.

49. Tom Meany, "Cronin Proves Real Hero," *New York World-Telegram*, October 3, 1933.

50. Hirshberg, *From Sandlots*, 98.

51. *San Francisco Chronicle*, October 16, 1933.

52. *Washington Post*, December 15, 1933.

53. Hirshberg, *From Sandlots*, 99.

54. Shirley Povich, "Joe Cronin Wedded to Baseball as a Lifelong Career," *Washington Post*, April 29, 1934.

55. Shirley Povich, *Washington Post*, December 7, 1935.

56. *Chicago Daily Tribune*, February 6, 1934.

57. *The Sporting News*, April 5, 1934.

58. *Washington Post*, March 11, 1934.

59. *Washington Post*, March 16, 1934.

60. Kirkpatrick, *Cecil Travis*.

61. *Washington Post*, March 21, 1934.

62. Deveaux, *The Washington Senators*, 125–27.

63. Arch Ward, *Chicago Daily Tribune*, June 16, 1934.

64. *Chicago Daily Tribune*, June 20, 1934.

65. *Washington Post*, July 1, 1934.

66. *Washington Post*, July 8, 1934.

67. *New York Times*, July 11, 1934.

68. *Washington Post*, July 12, 1934.

69. *Washington Post*, August 16, 1934.

70. *Washington Post*, September 4, 1934.

71. Hirshberg, *From Sandlots*, 102.

72. Cathedral of St. Mathew the Apostle (http://www.stmatthewscathedral .org/).

73. *Washington Post*, February 15, 1933.

74. *Washington Post*, September 4, 1934.

75. Cronin's salary with the Red Sox was widely reported as $30,000 for five years, and this has been repeated over the years. However his contract card at the Hall of Fame clearly states $27,000.

76. Joe Williams, "How Cronin Deal Was Made," *New York World-Telegram*, December 1, 1934.

77. *Washington Post*, October 27, 1934.

78. *The Sporting News*, July 30, 1952, 12.

79. *The Sporting News*, July 30, 1952, 12.

80. Dan Daniel, "Daniel's Dope," *New York World-Telegram*, undated clipping in Cronin's Hall of Fame file.

81. Associated Press, "Cronin, On Coast, Is Delighted," *New York Times*, October 27, 1934.

5. RICH KID

1. Glenn Stout and Richard L. Johnson, *Red Sox Century* (Boston: Houghton-Mifflin, 2000), 183–86.

2. Stout and Johnson, *Red Sox Century*, 182.

3. Stout and Johnson, *Red Sox Century*, 183–86.

4. Al Hirshberg, *Red Sox, the Bean and the Cod* (Boston: Waverly House, 1947).

5. Hirshberg, *Red Sox*.

6. *Boston Sunday Advertiser*, February 26, 1933.

7. *The Sporting News*, November 26, 1947.

8. Joe Cashman, quoted in Peter Golenbock, *Fenway—An Unexpurgated History of the Boston Red Sox* (New York: Putnam, 1992), 88.

9. Robert Creamer, *Babe* (New York: Simon and Schuster, 1974), 377–78.

10. Ed Hughes, *Brooklyn Daily Eagle*, reprinted in *The Sporting News*, November 25, 1934.

11. Shirley Povich, *Washington Post*, August 11, 1933.

12. *The Sporting News*, January 20, 1944.

13. Paul Shannon, *The Sporting News*, December 13, 1934.

14. *Washington Post*, February 7, 1935.

15. Paul Shannon, *The Sporting News*, December 20, 1934.

16. Arch Ward, "Talking It Over," *Chicago Daily Tribune*, February 6, 1935.

17. *Chicago Daily Tribune*, February 3, 1935.

18. *Washington Post*, February 17, 1935; February 24, 1935; March 1, 1935.

19. John Drebinger, "Red Sox Beat Yanks, 7–4, To Annex Fourth in Row," *New York Times*, April 24, 1935.

20. Shirley Povich, *Washington Post*, April 27, 1935.

21. Arch Ward, "Talking It Over," *Chicago Daily Tribune*, May 20, 1935.

22. *Boston Globe*, April 29, 1935.

23. *The Sporting News*, August 1, 1935.

24. *Washington Post*, August 22, 1937.

25. Jim Kaplan, *Lefty Grove—American Original* (Cleveland OH: SABR, 2000).

26. Jim Kaplan, *Lefty Grove*.

27. Donald Honig, *Baseball When the Grass Was Real* (New York: Coward, McCann & Geoghegan, 1975), 73.

28. Dick Thompson, *The Ferrell Brothers of Baseball* (Jefferson NC: McFarland, 2005), 109–10.

29. Dan Daniel, *New York World-Telegram*, August 24, 1938.

30. Shirley Povich, *Washington Post*, December 21, 1934.

31. Thompson, *The Ferrell Brothers*, 11–14.

32. Honig, *Baseball*, 33.

33. *New York Times*, August 8, 1935.

34. *Washington Post*, September 3, 1935.

35. Paul Shannon, *The Sporting News*, September 26, 1935.

36. Shirley Povich, *Washington Post*, April 11, 1935.

37. *Washington Post*, September 8, 1935.

38. Shirley Povich, *Washington Post*, December 7, 1935.

39. *The Sporting News*, October 10, 1935.

40. *Chicago Daily Tribune*, October 3, 1935.

41. Paul Shannon, *The Sporting News*, November 28, 1935.

42. *Washington Post*, January 14, 1936.

43. *Los Angeles Times*, January 20, 1936.

44. *Los Angeles Times*, March 8, 1936.

45. *Chicago Daily Tribune*, February 4, 1936.

46. *Washington Post*, February 9, 1936.

47. Mrs. Joe Cronin, "The Private Life."

48. *Washington Post*, March 29, 1936.

49. *Los Angeles Times*, April 10, 1936.

50. *Washington Post*, April 12, 1936.

51. Bob Ray, *Los Angeles Times*, April 20, 1936.

52. Shirley Povich, *Washington Post*, April 21, 1936.

53. Elden Auker, *Sleeper Cars and Flannel Uniforms* (Chicago: Triumph, 2001).

54. *The Sporting News*, June 11, 1936.

55. Armour and Levitt, *Paths to Glory*.

56. *Chicago Daily Tribune*, July 15, 1936.

57. Bob Ray, *Los Angeles Times*, July 16, 1936.

58. Thompson, *The Ferrell Brothers*, 197.

59. *New York Times*, August 22, 1936.

60. *Washington Post*, August 22, 1936.

61. *Washington Post*, August 22, 1936.

62. *Boston Globe*, August 22, 1936.

63. Linn, "Joe Cronin."

64. *Chicago Daily Tribune*, August 23, 1936.

65. *The Sporting News*, September 3, 1936.

66. J. G. Taylor Spink, "Three and One," *The Sporting News*, April 1, 1937.

67. Dan Daniel, *New York World-Telegram*, August 24, 1938.

68. *Washington Post*, August 26, 1936.

69. *Washington Post*, October 17, 1936.

70. *New York Times*, December 22, 1936.

6. Comeback

1. Dan Daniel, "Rambling around the Circuit," *The Sporting News*, May 6, 1937.

2. Joe Williams, *New York World-Telegram*, May 28, 1938.

3. *Chicago Daily Tribune*, January 14, 1937.

4. *The Sporting News*, October 1, 1936.

5. *Chicago Daily Tribune*, September 16, 1936.

6. Dan Daniel, "Rambling around the Circuit," *The Sporting News*, November 26, 1936.

7. *The Sporting News*, January 21, 1937.

8. Fred Lieb, "Joe Cronin, No Longer on the Spot," *The Sporting News*, March 25, 1937.

9. "Major League Notes," *The Sporting News*, March 18, 1937.

10. *Boston Globe*, April 5, 1927.

11. *Boston Globe*, April 12, 1927.

12. "Spring Training Notes," *The Sporting News*, April 22, 1937.

13. Bobby Doerr, interview by author, July 5, 2007.

14. Doerr, interview.

15. W. Harrison Daniel, *Jimmie Foxx—Life and Times* (Jefferson NC: McFarland, 1996), 102.

16. *Boston Globe*, May 14, 1937.

17. *Washington Post*, May 18, 1937.

18. *Washington Post*, May 25, 1937.

19. *Washington Post*, April 28, 1937.

20. Bill King, Associated Press, as referenced in *The Sporting News*, June 17, 1936.

21. *New York Journal-American*, as reported in *Lowell Sun*, August 18, 1937.

22. *Washington Post*, August 19, 1937; August 22, 1937; *New York Times*, August 19, 1937; *The Sporting News*, August 25, 1937; *Valparaiso (IN) Vidette-Messenger*, August 19, 1937.

23. *Washington Post*, August 20, 1937.

24. *Washington Post*, January 5, 1938.

25. *Washington Post*, December 4, 1937.

26. *Washington Post*, December 16, 1937.

27. *The Sporting News*, December 7, 1937.

28. Leigh Montville, *Ted Williams: The Biography of an American Hero* (New York: Doubleday, 2004).

29. Paul Shannon, *The Sporting News*, April 28, 1938.

30. Paul Shannon, *The Sporting News*, April 7, 1938.

31. Shirley Povich, *Washington Post*, April 3, 1938.

32. Ed Linn, "Joe Cronin."

33. *New York Times*, May 6, 1938; *Los Angeles Times*, May 8, 1938.

34. *New York Times*, May 31, 1938; *Boston Globe*, May 31, 1938.

35. *New York Times*, May 31, 1938; *New York Times*, June 1, 1938; Ed Linn, *The Great Rivalry* (New York: Ticknor and Fields, 1991).

36. Bob Ryan, *Boston Globe*, April 2, 2004.

37. Arch Ward, *Chicago Daily Tribune*, June 4, 1938.

38. Shirley Povich, *Washington Post*, June 2, 1938.

39. Ed McAuley, *Cleveland News*, reprinted in *The Sporting News*, August 11, 1938.

40. Kaplan, *Lefty Grove*.

41. Shirley Povich, *Washington Post*, August 28, 1938.

42. *The Sporting News*, October 6, 1938.

43. Joe Williams, *New York World-Telegram*, April 1, 1939.

44. *Washington Post*, November 1, 1938.

45. *Washington Post*, November 3, 1938; November 8, 1938.

46. Shirley Povich, *Washington Post*, October 29, 1938.

47. Jack Malaney, *Boston Post*, reprinted in *The Sporting News*, February 2, 1939.

48. *New York World-Telegram*, December 4, 1938; December 5, 1938; December 7, 1938.

49. *The Sporting News*, September 15, 1938.

50. *Hartford Courant*, September 9, 1938.

51. *Boston Globe*, March 28, 1939.

52. *Washington Post*, December 16, 1938.

53. *The Sporting News*, March 30, 1939.

54. *Boston Post*, March 27, 1939.

55. *The Sporting News*, April 6, 1939.

56. *New York Times*, July 19, 1939.

57. Stout and Johnson, *Red Sox Century*.

58. *The Sporting News*, June 2, 1948, 34.

59. *The Sporting News*, May 8, 1941.

60. Honig, *Baseball*, 206.

61. John P. Carmichael, *Chicago Daily News*, reprinted in *The Sporting News*, April 20, 1939.

62. *Washington Post*, June 8, 1939.

63. James P. Dawson, *New York Times*, July 10, 1939.

64. *The Sporting News*, August 17, 1939.

65. *New York Times*, September 30, 1939.

7. WINDING DOWN

1. U.S. Department of Labor, http://www.bls.gov/opub/cwc/cm20030124ar03p1.htm; Michigan Historical Center, http://www.michigan.gov/hal/0,1607,7-160-15481_19268_20778-52530—,00.html; U.S. Government info, http://usgovinfo.about.com/library/blminwage.htm.

2. Charles Alexander, *Breaking the Slump: Baseball in the Depression Era* (New York: Columbia University Press, 2002).

3. Maureen Cronin, interview, January 2007; William Curran, *Mitts* (New York: Morrow, 1985).

4. Joe Williams, *New York World-Telegram*, December 1, 1934.

5. *The Sporting News*, October 26, 1939; November 2, 1939; November 23, 1939; *New York Times*, October 28, 1939.

6. *The Sporting News*, November 16, 1939.

7. *Los Angeles Times*, November 15, 1939.

8. *New York Times*, December 7, 1939.

9. Shirley Povich, *Washington Post*, December 7, 1939.

10. *Christian Science Monitor*, December 8, 1939.

11. *Hartford Courant*, February 2, 1940.

12. *The Sporting News*, February 15, 1940; February 29, 1940; *Washington Post*, February 29, 1940.

13. *The Sporting News*, March 21, 1940.

14. *The Sporting News*, May 30, 1940.

15. Daniel, *Jimmie Foxx*, 121–22.

16. Dom DiMaggio, interview by author, November 19, 2007.

17. *The Sporting News*, August 8, 1940.

18. *New York Times*, September 30, 1940, 24.

19. *The Sporting News*, July 18, 1940.

20. Golenbock, *Fenway*.

21. See especially Cramer's comments in Golenbock, *Fenway*.

22. Philip J. Lowry, *Green Cathedrals* (Cleveland OH: SABR, 2006).

23. Montville, *Ted Williams*, 65.

24. Austen Lake, *Boston Evening Transcript*, August 13, 1940.

25. *The Sporting News*, June 13, 1940.

26. Montville, *Ted Williams*, 65.

27. *The Sporting News*, August 1, 1940.

28. *The Sporting News*, January 9, 1941.

29. Ted Williams, as told to John Underwood, *My Turn at Bat* (New York: Simon and Schuster, 1969).

30. Stout and Johnson, *Red Sox Century*.

31. Shirley Povich, "This Morning," *Washington Post*, October 11, 1940.

32. For one example, see *Los Angeles Times*, January 5, 1941.

33. *The Sporting News*, January 23, 1941.

34. *New York Times*, December 11, 1940.

35. *New York Times*, December 10, 1940.

36. *The Sporting News*, November 21, 1940.

37. George Kirksey, "Yawkey Plans No Radical Changes at Boston," *New York Times*, October 30, 1940.

38. *The Sporting News*, November 28, 1940.

39. *The Sporting News*, March 6, 1941.

40. *The Sporting News*, April 17, 1941.

41. *Washington Post*, April 17, 1941; April 22, 1941.

42. *The Sporting News*, May 8, 1941.

43. Michael "Corky" Cronin, interview with author, January 2008.

44. Montville, *Ted Williams*.

45. Montville, *Ted Williams*.

46. Montville, *Ted Williams*.

47. Bill Nowlin, *On Deck*, a publication of the Ted Williams Museum, 2002.

48. *The Sporting News*, January 8, 1942.

49. Joe Williams, *New York World-Telegram*, October 27, 1941.

50. *Chicago Daily Tribune*, December 11, 1941.

51. *The Sporting News*, June 4, 1942.

52. Daniel, *Jimmie Foxx*.

53. Kaplan, *Lefty Grove*.

54. *The Sporting News*, December 18, 1941.

8. War

1. George Q. Flynn, *The Draft—1940–1973* (Lawrence: University Press of Kansas, 1993).

2. Flynn, *The Draft*.

3. David Pietrusza, *Judge and Jury—The Life and Times of Judge Kenesaw Mountain Landis* (South Bend IN: Diamond Communications, 1998).

4. *Washington Post*, January 25, 1942.

5. *Washington Post*, January 31, 1942.

6. *The Sporting News*, January 29, 1942.

7. Montville, *Ted Williams*.

8. Bill Nowlin, *Ted Williams at War* (Boston: Rounder, 2007).

9. Johnny Pesky, interview with author, July 7, 2007.

10. Bill Nowlin, *Johnny Pesky—Mr. Red Sox* (Boston: Rounder, 2004).

11. Daniel, *Jimmie Foxx*.

12. *The Sporting News*, August 27, 1942.

13. Montville, *Ted Williams*.

14. Dan Daniel, *The Sporting News*, July 9, 1942.

15. *The Sporting News*, July 30, 1942.

16. *The Sporting News*, June 4, 1942.

17. *The Sporting News*, June 4, 1942.

18. *Chicago Daily Tribune*, January 29, 1943; *The Sporting News*, February 11, 1943.

19. *The Sporting News*, January 28, 1943; *New York Times*, February 11, 1943.

20. *The Sporting News*, October 22, 1942; *The Sporting News*, October 29, 1942; January 28, 1943.

21. *The Sporting News*, April 8, 1943; *New York Times*, February 11, 1943.

22. *The Sporting News*, June 24, 1943.

23. *The Sporting News*, July 8, 1943.

24. *The Sporting News*, September 23, 1943.

25. William B. Mead, *Even the Browns—The Zany, True Story of Baseball in the Early Forties* (Chicago: Contemporary Books, 1978).

26. *The Sporting News*, May 18, 1944; June 1, 1944.

27. *Christian Science Monitor*, September 30, 1943; *New York Times*, October 3, 1943.

28. *The Sporting News*, October 14, 1943.

29. *Christian Science Monitor*, January 19, 1944.

30. Mead, *Even the Browns*.

31. Ed Rumill, *Christian Science Monitor*, September 25, 1943.

32. *The Sporting News*, October 28, 1943.

33. *The Sporting News*, October 14, 1943.

34. *The Sporting News*, April 6, 1944.

35. *The Sporting News*, May 11, 1944.

36. *Washington Post*, September 12, 1944.

37. *Yank*, June 11, 1944; *The Sporting News*, August 17, 1944.

38. Mead, *Even the Browns*.

39. Mead, *Even the Browns*.

40. Mead, *Even the Browns*.

41. *The Sporting News*, January 18, 1945.

42. *Washington Post*, January 17, 1945.

43. *New York Times*, January 23, 1945.

44. *New York Times*, March 16, 1945.

45. *New York Times*, March 20, 1945.

46. *New York Times*, April 11, 1945.

47. *Washington Post*, April 13, 1945.

48. Wendell Smith, "Red Sox Consider Negroes," *Pittsburgh Courier*, April 21, 1945.

49. Glenn Stout, "Tryout and Fallout—Race, Jackie Robinson and the Red Sox," *The Massachusetts Historical Review* 6 (2004), www.historycooperative.org/journals/mhr/6/stout.html.

50. *Boston Daily Record*, April 27, 1945.

51. Marie Brenner, "A Rookie in Pearls," *Esquire*, July 1980.

52. Stout, "Tryout."

53. Smith, "Red Sox Consider."

54. *New York Times*, April 18, 1945.

55. *The Sporting News*, June 14, 1945.

56. *The Sporting News*, May 23, 1946.

57. *The Sporting News*, July 5, 1945.

9. Bench Manager

1. *Christian Science Monitor*, November 6, 1945.

2. Mead, *Even the Browns*.

3. Al Hirshberg, *American Legion Magazine*, August 1956.

4. *The Sporting News*, February 14, 1946.

5. *The Sporting News*, November 1, 1945.

6. *The Sporting News*, January 24, 1946.

7. Mrs. Joe Cronin, "My Husband Manages."

8. Montville, *Ted Williams*.

9. Bert Dunne, *Play Ball, Son!* (Self-published pamphlet, 1945).

10. Bert Dunne, *Play Ball!* (Garden City NJ: Doubleday, 1947).

11. William Marshall, *Baseball's Pivotal Era—1945–1951* (Lexington: University of Kentucky, 1999).

12. Marshall, *Baseball's Pivotal Era*.

13. *The Sporting News*, May 16, 1946.

14. Harold Kaese, "What's the Matter with the Red Sox?" *Saturday Evening Post*, March 23, 1946.

15. *The Sporting News*, March 21, 1946.

16. *Cleveland News*, reprinted in *The Sporting News*, March 28, 1946.

17. *New York Mirror*, reprinted in *The Sporting News*, April 11, 1946.

18. *The Sporting News*, April 4, 1946.

19. *The Sporting News*, May 16, 1946.

20. *The Sporting News*, June 12, 1946.

21. Frederick Turner, *When the Boys Came Back* (New York: Henry Holt, 1996).

22. Ed Rumill, *Christian Science Monitor*, September 14, 1946.

23. Turner, *When the Boys Came Back*.

24. *The Sporting News*, September 28, 1946; *Christian Science Monitor*, September 17, 1946.

25. *The Sporting News*, September 28, 1946.

26. Fred Lieb, *The Boston Red Sox* (New York: Putnam, 1947).

27. *The Sporting News*, May 16, 1946.

28. *Los Angeles Times*, October 1, 1946.

29. *Christian Science Monitor*, September 30, 1946.

30. *Boston Evening Post*, as quoted in Phil Bergen, "The Curse of Mickey Haefner," *The National Pastime* (Cleveland OH: SABR, 1999).

31. Bergen, "The Curse of Mickey Haefner."

32. Dan Daniel, *The Sporting News*, October 16, 1946; Montville, *Ted Williams*.

33. *New York Times*, October 12, 1946, 24.

34. DiMaggio, interview.

35. Turner, *When the Boys Came Back*.

36. DiMaggio, interview.

37. Harold Kaese, *Boston Globe*, reprinted in *The Sporting News*, October 30, 1946, 7.

38. Shirley Povich, *Washington Post*, October 20, 1946.

39. Joe Williams, *New York World-Telegram*, September 20, 1947.

40. Dan Daniel, *New York World-Telegram*, October 21, 1946.

41. Mrs. Joe Cronin, "My Husband Manages."

42. Maureen Cronin, interview, February, 2, 2007.

43. *The Sporting News*, October 9, 1946; Maureen Cronin, interview, February, 2, 2007.

44. Linn, "Joe Cronin."

45. Rick Huhn, *Eddie Collins* (Jefferson NC: McFarland, 2008).

46. Harold Kaese, "So You Think You Know Ted Williams?" *Sport*, August 1947, 14.

47. *Christian Science Monitor*, February 25, 1947.

48. Shirley Povich, *Washington Post*, April 16, 1947.

49. *The Sporting News*, September 17, 1947.

50. Arthur Daley, *New York Times*, June 17, 1947.

51. *New York Times*, May 8, 1947.

52. *The Sporting News*, July 16, 1947.

53. *Washington Post*, July 9, 1947; *Boston Post*, August 19, 1947; *The Sporting News*, July 22, 1947; April 4, 1951; Ellis Veach, *East St. Louis (IL) Journal*, as reported in *The Sporting News*, August 20, 1947.

54. Al Hirshberg, *What's the Matter with the Red Sox?* (New York: Dodd, Mead, 1973).

55. *The Sporting News*, October 8, 1947.

56. Bill James, *The Bill James Guide to Baseball Managers* (New York: Scribner, 1997).

57. Daniel R. Levitt, *Ed Barrow—The Bulldog Who Built the Bombers* (Lincoln: University of Nebraska Press, 2008).

58. Alan H. Levy, *Joe McCarthy* (Jefferson NC: McFarland, 2005).

59. Levy, *Joe McCarthy*.

60. *The Sporting News*, October 15, 1947.

61. See, for example, Joe Williams, *New York World-Telegram*, October 15, 1947.

10. General Manager

1. *Christian Science Monitor*, September 30, 1947.

2. John Harrington, interview by author, August 2007.

3. *The Sporting News Official Baseball Guide*, 1948.

4. Maureen Cronin, interview, July 2007.

5. *The Sporting News*, October 8, 1947.

6. *St. Louis Star-Times*, November 21, 1947, as reported in *Chicago Daily Tribune*, November 22, 1947.

7. *The Sporting News*, November 26, 1947.

8. *New York Times*, November 18, 1947.

9. *American Legion Magazine*, August 1956.

10. *The Sporting News*, November 26, 1947.

11. *The Sporting News*, November 26, 1947.

12. Dan Daniel, *The Sporting News*, November 26, 1947.

13. *New York Times*, November 25, 1947.

14. *Christian Science Monitor*, December 11, 1947; *The Sporting News*, December 24, 1947.

15. *The Sporting News*, December 24, 1947.

16. Shirley Povich, *Washington Post*, December 12, 1947.

17. *The Sporting News*, December 24, 1947, 24.

18. *Hartford Courant*, *Christian Science Monitor*, *The Sporting News*, several issues.

19. Levy, *Joe McCarthy*.

20. Ed Rumill, *Christian Science Monitor*, February 15, 1973, 12.

21. Levy, *Joe McCarthy*, quote is unsourced.

22. Williams, *My Turn at Bat*.

23. Alan Levy, "Joe McCarthy and the Fourth Estate—A Window onto Baseball and Media Relations in the Mid-Twentieth Century," *The Cooperstown Symposium 2003–2004* (Jefferson NC: McFarland, 2005), 156–79.

24. *The Sporting News*, February 18, 1948, 16.

25. Shirley Povich, *Washington Post*, March 17, 1948, 12.

26. Williams, *My Turn At Bat*; Pesky, DiMaggio, and Doerr, interviews.

27. Arthur Daley, "Sports of the *Times*," *New York Times*, March 7, 1948.

28. Armour and Levitt, *Paths to Glory*.

29. *The Sporting News*, October 8, 1947; *The Sporting News*, February 18, 1948.

30. *The Sporting News*, April 14, 1948.

31. Pesky, DiMaggio, and Doerr, interviews.

32. *The Sporting News*, January 21, 1948; January 28, 1948.

33. *The Sporting News*, April 28, 1948.

34. *The Sporting News*, June 2, 1948, 33.

35. *The Sporting News*, June 9, 1948, 7.

36. *The Sporting News*, June 2, 1948, 14.

37. *The Sporting News*, June 9, 1948, 7.

38. *New York Times*, April 27, 1944, 16.

39. *New York Times*, August 5, 1945, 49.

40. Levy, "Joe McCarthy and the Fourth Estate," 156–79.

41. Al Hirshberg, *The Boston Post*, September 9, 1948.

42. Al Hirshberg, *The Boston Post*, September 9, 1948.

43. Ed Linn, *Hitter—The Life and Turmoils of Ted Williams* (New York: Harcourt and Brace, 1993), 307–9.

44. *The Sporting News*, June 16, 1948.

45. *The Sporting News*, August 28, 1948.

46. David Kaiser, *Epic Season—The 1948 American League Pennant Race* (Amhurst: University of Massachusetts Press, 1998), 195.

47. *New York Times*, October 7, 1948, 41.

48. *The Sporting News*, February 16, 1979, 14.

49. Shirley Povich, *Washington Post*, January 11, 1949, 12.

50. *The Sporting News*, December 1, 1948.

51. *The Sporting News*, March 16, 1949, 18.

52. *The Sporting News*, January 19, 1949, 16.

53. Cliff Kachline, e-mail to author, July 23, 2008. Kachline worked for *The Sporting News* at the time.

54. *The Sporting News Official Baseball Guide*, 1949, 1950.

55. *The Sporting News Official Baseball Guide*, 1950, 93.

56. Shirley Povich, *Washington Post*, December 15, 1949, b6.

57. Levy, *Joe McCarthy*, 357.

58. David Halberstam, *Summer of '49* (New York: Morrow, 1989), 277.

59. U.S. House of Representatives, Hearings before the Subcommittee on the Study of Monopoly Power of the Committee on the Judiciary: Organized Baseball (82d Cong., 1st sess., 1952). Courtesy Dan Levitt.

60. For a lengthy treatment of these teams, see Armour and Levitt, *Paths to Glory*.

61. Halberstam, *Summer of '49*, 277.

62. Doerr, interview.

63. *New York Times*, October 4, 1949.

64. *The Sporting News*, November 9, 1949.

65. *New York Times*, December 24, 1949.

66. *The Sporting News*, February 15, 1950; *Chicago Tribune*, February 7, 1950.

67. *New York Times*, March 4, 1950; March 10, 1950.

68. *The Sporting News*, May 10, 1950.

69. Levy, *Joe McCarthy*, 370.

70. *Hartford Courant*, May 13, 1950, 11.

71. Levy, *Joe McCarthy*, 374; Golenbock, *Fenway*, 186; *Hartford Courant*, June 23, 1950, 1.

72. Golenbock, *Fenway*, 187.

73. Ed Rumill, *Christian Science Monitor*, October 2, 1950, 14.

11. OPPORTUNITY LOST

1. *Hartford Courant*, June 14, 1944, 13; *Chicago Daily Tribune*, June 12, 1945, 17; *New York Times*, June 27, 1945, 23; *Washington Post*, February 15, 1946.

2. *The Sporting News Official Baseball Guide*, 1947, 146.

3. *Hartford Courant*, August 8, 1948, c3; *Hartford Courant*, October 28, 1949, 21.

4. *Christian Science Monitor*, July 7, 1948, 12.

5. Dan Parker, "Bonus Players Are Poison," *Sport*, May 1950, 15.

6. *The Sporting News Official Baseball Guide*, 1951, 151.

7. *Los Angeles Times*, June 5, 1951.

8. *Washington Post*, June 22, 1952, c4.

9. *The Sporting News*, September 17, 1952.

10. *The Sporting News Official Baseball Guide*, 1953, 97.

11. Shirley Povich, *Washington Post*, August 5, 1952, 13.

12. *The Sporting News*, June 25, 1952.

13. *The Sporting News Official Baseball Guide*, 1953, 97.

14. *The Sporting News*, September 10, 1952.

15. *Hartford Courant*, September 9, 1953.

16. *The Sporting News*, March 17, 1954, 7.

17. Milton Gross, "They've Got to Change the Bonus Rule," *Sport*, January 1956.

18. Brent Kelley, *Baseball's Biggest Blunder* (Lanham MD: Scarecrow Press, 1997).

19. *New York Times*, December 12, 1957, 40; *Chicago Daily Tribune*, December 24, 1957, A3; *Christian Science Monitor*, May 20, 1958; *New York Times*, May 22, 1958; June 14, 1958; *Los Angeles Times*, June 29, 1958.

20. Al Hirshberg, "The Sad Case of the Red Sox," *Saturday Evening Post*, May 21, 1960.

21. For a detailed numerical analysis of the integration of the game, see Mark Armour, "The Effects of Integration, 1947–1986," *The Baseball Research Journal 2007* (Cleveland OH: SABR, 2007), 53–57.

22. Hirshberg, *What's the Matter?* 145–46.

23. Jules Tygiel, *Baseball's Great Experiment* (New York: Oxford, 1983).

24. For his forthcoming book on George Scott, Ron Anderson interviewed Digby extensively, including about the Mays story.

25. Willie Mays, as told to Charles Einstein, *My Life In and Out of Baseball* (New York: Dutton, 1966); Willie Mays, with Lou Sahadi, *Say Hey—The Autobiography of Willie Mays* (New York: Simon and Shuster, 1988).

26. *The Sporting News*, November 11, 1949, 6.

27. David Nevard, with David Marasco, "Who Was Piper Davis," The Buffalo

Head Society, 2001, http://home.comcast.net/~buffalohead/piper.htm.

28. *Pittsburgh Courier*, December 17, 1949.

29. Al Hirshberg, "Boston Needs a Negro Big-Leaguer," *Our Sports*, July 1953; *The Sporting News*, December 24, 1952.

30. Nevard, "Who Was Piper Davis."

31. Hirshberg, "Boston Needs"; *The Sporting News*, December 24, 1952.

32. Shirley Povich, *Washington Post*, January 4, 1953; Larry Moffi and Jonathan Kronstadt, *Crossing the Line—Black Major Leaguers 1947–1959* (Jefferson NC: McFarland, 1994).

33. Moffi and Kronstadt, *Crossing the Line.*

34. Hirshberg, *What's the Matter?* 143.

35. Howard Bryant. *Shut Out—A Story of Race and Baseball in Boston* (New York: Routledge, 2002).

36. *Chicago Defender*, December 25, 1954, 11.

37. Hirshberg, "The Sad Case."

38. *Hartford Courant*, June 28, 1958, 13B.

39. Tygiel, *Baseball's Great Experiment*, 332.

40. Hirshberg, *What's the Matter?* 142.

41. Tygiel, *Baseball's Great Experiment*, 329–30.

42. Jules Tygiel, e-mail to author, May 2007.

43. *The Sporting News*, February 17, 1954, 4.

44. *Hartford Courant*, January 15, 1958; *Christian Science Monitor*, January 16, 1957.

12. YOUTH MOVEMENT

1. *Washington Post*, December 14, 1950, B6.

2. *The Sporting News*, November 29, 1950.

3. See especially Joe Williams, "Why I Would Trade Ted Williams," *Sport*, February 1951, 10.

4. *The Sporting News*, January 17, 1951.

5. Tommy and Michael "Corky" Cronin, interviews by author, June 2008.

6. Rick Huhn, *Eddie Collins* (Jefferson NC: McFarland, 2008), 314.

7. *Washington Post*, September 24, 1951, 9.

8. *Washington Post*, September 24, 1951, 9.

9. Doerr, interview by author.

10. *Los Angeles Times*, September 20, 1951, C1.

11. *Chicago Tribune*, October 23, 1951, B1.

12. *The Sporting News*, October 31, 1951.

13. Williams, *My Turn at Bat*, 173–74.

14. Nowlin, *Ted Williams at War*, 86.

15. *The Sporting News*, January 16, 1952.

16. *The Sporting News*, November 28, 1951; February 6, 1952.

17. Harold Kaese, "Boston's Shortstop Gamble," *Sport*, August 1952, 20.

18. Shirley Povich, *Washington Post*, April 17, 1952.

19. *The Sporting News*, March 19, 1952, 1.

20. Kaese, "Boston's Shortstop Gamble," 20.

21. *Chicago Tribune*, July 29, 1952, B1.

22. *The Sporting News*, July 9, 1952.

23. *The Sporting News*, June 25, 1952; July 2, 1952.

24. *The Sporting News*, July 16, 1952.

25. *The Sporting News*, July 30. 1952.

26. Jim Piersall and Al Hirshberg, *Fear Strikes Out* (New York: Little Brown, 1955); *The Sporting News*, June 25, 1952; July 2, 1952.

27. Bob Kohler, "Striking Fear on the Court," *Boston Globe*, October 5, 2006.

28. *Los Angeles Times*, September 12, 1952.

29. Will McDonough, "A Man for One Season Every Day of His Life," *Boston Globe*, undated clipping in Cronin's Hall of Fame file, circa September 8, 1984.

30. Piersall and Hirshberg, *Fear Strikes Out*.

31. *The Sporting News*, October 15, 1952, 30.

32. *The Sporting News*, January 28, 1953, 14.

33. *The Sporting News*, May 28, 1953.

34. Doug Segrest, *The Birmingham News*, May 28, 2008.

35. James R. Walker and Robert V. Bellamy Jr., *Center Field Shot—A History of Baseball on Television* (Lincoln: University of Nebraska Press, 2008), 22–31.

36. *The Sporting News*, February 15, 1950, 1–2.

37. Grantland Rice, "Is Baseball Afraid of Television?" *Sport*, April 1951.

38. *The Sporting News*, April 22, 1953.

39. Saul Wisnia, *The Jimmy Fund of Dana-Farber Cancer Institute* (Charleston SC: Arcadia, 2002).

40. *New York Times*, May 13, 1953.

41. Golenbock, *Fenway*, 195.

42. *The Sporting News*, May 20, 1953.

43. Arthur Daley, *New York Times*, July 15, 1953, 30; *Hartford Courant*, July 15, 1953, 13.

44. *Christian Science Monitor*, September 26, 1953, 7.

45. Nowlin, *Ted Williams at War*, 150–56.

46. *Christian Science Monitor*, August 18, 1953, 7.

47. *The Sporting News*, May 13, 1953.

48. *The Sporting News*, January 6, 1954, 22; January 27, 1954.

49. *The Sporting News*, January 20, 1954.

50. *New York Times*, November 4, 1953; *The Sporting News*, November 18, 1953.

51. Mickey McDermott, with Howard Eisenberg, *A Funny Thing Happened on the Way to Cooperstown* (Chicago: Triumph Books, 2003); *The Sporting News*, December 30, 1953.

52. Al Stump, "How Jackie Jensen Found Himself," *Sport*, February 1955, 94.

53. *The Sporting News*, February 17, 1954.

54. Andy Dabilis, "Lynn Will Never Forget Harry Agganis's Athletic Skill—or His Character," *Boston Globe*, July 2, 1995; Michael Madden, "AGGANIS," *Boston Globe*, June 6, 1995.

55. *The Sporting News*, June 23, 1954.

56. *The Sporting News*, June 30, 1954, 18.

57. *The Sporting News*, October 20, 1954.

58. *The Sporting News*, October 20, 1954.

13. POWER AND GLORY

1. *The Sporting News*, March 16, 1955.

2. *The Sporting News*, May 18, 1955, 1–2.

3. *The Sporting News*, May 25, 1955, 1.

4. *The Sporting News*, June 15, 1955, 2.

5. *Hartford Courant*, October 24, 1954.

6. *Christian Science Monitor*, February 3, 1955; *The Sporting News*, December 15, 1954; April 6, 1955.

7. *The Sporting News*, October 6, 1954; October 20, 1954.

8. Montville, *Ted Williams*.

9. *The Sporting News*, July 6, 1955.

10. Maureen Cronin, interview, February 1, 2007.

11. *Washington Post*, October 28, 1955, 1.

12. Jim McCulley, "Cronin: D.C.'s Boy Wonder Boston's Man," *New York Daily News*, February 2, 1959.

13. *The Sporting News*, December 7, 1955.

14. *Christian Science Monitor*, November 29, 1955, 16.

15. Arthur Daley, *New York Times*, December 4, 1955, s2.

16. *Los Angeles Times*, December 19, 1955, C1.

17. Bob Stevens, *San Francisco Chronicle*, December 10, 1955, 1H.

18. *New York Times*, November 10, 1955, 49.

19. *The Sporting News*, February 1, 1956, 6.

20. *The Sporting News*, February 8, 1956, 7–8.

21. Arthur Daley, *New York Times*, January 30, 1956, 36.

22. *The Sporting News*, August 1, 1956.

23. *Christian Science Monitor*, July 24, 1956, 10.

24. *Los Angeles Times*, July 19, 1956.

25. *Chicago Daily Tribune*, July 22, 1956.

26. Montville, *Ted Williams*, 197–98.

27. Montville, *Ted Williams*; *Los Angeles Times*, August 8, 1956.

28. *The Sporting News*, August 15, 1956, 6.

29. Montville, *Ted Williams*.

30. Williams, *My Turn at Bat*.

31. *The Sporting News*, August 29, 1956.

32. *The Sporting News Official Baseball Guide*, 1957; *The Sporting News*, August 8, 1956.

33. *The Sporting News Official Baseball Guide*, 1957; *The Sporting News*, August 22, 1956.

34. *The Sporting News*, September 26, 1956.

35. *San Francisco News*, September 29, 1956.

36. *The Sporting News*, December 12, 1956, 10; December 19, 1956, 19.

37. *Hartford Courant*, March 19, 1957.

38. *The Sporting News*, April 3, 1956, 1–2.

39. *The Sporting News*, April 3, 1956, 32.

40. *Los Angeles Times*, March 27, 1957, c1.

41. *Christian Science Monitor*, March 26, 1957, 14.

42. Golenbock, *Fenway*, 218–19.

43. *The Sporting News*, October 16, 1957, 6; October 23, 1957, 21.

44. *The Sporting News*, October 23, 1957; October 30, 1957.

45. *Washington Post*, December 2, 1958.

46. *American Legion Magazine*, August 1956.

47. *Chicago Daily Tribune*, July 20, 1958.

48. *Washington Post*, February 2, 1958; *Chicago Daily Tribune*, March 12, 1958; *Washington Post*, March 14, 1958.

49. *Washington Post*, January 24, 1958; Daniel, *Jimmie Foxx*; John Bennett, "Jimmie Foxx," sabr's Baseball Biography Project, www.bioproj.sabr.org.

50. *The Sporting News*, April 16, 1958, 24.

51. William M. Simons, "Pitcher at Twilight: Bill Monboquette and the American Dream," *The Cooperstown Symposium on Baseball and American Culture*, 2002 (Jefferson nc: McFarland, 2002).

52. *The Sporting News*, October 1, 1958.

53. *Los Angeles Times*, July 7, 1958; *The Sporting News*, September 3, 1958.

54. *The Sporting News*, November 12, 1958, 2.

55. *The Sporting News*, December 17, 1958, 1; *New York Times*, January 7, 2008.

56. *The Sporting News Official Baseball Guide*, 1959; *The Sporting News*, January 21, 1959.

14. Mr. President

1. Bob Addie, *Washington Post*, March 4, 1960, c3.

2. McCulley, "Cronin."

3. Bob Addie, *Washington Post*, March 25, 1960, c3.

4. McCulley, "Cronin."

5. Arthur Daley, *New York Times*, January 19, 1959.

6. *The Sporting News*, April 15, 1959, 29.

7. Leonard Koppett, *Koppett's Concise History of Baseball* (Philadelphia: Temple University Press, 1998), 272–77.

8. *New York Times*, July 28, 1959, 30.

9. Koppett, *Koppett's Concise History*, 272–77.

10. *Daily Defender*, December 1, 1959, 34.

11. *The Sporting News*, November 18, 1959.

12. Koppett, *Koppett's Concise History*, 277–80.

13. Shirley Povich, *Washington Post*, October 26, 1960, 31.

14. *New York Times*, October 28, 1961, 34; November 2, 1961, 46.

15. Dan Daniel, *The Sporting News*, November 9, 1960.

16. Joe Williams, *New York World-Telegram*, March 7, 1961.

17. *Christian Science Monitor*, December 15, 1960, 10.

18. *Christian Science Monitor*, May 13, 1961, 11.

19. *Washington Post*, January 18, 1961.

20. *The Sporting News*, May 27, 1959.

21. *New York World-Telegram-Sun*, July 24, 1959; Larry Gerlach, correspondence with author.

22. John Rice, interview by author, December 1, 2007.

23. *New York Times*, May 5, 1959.

24. *New York Times*, July 18, 1959; *Chicago Tribune*, July 24, 1959.

25. *The Sporting News*, August 3, 1960.

26. SABR's ejection database, compiled by Doug Pappas. Courtesy David Vincent.

27. *The Sporting News*, September 14, 1960; September 21, 1960; September 28, 1960.

28. *The Sporting News*, June 29, 1960.

29. *The Sporting News*, May 20, 1959.

30. *The Sporting News*, May 11, 1963.

31. *Washington Post*, June 21, 1964.

32. *Christian Science Monitor*, June 3, 1959, 11.

33. *The Sporting News*, July 22, 1959.

34. *Chicago Daily Tribune*, December 24, 1959.

35. *New York Times*, September 21, 1961; *The Sporting News*, October 4, 1961.

36. *The Sporting News*, October 27, 1962; November 3, 1962; November 10, 1962.

37. *The Sporting News*, December 1, 1962; December 8, 1962.

38. *The Sporting News*, April 20, 1974, 10.

39. *New York Times*, August 3, 1961.

40. *New York World-Telegram-Sun*, August 17, 1961.

41. *New York Times*, October 15, 1961.

42. *The Sporting News Official Baseball Guide*, 1962, 111.

43. *Christian Science Monitor*, November 27, 1961.

44. *The Sporting News*, February 2, 1963; February 9, 1963; *Washington Post*, March 10, 1963, C1.

45. *The Sporting News*, April 13, 1963.

46. *Los Angeles Times*, September 8, 1963.

47. Al Hirshberg, "Is the American League Really That Bad?" *Sport*, March 1964, 26–29.

48. *New York World-Telegram-Sun*, June 18, 1964.

49. Bud Furillo, *Los Angeles Examiner*, reprinted in *The Sporting News*, May 1, 1962.

50. *Los Angeles Times*, August 20, 1963, B1.

51. Dan Daniel, *New York World-Telegram*, April 12, 1960.

15. New Order

1. Armour and Levitt, *Paths to Glory*.

2. *The Sporting News*, June 28, 1961.

3. Armour and Levitt, *Paths to Glory*.

4. *Chicago Daily Tribune*, December 15, 1961, C1.

5. *The Sporting News*, December 28, 1963.

6. *Washington Post*, September 20, 1962, B13; *The Sporting News*, October 13, 1962.

7. *Washington Post*, January 10, 1964.

8. Armour and Levitt, *Paths to Glory*; *The Sporting News*, July 20, 1963; January 11, 1964; *Washington Post*, January 10, 1964.

9. *The Sporting News*, February 22, 1964; February 29, 1964; March 7, 1964.

10. *Chicago Tribune*, April 5, 1964, B4; April 7, 1964, B3.

11. *New York Times*, April 12, 1964; *Hartford Courant*, April 12, 1964, C1; *Chicago Tribune*, April 14, 1964, C1.

12. Armour and Levitt, *Paths to Glory*.

13. Bowie Kuhn, *Hardball—The Education of a Baseball Commissioner* (New York: Times Books, 1987).

14. Harrington, interview, July 2007.

15. *Christian Science Monitor*, August 7, 1964; *Washington Post*, August 8, 1964.

16. *New York Journal-American*, October 20, 1965.

17. *Hartford Courant*, August 26, 1984.

18. *The Sporting News Official Baseball Guide*, 1965, 153–57.

19. *New York Times*, August 14, 1964; *Christian Science Monitor*, August 15, 1964, 5.

20. Bill Veeck, with Ed Linn, *The Hustler's Handbook* (New York: Putnam, 1965).

21. *Washington Post*, August 21, 1964.

22. *Chicago Tribune*, September 10, 1964, 40.

23. *Chicago Tribune*, September 12 and 13, 1964; *Hartford Courant*, September 12, 1964, 15A.

24. *The Sporting News Official Baseball Guide*, 1965, 153–57; Koppett, *Koppett's Concise History*, 298; *New York Journal-American*, February 9, 1965.

25. *Washington Post*, March 3, 1965; July 13, 1965.

26. *Chicago Tribune*, December 9, 1964, E1.

27. Charles Dexter, "Sound Off! Joe Cronin: If He Were Commissioner," *Sport*, February, 1965, 64.

28. Leonard Koppett, "Baseball's Biggest Crisis," *Sport*, March 1965, 22.

29. *The Sporting News Official Baseball Guide*, 1966, 156.

30. Koppett, *Koppett's Concise History*, 303; *The Sporting News Official Baseball Guide*, 1966, 157–58.

31. *Washington Post*, February 12, 1965; July 4, 1965.

32. *Hartford Courant*, November 18, 1965, 21A; *Christian Science Monitor*, December 20, 1965, 7.

33. *New York World-Telegram-Sun*, March 31, 1965.

34. *New York Times*, July 20, 1965; *Hartford Courant*, July 21, 1965.

35. *New York Times*, May 28, 1964.

36. Larry Gerlach, *The Men in Blue* (New York: Viking, 1980), 169.

37. *Washington Post*, February 17, 1966; March 27, 1966.

38. Mark Armour, "Emmett Ashford—Entertainer and Pioneer," *The National Pastime* (Cleveland OH: SABR, 2007).

39. Armour, "Emmett Ashford."

40. *Chicago Defender*, March 28, 1963; *Los Angeles Times*, July 2, 1965.

41. *Los Angeles Herald-Examiner*, October 2, 1965; *New York Journal-American*, March 14, 1966.

42. Bob Sudyk, "Emmett Ashford: Only His Suit Is Blue," *The Sporting News*, April 23, 1966.

43. Sudyk, "Emmett Ashford."

44. Armour, "Emmett Ashford."

45. *Boston Globe*, August 16, 1970.

46. Harrington, interview, August 2007.

47. Gerlach, *The Men in Blue*, 284–85.

48. *Washington Post*, October 20, 1963.

49. *Chicago Daily Defender*, May 20, 1965.

50. Clifford Kachline, "Expansion 'Years Away,' Majors Insist," *The Sporting News*, December 18, 1965.

51. *Los Angeles Times*, September 12, 1967.

52. *Chicago Daily Defender*, October 19, 1967.

53. *The Sporting News Official Baseball Guide*, 1968; Armour and Levitt, *Paths to Glory*.

54. *Washington Post*, November 16, 1967.

55. Interview with Max Soriano, January 10, 1994, www.seattlepilots.com/msoriano.html.

56. *Los Angeles Times*, February 15, 1968.

16. UNREST

1. Arnold Hano, "Is Pitching Dominance Ruining Baseball," *Sport*, September 1968.

2. William M. Mead, *Two Spectacular Seasons* (New York: Macmillan, 1960), 187.

3. Mead, *Two Spectacular Seasons*.

4. *Washington Post*, August 30, 1968, D1.

5. Marvin Miller, interview by author, October 2007.

6. Marvin Miller, *A Whole Different Ballgame* (New York: Birch Lane Press, 1991), 80.

7. Miller, interview; *Washington Post*, August 11, 1967.

8. *Chicago American*, September 18, 1968; *The Sporting News Official Baseball Guide*, 1969, 195.

9. U.S. Senator Charles E. Goodell (NY), news release, April 16, 1969.

10. *The Sporting News Official Baseball Guide*, 1969, 195.

11. Goodell, news release.

12. *The Sporting News Official Baseball Guide*, 1971, 283–87.

13. *The Sporting News Official Baseball Guide*, 1971, 283–8.

14. Bill Valentine, interview by author, June 2007; Al Salerno, interview by author, June 2007.

15. Valentine, interview.

16. *The Sporting News Official Baseball Guide*, 1971.

17. Copy of Dewey Soriano's affidavit, acquired from Al Salerno in 2007.

18. Al Margulies, "What Ever Happened to Bill Valentine," *Referee*, March 1992.

19. Valentine, interview.

20. *The Sporting News Official Baseball Guide*, 1969, 185–87.

21. *The Sporting News Official Baseball Guide*, 1970, 263.

22. Kuhn, *Hardball*.

23. *Washington Post*, April 13, 1969.

24. *New York Times*, April 21, 1969, 60; *Washington Post*, April 21, 1969, D1.

25. Kuhn, *Hardball*.

26. *The Sporting News Official Baseball Guide*, 1969, 185–87.

27. *The Sporting News Official Baseball Guide*, 1970, 290–93.

28. *Chicago Tribune*, May 29, 1968, C1; *New York Times*, May 29, 1968, 29.

29. *New York Times*, July 11, 1968, 45.

30. Max Soriano interview, http://www.seattlepilots.com/msoriano.html.

31. *Chicago Daily Defender*, January 14, 1970.

32. *New York Times*, February 12, 1970, 62.

33. Kuhn, *Hardball*.

34. *Chicago Daily Tribune*, January 18, 1970, B2.

35. *Hartford Courant*, January 30, 1970, 25A.

36. *Hartford Courant*, June 3, 1970, 26A.

37. Brad Snyder, *A Well-Paid Slave—Curt Flood's Fight for Free Agency in Professional Sports* (New York: Viking, 2006), 181.

38. For a full treatment of this thesis, see Snyder, *A Well-Paid Slave*.

39. Mark Armour, "Alex Johnson," SABR's Biography Project, http://bioproj .sabr.org/.

40. Miller, interview.

41. *The Sporting News Official Baseball Guide*, 1972, 277–90.

42. Joe Cronin, interview with *Boston Herald-Traveler*, unknown date, 1972 (clipping in Cronin's Hall of Fame file).

43. Harrington, interview, August 2007.

44. Kuhn, *Hardball*.

45. *The Sporting News*, March 1, 1969, 20.

46. *Chicago Tribune*, January 12, 1973, C1.

47. Harrington, interview, August 2007.

48. *Hartford Courant*, June 30, 1973, 29.

49. *Washington Post*, August 28, 1973, D3.

50. *New York Times*, August 29, 1973.

51. *New York Times*, August 31, 1973.

52. *Los Angeles Times*, September 1, 1973; September 3, 1973.

53. Harrington, interview, August 2007.

54. *New York Times*, October 19, 1973.

55. *The Sporting News Official Baseball Guide*, 1974.

56. *The Sporting News Official Baseball Guide*, 1974.

17. AT REST

1. *The Sporting News*, February 16, 1974.

2. *New York Times*, January 12, 1975.

3. *The Sporting News*, February 17, 1976.

4. *The Sporting News*, February 23, 1974; December 21, 1974.

5. *The Sporting News*, January 22, 1977.

6. *The Sporting News*, July 22, 1980.

7. Maureen Cronin, interview, February 2007.

8. Roland Hemond, interview by author, June 2007.

9. Harrington, interview, August 2007.

10. Ben Henke, "Joe Cronin, Hall of Fame Player, Exec," *The Sporting News*, September 17, 1984.

11. AP wire clipping, September 8, 1984.

12. Dick Young, *The Sporting News*, September 24, 1984.

13. Bucky Walter, "Old Friends, Fans, Mourn Mission District's Cronin," *San Francisco Examiner*, September 8, 1984.

14. Will McDonough, "A Man for One Season."

15. Bob Addie, "The Last Time Washington Won a World Series," *Washington Post*, April 6, 1975.

Index